365 Ultimate Nut-Free Recipes

(365 Ultimate Nut-Free Recipes - Volume 1)

Linda Crawford

Copyright: Published in the United States by Linda Crawford/ © LINDA CRAWFORD

Published on December, 11 2020

All rights reserved. No part of this publication may be reproduced, stored in retrieval system, copied in any form or by any means, electronic, mechanical, photocopying, recording or otherwise transmitted without written permission from the publisher. Please do not participate in or encourage piracy of this material in any way. You must not circulate this book in any format. LINDA CRAWFORD does not control or direct users' actions and is not responsible for the information or content shared, harm and/or actions of the book readers.

In accordance with the U.S. Copyright Act of 1976, the scanning, uploading and electronic sharing of any part of this book without the permission of the publisher constitute unlawful piracy and theft of the author's intellectual property. If you would like to use material from the book (other than just simply for reviewing the book), prior permission must be obtained by contacting the author at author@thymerecipes.com

Thank you for your support of the author's rights.

Content

365 AWESOME NUT-FREE RECIPES 9

1. Alex Delicata's Dry Cure For Smoked Fish 9
2. Allergen Free Warm Apple Apricot Cake ... 9
3. Allergy Friendly Cookies 10
4. Amazingly Sweet Slow Roasted Tomatoes 10
5. Anxiety Free Angel Food Cake 11
6. Artichokes Bagna Cauda 11
7. Arugula Piña Colada Smoothie 12
8. Asparagus And Mushrooms With Fresh Coriander 12
9. Asparagus, Green Beans And Potatoes With Green Mole Sauce 13
10. Atjar Bloemkool (Pickled Cauliflower Indonesian Style) 13
11. Aunt Rosie's Oven Barbecued Spareribs .. 14
12. Avocado Salad 15
13. Baked Acorn Squash Stuffed With Wild Rice And Kale Risotto 15
14. Baked Apple Cruch 16
15. Baked Beans With Sweet Potatoes And Chipotles 17
16. Baked Clams Oreganate 17
17. Baked Halibut With Tomato Caper Sauce 18
18. Baked Ham 19
19. Banana Bread 19
20. Banana Wild Blueberry Smoothie With Chia Seeds 20
21. Barbecue Sauce With Honey 20
22. Barberry And Orange Tea 21
23. Barley Risotto With Cauliflower And Red Wine 21
24. Barley With Beets, Arugula And Goat Cheese 22
25. Barley And Herb Salad With Roasted Asparagus 23
26. Basic Smoked Fish 23
27. Basil Broth 24
28. Basil Butter Sauce 24
29. Basil Parmesan Focaccia With Fresh Tomatoes 25
30. Beef Stroganoff 26
31. Beet Salad With Chèvre Frais And Caraway 27
32. Beet And Beet Green Fritters 27
33. Beet And Chia Pancakes 28
34. Black Kale And Black Olive Salad 29
35. Black Quinoa, Fennel And Celery Salad 30
36. Black Rice And Arborio Risotto With Artichokes 30
37. Black Rice, Corn And Cranberries 31
38. Black And Arborio Risotto With Beets And Beet Greens 32
39. Black Eyed Pea Salad 33
40. Braised Red Cabbage With Apples 34
41. Braised Stuffed Artichoke A La Barigoule 34
42. Bread And Butter Pickles 35
43. Brioche Stuffing With Chestnuts And Figs 35
44. Broccoli Rabe With Raisins And Garlic 36
45. Broccoli, Cabbage And Kohlrabi Coleslaw With Quinoa 37
46. Broiled Fish With Chermoula 37
47. Broiled Tuna Steaks With Herb Vinaigrette 38
48. Broken Glass Pudding 38
49. Brother Bandera's Italian Easter Bread 39
50. Brown Rice With Carrots And Leeks 40
51. Buckwheat Crêpes With Caramelized Apples 40
52. Buckwheat And Black Kale With Brussels Sprouts 41
53. Bulgur, Prosciutto And Pea Salad With Mustard Dill Vinaigrette 42
54. Buttered Carrots 43
55. Buttermilk Chocolate Sauce 43
56. Buttermilk Mango Curry 43
57. Cabbage And Onion Marmalade 44
58. Cabbage, Onion And Millet Kugel 45
59. Caesar Salad 45
60. Cajun Cornbread Casserole 46
61. Campari Jelly 47
62. Caramel Ice Cream 47
63. Carrot And Avocado Salad With Crunchy Seeds 48
64. Cauliflower, Brussels Sprouts And Red Beans With Lemon And Mustard 49
65. Celery And Apple Salad 49
66. Charcoal Roasted Eggplant 50
67. Chard Leaves Stuffed With Rice And Herbs

- 50
68. Chard Quiche 51
69. Cherry Clafouti 51
70. Cherry Tomato And Goat Cheese Tart 52
71. Cherry Tomatoes With Cream And Caviar 53
72. Cherry Vanilla Semi Freddo 53
73. Chicken Bouillabaisse 54
74. Chicken Breasts With Lemon 55
75. Chicken Breasts With Sweet Red Peppers And Snow Peas 56
76. Chicken Fingers With Garlic Butter 56
77. Chicken With Olives, Prunes And Capers 57
78. Chicken And Chickpea Tagine 57
79. Chicken And Three Peppers Sausage 58
80. Chicken, Greek Style 59
81. Chocolate Lover's Angel Food Cake 59
82. Choux A La Creme 60
83. Cinnamon Curry Rice 61
84. Clam And Fregola Soup 62
85. Clams In Spinach And Garlic Broth 63
86. Cocoa Brownies 63
87. Corn Chowder 64
88. Corn Pudding With Roasted Garlic And Sage 64
89. Corn And Vegetable Gratin With Cumin . 65
90. Cornmeal Cranberry Drop Scones 65
91. Couscous Risotto 66
92. Couscous With Eggplant 67
93. Couscous With Thick Tomato Vegetable Sauce 67
94. Couscous With Tomatoes 68
95. Couscous And Pepper Salad 68
96. Creamy Ranch Dressing 69
97. Cumin Chicken With Black Bean Sauce ... 69
98. Curried Lentil And Grilled Chicken Casserole 70
99. Curried Rice 70
100. Curry Laced Moules À La Marinière With Fresh Peas 71
101. Dark Chocolate Cherry Ganache Bars 72
102. Dark Fruit And Creamy Cheese 72
103. Deconstructed Pumpkin Pie 73
104. Denesse Willey's Fresh Plum Cake 74
105. Deviled Crab 75
106. Dressing 75
107. Egg And Herb Salad 75

108. Eggs Poached In Red Wine Sauce (Les Oeufs Poches Au Vin Rouge) 76
109. Enfrijoladas 77
110. Fajitas (Meat Filled Tortillas With Hot Sauce) 78
111. Farfalle With Roasted Peppers 79
112. Fettucine With Salsa Cruda 79
113. Fish And Vegetables 80
114. Flaky Pie Crust 80
115. Focaccia With Tomatoes And Rosemary .. 81
116. Fried Chicken Salad 82
117. Fried Soft Shell Clams 83
118. Fried Winter Squash With Mint 83
119. Fruit Tarts 84
120. Ginger Butter Sauce 85
121. Ginger Pumpkin Ice Cream 85
122. Gluten Free Pumpkin Muffins With Crumble Topping 86
123. Gluten Free Whole Grain Cheese And Mustard Muffins 86
124. Goat Cheese Salad With Pancetta, Garlic And Figs 87
125. Grapefruit Vinaigrette With Greens Or Broccoli 87
126. Grapefruit And Navel Orange Gratin 88
127. Grated Carrot Salad With Dates And Oranges 89
128. Gratin Of Zucchini And Yellow Squash ... 89
129. Greek Rizogalo 90
130. Greek Zucchini And Herb Pie 90
131. Green Beans And Tomatoes 91
132. Green Goddess Dip 92
133. Green Mayonnaise 92
134. Green Sauce 93
135. Grilled Fish With Tomato Cilantro Vinaigrette 93
136. Grilled Lobster With Vietnamese Dipping Sauce 94
137. Grilled Medallions Of Venison With Black Bean Pancakes 94
138. Grilled Potatoes 95
139. Grilled Trout With Cucumber Tomato Relish 96
140. Grilled Veal Kidneys With Sage And Pancetta 96
141. Grilled Vegetables 97
142. Grits 97

143. Hake In Vegetable And Lemon Broth 98
144. Hash Browns 98
145. Herb Fritters 99
146. Homemade Twinkies 99
147. Hot Mayonnaise 100
148. Hot Or Cold Leek Soup 101
149. Howard Bulka's Strawberry Icebox Cake 101
150. Iced Tea 102
151. Jacques Pepin's Banana Ice Cream 102
152. Jerry Anne Cardamom Cake 103
153. Julia Alvarez's Pudin De Pan (Bread Pudding) 103
154. Kale And Quinoa Salad With Plums And Herbs 104
155. Kohlrabi Home Fries 105
156. Kohlrabi Risotto 105
157. Lapin A La Bourguignonne (Rabbit With Red Wine Sauce) 106
158. Lasagna With Spicy Roasted Cauliflower 107
159. Lebanese Tabbouleh 107
160. Leg Of Lamb With Julienned Vegetables 108
161. Lemon And Garlic Chicken With Mushrooms 109
162. Lentil, Celery And Tomato Minestrone .. 110
163. Lentils With Smoked Trout Rillettes 110
164. Light Red Sauce 111
165. Ligurian Kale Pie (Torta Di Verdura) 112
166. Lime Marinated Chicken Over 'Creamed' Corn 113
167. Lindy Boggs's Oven Fried Chicken 113
168. Linguine With Mussels Provencale 114
169. Linguine With Shrimp, Tomato And Fennel 114
170. Liz Haupert's Fried Chicken 115
171. Lobster With Pasta And Mint 116
172. Mackerel With Mediterranean Vegetables 116
173. Mango Buttermilk Smoothie 117
174. Mango Lassi Ice 117
175. Marinated Lamb Chops With Fennel And Black Olives 117
176. Mashed Potato And Broccoli Raab Pancakes 118
177. Mashed Potato And Cabbage Pancakes .. 119
178. Mashed Potatoes With Chives 119
179. Mashed Potatoes With Scallions 120
180. Medallion Of Pork With Sesame Seeds ... 120

181. Mint Ice Cream 121
182. Mississippi Mud Pie 122
183. Mixed Greens Galette With Onions And Chickpeas 123
184. Moroccan Lamb 124
185. Mulled Cider 124
186. Multigrain Seed Bread 125
187. Mushroom And Grain Cheeseburgers 125
188. Mushroom And Wild Rice Strudel 126
189. Mussels With Linguine 127
190. Napa Cabbage Salad 128
191. Octopus, Galician Style 128
192. Orange Chrysanthemum Iced Tea With Peach Ice Cubes 129
193. Orange Scented Lamb With Fennel And Greens 129
194. Pad Thai 130
195. Parsley Potatoes 130
196. Parsley And Cracked Wheat Salad 131
197. Pasta With Cauliflower, Spicy Tomato Sauce And Capers 131
198. Pasta With Fresh Tomato Sauce 132
199. Pasta With Mushrooms, Cauliflower And Peas 132
200. Pasta E Fagioli 133
201. Paupiettes Of Sole With Spinach And Mushroom Stuffing 134
202. Pear Smoothie With Spinach, Celery And Ginger 135
203. Penne With Mushroom Ragout And Spinach 135
204. Penne With Sun Dried Tomatoes And Chicken 136
205. Peppers Stuffed With Rice, Zucchini And Herbs 137
206. Perciatelli With Broccoli, Tomatoes And Anchovies 138
207. Phillip Schulz's Brine Cure For Smoked Bluefish 138
208. Pickled Broccoli Stems 139
209. Pierre Franey's Pasta With Clams 139
210. Pizza Fantasy 140
211. Pizza On The Grill 140
212. Platanos Maduros (Fried Yellow Plantains) 141
213. Poached Chicken Breasts With Tomatillos And Jalapeños 141

214. Pocket Sandwiches 142
215. Polenta With Parmesan And Tomato Sauce 143
216. Pork Chops Baked With Apples And Onions 143
217. Pork Loin With Mustard Seed Crust 144
218. Pork With Red Wine And Coriander 144
219. Potato Salad With White Wine 145
220. Potatoes And Carrots Family Style 145
221. Provencal Spinach Gratin 146
222. Provençal Onion Pizza 146
223. Purslane Salad With Cherries And Feta .. 147
224. Puréed Mushroom Soup 148
225. Puréed White Bean Soup With Pistou 149
226. Quesadilla With Mushroom Ragoût And Chipotles 149
227. Quick Pumpkin Sage Pasta 150
228. Quince Compote 150
229. Quinoa, Pea And Black Bean Salad With Cumin Vinaigrette 151
230. Raspberry Lime Iced Tea 151
231. Raspberry Rose Granita 152
232. Raspberry Rose Sorbet 152
233. Red Pepper Coulis 153
234. Red Quinoa, Cauliflower And Fava Bean Salad 153
235. Rendered Chicken Fat 154
236. Rhubarb Butterscotch Sauce 154
237. Rhubarb Soup 155
238. Rhubarb And Berry Crumble 155
239. Rice Bowl With Oven Baked Miso Tofu 156
240. Risotto With Broccoli 157
241. Risotto With Pumpkin 157
242. Roast Breast Of Turkey 158
243. Roast Leg Of Lamb With Moroccan Marinade 158
244. Roast Rabbit With Rosemary 159
245. Roasted Brussels Sprouts And Mushrooms With Gremolata And Quinoa 160
246. Roasted Cauliflower Gratin, With Tomatoes And Goat Cheese 160
247. Roasted Corn And Tomato Salsa 161
248. Roasted Cornish Hens With Rosemary And Garlic 162
249. Roasted Eggplant And Chickpeas With Tomato Sauce 163
250. Roasted Mushroom Base 163
251. Roasted Vegetable Sandwich With Parsley Arugula Salad 164
252. Romaine Salad With Cucumber, Red Onion And Feta 165
253. Rosemary Bread 166
254. Roti 166
255. Salad Astoria 167
256. Salmon Cakes With Dill 167
257. Salmon Fillets Braised In Red Wine 168
258. Salmon Rillettes 168
259. Salmon And Cucumber Tartare With Wasabi Sauce 169
260. Salsa Intravaia (A Meat And Wild Mushroom Sauce) 170
261. Salt Baked Chicken 170
262. Sauce Rémoulade 171
263. Sausage Stuffing 171
264. Sausages With Mushrooms And Red Wine 172
265. Sautéed Apple Rings 173
266. Sautéed Red Snapper With Rhubarb Sauce 173
267. Savory Bread Pudding With Swiss Chard And Red Pepper 174
268. Savory Oatmeal Pan Bread 175
269. Savory Soup, Fish And Potatoes Cold Tomato Soup 175
270. Savory Waffles 176
271. Savory Whole Wheat Buttermilk Scones With Rosemary And Thyme 176
272. Scallion Risotto 177
273. Schav 177
274. Sea Scallops On Asparagus 178
275. Sea Scallops With Tomatoes And Shallot Butter 179
276. Seared Sea Scallops With Lime Ginger Sauce And Caramelized Endive 180
277. Seared Wild Mushrooms 180
278. Seitan Roulade With Oyster Mushroom Stuffing 181
279. She Crab And Corn Salad 182
280. Shrimp And Blue Cheese Roulade 183
281. Shrimp Broth 183
282. Shrimp Risotto With Peas 183
283. Shrimp A La King 184
284. Shrimp In Spicy Tomato Sauce 185
285. Sirloin Steak With Crushed Peppercorns 185

286. Skillet Macaroni And Broccoli And Mushrooms And Cheese 186
287. Smoked Autumn Vegetables 187
288. Smoked Salmon Roulade 187
289. Smoked Vegetable Salad 188
290. Soft Shell Crabs With Tomato Buttermilk Sauce 188
291. Sole With Julienne Of Pumpkin 189
292. Sonia's Phyllo And Feta Torte With Dill And Nutmeg 189
293. Sour Cream Cheesecake With Vanilla Bean 190
294. Southern Mesclun Salad 191
295. Spaghetti With Cauliflower, Almonds, Tomatoes And Chickpeas 191
296. Spaghetti With Turkey And Tomato Sauce 192
297. Spaghettini With Spicy Lentil Sauce 193
298. Spartina's Roasted Cod With Nicoise Vinaigrette 193
299. Spiced Iced Tea 194
300. Spiced Lamb Sausage With Green Lentils 194
301. Spiced Lobster And Carrot Risotto 195
302. Spiced Pepper Purée 196
303. Spicy Celery With Garlic 196
304. Spicy Pork 197
305. Spinach Basil Pesto 197
306. Spring Lamb With Baby Greens 198
307. Spy Wednesday Biscuits 199
308. Steamed Cucumbers With Dill 200
309. Stracciatella With Spinach 200
310. Strata With Mushrooms And Chard 200
311. Strawberry Floating Islands 201
312. Strawberry Rhubarb Pie 202
313. Strawberry Moscato Sorbet 203
314. Stuffed Shells Filled With Spinach And Ricotta 203
315. Stuffed Strawberries 204
316. Succotash 204
317. Summer Squash Medley 205
318. Summer Tomato Gratin 205
319. Sunday Black Bean Soup 206
320. Sweet Potato And Green Bean Salad 207
321. Sweet Potato, Pumpkin And Apple Puree 207
322. Sweet And Pungent Apple And Cabbage Slaw 208
323. Tangerine Or Minneola Tart 208
324. Teff Pancakes With Chia, Millet And Blueberries 209
325. Thanksgiving Roasted Root Veggies 210
326. The Perfect Burger 210
327. Three Cheese Ravioli 211
328. Tijoe's Fungi 212
329. Toasted Corn Salsa 212
330. Tofu Scramble 213
331. Tomato Salad With Turkish Tahini Dressing 213
332. Tossed Green Salad 214
333. Tunisian Winter Squash Salad 214
334. Turkey And Vegetable Burgers 215
335. Turkish Shepherd's Salad 215
336. Veal Stew With Sauteed Artichokes 216
337. Veal" With Capers 216
338. Vegan Chocolate Chip Banana Cake 217
339. Vegetable Cakes 218
340. Vegetable And Ricotta Tortino 218
341. Vegetarian Apple Parsnip Soup 219
342. Warm Chickpeas And Greens With Vinaigrette 220
343. Warm Millet, Carrot And Kale Salad With Curry Scented Dressing 221
344. Warm Vanilla Cakes 222
345. Watercress And Red Onion Salad 222
346. Watermelon Granite 223
347. Wehani Rice Pudding 223
348. Wheat Berry And Tomato Salad 224
349. White Bean Burgers 224
350. White Beans With Celery 225
351. White Chocolate Spice Cupcakes 226
352. White Tepary Bean And Potato Purée ...227
353. Whole Rainbow Trout Baked In Foil 227
354. Whole Wheat Bread, Apple And Cranberry Dressing 228
355. Whole Wheat Focaccia With Cherry Tomatoes And Olives 229
356. Whole Wheat Penne Or Fusilli With Tomatoes, Shell Beans And Feta 230
357. Whole Wheat Sesame Rings (Simit) 231
358. Whole Wheat Buttermilk Scones With Raisins And Oatmeal 232
359. Wilted Salad Soup 232
360. Winter Squash, Leek And Farro Gratin

With Feta And Mint..233
361. Winter Tomato Quiche..............................234
362. Zucchini And Cheddar Cheese Soup 235
363. Zucchini Cake 235
364. Zucchini Salad...236
365. Zucchini And Apricot Muffins.................236

INDEX... 238

CONCLUSION.. 243

365 Awesome Nut-Free Recipes

***

1. Alex Delicata's Dry Cure For Smoked Fish

Serving: About 2 cups | Prep: | Cook: | Ready in: 10mins

Ingredients

- 1 cup kosher salt
- 1 cup brown sugar
- 1 teaspoon dry parsley
- 1 teaspoon dry basil
- ½ teaspoon ground white pepper
- ¼ teaspoon ground clove

Direction

- Combine all ingredients and mix well. Use 1 to 2 tablespoons, depending on the size of the fish pieces to be smoked, rubbed over the surface of the fish. Remainder may be stored in a covered glass jar in a cool dry place.

Nutrition Information

- 139: calories;
- 36 grams: carbohydrates;
- 35 grams: sugars;
- 86 milligrams: sodium;
- 0 grams: protein;

2. Allergen Free Warm Apple Apricot Cake

Serving: 1 bundt cake; 12 slices | Prep: | Cook: | Ready in: 1hours30mins

Ingredients

- Nonstick baking spray
- 3 cups flour
- 1 teaspoon salt
- ¾ teaspoon ground cinnamon
- 1 teaspoon baking soda
- 1 teaspoon baking powder
- 1 ½ cups canola oil
- 1 ½ cups sugar
- ½ cup applesauce (a 4-ounce snack pack contains about 1/2 cup)
- ⅓ cup apricot all-fruit spread (apricot jam)
- 3 cups 1/4-inch-thick diced pieces of peeled, cored Granny Smith apples (about 5 apples)

Direction

- Preheat oven to 350 degrees Fahrenheit.
- Spray a bundt-style pan with nonstick baking spray.
- Whisk together the flour, salt, cinnamon, baking soda and baking powder in a bowl and set aside.
- In a separate bowl, whip together the oil and sugar with an electric mixer, increasing gradually to high speed, for a total of 3 minutes. Add the applesauce and apricot spread and mix on high speed for another minute until creamy.
- Add the dry ingredients to the wet and mix on medium speed until well incorporated. Scrape down the sides of the bowl with a spatula and continue mixing. The batter will clump together.
- Add the apples to the batter and mix on low speed until well combined. Pour the batter (which will be very thick) into the prepared pan.

- Bake in the oven for 60 to 70 minutes, rotating the pan halfway through. Test the center of the cake for doneness with a toothpick; the toothpick should come out clean. The cake may take a bit longer to bake if the apples are particularly juicy, because the center will be extra moist. Turn the cake out of the pan onto a cooking rack immediately after removing from the oven.

Nutrition Information

- 520: calories;
- 28 grams: fat;
- 0 grams: trans fat;
- 17 grams: monounsaturated fat;
- 8 grams: polyunsaturated fat;
- 67 grams: carbohydrates;
- 3 grams: protein;
- 38 grams: sugars;
- 334 milligrams: sodium;
- 2 grams: saturated fat;

3. Allergy Friendly Cookies

Serving: 2 Dozen Cookies | Prep: | Cook: | Ready in: 45mins

Ingredients

- 1 teaspoon baking powder
- ½ teaspoon baking soda
- ¾ teaspoon salt
- 1 cup whole wheat pastry flour
- ½ cup all-purpose flour
- ½ cup Earth Balance brand organic whipped buttery spread
- ¾ cup sun butter
- ½ cup brown sugar
- ¾ cup powdered sugar
- ½ teaspoon vanilla extract
- ½ cup Enjoy Life brand semi-sweet chocolate mini-chips

Direction

- Preheat oven to 350 degrees. Blend baking powder, baking soda, salt and both flours. Set aside.
- With a stand mixer, blend buttery spread, sun butter, sugars and vanilla. Gradually pour the dry mixture into the wet mixture and combine.
- Add chocolate chips.
- Refrigerate dough for 30 minutes. Remove, and use a tablespoon or a small scoop to create two dozen dough balls. With the palms of your hands, flatten balls into disks. Place on parchment-lined cookie sheet.
- Bake for 10-12 minutes. Remove from oven and place cookies on a wire rack to cool.

Nutrition Information

- 154: calories;
- 79 milligrams: sodium;
- 11 grams: fat;
- 5 grams: saturated fat;
- 4 grams: monounsaturated fat;
- 15 grams: carbohydrates;
- 9 grams: sugars;
- 0 grams: trans fat;
- 1 gram: protein;

4. Amazingly Sweet Slow Roasted Tomatoes

Serving: Serves 4 as a snack, side dish or sauce. | Prep: | Cook: | Ready in: 3hours

Ingredients

- 1 pound small plum tomatoes, halved lengthwise
- Coarse salt to taste
- A tiny amount of sugar
- 1 tablespoon extra virgin olive oil

Direction

- Preheat the oven to 300 degrees. Put the halved tomatoes in a bowl and toss with the olive oil. Oil a rack that will fit on top of a baking sheet. Place foil on the baking sheet and oil the foil, and place the rack on top. Place the tomatoes, cut side up, on the rack. Sprinkle with coarse salt and a tiny amount of sugar. Place in the oven and roast for 2 hours. Remove from the heat and allow to cool for about 30 minutes. The tomatoes will look a little dry on the surfaces and the skin will be tough. But when you bite into the tomatoes you'll experience a rush of incredibly sweet juice and pulp. If you want to use these for a sauce, put through the fine blade of a food mill.

Nutrition Information

- 56: calories;
- 4 grams: sugars;
- 0 grams: polyunsaturated fat;
- 2 grams: monounsaturated fat;
- 6 grams: carbohydrates;
- 1 gram: protein;
- 275 milligrams: sodium;

5. Anxiety Free Angel Food Cake

Serving: 1 cake (10 to 12 servings) | Prep: | Cook: | Ready in: 15mins

Ingredients

- 1 12-ounce bag frozen raspberries, or 2 cups fresh raspberries, pureed and strained
- 1 1-pound bag frozen mango chunks, or 2 large, peeled and pitted mangoes, pureed
- 2 tablespoons unsalted butter
- 6 ounces semisweet chocolate
- 1 9- or 10-inch angel food cake (purchased from a bakery or supermarket)
- 1 ½ cups fresh pineapple chunks
- Lightly sweetened whipped cream (canned or homemade)
- 1 cup all-natural jelly beans
- Vanilla bean ice cream

Direction

- Combine the raspberry and mango purees, and mix well. Using a double-boiler or microwave oven, melt together the butter and chocolate. Mix well and transfer to a serving dish.
- Place the cake on a platter and fill the center hole with pineapple chunks. Drizzle some of the fruit puree over the cake and place the rest in a bowl to serve separately. Squirt or spoon puffs of whipped cream on top of the cake. Sprinkle jelly beans on and around the cake. To serve, place a slice of cake and some pineapple on a plate and garnish with a scoop or two of ice cream. Pass chocolate sauce and fruit puree separately.

6. Artichokes Bagna Cauda

Serving: 4 servings | Prep: | Cook: | Ready in: 55mins

Ingredients

- 4 globe artichokes
- Juice 1/2 lemon
- ¾ cup olive oil
- 1 tablespoon unsalted butter
- 1 clove garlic, minced (green part removed)
- 6 anchovy fillets, chopped
- 3 tablespoon Italian parsley, chopped
- Freshly ground pepper to tast

Direction

- Trim the stalks from the artichokes. Place three inches water in a large pot (do not use aluminum) and add the lemon juice. Simmer the artichokes until done (about 30 minutes). Drain upside down and serve at room temperature.

- Meanwhile, make the sauce. Heat the olive oil in a small pan and add the butter. When it has melted, add the garlic and saute for one to two minutes. Do not allow it to brown. Add the anchovies and cook over low heat, stirring constantly, until they have reduced to a paste. Add the parsley and pepper and cool.
- Serve the sauce on the side with the artichokes, using it as a dip.

Nutrition Information

- 421: calories;
- 8 grams: saturated fat;
- 31 grams: monounsaturated fat;
- 5 grams: polyunsaturated fat;
- 3 grams: protein;
- 1 gram: sugars;
- 264 milligrams: sodium;
- 44 grams: fat;
- 0 grams: trans fat;
- 6 grams: carbohydrates;

7. Arugula Piña Colada Smoothie

Serving: 1 generous serving | Prep: | Cook: |Ready in:

Ingredients

- ¼ cup freshly squeezed orange juice
- ½ cup light coconut milk
- 1 ¼ cups chopped pineapple (about 180 grams)
- 1 cup arugula (30 grams), rinsed
- 1 quarter-size piece of ginger, peeled
- 2 or 3 ice cubes

Direction

- Place all of the ingredients in a blender and blend for 1 full minute. Pour into a glass, garnish with an orange slice and enjoy.

8. Asparagus And Mushrooms With Fresh Coriander

Serving: Four to six servings | Prep: | Cook: |Ready in: 15mins

Ingredients

- 1 pound fresh asparagus spears, trimmed of woody sections and scraped
- 2 tablespoons olive oil
- ½ pound sliced mushrooms (about 2 cups)
- 2 tablespoons chopped shallots
- ½ teaspoon salt
- Freshly ground black pepper to taste
- 4 tablespoons chopped fresh coriander leaves

Direction

- Cut the asparagus spears on the diagonal into one-inch pieces.
- Heat the olive oil in a nonstick frying pan. Add the mushrooms and saute over over high heat, tossing, until the mushrooms are lightly browned. Add the asparagus pieces. Cook, stirring and tossing, for about a minute. Add the shallots, salt and pepper. Sprinkle with the coriander. Cook for 30 seconds and serve.

Nutrition Information

- 64: calories;
- 5 grams: carbohydrates;
- 1 gram: polyunsaturated fat;
- 3 grams: protein;
- 2 grams: sugars;
- 198 milligrams: sodium;

9. Asparagus, Green Beans And Potatoes With Green Mole Sauce

Serving: Serves 4 | Prep: | Cook: | Ready in: 50mins

Ingredients

- ½ cup hulled untoasted pumpkin seeds
- ½ pound tomatillos, husked, rinsed and coarsely chopped
- 1 serrano chile or 1/2 jalapeño (more to taste), stemmed and roughly chopped
- 3 romaine lettuce leaves, torn into pieces (about 1 1/2 cups / 1 1/2 ounces)
- ¼ small white onion, coarsely chopped, soaked for 5 minutes in cold water, drained and rinsed (optional)
- 2 garlic cloves, halved, green shoots removed
- ¼ cup loosely packed chopped cilantro, plus additional for garnish
- ½ teaspoon cumin seeds, lightly toasted and ground
- 1 ½ cups vegetable stock, garlic broth or chicken stock
- 1 tablespoon canola or extra-virgin olive oil
- Salt to taste
- ½ to ¾ pound asparagus
- ½ to ¾ pound green beans
- ¾ to 1 pound boiling potatoes or Yukon golds, cut in wedges

Direction

- Heat a heavy Dutch oven or saucepan over medium heat and add pumpkin seeds. Wait until you hear one pop, then stir constantly until they have puffed and popped, and smell toasty. They should not get any darker than golden or they will taste bitter. Transfer to a bowl or a baking sheet and allow to cool.
- Place cooled pumpkin seeds in a blender and add tomatillos, chiles, lettuce, onion, garlic, cilantro, cumin, salt, and 1/2 cup of the stock. Cover blender and blend mixture until smooth, stopping blender to stir if necessary.
- Heat oil in the Dutch oven or heavy saucepan over medium-high heat. Drizzle in a bit of the blended mixture and if it sizzles, add the rest. Cook, stirring, until mixture darkens and thickens, about 5 minutes. (Hold the lid above the pot to shield you and your stove from splatters.) Add remaining stock, bring to a simmer, reduce heat to medium-low and simmer uncovered, stirring often, until sauce is thick and creamy, 15 to 20 minutes. Season to taste with salt. You should have about 2 cups.
- Steam potato wedges above 1 inch boiling water for 10 to 15 minutes, until tender. Steam asparagus and green beans for 5 minutes, or blanch for the same amount of time in salted boiling water. Transfer to a bowl of cold water, drain and drain again on a kitchen towel.
- Arrange the vegetables on a platter or plates and spoon mole sauce over, or heat through in the sauce, in the saucepan. Serve with rice or corn tortillas if desired.

Nutrition Information

- 289: calories;
- 2 grams: saturated fat;
- 0 grams: trans fat;
- 6 grams: monounsaturated fat;
- 4 grams: polyunsaturated fat;
- 13 grams: protein;
- 34 grams: carbohydrates;
- 8 grams: sugars;
- 979 milligrams: sodium;

10. Atjar Bloemkool (Pickled Cauliflower Indonesian Style)

Serving: Four to six servings as a side dish | Prep: | Cook: | Ready in: 15mins

Ingredients

- 1 head cauliflower, about 1 1/2 pounds

- 1 teaspoon fresh or frozen turmeric, minced (see note)
- 1 teaspoon ginger, minced
- 2 cloves garlic, minced
- 1 cup white vinegar
- ½ cup sugar
- 1 teaspoon salt
- 1 ½ cups water

Direction

- Cut the florets from the cauliflower into pieces two and a half inches in length by about one and a half inches wide. Wash and drain them.
- Place eight cups of water in a large pot. Bring the water to a boil. Add the cauliflower and cook for 10 to 15 seconds, until the florets whiten slightly. Remove the pot from the heat and run cold water into it. Drain the cauliflower, put it back in the pot, run cold water over it again. Drain. Place in a large bowl and reserve.
- In the pot, place all the other ingredients and bring to a boil. Stir to dissolve the sugar. Turn off the heat, pour the mixture over the cauliflower florets and mix well so that the cauliflower is covered and the florets turn bright yellow. Place the bowl, covered, in the refrigerator for at least 12 hours, or overnight. Serve cold. Leftover cauliflower florets may be kept in a jar, refrigerated, for about four to six weeks.

Nutrition Information

- 97: calories;
- 22 grams: carbohydrates;
- 2 grams: protein;
- 18 grams: sugars;
- 418 milligrams: sodium;
- 0 grams: polyunsaturated fat;

11. Aunt Rosie's Oven Barbecued Spareribs

Serving: 6 to 8 servings | Prep: | Cook: | Ready in: 2hours15mins

Ingredients

- 2 slabs of lean spareribs, about 4 pounds each
- Salt to taste if desired
- Freshly ground pepper to taste
- The barbecue sauce:
- 8 tablespoons unsalted butter
- 2 teaspoons finely minced garlic
- 2 cups finely chopped onions
- 2 cups tomato ketchup
- ¼ cup soy sauce
- 1 ½ tablespoons chili powder
- ¼ teaspoon Tabasco sauce or more, according to taste
- ¼ cup sherry wine vinegar or red wine vinegar
- 3 tablespoons dark brown sugar

Direction

- Preheat oven to 400 degrees.
- Sprinkle spareribs with salt and pepper. Arrange slabs in each of two large baking dishes. Bake one hour in oven. Turn ribs and bake 10 minutes longer. Pour off fat.
- Meanwhile, heat the butter in a large saucepan and add the garlic and onions. Cook, stirring, until onions are wilted. Add the ketchup, soy sauce, chili powder, Tabasco sauce, vinegar and sugar. There should be about three cups of sauce. Bring to a boil and let simmer about five minutes.
- Brush each slab of ribs on the underside with sauce and return to oven, brushed side up. Bake 30 minutes, brushing every 10 minutes on the same side with the sauce.
- Turn the ribs. Brush generously with all the remaining sauce. Return to the oven and bake 30 minutes.
- Cut the spareribs into individual rib servings. Serve hot or cold.

12. Avocado Salad

Serving: Four to six servings | Prep: | Cook: |Ready in: 10mins

Ingredients

- 3 Haas avocados, ripe but not too soft, peeled and diced
- ¼ cup diced scallions
- 1 large red bell pepper, diced
- 1 medium red onion, peeled and diced
- 1 medium cucumber, peeled, seeded and cut into 1/8-inch slices
- 2 small tomatoes, seeded and diced
- ¼ cup fresh lime juice
- 2 tablespoons extra-virgin olive oil
- Salt and freshly ground pepper to taste

Direction

- Toss together the avocado, scallions, red pepper and onion. Add the cucumber and tomatoes. Add the lime juice and then the olive oil. Season with salt and pepper.

Nutrition Information

- 234: calories;
- 3 grams: protein;
- 13 grams: monounsaturated fat;
- 550 milligrams: sodium;
- 19 grams: fat;
- 2 grams: polyunsaturated fat;
- 16 grams: carbohydrates;
- 9 grams: dietary fiber;
- 4 grams: sugars;

13. Baked Acorn Squash Stuffed With Wild Rice And Kale Risotto

Serving: 6 to 8 generous servings | Prep: | Cook: |Ready in: 2hours30mins

Ingredients

- 6 small acorn squash
- 1 bunch kale or 1 10-ounce package stemmed and washed kale, stems picked out and discarded
- Salt to taste
- 1 cup cooked wild rice (1/3 cup uncooked)*
- 1 quart vegetable stock
- 2 tablespoons extra virgin olive oil
- ½ cup minced onion
- ⅔ cup arborio rice
- 1 plump garlic clove, minced
- ½ cup dry white wine, like pinot grigio or sauvignon blanc
- ¼ cup chopped fresh dill
- ¼ cup chopped flat-leaf parsley
- Freshly ground pepper to taste
- ¼ to ½ cup freshly grated Parmesan cheese (1 to 2 ounces) (optional)
- Cayenne or freshly grated nutmeg to taste (optional)

Direction

- Heat the oven to 425 degrees. Line a baking sheet with foil and brush the foil with olive oil. Place the squash in the oven and bake 30 minutes. Each squash should be intact but beginning to give on the side it's resting on, and soft enough to cut through. Remove from the oven and let sit for 15 minutes, until the squash has cooled slightly. Then, resting a squash on the slightly flattened side that it was sitting on in the oven, cut away the top third. You will be putting the top "cap" back on once the squash is filled, so cut it off in one neat slice. Scrape out the seeds and membranes from both pieces and set aside. Repeat for the remaining squash. Turn the oven heat down to

350 degrees. Oil a baking dish or sheet pan that can accommodate all of the squash
- Meanwhile, blanch the kale in a large pot of salted boiling water for 2 to 4 minutes, until just tender. Transfer to a bowl of cold water, drain and squeeze out excess water. Chop medium-fine and set aside. Cook the wild rice, following the directions below, and set aside
- Put the stock into a saucepan and bring it to a simmer over low heat, with a ladle nearby. Heat 1 tablespoon of the olive oil over medium heat in a wide, heavy nonstick saucepan or skillet. Add the onion and a generous pinch of salt, and cook gently until it is just tender, 3 to 5 minutes
- Add the arborio rice and garlic and stir until the grains separate and begin to crackle. Add the wine and stir until it has been absorbed. Begin adding the simmering stock, a couple of ladlefuls (about 1/2 cup) at a time. The stock should just cover the rice, and should be bubbling, not too slowly but not too quickly. Cook, stirring often, until it is just about absorbed. Add another ladleful or two of the stock and continue to cook in this fashion, adding more stock and stirring when the rice is almost dry. You do not have to stir constantly, but stir often. Continue to add stock and stir until the rice is almost tender, about 20 minutes. The rice should still be a little chewy. Add another ladleful of stock and stir in the kale, wild rice and herbs. Stir together until the stock is just about absorbed, about 5 minutes, and add another ladleful of stock. Remove from the heat. Add pepper, taste and adjust seasonings. Stir in the remaining olive oil and the Parmesan if using
- Season the surface of the acorn squash with salt, pepper and nutmeg or cayenne (if desired). Fill the hollowed-out squash with the risotto. Place the tops back on the squash and put them in the baking dish or on the sheet pan
- Bake 40 minutes, or until the squash is tender all the way through when pierced with a knife

Nutrition Information

- 241: calories;
- 1 gram: sugars;
- 3 grams: monounsaturated fat;
- 48 grams: carbohydrates;
- 6 grams: dietary fiber;
- 5 grams: protein;
- 1047 milligrams: sodium;
- 4 grams: fat;

14. Baked Apple Crunch

Serving: 6 servings | Prep: | Cook: | Ready in: 1hours15mins

Ingredients

- For the filling:
- 2 pounds tart apples, peeled, cored and sliced 1/4-inch thick
- ½ cup sugar
- 1 teaspoon cinnamon
- ½ teaspoon nutmeg
- ½ teaspoon ground cloves
- For the crunch:
- ½ cup flour
- 4 tablespoons sugar
- 3 tablespoons butter
- 1 teaspoon vanilla extract
- Confectioners' sugar for garnish

Direction

- To make the filling, combine the apples, sugar, cinnamon, nutmeg and cloves in a large bowl. Stir to coat the apples. Spoon the mixture into an 8- to 9-inch pie plate and set aside.
- Preheat oven to 350 degrees.
- To make the crunch, combine flour, sugar, butter and vanilla in a medium-size bowl. Work mixture between fingers and drop crumbs on top of apple filling.

- Bake for one hour, or until topping is a light gold. Allow to cool slightly, sprinkle with confectioners' sugar and serve.

Nutrition Information

- 278: calories;
- 6 grams: fat;
- 54 grams: carbohydrates;
- 5 grams: dietary fiber;
- 3 milligrams: sodium;
- 4 grams: saturated fat;
- 0 grams: polyunsaturated fat;
- 2 grams: protein;
- 40 grams: sugars;

15. Baked Beans With Sweet Potatoes And Chipotles

Serving: 6 servings | Prep: | Cook: |Ready in: 3hours

Ingredients

- 1 pound red beans, San Franciscano beans, or pintos, washed, picked over for stones, and soaked in 2 quarts water for 4 hours or overnight
- 1 bay leaf
- 2 tablespoons extra virgin olive oil
- 1 yellow or red onion, chopped
- Salt to taste
- 2 to 4 garlic cloves (to taste), minced
- ¼ cup tomato paste
- 2 tablespoons honey or agave nectar
- 2 chipotles in adobo, seeded and minced
- 2 large sweet potatoes (1 1/2 to 2 pounds), peeled and cut in large dice

Direction

- Place beans and soaking water in an ovenproof casserole. Add bay leaf and bring to a gentle boil over medium heat. Reduce heat to low, cover and simmer 1 hour. Check beans at regular intervals to make sure they are submerged, and add water as necessary.
- Meanwhile, heat oven to 300 degrees . Heat 1 tablespoon of the oil in a heavy skillet and add onion. Cook, stirring often, until tender, about 5 minutes. Add a generous pinch of salt and the garlic and cook, stirring, until garlic is fragrant, 30 seconds to a minute. Stir onion and garlic into beans, along with salt to taste, tomato paste, honey or agave nectar, and chipotles, and stir together. Add sweet potatoes and bring back to a simmer, drizzle with remaining olive oil, and place in oven.
- Bake 1 to 1 1/2 hours, until beans are thoroughly soft and sweet potatoes are beginning to fall apart, checking and stirring from time to time to make sure that beans are submerged. Either add liquid or push them down into the simmering broth if necessary. Remove from heat and serve hot or warm.

Nutrition Information

- 190: calories;
- 644 milligrams: sodium;
- 6 grams: dietary fiber;
- 14 grams: sugars;
- 1 gram: polyunsaturated fat;
- 3 grams: monounsaturated fat;
- 36 grams: carbohydrates;
- 4 grams: protein;
- 5 grams: fat;

16. Baked Clams Oreganate

Serving: 6 to 8 servings | Prep: | Cook: |Ready in: 30mins

Ingredients

- 1 ½ cups bread crumbs
- ½ tablespoon minced flat-leaf parsley
- 1 small clove garlic, minced
- 1 teaspoon dried oregano, or to taste

- Salt and fresh-ground black pepper to taste
- 4 tablespoons extra virgin olive oil
- ⅔ cup chicken stock
- 36 littleneck clams on half shell
- Lemon wedges for garnish

Direction

- Heat broiler. Place rack in lowest setting, or about 12 inches from heat.
- Combine bread crumbs, parsley, garlic, oregano and salt and pepper. Add olive oil, and toss until crumbs are evenly coated. Stir in broth, mixing to blend. Mixture will be quite damp.
- Put a rounded teaspoon of the crumb mixture on each clam, smoothing the top. Arrange clams on baking sheet with sides, and pour in about 1/8 inch water. Broil until topping is lightly browned, about 7 minutes. Serve with lemon wedges.

Nutrition Information

- 204: calories;
- 2 grams: sugars;
- 569 milligrams: sodium;
- 18 grams: carbohydrates;
- 13 grams: protein;
- 9 grams: fat;
- 1 gram: dietary fiber;
- 0 grams: trans fat;
- 5 grams: monounsaturated fat;

17. Baked Halibut With Tomato Caper Sauce

Serving: Serves 6 | Prep: | Cook: | Ready in: 1hours

Ingredients

- For the tomato caper sauce
- 1 tablespoon extra virgin olive oil
- ½ medium onion, finely chopped
- 4 plump garlic cloves, minced or mashed in a mortar and pestle
- ¼ cup capers, drained, rinsed and finely chopped or mashed with the garlic in a mortar and pestle
- 2 pounds tomatoes, peeled, seeded and finely chopped, or 1 28-ounce can diced tomatoes with juice
- Salt, preferably kosher salt
- freshly ground pepper to taste
- Pinch of sugar
- 1 teaspoon chopped fresh thyme leaves
- 1 tablespoon slivered fresh basil leaves
- For the baked halibut
- 1 recipe tomato-caper sauce, above
- 6 6-ounce halibut fillets (Choose Pacific halibut over Atlantic halibut. According to the Environmental Defense Fund and the Blue Ocean Institute, Pacific halibut fisheries have been properly managed, but they are overfished in the Atlantic.)
- Salt, preferably kosher salt
- freshly ground pepper
- 1 tablespoon extra-virgin olive oil
- 6 lemon slices

Direction

- Heat the olive oil in a large, heavy skillet over medium heat, and add the onion. Cook, stirring often, until tender, three to five minutes, and add the garlic and the capers. Cook, stirring, for three to five minutes, until the onion has softened thoroughly and the mixture is fragrant. Add the tomatoes, salt, pepper and a pinch of sugar. Stir in the thyme, bring to a simmer and cook, stirring often, for 15 to 20 minutes, until the sauce is thick and fragrant. Taste and adjust seasonings. Serve hot or cold.
- Make the sauce as directed and keep warm.
- Preheat the oven to 450 degrees. Oil a baking dish large enough for the fish to lie flat. Season the fish with salt and pepper, and arrange in the baking dish. Drizzle the olive oil over the fillets, and place a round of lemon on each one. Cover the dish tightly with foil, and place

in the oven. Bake 15 minutes. Check the fish; if you can cut into it with a fork, it is done. If it doesn't yield, (halibut fillets tend to be thick can take time to cook), cover and return to the oven for five minutes. Remove from the oven, and check again. Remove the lemon slices from the fish.
- Place a spoonful of sauce on each plate, and place a piece of fish partially on top. Spoon some of the liquid from the baking dish over the fish. If you wish, top the fish with another spoonful of sauce, garnish with basil leaves and serve.

Nutrition Information

- 254: calories;
- 1 gram: polyunsaturated fat;
- 4 grams: monounsaturated fat;
- 15 grams: carbohydrates;
- 6 grams: sugars;
- 34 grams: protein;
- 984 milligrams: sodium;
- 8 grams: fat;

18. Baked Ham

Serving: Twenty to 30 servings | Prep: | Cook: | Ready in: 4hours45mins

Ingredients

- 1 18-pound smoked ham, bone in
- 1 cup white vinegar
- 1 tablespoon ground cloves
- 1 teaspoon nutmeg
- Freshly ground pepper to taste
- 1 cup dark brown sugar
- ½ teaspoon mace
- 2 tablespoons American-style spicy mustard
- Juice of one orange

Direction

- Preheat the oven to 425 degrees.
- Remove the skin from the ham, if necessary, leaving at least a one-half-inch-thick layer of fat around it. Score the ham, place it in a large baking pan and pour the vinegar over it. Combine half of the ground cloves, all the nutmeg and pepper and rub all over the ham.
- Bake for 30 minutes. Lower the temperature to 325 degrees and bake for three and one-half hours.
- Meanwhile, in a small bowl, combine the brown sugar, mace, mustard, orange juice and remaining ground cloves. After the baking is finished, turn off the oven and brush the ham with the mixture. Return the ham to the turned-off oven for 30 minutes.

Nutrition Information

- 413: calories;
- 57 grams: protein;
- 8 grams: fat;
- 0 grams: trans fat;
- 1 gram: dietary fiber;
- 6 grams: sugars;
- 2842 milligrams: sodium;
- 3 grams: saturated fat;
- 4 grams: monounsaturated fat;
- 30 grams: carbohydrates;

19. Banana Bread

Serving: Sixteen servings | Prep: | Cook: | Ready in: 1hours

Ingredients

- Vegetable oil cooking spray
- 3 ripe bananas, mashed
- 1 ½ teaspoons vanilla extract
- 1 egg, lightly beaten
- ⅓ cup honey
- 1 ¼ cups whole-wheat flour
- 2 teaspoons baking powder

- ⅓ cup margarine, melted

Direction

- Preheat the oven to 350 degrees. Spray a 9-inch-by-5-inch loaf pan with the vegetable oil. In a large bowl, combine the mashed bananas, vanilla, egg and honey until well mixed. In another bowl, stir the flour and baking powder together.
- Very lightly stir the flour mixture into the banana mixture. Add the margarine and stir just until combined; do not overmix. Scrape the batter into the prepared pan. Bake until a toothpick inserted into the center of the cake comes out clean, about 45 minutes to 1 hour.

Nutrition Information

- 117: calories;
- 5 grams: fat;
- 1 gram: polyunsaturated fat;
- 2 grams: protein;
- 18 grams: carbohydrates;
- 9 grams: sugars;
- 80 milligrams: sodium;

20. Banana Wild Blueberry Smoothie With Chia Seeds

Serving: 1 serving | Prep: | Cook: | Ready in:

Ingredients

- 1 tablespoon soaked chia seeds (1 teaspoon dry unsoaked)
- 1 small banana (about 4 ounces without the skin)
- ½ cup frozen organic wild blueberries
- 1 cup buttermilk
- 1 teaspoon honey

Direction

- To soak the chia seeds, place in a jar or bowl and add 4 tablespoons water for every tablespoon of chia seeds. Place in the refrigerator for several hours or overnight. The seeds and water will be become gelatinous.
- Scoop up a tablespoon of seeds with the gooey liquid and place in a blender (don't worry, your smoothie won't have this consistency). Add the remaining ingredients and blend for 1 full minute at high speed.

Nutrition Information

- 307: calories;
- 2 grams: saturated fat;
- 1 gram: monounsaturated fat;
- 471 milligrams: sodium;
- 10 grams: dietary fiber;
- 30 grams: sugars;
- 11 grams: protein;
- 6 grams: fat;
- 0 grams: trans fat;
- 3 grams: polyunsaturated fat;
- 55 grams: carbohydrates;

21. Barbecue Sauce With Honey

Serving: None | Prep: | Cook: | Ready in:

Ingredients

- 2 tablespoons olive oil
- 1 ½ cups finely chopped onions
- 2 tablespoons finely chopped garlic
- 1 28-ounce can crushed tomatoes
- 1 6-ounce can tomato paste
- ½ cup red-wine vinegar
- ¼ cup Worcestershire sauce
- 1 tablespoon chili powder
- 1 tablespoon ground coriander
- 3 tablespoons lemon juice
- ¼ teaspoon red pepper flakes
- 1 tablespoon Tabasco sauce, or to taste

- 2 tablespoons chopped fresh oregano, or 1 tablespoon dried
- 2 teaspoons ground cumin
- 2 bay leaves
- 4 sprigs fresh thyme, or 1 teaspoon dried
- 1 teaspoon freshly ground black pepper
- 4 tablespoons honey
- Salt to taste

Direction

- Heat the oil in a saucepan and add the onions. Cook, stirring, until wilted. Add the garlic, cook briefly and add the remaining ingredients. Bring to a simmer and cook, stirring often, about 30 minutes. Let the sauce cool and use for basting. This sauce is good for any barbecued meat and keeps very well refrigerated.

Nutrition Information

- 120: calories;
- 0 grams: saturated fat;
- 2 grams: monounsaturated fat;
- 1 gram: polyunsaturated fat;
- 23 grams: carbohydrates;
- 4 grams: dietary fiber;
- 14 grams: sugars;
- 385 milligrams: sodium;
- 3 grams: protein;

22. Barberry And Orange Tea

Serving: Serves 2 | Prep: | Cook: | Ready in: 30mins

Ingredients

- 20 grams dried barberries (2 heaped tablespoons)
- 3 strips orange zest
- 1 or 2 slices orange
- 2 cloves
- 2 ½ cups boiling water
- 2 teaspoons honey

Direction

- Place the dried barberries in a teapot or pyrex measuring cup. Add the orange zest, orange slices and cloves. Pour on the boiling water. Stir in the honey. Cover and allow the mixture to steep for 15 to 30 minutes. Strain and reheat gently if desired but do not boil.

Nutrition Information

- 51: calories;
- 0 grams: protein;
- 14 grams: carbohydrates;
- 1 gram: dietary fiber;
- 12 grams: sugars;
- 13 milligrams: sodium;

23. Barley Risotto With Cauliflower And Red Wine

Serving: Serves 6 | Prep: | Cook: | Ready in: 30mins

Ingredients

- 7 to 8 cups vegetable or chicken stock, as needed
- Salt
- 2 tablespoons extra virgin olive oil
- 1 small or 1/2 medium onion, minced
- 2 large garlic cloves, minced or pressed
- 1 ½ cups barley
- 1 medium cauliflower, separated into small florets or sliced 1/2 inch thick
- 1 cup robust red wine, such as a Côtes du Rhône
- 3 tablespoons chopped flat-leaf parsley
- 2 ounces Parmesan cheese, grated (1/2 cup)
- Freshly ground pepper

Direction

- Season the stock well with salt and bring to a simmer in a medium saucepan.
- Heat the oil over medium heat in a large, heavy nonstick frying pan or a wide, heavy saucepan. Add the onion. Cook, stirring, until the onion begins to soften, about three minutes. Add the garlic, cauliflower and barley. Cook, stirring, for a couple of minutes, until the grains of barley are separate and beginning to crackle.
- Add the red wine and cook, stirring, until there is no more wine visible in the pan. Stir in enough of the simmering stock to just cover the barley. The stock should bubble slowly. Cook, stirring often, until it is just about absorbed. Add more stock and continue to cook in this fashion, not too fast and not too slowly, adding more stock when the barley is almost dry, until the barley is tender but still chewy. Taste and add salt if necessary.
- Add another ladleful of stock to the barley. Stir in the parsley and Parmesan, and immediately remove from the heat. Add freshly ground pepper, taste one last time and adjust salt. Serve at once.

Nutrition Information

- 418: calories;
- 54 grams: carbohydrates;
- 11 grams: dietary fiber;
- 19 grams: protein;
- 12 grams: fat;
- 4 grams: saturated fat;
- 1207 milligrams: sodium;
- 6 grams: monounsaturated fat;
- 2 grams: polyunsaturated fat;
- 8 grams: sugars;

24. Barley With Beets, Arugula And Goat Cheese

Serving: 4 servings | Prep: | Cook: | Ready in: 1hours30mins

Ingredients

- 1 small beet
- 2 tablespoons olive oil
- ½ small onion, diced small
- 1 clove garlic
- 1 cup barley
- 2 cups water or broth
- 1 cup arugula
- Salt and pepper
- ¼ cup goat cheese

Direction

- Heat the oven to 400 degrees. Wrap the beet in foil and roast in oven for 40 minutes, until it can be easily pierced with a knife. Allow to cool slightly. Peel the beet by wrapping it in plastic wrap and rubbing off the skin. Dice into 1/2 inch pieces.
- In a medium saucepan, heat the oil. Add the onion and cook until it becomes translucent, about 3 minutes. Add the garlic and cook for 1 minute. Add the barley and the broth. Stir, cover and simmer for 20 minutes, or until the barley is cooked and tender. Stir in the arugula and the beets. Season with salt and pepper. Crumble the goat cheese on top.

Nutrition Information

- 265: calories;
- 1 gram: polyunsaturated fat;
- 37 grams: carbohydrates;
- 9 grams: dietary fiber;
- 8 grams: protein;
- 490 milligrams: sodium;
- 10 grams: fat;
- 6 grams: monounsaturated fat;
- 3 grams: saturated fat;
- 2 grams: sugars;

25. Barley And Herb Salad With Roasted Asparagus

Serving: Serves 4 as a main dish salad, 6 as a side | Prep: | Cook: | Ready in: 1hours

Ingredients

- 1 cup barley
- 3 cups water
- Salt, preferably kosher salt, to taste
- 1 pound thick-stemmed asparagus
- 2 tablespoons extra- virgin olive oil
- Freshly ground pepper to taste
- ½ cup chopped fresh herbs, such as parsley, marjoram, chives, tarragon and thyme
- For the vinaigrette
- 1 ½ tablespoons fresh lemon juice
- 1 tablespoon sherry vinegar
- Salt to taste
- 1 teaspoon lemon zest
- 1 small garlic clove, puréed
- ½ teaspoon dry mustard or 1 teaspoon Dijon mustard
- 6 tablespoons extra- virgin olive oil
- Lemon wedges or sliced lemon for garnish (optional)

Direction

- Heat a 3- quart saucepan over medium-high heat and add barley. Toast in the pan, shaking pan or stirring grains until they begin to smell a little bit like popcorn. Add water and bring to a boil. Add salt to taste (I suggest 1/2 to 3/4 teaspoon for 1 cup barley), reduce heat, cover and simmer 45 to 50 minutes, until barley is tender (it will always be chewy). Drain off any liquid remaining in the pot through a strainer (set it over a bowl if you think you might want to use the barley water in a stock or risotto – it'll keep for a day in the refrigerator). Shake strainer and return barley to the pot. Cover pot with a clean dishtowel and return the lid. Allow barley to sit for 10 to 15 minutes.
- Meanwhile, roast asparagus and make dressing. Preheat oven to 425 degrees F. Line a baking sheet with parchment. Snap off woody ends of the asparagus and place on parchment-lined baking sheet. Add olive oil and salt and pepper to taste and toss together until all of the asparagus is coated with oil (I do this with my hands). Make sure that asparagus is in one layer on the baking sheet in the pan and place in oven. Roast for about 12 minutes, or until tender and beginning to shrivel. It should be browned in spots. Remove from heat.
- Whisk together lemon juice, vinegar, salt, lemon zest, garlic, and mustard. Whisk in olive oil.
- Transfer cooked barley to a large bowl. Add herbs and vinaigrette and toss together until barley is evenly coated with dressing. Arrange on a platter or on plates. Lay stalks of roasted asparagus on over the top, and serve.

Nutrition Information

- 449: calories;
- 895 milligrams: sodium;
- 29 grams: fat;
- 0 grams: trans fat;
- 20 grams: monounsaturated fat;
- 43 grams: carbohydrates;
- 3 grams: sugars;
- 4 grams: polyunsaturated fat;
- 12 grams: dietary fiber;
- 10 grams: protein;

26. Basic Smoked Fish

Serving: About 1 1/2 pounds smoked fish | Prep: | Cook: | Ready in: 12hours20mins

Ingredients

- 2 fish fillets weighing approximately 1 pound each (bluefish, mackerel, salmon, haddock)
- 1 quart liquid brine or 4 table spoons dry cure (see recipe)
- 4 or 5 hardwood chunks, shavings or sawdust (see note)
- Charcoal, if necessary (see note)

Direction

- If using liquid brine, place the fish fillets in a ceramic, glass or stainless-steel (not aluminum) bowl with the brine. If using dry cure, rub each fillet top and bottom with the dry mixture and place in a ceramic, glass or stainless-steel (not aluminum) baking dish. Cover and refrigerate about 6 hours, or overnight.
- Remove fillets from bowl or dish and rinse them under running water quickly to remove surface salt. If using dry cure, do not rub off all the seasonings. Place fillets on a cake rack or raised grid surface that allows air to circulate beneath them. Leave to dry about 3 hours, or until a dry shiny surface forms.
- When fillets are sufficiently dry, build a charcoal fire, if necessary (it will take about 30 minutes for the charcoal to reach the desired state). If using wood chunks, let them soak in a bucket of water for half an hour. If using an electric smoker, turn it on just before using and place sawdust or wood shavings in the smoking pan.
- Place fillets on the smoker grid. Close vents, or place lid on smoker. Regulate vents, if possible, so that heat stays at around 110 to 120 degrees Fahrenheit. Leave the fish 1 to 2 hours or longer, checking periodically and, if possible, replenishing fuel or smoking medium as necessary. The fish will be done more quickly at higher temperatures. At temperatures of 175 to 200 degrees, for example, fish will be done in about 1 hour.
- Remove fillets from smoker when they are dry and yellowish in color. Serve immediately, or refrigerate and serve cold or as an ingredient in other recipes.

27. Basil Broth

Serving: 1 quart | Prep: | Cook: | Ready in: 2hours30mins

Ingredients

- 1 pound celery root, peeled and chopped
- 1 pound leeks, cleaned and chopped
- 1 pound white onions, unpeeled, chopped
- 1 pound celery, chopped
- ¼ pound parsnips, chopped
- 2 gallons water
- 1 pound fresh basil, well rinsed

Direction

- Put all ingredients but the basil in a large pot over medium heat and simmer 1 1/2 hours. Strain, and discard the vegetables. Return the broth to a pan over medium heat and continue cooking until it cooks down to 1 quart.
- Remove from heat, add the basil to the broth and steep 1 minute. Strain. Discard the basil. In a well-covered container in the refrigerator, the broth will keep for up to 5 days.

Nutrition Information

- 1: calories;
- 0 grams: protein;
- 4 milligrams: sodium;

28. Basil Butter Sauce

Serving: 4 servings | Prep: | Cook: | Ready in: 10mins

Ingredients

- 5 tablespoons butter
- 1 tablespoon finely chopped shallots
- 8 leaves fresh basil, coarsely chopped

- ¼ cup white-wine vinegar
- ¼ cup heavy cream
- Salt to taste if desired
- Freshly ground pepper to taste

Direction

- Heat 1 tablespoon butter in a small saucepan, and add shallots. Cook briefly, and add basil and vinegar. Bring to a boil, and cook until reduced to 2 tablespoons.
- Add cream, and bring to a rapid boil. Cook this until reduced to 1/3 cup. Remove the sauce from the heat, and immediately add the remaining 4 tablepoons of butter, salt and pepper, stirring rapidly with a wire whisk.

Nutrition Information

- 184: calories;
- 13 grams: saturated fat;
- 1 gram: protein;
- 5 grams: monounsaturated fat;
- 0 grams: dietary fiber;
- 119 milligrams: sodium;
- 20 grams: fat;

29. Basil Parmesan Focaccia With Fresh Tomatoes

Serving: Eight to 10 generous first-course servings | Prep: | Cook: | Ready in: 2hours35mins

Ingredients

- The bread:
- 1 medium onion, peeled and finely chopped
- 1 package rapid-rise or regular active dry yeast
- ½ cup warm water between 105 and 115 degrees
- 3 cups unbleached all-purpose flour
- 6 tablespoons olive oil
- 1 cup freshly grated Parmesan cheese
- ¼ cup finely chopped fresh basil
- 2 teaspoons salt
- 2 teaspoons coarse or kosher salt
- The topping:
- 5 tablespoons olive oil
- 2 large cloves garlic, peeled and minced
- ½ cup finely chopped fresh basil
- 2 teaspoons salt
- Freshly ground black pepper
- 3 to 4 large tomatoes, thinly sliced
- 3 tablespoons freshly grated Parmesan cheese

Direction

- Place the chopped onion in a bowl and pour boiling water over it. After 15 seconds, drain and blot dry with paper towels. Set aside.
- Combine the yeast with the half-cup of water. Add one and a half cups of the flour and mix. Turn the dough out on a lightly floured board and knead it for about eight minutes until it is smooth and elastic. Pour one tablespoon of the olive oil in a bowl, add the dough, turning once to cover with the oil. Drape a lightly dampened towel over the bowl and let the dough rise in a warm, draft-free spot until doubled in bulk. This will take one and a half hours with rapid-rise yeast, or three hours with regular yeast.
- Punch down the dough, add the onion, a quarter-cup of water, three tablespoons of olive oil, the cup of Parmesan cheese, the remaining flour, the basil and two teaspoons salt, and mix. Turn the dough out onto a lightly floured board and knead it for eight minutes, or until it is smooth and elastic, adding small amounts of additional flour if needed.
- Preheat the oven to 400 degrees.
- Roll the dough into a large circle measuring about 15 inches in diameter and about a quarter-inch thick, and transfer it to a heavy cookie sheet. Using your fingertips, make several indentations in the dough, so the surface is irregular. Brush with two tablespoons of olive oil and sprinkle on two teaspoons of coarse salt. Bake in the top half of

the oven for 20 to 25 minutes, or until the focaccia is golden brown and crisp. (You may prepare the recipe ahead to this point, but leave the baked focaccia at room temperature.)
- To prepare the topping, combine the olive oil, garlic, basil, salt and pepper. Lay the sliced tomatoes in an overlapping pattern on the focaccia and spoon the olive-oil mixture over them. Return the focaccia to the oven for two minutes. Sprinkle with three tablespoons of Parmesan and return the focaccia to the oven just until the cheese is melted and lightly browned, about one to two minutes. Remove from the oven and cut into large slices. Serve.

Nutrition Information

- 358: calories;
- 352 milligrams: sodium;
- 20 grams: fat;
- 5 grams: saturated fat;
- 12 grams: protein;
- 2 grams: sugars;
- 34 grams: carbohydrates;
- 3 grams: dietary fiber;

30. Beef Stroganoff

Serving: 4 servings | Prep: | Cook: | Ready in: 1hours

Ingredients

- Kosher salt and freshly ground black pepper
- 1 ½ pounds sirloin roast, or beef tenderloin, if you're feeling fancy
- 2 tablespoons all-purpose flour
- 1 ½ teaspoons hot paprika
- 1 tablespoon neutral oil, such as canola or grapeseed
- 4 tablespoons unsalted butter
- ½ pound button mushrooms, cleaned and cut into quarters
- 2 small shallots, thinly sliced
- 12 ounces wide egg noodles
- ¼ cup dry white wine
- 1 cup heavy cream or crème fraîche
- 1 ½ teaspoons Worcestershire sauce
- 1 ½ teaspoons Dijon mustard
- Chopped fresh parsley, for garnish

Direction

- Bring a large pot of salted water to a boil.
- Cut the beef against the grain into 1/2-inch slices, pound lightly, then cut those slices into 1-inch-wide strips.
- Add the flour, paprika, 1 1/2 teaspoons salt and 1 1/2 teaspoons pepper to a large shallow bowl and toss to combine. Dredge the strips of meat in the flour mixture, shake them to remove excess flour, then transfer them to a rimmed baking sheet.
- Place a large skillet over high heat and swirl in the oil. When the oil begins to shimmer, sauté the beef slices, in two batches, until they are well browned on both sides but rare inside, 3 to 4 minutes per batch. Transfer the seared meat to the baking sheet. Turn the heat down slightly.
- Add 1 tablespoon of the butter to the pan. When it has melted and started to foam, add the mushrooms, toss to coat them with the fat, and season with salt and pepper. Cook, stirring frequently, until the mushrooms have released their moisture and are a deep, dark brown, 12 to 15 minutes. About halfway into the process, add the sliced shallots and 1 tablespoon butter and stir to combine.
- While the mushrooms cook, add the noodles to the boiling water, and cook until just done, about 10 minutes. Drain the noodles, and toss with the remaining 2 tablespoons butter. Set aside.
- When the mushrooms and shallots are soft and caramelized, deglaze the pan with the wine, scraping at all the stuck-on bits on the pan's surface. When the wine has reduced by about half, slowly stir in the cream, followed by the Worcestershire and mustard. Add the meat, along with any accumulated juices, and stir to combine. Cook, stirring occasionally,

until the dish is hot and the beef is medium-rare, 2 to 3 minutes. Taste, and adjust the seasonings.
- Serve the noodles under or alongside the stroganoff; sprinkle stroganoff with parsley.

31. Beet Salad With Chèvre Frais And Caraway

Serving: 8 servings. | Prep: | Cook: | Ready in: 4hours

Ingredients

- Roasted Beets
- 1 ½ to 2 pounds large red beets
- 1 ½ to 2 pounds large Chioggia beets
- 1 ½ to 2 pounds large golden beets
- ½ cup olive oil
- ½ cup salt
- 4 tablespoons sugar
- 3 cups red wine vinegar
- Goat Cheese Mousse
- 1 ½ cups skim milk
- 1 cup chèvre
- ¾ cup cream
- ⅔ cup sheep's milk yogurt
- 2 tablespoons lime juice
- 2 tablespoons salt
- 1 N2O charger
- Caraway Tuiles
- 2 tablespoons caraway seeds
- ⅔ cup rye flour
- ½ cup flour
- 1 teaspoon baking soda
- ½ cup butter, melted
- ¾ cup glucose syrup
- 4 egg whites
- Rye Crumble
- ½ cup butter, room temperature
- ¼ cup sugar
- 1 cup rye flour
- 1 cup bread flour
- 2 tablespoons caraway seeds
- 1 tablespoon plus 1 teaspoon salt
- 1 tablespoon milk
- Beet Vinaigrette
- 2 cups red beet juice
- ½ cup white balsamic vinegar
- 1 tablespoon caraway seeds
- 1 teaspoon black peppercorns
- 1 cup raspberries
- 1 teaspoon salt
- ¼ teaspoon xanthan gum (6/10 grams)
- 2 tablespoons olive oil
- To finish the salad
- Roasted Beets
- 2 tablespoons olive oil
- Fleur de sel
- Caraway Tuiles
- Goat Cheese Mousse
- 3 tablespoons Beet Vinaigrette
- 3 teaspoons Rye Crumble
- 32 dill blossoms

Direction

-
-
-
-
-
-
-

32. Beet And Beet Green Fritters

Serving: 16 to 18 fritters, serving 5 to 6 | Prep: | Cook: | Ready in: 2hours30mins

Ingredients

- 1 bunch beets, with greens, peeled and grated on the wide holes of a grater or food processor (about 1 to 1 1/4 pounds beets)
- Salt
- Greens from 1 bunch beets, stemmed and washed in 2 changes of water
- 2 eggs
- ½ cup chopped mixed fresh herbs, like as fennel, dill, mint, parsley

- 2 teaspoons ground cumin
- 1 teaspoon ground caraway
- 1 cup fresh or dry bread crumbs (more as necessary)
- Freshly ground pepper
- 2 ounces feta, crumbled (1/2 cup)
- All-purpose flour as needed and for dredging
- ¼ cup canola oil
- ¼ cup extra virgin olive oil
- Plain Greek-style yogurt or aioli for serving

Direction

- Salt the beets generously and leave them to drain in a colander placed in the sink or in a bowl for 1 hour, tossing and squeezing the beets from time to time (wear rubber gloves to protect your hands from the color). After an hour, take up the grated beets by the handful, squeeze out as much liquid as you can and transfer to a bowl.
- While the beets are draining, heat a large pot of water over high heat and stem and wash the beet greens in 2 changes of water. When the water comes to a boil, salt generously and add the beet greens. Cook for about 1 minute, until tender, and transfer to a bowl of ice water. Let sit for a few minutes, then drain, squeeze dry and chop fine. Alternatively, steam the greens for 2 minutes above 1 inch of boiling water.
- In a large bowl, beat the eggs and add the grated beets, herbs, cumin, caraway, beet greens, bread crumbs, salt and pepper to taste, and feta. Mix together well. Take up a small handful (one to 2 tablespoons) of the mixture, and if it presses neatly into a patty, it is the right consistency. If it seems wet, add more bread crumbs or a few tablespoons of all-purpose flour. When the mixture has the right consistency, cover the bowl with plastic wrap and refrigerate for one hour or longer.
- Combine the oils in a large frying pan and heat until rippling, about 275 degrees. Meanwhile, take up heaped tablespoons of the beet mixture and form patties. Lightly dredge in flour. Carefully transfer to the pan, taking care to fry them in batches so you don't crowd the pan, and fry until patties are golden brown on both sides. Use tongs, a slotted spatula or a spider to turn the fritters over. Remove from the oil and drain briefly on a rack, then serve, with yogurt or aioli if desired.

Nutrition Information

- 364: calories;
- 518 milligrams: sodium;
- 24 grams: fat;
- 5 grams: saturated fat;
- 6 grams: dietary fiber;
- 12 grams: sugars;
- 9 grams: protein;
- 0 grams: trans fat;
- 14 grams: monounsaturated fat;
- 4 grams: polyunsaturated fat;
- 31 grams: carbohydrates;

33. Beet And Chia Pancakes

Serving: About 15 pancakes | Prep: | Cook: |Ready in: 1hours30mins

Ingredients

- 1 large or 2 medium beets (enough for 1/2 cup puréed roasted beets)
- 125 grams (1 cup) whole wheat flour or teff flour (or a combination)
- 60 grams (1/2 cup) unbleached all-purpose flour
- 10 grams (2 teaspoons) baking powder
- 5 grams (1 teaspoon) baking soda
- 2 grams (rounded 1/4 teaspoon) salt
- 1 tablespoon sugar, honey, or agave syrup (optional)
- 2 eggs
- 5 grams (1 teaspoon) vanilla
- 1 ½ cups buttermilk or 1 cup yogurt + 1/2 cup milk
- 35 grams (3 tablespoons) chia seeds

- 3 tablespoons sunflower, grapeseed or canola oil

Direction

- Preheat the oven to 425 degrees. Cut the greens away from the beets, leaving about 1/4 inch of stems. Scrub the beets and place in a baking dish (or lidded ovenproof casserole). Add 1/2 inch water to the dish. Cover tightly. Place in the oven and roast medium beets (4 to 6 ounces) for 50 minutes, large beets (8 ounces) 60 minutes, or until very soft and easily penetrated with the tip of a knife. Remove from the oven and allow to cool in the covered baking dish. Cut away the ends and slip off the skins. Purée in a food processor fitted with the steel blade until smooth. Measure out 1/2 cup. Freeze any extra.
- Sift together the flours, baking powder, baking soda, salt, and sugar (if using sugar). In a medium-size bowl, beat together the eggs, buttermilk or yogurt and milk, oil, vanilla, beet purée and honey or agave nectar (if using). Quickly whisk in the flour mixture and fold in the chia seeds.
- Heat a large skillet or griddle over medium-high heat and brush with butter or oil. Drop the pancakes by the scant 1/4 cup onto the hot pan or griddle. Cook until bubbles break through and turn the pancakes. They will be quite moist so make sure to wait long enough so that they don't fall apart when you turn them. Cook for 1 to 2 minutes on the other side, until lightly browned. Remove to a rack. Serve with maple syrup and butter.

Nutrition Information

- 101: calories;
- 2 grams: sugars;
- 12 grams: carbohydrates;
- 4 grams: protein;
- 203 milligrams: sodium;
- 5 grams: fat;
- 1 gram: saturated fat;
- 0 grams: trans fat;

34. Black Kale And Black Olive Salad

Serving: 4 servings. | Prep: | Cook: | Ready in: 10mins

Ingredients

- 1 large bunch black kale (about 1 pound), cut into thin ribbons
- ½ cup black olives, pitted and chopped
- ¼ cup grated Parmesan or other hard cheese
- ¼ cup olive oil
- 2 tablespoons sherry vinegar
- Salt
- Black pepper

Direction

- Combine the kale, olives and cheese in a large bowl. Drizzle with the oil and vinegar, sprinkle with salt (not too much) and lots of pepper, and toss
- Taste and adjust the seasoning if necessary. Serve immediately or refrigerate for up to an hour.

Nutrition Information

- 223: calories;
- 0 grams: trans fat;
- 2 grams: polyunsaturated fat;
- 7 grams: protein;
- 365 milligrams: sodium;
- 4 grams: saturated fat;
- 19 grams: fat;
- 12 grams: monounsaturated fat;
- 11 grams: carbohydrates;
- 5 grams: dietary fiber;
- 3 grams: sugars;

35. Black Quinoa, Fennel And Celery Salad

Serving: Serves 4 | Prep: | Cook: | Ready in: 5mins

Ingredients

- 1 medium-size fennel bulb (about 10 ounces), quartered, cored and very thinly sliced
- 1 long or 2 shorter celery sticks, very thinly sliced
- 2 cups cooked black quinoa (about 3/4 cup uncooked)
- ¼ cup chopped flat-leaf parsley
- 2 tablespoons chopped chives
- 2 tablespoons freshly squeezed lemon juice
- 1 small garlic clove, puréed
- Salt and freshly ground pepper to taste
- 5 tablespoons extra virgin olive oil

Direction

- In a salad bowl, combine the sliced fennel and celery, the quinoa, parsley and chives.
- In a small bowl or measuring cup, whisk together the lemon juice, garlic, salt, pepper and olive oil. Toss with the salad and serve.

Nutrition Information

- 289: calories;
- 19 grams: fat;
- 3 grams: polyunsaturated fat;
- 13 grams: monounsaturated fat;
- 27 grams: carbohydrates;
- 5 grams: protein;
- 4 grams: sugars;
- 474 milligrams: sodium;

36. Black Rice And Arborio Risotto With Artichokes

Serving: 6 servings | Prep: | Cook: | Ready in: 2hours

Ingredients

- 1 cup black rice, like Lundberg Black Japonica or Forbidden Rice, cooked (3 cups cooked)
- 8 baby artichokes, trimmed and quartered, or 1 12-ounce package frozen artichoke hearts, thawed
- 1 lemon, cut in half
- About 7 cups chicken or vegetable stock, as needed
- 2 tablespoons extra virgin olive oil
- ½ cup minced onion
- Salt to taste
- 2 garlic cloves, minced
- ⅔ cup arborio rice
- 1 teaspoon fresh thyme leaves, or 1/2 teaspoon dried thyme
- ½ cup dry white wine, like pinot grigio or sauvignon blanc
- ¼ cup chopped fresh parsley
- 2 teaspoons lemon zest
- 2 teaspoons fresh lemon juice
- ¼ to ½ cup grated Parmesan cheese, or a mixture of Parmesan and pecorino Romano (optional)
- Freshly ground pepper

Direction

- To cook the black rice, combine with 2 cups water in a saucepan, add salt to taste and bring to a boil. Reduce the heat, cover and simmer 30 to 40 minutes, until all of the liquid has been absorbed by the rice. Remove from the heat, remove the lid from the pan and place a dish towel over the pan, then return the lid. Let sit for 10 to 15 minutes.
- To trim the artichokes, fill a bowl with water and add the juice of 1/2 lemon. Cut the stems off the artichokes and, with a sharp knife, cut away the tops — about 1/2 inch from the top for baby artichokes. Rub the cut parts with the other half of the lemon. Break off the tough outer leaves until you reach the lighter green leaves near the middle. With a paring knife, trim the bottom of the bulb right above the stem by holding the knife at an angle and

cutting around the artichoke, until you reach the light-colored flesh beneath the tough bottoms of the leaves. Cut in quarters and cut away the chokes. Place in the bowl of acidulated water until ready to cook.
- Put your stock or broth into a saucepan and bring it to a simmer on the stove, with a ladle nearby or in the pot. Make sure that it is well seasoned.
- Drain the artichoke hearts and pat dry. Heat the oil in a wide, heavy nonstick skillet or saucepan over medium heat. Add the onion and salt to taste, and cook gently until tender, 3 to 5 minutes. Add the artichoke hearts and the garlic and stir for 2 to 3 minutes, until the artichoke hearts are beginning to color.
- Stir in the arborio rice and thyme and stir until the grains become separate and begin to crackle. Add the wine and cook, stirring, until the wine has just about evaporated and been absorbed by the rice. Stir in enough of the simmering stock to just cover the rice. The stock should bubble slowly. Cook, stirring often, until it is just about absorbed. Add another ladleful or two of the stock and continue to cook in this fashion, not too fast and not too slowly, adding more stock when the rice is almost dry and stirring often, for about 20 minutes. When the rice is tender all the way through but still chewy, it is done. Add pepper, taste and adjust seasoning.
- Mince the parsley and lemon zest together, and add to the risotto with the black rice, along with another ladleful or two of stock and freshly ground pepper. Simmer, stirring often, for 5 minutes. Remove from the heat, add another small ladleful of stock and a teaspoon or two of lemon juice, and stir in the cheese if using. Serve right away, in wide soup bowls or on plates, spreading the risotto in a thin layer rather than a mound.

Nutrition Information

- 461: calories;
- 14 grams: dietary fiber;
- 7 grams: sugars;
- 18 grams: protein;
- 9 grams: fat;
- 2 grams: polyunsaturated fat;
- 5 grams: monounsaturated fat;
- 77 grams: carbohydrates;
- 1369 milligrams: sodium;

37. Black Rice, Corn And Cranberries

Serving: 8 servings | Prep: | Cook: | Ready in: 45mins

Ingredients

- 1 cup black rice or wild rice
- 3 tablespoons olive oil or other healthy vegetable oil
- 3 to 4 cloves garlic, minced
- 3 to 4 scallions, green and white parts, thinly sliced
- 2 cups thawed frozen corn kernels
- ¼ cup lemon or lime juice, or to taste
- ¼ to ½ cup chopped cilantro leaves, to taste
- 2 teaspoons ground cumin
- ½ teaspoon dried oregano
- ¼ teaspoon dried thyme
- ½ cup dried cranberries
- Salt and freshly ground pepper to taste
- ¼ cup toasted pumpkin seeds for topping

Direction

- If using black rice, combine in a saucepan with 2 cups water. Bring to a rapid simmer, then lower the heat, cover, and simmer gently until the water is absorbed, about 30 minutes. If you'd like a more tender grain, add 1/2 cup additional water and cook until absorbed. If using wild rice, combine with 3 cups of water and cook as directed above.
- Just before the rice is done, heat half the oil in a large skillet. Add the garlic and sauté over low heat until golden. Add the scallions and

corn kernels and sauté just until warmed through.
- Transfer the cooked rice to the skillet. Turn the heat up to medium-high, then add the lime juice, cilantro, cumin, oregano, thyme, cranberries, and remaining oil. Gently stir the mixture, then season to taste with salt and pepper.
- To serve, transfer to an attractive serving platter and sprinkle the pumpkin seeds over the top.

Nutrition Information

- 209: calories;
- 206 milligrams: sodium;
- 6 grams: sugars;
- 1 gram: polyunsaturated fat;
- 4 grams: monounsaturated fat;
- 35 grams: carbohydrates;
- 3 grams: protein;

38. Black And Arborio Risotto With Beets And Beet Greens

Serving: 6 servings | Prep: | Cook: | Ready in: 2hours

Ingredients

- 1 cup black rice, like Lundberg Black Japonica or Forbidden Rice, cooked (3 cups cooked black rice)
- 1 quart chicken or vegetable stock, as needed
- 1 bunch beet greens, stemmed and washed
- 2 tablespoons extra virgin olive oil
- ½ cup finely chopped onion
- ⅔ cup arborio rice
- 2 garlic cloves, minced
- ½ cup dry white wine
- ¾ pound beets (1 bunch small), roasted, skinned and diced
- Salt
- Freshly ground pepper
- 1 to 2 ounces Parmesan cheese, grated (1/4 to 1/2 cup, to taste, optional)
- 2 tablespoons finely chopped flat-leaf parsley

Direction

- To cook the black rice, combine with 2 cups water in a saucepan, add salt to taste and bring to a boil. Reduce the heat, cover and simmer 30 to 40 minutes, until all of the liquid has been absorbed by the rice. Remove from the heat, remove the lid from the pan and place a dish towel over the pan, then return the lid. Let sit for 10 to 15 minutes.
- Bring the stock to a simmer in a saucepan. Season well and turn the heat to low. Stack the stemmed, washed greens and cut crosswise into 1-inch-wide strips.
- Heat the oil over medium heat in a large nonstick frying pan or wide, heavy saucepan and add the onion. Cook, stirring, until the onion begins to soften, about 3 minutes, and add the rice and garlic. Cook, stirring, until the grains of rice are separate and beginning to crackle, about 3 minutes.
- Stir in the wine and cook over medium heat, stirring constantly. The wine should bubble, but not too quickly. You want some of the flavor to cook into the rice before it evaporates. When the wine has just about evaporated, stir in a ladleful or two of the simmering stock (about 1/2 cup), enough to just cover the rice. The stock should bubble slowly (adjust heat accordingly). Cook, stirring often, until it is just about absorbed. Add another ladleful or two of the stock and continue to cook in this fashion, not too fast and not too slowly, stirring often and adding more stock when the rice is almost dry, for 10 minutes.
- Stir in the greens, the diced beets and black rice and continue adding more stock, enough to barely cover the rice, and stirring often, for another 10 to 15 minutes. The arborio rice should be chewy but not hard in the middle – and definitely not soft like steamed rice. If it is still hard in the middle, you need to continue

adding stock and stirring for another 5 minutes or so. Now is the time to ascertain if there is enough salt. Add if necessary.
- When the rice is cooked through, add a generous amount of freshly ground pepper, and stir in another ladleful of stock, the Parmesan and the parsley. Remove from the heat. The risotto should be creamy; if it isn't, add a little more stock. Stir once, taste and adjust seasonings, and serve.

Nutrition Information

- 267: calories;
- 1 gram: polyunsaturated fat;
- 4 grams: dietary fiber;
- 40 grams: carbohydrates;
- 8 grams: protein;
- 768 milligrams: sodium;
- 7 grams: sugars;

39. Black Eyed Pea Salad

Serving: 4 servings | Prep: | Cook: | Ready in: 2hours

Ingredients

- 1 cup black-eyed peas, rinsed and picked over
- 3 large garlic cloves, 2 of them crushed and left in the skin, 1 of them minced
- ½ onion, intact
- 1 bay leaf
- Salt to taste
- 2 medium tomatoes, in season only, diced
- 1 medium fennel bulb (about 1/2 pound), trimmed, quartered, cored and sliced very thin across the grain
- 1 tablespoon fresh lemon juice
- 2 tablespoons red wine vinegar or cider vinegar
- 3 tablespoons extra virgin olive oil
- 1 teaspoon cumin seeds, lightly toasted and ground
- Freshly ground black pepper to taste
- ⅓ cup chopped flat-leaf parsley
- ⅓ cup chopped fresh dill
- ⅓ cup chopped chives
- 2 ounces feta, crumbled

Direction

- Place the black-eyed peas, whole crushed garlic cloves, halved onion and bay leaf in a large, heavy saucepan and add enough water to cover by 2 inches. Bring to a boil, add salt to taste, reduce the heat, cover and simmer until tender but intact, about 45 minutes. Remove from the heat, remove the lid and allow the black-eyed peas to cool for 30 minutes. Remove and discard the onion. Remove the garlic cloves, squeeze the cooked garlic out of the skins and back into the black-eyed peas, and drain through a strainer set over a bowl.
- Transfer the black-eyed peas to a large bowl. Whisk together the lemon juice, vinegar, minced garlic, cumin, salt, pepper and olive oil. Toss with the beans. Add the remaining ingredients except the feta and toss together. If you want a bit more liquid with the beans, add back some of the broth (I found the dressing to be sufficient). Marinate in the refrigerator for at least 30 minutes before serving. Sprinkle the feta over the top and serve.

Nutrition Information

- 210: calories;
- 1 gram: polyunsaturated fat;
- 5 grams: protein;
- 6 grams: sugars;
- 512 milligrams: sodium;
- 14 grams: fat;
- 4 grams: saturated fat;
- 8 grams: monounsaturated fat;
- 18 grams: carbohydrates;

40. Braised Red Cabbage With Apples

Serving: 6 to 8 servings | Prep: | Cook: |Ready in: 1hours15mins

Ingredients

- 1 large red cabbage, 2 to 2 1/2 pounds, quartered, cored and cut crosswise in thin strips
- 2 tablespoons canola oil
- 1 small onion, thinly sliced
- 2 tart apples, such as Braeburn or granny smith, peeled, cored and sliced
- About 1/3 cup balsamic vinegar
- ¼ teaspoon ground allspice
- Salt
- freshly ground pepper to taste

Direction

- Prepare the cabbage, and cover with cold water while you prepare the remaining ingredients. Heat the oil over medium heat in a large, lidded skillet or casserole, and add the onion. Cook, stirring, until just about tender, about three minutes. Add 2 tablespoons of the balsamic vinegar and cook, stirring, until the mixture is golden, about three minutes, then add the apples and stir for two to three minutes.
- Drain the cabbage and add to the pot. Toss to coat thoroughly, then stir in the allspice, another 2 tablespoons balsamic vinegar, and salt to taste. Toss together. Cover the pot, and cook over low heat for one hour, stirring from time to time. Add freshly ground pepper, taste and adjust salt, and add another tablespoon or two of balsamic vinegar as desired.

Nutrition Information

- 102: calories;
- 0 grams: trans fat;
- 2 grams: protein;
- 1 gram: polyunsaturated fat;
- 17 grams: carbohydrates;
- 10 grams: sugars;
- 453 milligrams: sodium;
- 4 grams: dietary fiber;

41. Braised Stuffed Artichoke A La Barigoule

Serving: 4 servings | Prep: | Cook: |Ready in: 2hours

Ingredients

- 4 artichokes
- 1 white onion, peeled and minced
- 1 carrot, peeled and minced
- 2 cloves garlic, minced
- ½ cup olive oil
- 4 cups white wine
- 1 cup vegetable or chicken broth
- 2 cups mashed potatoes
- 1 cup basil leaves
- Salt and freshly ground black pepper to taste
- 1 cup asparagus tips
- 1 large tomato, peeled, seeded and minced
- 26 black olives, pitted and chopped

Direction

- Use scissors to remove the thorny ends of the artichoke leaves. Use a knife to remove the stem so the artichokes will sit flat. In a heavy pot, combine the onion, carrot and garlic with 4 tablespoons of the olive oil over low heat and cook until the onion is tender and gold, about 10 minutes. Add the white wine and simmer 2 minutes. Add the artichokes, cover, and cook about 1 hour, until tender. Remove the artichokes from the pot and set aside; reserve the broth.
- Put the mashed potatoes in a mixing bowl. Mince the basil, and in another bowl combine it well with 2 tablespoons of olive oil. Whisk 3 tablespoons of the basil mixture into the potatoes, add salt and pepper and set aside. Use a spoon to remove the thistly choke from

the center of each artichoke. Spoon the potato mixture into the center of each and set aside.
- Return the broth in the pot to the stove over medium heat. Add the asparagus and simmer 10 minutes. Add the tomato and olives and simmer 2 minutes. Put the artichokes back in the pot and cook until completely warm, about 5 minutes. Put each artichoke in the center of a shallow bowl. Whisk the remaining basil paste into the broth, gently ladle it around the artichokes, and serve.

Nutrition Information

- 638: calories;
- 7 grams: protein;
- 41 grams: carbohydrates;
- 8 grams: sugars;
- 1455 milligrams: sodium;
- 34 grams: fat;
- 5 grams: polyunsaturated fat;
- 0 grams: trans fat;
- 23 grams: monounsaturated fat;

42. Bread And Butter Pickles

Serving: 8 pint jars | Prep: | Cook: | Ready in: 35mins

Ingredients

- 8 medium cucumbers, sliced into 1/8-inch-thick rounds
- ⅓ cup kosher salt
- 4 medium onions, peeled and thinly sliced
- 1 green bell pepper, stemmed, seeded and cut into 1/4-inch dice
- 1 red bell pepper, stemmed, seeded and cut into 1/4-inch dice
- 3 cups white vinegar
- 3 cups sugar
- 1 tablespoon mustard seeds
- 1 teaspoon celery seeds

Direction

- In a large bowl, toss the cucumbers and salt and let stand for 4 hours or, refrigerated, overnight.
- Have ready 8 hot, sterilized pint (2-cup) jars and lids. (See pickled peppers for sterilizing instructions.) Place the cucumber slices and their liquid in a large kettle and add remaining ingredients. Place over high heat and bring just to a boil. Remove from heat. Gently pack the cucumbers into the jars, leaving 1/4inch of space below the lip. Pour enough liquid into the jars to cover the ingredients. Wipe rims with a clean, damp towel and screw lids on securely but not too tightly.
- Fill a large kettle fitted with a rack halfway with water and bring to a boil. Meanwhile, bring a teapot full of water to a boil. Place the filled jars on the rack (do not let them touch -- work in batches if necessary) and pour in boiling water from the teapot until jar tops are covered by 2 inches. Bring to a boil and boil 10 minutes.
- Using tongs, remove jars from the kettle. Using potholders, tighten lids. Allow to cool. Store in a cool, dark place.

Nutrition Information

- 377: calories;
- 1 gram: fat;
- 0 grams: polyunsaturated fat;
- 91 grams: carbohydrates;
- 3 grams: protein;
- 82 grams: sugars;
- 1139 milligrams: sodium;

43. Brioche Stuffing With Chestnuts And Figs

Serving: 10 servings | Prep: | Cook: | Ready in: 1hours

Ingredients

- ½ loaf of brioche

- ½ cup (1 stick) butter
- ½ cup celery, medium fine dice
- ½ cup fennel, medium fine dice
- ¼ cup Fiji apple, medium fine dice
- 1 cup Spanish onion, medium fine dice
- 1 pound vegetarian sausage, finely diced (optional)
- ⅔ cup glazed chestnuts, medium fine dice
- ⅔ cup dried figs, medium fine dice
- ⅓ cup reduced (syrupy) vegetable stock
- 2 cups vegetable stock
- 1 tablespoon salt
- 2 eggs
- 2 teaspoons fresh thyme leaves, chopped
- 2 teaspoons fresh sage leaves, chopped
- 2 teaspoons fresh marjoram leaves, chopped
- 1 pinch quatre épices
- 2 teaspoons ground pepper

Direction

- Dice brioche into a medium-fine dice and allow to dry in a low oven or overnight at room temperature. Once dry, you will have about 2 cups total.
- Melt 1/4 cup (1/2 stick) of butter in a sauté pan. Sweat the celery, fennel, apple and onion until translucent and soft. ("Sweating" vegetables means slowly cooking them over low heat until soft but not brown.)
- In a second sauté pan, melt the remaining butter and cook sausage gently. Combine the butter and sausage with the diced brioche, celery and onion mixture, chestnuts, figs, reduced stock and stock in a large bowl and toss gently. Season with salt to taste. Gently add eggs and toss to combine. Finish with chopped herbs, spices and pepper.
- Bake in a 9- by 13-inch baking dish at 350 degrees Fahrenheit for 40 minutes or until browned and hot throughout.

Nutrition Information

- 221: calories;
- 2 grams: dietary fiber;
- 6 grams: sugars;
- 341 milligrams: sodium;
- 4 grams: protein;
- 12 grams: fat;
- 7 grams: saturated fat;
- 0 grams: trans fat;
- 3 grams: monounsaturated fat;
- 1 gram: polyunsaturated fat;
- 26 grams: carbohydrates;

44. Broccoli Rabe With Raisins And Garlic

Serving: 6 servings | Prep: | Cook: | Ready in: 25mins

Ingredients

- 2 pounds broccoli rabe, washed, trimmed and chopped
- 4 tablespoons extra-virgin olive oil
- 2 cloves garlic, minced
- ½ cup raisins
- ¾ teaspoon kosher salt
- ½ teaspoon dried red pepper flakes

Direction

- Bring a gallon of water to a boil in a large pot. Blanche the rabe for 7 minutes and cool under cold running water. Drain.
- Heat 2 tablespoons of the olive oil in a large skillet over medium heat. Add the garlic and toss, cooking for about 2 minutes, until golden. Add the cooked rabe, raisins, salt and pepper flakes. Shake the skillet and cook until hot, about 7 minutes.
- Pour the remaining oil over the vegetables and adjust seasoning. Serve hot or at room temperature.

Nutrition Information

- 151: calories;
- 14 grams: carbohydrates;

- 5 grams: protein;
- 8 grams: sugars;
- 287 milligrams: sodium;
- 10 grams: fat;
- 1 gram: polyunsaturated fat;
- 7 grams: monounsaturated fat;

45. Broccoli, Cabbage And Kohlrabi Coleslaw With Quinoa

Serving: 3 generous servings. | Prep: | Cook: | Ready in: 1hours

Ingredients

- 3 ½ cups mixed shredded broccoli stems, green cabbage and kohlrabi (peel broccoli stems and kohlrabi before shredding) (about 3/4 pound)
- Salt to taste
- ½ cup cooked quinoa
- 2 tablespoons chopped fresh dill
- ½ teaspoons nigella seeds (optional)
- 3 tablespoons fresh lemon juice
- 1 tablespoon seasoned rice vinegar
- 2 teaspoons Dijon mustard
- 2 tablespoons grapeseed or canola oil
- ¼ cup plain low-fat yogurt
- Freshly ground pepper
- ½ cup low-fat cottage cheese (optional)

Direction

- Toss the shredded vegetables with salt to taste and place in a strainer set over a bowl. Refrigerate and let sit for 45 minutes to an hour. Discard the water that accumulates in the bowl and squeeze the shredded vegetables to extract more water. (Note: If you are on a no-sodium diet, omit this step). Transfer to a bowl and toss with the quinoa, dill and nigella seeds.
- In a small bowl or measuring cup, mix together the lemon juice, rice vinegar, salt, pepper, Dijon mustard, oil and yogurt. Toss with the shredded vegetables. Add the cottage cheese to the salad and toss, or serve with the cottage cheese spooned on top. Refrigerate in a bowl or in containers until ready to take to work.

Nutrition Information

- 247: calories;
- 1 gram: saturated fat;
- 3 grams: polyunsaturated fat;
- 10 grams: protein;
- 1055 milligrams: sodium;
- 11 grams: sugars;
- 0 grams: trans fat;
- 6 grams: monounsaturated fat;
- 33 grams: carbohydrates;
- 12 grams: dietary fiber;

46. Broiled Fish With Chermoula

Serving: Serves 4 | Prep: | Cook: | Ready in: 45mins

Ingredients

- 1 ½ to 2 pounds firm white fish fillets, such as halibut, mahi mahi, striped bass
- Salt and freshly ground pepper
- 1 recipe chermoula (see recipe)
- Additional lemon juice and wedges or olive oil to taste

Direction

- Season the fish with salt and pepper. In a large baking dish combine the fish with half the chermoula and toss together until the fish is coated. If the chermoula is thick it may be easier to spread it onto the fish with a spatula. Refrigerate for 15 to 30 minutes while you preheat the broiler or prepare a grill.
- If using a broiler, line a sheet pan with foil and brush the foil with olive oil, or oil a shallow baking dish. Place the fish in the pan in a

single layer. If desired drizzle on a little more olive oil or lemon juice. Place under the broiler, close to the heat (about 2 1/2 inches below) and broil 5 minutes. Check the fish; the timing depends on how thick the fillets are; figure on 4 to 5 minutes per 1/2 inch of thickness. It is done when it is opaque and you can pull it apart with a fork. Using a spatula, transfer the fish from the sheet pan or baking dish to a platter or to individual plates. Tip the juices in the pan over the fish fillets. Pass the remaining chermoula and lemon wedges at the table.

Nutrition Information

- 163: calories;
- 0 grams: sugars;
- 1 gram: dietary fiber;
- 3 grams: carbohydrates;
- 14 grams: protein;
- 333 milligrams: sodium;
- 11 grams: fat;
- 2 grams: saturated fat;

47. Broiled Tuna Steaks With Herb Vinaigrette

Serving: 4 servings | Prep: | Cook: | Ready in: 1hours10mins

Ingredients

- Salt and freshly ground pepper to taste
- 1 teaspoon grated fresh ginger
- 4 sprigs fresh thyme, chopped coarse, or 1 teaspoon dried
- 2 tablespoons dark soy sauce
- 1 tablespoon fresh lemon juice
- 2 tablespoons olive oil
- 4 tuna steaks, each about 1 inch thick, 2 pounds total weight
- Tomato and herb vinaigrette (see recipe)

Direction

- Preheat the broiler or an outdoor grill.
- In a mixing bowl, blend the salt, pepper, ginger, thyme, soy sauce, lemon juice and olive oil. Brush the mixture all over the tuna. Cover with plastic wrap and let stand about an hour or until ready to broil.
- Arrange the steaks on a rack and place under the broiler or over the grill about 4 inches from the source of heat. Broil about 3 minutes. If using the oven, leave the door partly open. Turn the steaks, continue broiling, leaving the door partly open, for another 3 minutes. The center should remain pink.
- Serve with tomato and herb vinaigrette on the side.

Nutrition Information

- 579: calories;
- 2 grams: saturated fat;
- 5 grams: carbohydrates;
- 1 gram: polyunsaturated fat;
- 3 grams: dietary fiber;
- 112 grams: protein;
- 9 grams: fat;
- 0 grams: sugars;
- 1120 milligrams: sodium;

48. Broken Glass Pudding

Serving: Six or more servings | Prep: | Cook: | Ready in: 1hours30mins

Ingredients

- ¼ teaspoon unsalted butter
- ⅔ cup, plus 2 tablespoons, sugar
- 2 eggs, plus 2 egg yolks
- 2 cups milk
- 1 cup heavy cream
- 1 teaspoon vanilla extract

- 2 pints fresh strawberries, raspberries or blackberries

Direction

- Adjust oven rack to middle shelf and preheat the oven to 350 degrees.
- Lightly butter a small baking pan and set aside.
- Dissolve two-thirds of a cup of sugar with one cup water and heat in a heavy saucepan over medium heat. When the sugar begins to turn golden, rotate the pan to even the color. When the color is a rich amber, pour half the caramel into a one-quart souffle dish and the remainder on the buttered baking pan. Rotate the souffle dish to coat the bottom and even the sugar on the baking pan to coat as much as possible. Set aside to cool.
- Whisk the eggs and yolks in a large mixing bowl until creamy and set aside.
- In a saucepan, heat the milk and a half cup of heavy cream with the remaining two tablespoons of sugar. When the mixture begins to simmer, remove from the heat and slowly whisk into the egg mixture. Add the vanilla and strain the mixture into the souffle dish.
- Place the souffle dish in a roasting pan and set on the oven rack. Add boiling water into the roasting pan until it reaches halfway up the side. Bake for 45 minutes or until a sharp paring knife inserted into the center of the pudding comes out clean. Cool and refrigerate.
- Pull the remaining cooled caramel from the baking pan and crack into random inch-size pieces. Place the pieces in a tightly sealed container and refrigerate until ready to serve.
- When ready to serve, whip the remaining cream and set aside. Sprinkle half the broken caramel over the pudding. Spread the whipped cream over the pudding and cover with the remaining "glass." Serve with fresh berries.

Nutrition Information

- 268: calories;
- 20 grams: fat;
- 13 grams: sugars;
- 7 grams: protein;
- 74 milligrams: sodium;
- 1 gram: polyunsaturated fat;
- 16 grams: carbohydrates;
- 2 grams: dietary fiber;
- 12 grams: saturated fat;
- 0 grams: trans fat;
- 6 grams: monounsaturated fat;

49. Brother Bandera's Italian Easter Bread

Serving: 1 loaf of 12 servings | Prep: | Cook: | Ready in: 2hours45mins

Ingredients

- 4 ½ cups flour (approximately)
- 1 package active dry yeast
- 1 teaspoon salt
- ½ cup sugar
- ½ teaspoon nutmeg, preferably freshly ground
- ¼ teaspoon allspice
- ½ teaspoon grated lemon peel
- ⅔ cup skim milk
- 3 tablespoons unsalted butter, in pieces
- 4 eggs
- ⅓ cup chopped candied fruit peel
- Oil for bowl and pan

Direction

- Place 2 1/2 cups of the flour in a mixing bowl, and mix in the yeast, salt, sugar, nutmeg, allspice and lemon peel.
- Warm the milk and butter in a saucepan to 120 degrees, stir to melt the butter and pour into the bowl with the dry ingredients. Lightly beat 3 of the eggs, add them and mix all the ingredients together. Gradually add enough of the remaining flour to make a soft dough.

- Turn the dough out onto a floured board, flatten it and knead in the fruit peel. Knead the dough about 10 minutes, adding additional flour as necessary to make a soft dough that is barely sticky.
- Lightly oil a bowl, place the dough in it, turn it, cover the bowl and set the dough aside to rise until doubled, about 1 hour.
- Punch the dough down, and divide it in four pieces. Roll each of the pieces into a tight ball and place them in an oiled 10-inch cake pan. Cover, and allow to rise in a warm place about 30 minutes.
- Preheat oven to 350 degrees. Beat the remaining egg with 1 tablespoon of water, and brush this mixture lightly onto the dough. Place in the oven and bake about 45 minutes, until nicely browned. Allow to cool before cutting.

Nutrition Information

- 296: calories;
- 3 grams: saturated fat;
- 0 grams: trans fat;
- 1 gram: polyunsaturated fat;
- 51 grams: carbohydrates;
- 8 grams: protein;
- 6 grams: fat;
- 2 grams: dietary fiber;
- 14 grams: sugars;
- 227 milligrams: sodium;

50. Brown Rice With Carrots And Leeks

Serving: Serves four | Prep: | Cook: | Ready in: 1hours

Ingredients

- 2 tablespoons extra virgin olive oil
- 1 pound leeks, white and light green parts only, trimmed, cut in half lengthwise, washed thoroughly and cut in 1/2-inch slices
- ½ pound carrots, peeled and sliced
- 2 garlic cloves, halved, green shoots removed and thinly sliced
- 1 cup brown rice (short- or long-grain)
- Salt to taste
- 2 ½ cups water
- 2 to 3 tablespoons freshly squeezed lemon juice, to taste

Direction

- Heat the olive oil over a medium-sized, heavy skillet or saucepan, and add the leeks and carrots. Cook, stirring, until the leeks are tender and translucent and the carrots have softened slightly, about five minutes. Add the garlic and salt to taste. Cook, stirring, until the garlic smells fragrant, about a minute. Add the rice and about 1/2 teaspoon salt, and stir to coat the grains with olive oil. Add the water, and bring to a boil. Reduce the heat, cover and simmer over low heat until the rice is tender, about 45 minutes. Remove from the heat, and do not remove the cover for 10 minutes. Then stir in the lemon juice, and taste and adjust salt. Serve hot or warm.

Nutrition Information

- 328: calories;
- 890 milligrams: sodium;
- 9 grams: fat;
- 1 gram: polyunsaturated fat;
- 5 grams: dietary fiber;
- 59 grams: carbohydrates;
- 7 grams: sugars;
- 6 grams: protein;

51. Buckwheat Crêpes With Caramelized Apples

Serving: 12 crêpes, serving 6 | Prep: | Cook: | Ready in: 1hours

Ingredients

- For the crêpes
- 250 grams (1 cup) low-fat or whole milk
- 75 grams (1/3 cup) water
- 3 large eggs
- 3 grams (scant 1/2 teaspoon) salt
- 75 grams (2/3 cup) buckwheat flour
- 62 grams (about 1/2 cup) unbleached all-purpose flour
- 45 grams (3 tablespoons) melted butter or grapeseed oil
- For the Apples
- 30 grams (2 tablespoons) butter
- 15 grams (1 tablespoon) turbinado sugar
- 2 tart apples, such as Pink Lady, Gravenstein, Braeburn or Granny Smith, cored, peeled if desired, and sliced very thin
- ½ teaspoon cinnamon
- ¼ teaspoon freshly grated nutmeg
- Yogurt or crème fraîche for serving

Direction

- Place milk, water, eggs and salt in a blender. Cover blender and turn on at low speed. Add flours, then butter or oil and increase speed to high. Blend for 1 minute. Transfer to a bowl, cover and refrigerate for 1 to 2 hours.
- Place a nonstick or seasoned 8-inch crêpe pan over medium heat. Brush with butter or oil and when pan is hot, just before it begins to smoke, remove from the heat and ladle in about 3 tablespoons batter. Tilt or swirl pan to distribute batter evenly and return to the heat. Cook for about 1 minute, until you can easily loosen the edges with a spatula. Turn and cook on the other side for 20 to 30 seconds. Reverse onto a plate. Continue until all of batter is used up. Keep warm in a low oven.
- To make the caramelized apples, heat a large, heavy skillet over medium-high heat. Add butter. When it begins to color add sugar, apples, cinnamon and nutmeg. Turn heat to high and cook the apples, shaking and flipping them in the pan or stirring with a heat-proof spatula, until they have softened and caramelized, 5 to 10 minutes.
- Place a warm crêpe on a plate and spoon apples onto one half. Fold the crêpe over, then fold over again (to a quarter circle) to make room for another crêpe. Repeat with another crêpe. Top with a spoonful of crème fraiche or yogurt, and serve.

Nutrition Information

- 288: calories;
- 30 grams: carbohydrates;
- 3 grams: dietary fiber;
- 7 grams: protein;
- 251 milligrams: sodium;
- 16 grams: fat;
- 5 grams: saturated fat;
- 4 grams: monounsaturated fat;
- 6 grams: polyunsaturated fat;
- 11 grams: sugars;
- 0 grams: trans fat;

52. Buckwheat And Black Kale With Brussels Sprouts

Serving: 8 servings | Prep: | Cook: | Ready in: 30mins

Ingredients

- 3 medium onions, minced
- 3 cloves garlic, minced
- 1 tablespoon olive oil
- 3 cups buckwheat
- Salt
- Pepper
- 6 cups water
- 1 bunch black kale, blanched and finely chopped
- 2 parsnips, diced and blanched
- 1 tablespoon whipped cream
- 1 tablespoon chopped parsley
- 1 small red onion, sliced and sautéed

- 12 large shiitake mushrooms, quartered and sautéed
- 12 brussels sprouts, quartered or split into leaves (roasted in 375 degree oven until just tender).

Direction

- In a saucepan over medium heat, sweat the onions and garlic by cooking them in 1 tablespoon oil until they release some of their moisture and become slightly translucent, about 5 minutes
- Add buckwheat, and season with salt and pepper to taste. Cover with water and bring to a simmer for approximately 5 minutes. Remove from the heat and let buckwheat rest in water for approximately 10 minutes. Strain excess water. (Note: Do not let buckwheat rest too long or it will become too thick.)
- Once the buckwheat has been drained, immediately add kale and parsnips. Add whipped cream and parsley, and stir gently. Add vegetable stock as needed to reach desired consistency. Garnish by topping with shiitake mushrooms, onions and roasted brussels sprouts.

Nutrition Information

- 328: calories;
- 2 grams: monounsaturated fat;
- 66 grams: carbohydrates;
- 13 grams: protein;
- 6 grams: sugars;
- 1017 milligrams: sodium;
- 5 grams: fat;
- 1 gram: polyunsaturated fat;

53. Bulgur, Prosciutto And Pea Salad With Mustard Dill Vinaigrette

Serving: Four servings | Prep: | Cook: | Ready in: 1hours10mins

Ingredients

- The salad:
- ⅔ cup bulgur wheat
- 3 cups boiling water
- 1 cup cooked peas, cooled
- 1 cup prosciutto, cut into 1 1/4-inch strips
- 1 tablespoon chopped fresh dill
- The vinaigrette:
- 1 shallot, peeled and minced
- 1 teaspoon Dijon mustard
- 2 teaspoons white-wine vinegar
- 2 tablespoons olive oil
- 1 tablespoon water
- ¼ teaspoon salt
- Freshly ground pepper to taste
- 1 tablespoon chopped fresh dill

Direction

- To make the salad, place the bulgur in a large bowl and pour the boiling water over it. Let stand for 1 hour. Drain well. Toss with the peas and prosciutto.
- To make the vinaigrette, whisk together the shallot, mustard and vinegar in a medium bowl. Slowly whisk in the olive oil. Whisk in the water, salt, pepper and dill. Toss the vinaigrette with the salad. Divide among 4 plates, sprinkle with the remaining dill and serve.

Nutrition Information

- 252: calories;
- 973 milligrams: sodium;
- 10 grams: fat;
- 0 grams: trans fat;
- 1 gram: polyunsaturated fat;

- 26 grams: carbohydrates;
- 3 grams: sugars;
- 15 grams: protein;
- 2 grams: saturated fat;
- 6 grams: dietary fiber;

54. Buttered Carrots

Serving: 4 servings | Prep: | Cook: | Ready in: 15mins

Ingredients

- 1 pound carrots, trimmed and scraped
- Salt and freshly ground pepper to taste
- ½ teaspoon sugar
- ¼ cup water
- 1 tablespoon butter
- 2 tablespoons finely chopped parsley

Direction

- Cut the carrots into very thin slices. Place them in a small skillet and add salt, pepper, sugar, water and butter.
- Cover the pan and cook over medium heat, shaking the skillet occasionally. Cook about 8 minutes until the carrots are tender, the liquid has disappeared and the carrots are slightly glazed. Take care they do not burn. Sprinkle the parsley over them and serve.

Nutrition Information

- 76: calories;
- 12 grams: carbohydrates;
- 6 grams: sugars;
- 313 milligrams: sodium;
- 3 grams: dietary fiber;
- 2 grams: saturated fat;
- 0 grams: polyunsaturated fat;
- 1 gram: protein;

55. Buttermilk Chocolate Sauce

Serving: 3/4 cup | Prep: | Cook: | Ready in: 5mins

Ingredients

- ⅓ cup Dutch-processed cocoa, like Droste or Lindt
- ¼ cup firmly packed light-brown sugar
- ½ cup nonfat or low-fat buttermilk

Direction

- Combine cocoa and brown sugar in a small saucepan. Gradually add the buttermilk, stirring to blend smoothly with a wooden spoon. Cook, over medium heat, stirring with a whisk, until the sugar dissolves, about two minutes. Remove from heat. The sauce will thicken as it cools and will keep in the refrigerator for several weeks in a tightly closed container.

Nutrition Information

- 214: calories;
- 51 grams: carbohydrates;
- 6 grams: protein;
- 169 milligrams: sodium;
- 2 grams: saturated fat;
- 1 gram: monounsaturated fat;
- 0 grams: polyunsaturated fat;
- 40 grams: sugars;
- 3 grams: fat;

56. Buttermilk Mango Curry

Serving: Serves 4 | Prep: | Cook: | Ready in: 25mins

Ingredients

- ½ cup grated unsweetened coconut
- ¼ teaspoon cumin
- ½ teaspoon cayenne
- ¼ teaspoon turmeric

- 1 ripe but firm mango
- 2 green chilies (Serrano or Thai), split
- 1 teaspoon salt
- 2 cups buttermilk
- 1 ½ tablespoons vegetable oil
- ½ teaspoon mustard seeds
- ¼ teaspoon fenugreek seeds
- 1 dried red chili
- 10 to 12 curry leaves

Direction

- In a blender, combine the coconut, cumin, 1/4 teaspoon cayenne, 1/8 teaspoon turmeric and 1/2 cup of water. Blend to a paste.
- Peel, seed and cut mango into 1/2-inch cubes (about 1 cup). In a saucepan, combine the mango, green chilies, remaining cayenne and turmeric, salt and 1 cup water. Simmer until the mango is soft.
- Add the coconut paste and buttermilk and stir over medium heat; do not let it boil. When the mixture is hot, remove it from the heat.
- In a small pan, heat the oil over medium-high heat. Add the mustard seeds and cover. After the seeds begin popping, add the fenugreek and chili. When the fenugreek is toasted, toss in the curry leaves, then pour this into the buttermilk mixture. Serve warm over rice.

Nutrition Information

- 234: calories;
- 7 grams: saturated fat;
- 25 grams: carbohydrates;
- 4 grams: dietary fiber;
- 19 grams: sugars;
- 6 grams: protein;
- 576 milligrams: sodium;
- 14 grams: fat;
- 0 grams: trans fat;
- 5 grams: monounsaturated fat;
- 1 gram: polyunsaturated fat;

57. Cabbage And Onion Marmalade

Serving: One 12- to 14-inch pizza, 8 slices | Prep: | Cook: | Ready in: 2hours

Ingredients

- 2 tablespoons olive oil
- 1 to 1 ¼ pounds onions, quartered lengthwise and thinly sliced across the grain
- 1 pound cabbage, shredded or finely chopped
- Salt and freshly ground pepper
- 3 garlic cloves, minced
- 2 teaspoons fresh thyme leaves, or 1 teaspoon dried thyme
- 1 tablespoon capers, drained, rinsed and mashed in a mortar and pestle or finely chopped
- For pizza:
- ½ recipe whole-wheat pizza dough
- 12 anchovy fillets, soaked in water for 5 minutes, drained, rinsed and dried on paper towels (optional)
- 12 Niçoise olives (optional)

Direction

- Heat the olive oil in a large, heavy nonstick skillet over medium heat. Add the onions and cabbage with a generous pinch of salt and cook, stirring, until they begin to soften, about 5 minutes. Add another generous pinch of salt, cover the pan and turn the heat to low. Cook slowly for one hour, stirring often, until the mixture has melted down to a sweet, soft, golden marmalade. Add the garlic, thyme, capers, and salt and pepper to taste. Cover and cook for another 15 minutes. Uncover, and if there is a lot of liquid in the pan, cook until the liquid in the pan has cooked off.
- For pizza, preheat the oven to 450 degrees, preferably with a baking stone in it. Roll out the pizza dough and line a 12- to 14-inch pan. Brush the remaining tablespoon of oil over the bottom but not the rim of the crust. Spread the onion and cabbage mixture over the crust in an even layer. Cut the anchovies in half and decorate the top of the crust with them,

making 12 small x's and placing an olive in the middle of each x. Place on top of the pizza stone and bake 10 to 15 minutes, until the edges of the crust are brown and the topping is beginning to brown. Remove from the heat. Serve hot or warm or at room temperature.

Nutrition Information

- 149: calories;
- 1 gram: polyunsaturated fat;
- 3 grams: monounsaturated fat;
- 23 grams: carbohydrates;
- 4 grams: protein;
- 6 grams: sugars;
- 437 milligrams: sodium;
- 5 grams: fat;

58. Cabbage, Onion And Millet Kugel

Serving: 6 servings | Prep: | Cook: | Ready in: 2hours

Ingredients

- ½ medium head cabbage (1 1/2 pounds), cored and cut in thin strips
- Salt to taste
- 2 tablespoons extra virgin olive oil
- 1 medium onion, finely chopped
- ¼ cup chopped fresh dill
- Freshly ground pepper
- 1 cup low-fat cottage cheese
- 2 eggs
- 2 cups cooked millet

Direction

- Preheat the oven to 375 degrees. Oil a 2-quart baking dish. Toss the cabbage with salt to taste and let it sit for 10 minutes
- Meanwhile, heat 1 tablespoon of the oil over medium heat in a large, heavy skillet and add the onion. Cook, stirring, until it begins to soften, about 3 minutes, then add a generous pinch of salt and turn the heat to medium-low. Cook, stirring often, until the onion is soft and beginning to color, about 10 minutes. Add the cabbage, turn the heat to medium, and cook, stirring often, until the cabbage is quite tender and fragrant, 10 to 15 minutes. Stir in the dill, taste and adjust salt, and add pepper to taste. Transfer to a large bowl
- In a food processor fitted with the steel blade, purée the cottage cheese until smooth. Add the eggs and process until the mixture is smooth. Add salt (I suggest about 1/2 teaspoon) and pepper and mix together. Scrape into the bowl with the cabbage. Add the millet and stir everything together. Scrape into the oiled baking dish. Drizzle the remaining oil over the top and place in the oven
- Bake for about 40 minutes, until the sides are nicely browned and the top is beginning to color. Remove from the oven and allow to cool for at least 15 minutes before serving. Serve warm or at room temperature, cut into squares or wedges

Nutrition Information

- 198: calories;
- 2 grams: saturated fat;
- 0 grams: trans fat;
- 4 grams: dietary fiber;
- 1 gram: polyunsaturated fat;
- 24 grams: carbohydrates;
- 6 grams: sugars;
- 7 grams: fat;
- 10 grams: protein;
- 575 milligrams: sodium;

59. Caesar Salad

Serving: Six servings | Prep: | Cook: | Ready in: 20mins

Ingredients

- 5 anchovies
- 1 teaspoon cracked black peppercorns
- ½ cup, plus 1/2 teaspoon, extra-virgin olive oil
- ½ cup freshly grated Parmesan cheese
- 1 egg
- 1 clove garlic, peeled
- 1 tablespoon red-wine vinegar
- 2 tablespoons fresh lemon juice
- 1 ½ teaspoons dry mustard
- 3 dashes Tabasco
- 3 dashes Worcestershire sauce
- ½ loaf sourdough baguette or hearty French or Italian bread with crust, diced for croutons
- 2 medium heads Romaine lettuce

Direction

- Combine the anchovies, black pepper and a half-cup of the olive oil in a blender or food processor. Puree about five minutes until very smooth. Add the grated Parmesan and blend briefly to combine. Measure and reserve one-third cup of the anchovy mixture for use with the croutons.
- Bring a small saucepan water to a boil. Place a refrigerated egg on a slotted spoon and submerge in boiling water. Cook one-and-a-half minutes, remove from the water and reserve.
- Puree the garlic with the remaining half teaspoon of olive oil in a blender, or mash together with a mortar and pestle.
- Place the garlic and the remaining dressing ingredients in a large bowl and whisk in the anchovy mixture. Crack open the egg and spoon it (including the parts that are uncooked) into the mixture. Whisk until well combined.
- Combine the reserved anchovy mixture with the diced bread in a bowl and toss to coat. Heat a dry cast-iron skillet over medium-high heat and cook the croutons, stirring constantly until golden and crisp.
- Wash and dry the lettuce. Discard the tough outer leaves and break the remaining leaves into bite-sized pieces. Place in a salad bowl along with the dressing and toss well. Add the toasted croutons, toss again and serve.

Nutrition Information

- 172: calories;
- 450 milligrams: sodium;
- 6 grams: fat;
- 2 grams: monounsaturated fat;
- 5 grams: dietary fiber;
- 3 grams: sugars;
- 10 grams: protein;
- 0 grams: trans fat;
- 1 gram: polyunsaturated fat;
- 22 grams: carbohydrates;

60. Cajun Cornbread Casserole

Serving: 4 servings | Prep: | Cook: | Ready in: 1hours15mins

Ingredients

- 1 15-ounce can diced tomatoes, undrained
- 1 small onion, diced
- 2 celery stalks, minced
- 3 garlic cloves, minced
- 1 bell pepper, seeded and diced
- 2 tablespoons Cajun seasoning (commercial blend, or make your own)
- 1 15-ounce can kidney beans, drained and rinsed
- 1 cup cornmeal
- 1 ½ teaspoons baking powder
- Pinch of salt
- 1 to 2 tablespoons raw sugar (optional)
- ¾ cup nondairy milk
- ¼ cup unsweetened applesauce

Direction

- Preheat oven to 400 degrees. Grease an 8- or 9-inch square baking pan or casserole dish.

- Drain tomato juices into a skillet, and chop tomatoes into smaller pieces. Set chopped tomatoes aside to use in Step 5.
- Add water as necessary until a thin layer of liquid covers the skillet.
- Sauté onion, celery, garlic and bell pepper over high heat until onion is translucent, bell pepper slices are tender and all of the water has evaporated, about 4 minutes.
- Turn off heat, and mix in 1 to 2 tablespoons of Cajun Seasoning, chopped tomatoes and kidney beans, stirring to combine. Set aside.
- In a small mixing bowl, whisk cornmeal, baking powder, salt and, if desired, additional Cajun Seasoning (several dashes, so the mix looks speckled when stirred). You can also add 1 to 2 teaspoons of sugar if you like a sweet cornbread topping. Then stir in nondairy milk and applesauce. It should be thick but spreadable, like hummus, and not dry.
- Pour bean mixture into your baking dish, and pat down firmly with a spatula. Spread cornbread mixture on top, and bake for 30 to 35 minutes, or until the cornbread is a deep golden, cracked and firm to the touch. Allow to set out for 15 minutes before serving.

Nutrition Information

- 316: calories;
- 3 grams: fat;
- 61 grams: carbohydrates;
- 11 grams: protein;
- 592 milligrams: sodium;
- 2 grams: saturated fat;
- 1 gram: polyunsaturated fat;
- 10 grams: dietary fiber;
- 9 grams: sugars;

61. Campari Jelly

Serving: 4 to 6 servings | Prep: | Cook: |Ready in: 20mins

Ingredients

- ½ cup sugar
- ½ cup Campari, at room temperature
- 1 packet unflavored gelatin
- ¾ cup sparkling water
- 1 teaspoon silver mini dragées, optional
- Orange jellies (see recipe)

Direction

- Make simple syrup: Place sugar in a saucepan, add 2/3 cup water, bring to a simmer and cook just until sugar dissolves. Allow to cool to room temperature.
- In a bowl, mix Campari and simple syrup. Place gelatin in a small metal bowl or 1-cup metal measuring cup and pour 1/4 cup Campari mixture over it to soften it. When gelatin is soft, place bowl or cup in a shallow pan with simmering water below rim of bowl or cup. Simmer until gelatin mixture liquefies. Slowly whisk liquid gelatin into rest of Campari mixture. Stir in sparkling water.
- If using candies, divide them among 4 4-ounce or 6 3-ounce metal or silicon molds. Strain Campari mixture into molds. Refrigerate until firm, at least 4 hours. Unmold onto dessert plates by first dipping molds in hot water for count of 20. Return plates to refrigerator for at least 1 hour before serving. Serve with orange jellies.

62. Caramel Ice Cream

Serving: About 1 1/2 quarts, 6 to 8 servings | Prep: | Cook: | Ready in: 30mins

Ingredients

- For the caramel:

- 1 ¼ cups heavy cream
- 1 ½ cups sugar
- ½ cup (1 stick) butter
- For the ice cream base:
- 2 cups heavy cream
- 1 cup milk
- 6 egg yolks
- ¾ cup sugar

Direction

- To make the caramel: in a heavy-bottomed saucepan, scald the cream and keep warm. In another saucepan combine the sugar with 1/2 cup water over medium heat and stir until the sugar dissolves and the liquid is clear. Turn heat to high and boil the mixture, without stirring, until it is a light to medium amber color, about 10 minutes. Remove from the heat and slowly stir in the cream. (Protect your face and hands, because the cream will spatter.) Stir until smooth, whisk in the butter and let cool.
- To make the ice cream base: In a heavy-bottomed saucepan, scald the cream and milk. In the top of a double boiler set over simmering water, whisk egg yolks and sugar. Add the scalded cream mixture, turn up the heat until the water is boiling and whisk the mixture continuously until it is thick enough to coat the back of a spoon. Remove the pan from the heat and whisk in the caramel.
- Chill overnight and freeze in an ice-cream maker according to the manufacturer's directions.

Nutrition Information

- 704: calories;
- 2 grams: polyunsaturated fat;
- 60 grams: sugars;
- 57 milligrams: sodium;
- 51 grams: fat;
- 31 grams: saturated fat;
- 0 grams: trans fat;
- 15 grams: monounsaturated fat;
- 61 grams: carbohydrates;
- 5 grams: protein;

63. Carrot And Avocado Salad With Crunchy Seeds

Serving: 4 servings | Prep: | Cook: | Ready in: 1hours30mins

Ingredients

- For the salad
- 1 tablespoon sunflower seeds
- 1 tablespoon pumpkin seeds
- 1 tablespoon white sesame seeds
- Cumin and Citrus Roasted Carrots
- 1 avocado, halved, pitted, peeled and cut into thin wedges
- 4 cups sprouts, preferably a mix of radish and beet
- 1 tablespoon plus 1 teaspoon sour cream
- Garnish
- Edible flowers, for garnish, optional
- Cumin and Citrus Roasted Carrots
- 1 pound medium carrots, peeled
- 3 garlic cloves
- 1 teaspoon cumin seeds
- 1 teaspoon fresh thyme leaves
- ¼ teaspoon crushed red chile flakes
- Kosher salt and freshly ground black pepper, plus more to taste
- 1 tablespoon red wine vinegar
- ¼ cup plus 2 tablespoons extra-virgin olive oil
- 1 ½ oranges
- 2 lemons, halved

Direction

-
-

Nutrition Information

- 457: calories;
- 33 grams: fat;

- 5 grams: polyunsaturated fat;
- 21 grams: sugars;
- 7 grams: protein;
- 973 milligrams: sodium;
- 0 grams: trans fat;
- 41 grams: carbohydrates;
- 14 grams: dietary fiber;

64. Cauliflower, Brussels Sprouts And Red Beans With Lemon And Mustard

Serving: 4 servings | Prep: | Cook: | Ready in: 30mins

Ingredients

- 1 medium cauliflower
- 2 teaspoons Dijon mustard
- 2 tablespoons fresh lemon juice
- ¼ cup water, stock or drained cooking liquid from the accompanying grain (optional)
- 2 tablespoons extra virgin olive oil
- ¾ pound brussels sprouts, trimmed and quartered
- Salt and freshly ground pepper to taste
- 1 can red beans, drained and rinsed
- 2 ½ tablespoons chopped fresh dill
- Suggested grain for serving: quinoa (1/2 to 3/4 cup per person)
- Optional: Lemon-flavored olive oil for drizzling

Direction

- Quarter and core the cauliflower, then slice thin so that it falls apart into small, thin pieces. Whisk together the Dijon mustard, lemon juice, 1 tablespoon of the olive oil, and water or stock in a small bowl and set aside.
- Heat the olive oil over medium-high heat in a well-seasoned wok or in a large, heavy nonstick skillet. Add the cauliflower and brussels sprouts and cook, stirring often, for 5 minutes, until the vegetables are seared and beginning to soften. Add salt and pepper and continue to cook, stirring or tossing (as you would a stir-fry), for another 5 minutes, or until the cauliflower and the brussels sprouts are just tender and flavorful.
- Add the beans, dill and lemon-mustard mixture and stir together for another minute or two. Taste, adjust seasonings, and remove from the heat. Serve with quinoa or another grain of your choice. If desired, add a drizzle of lemon-flavored olive oil to each serving.

65. Celery And Apple Salad

Serving: 6 servings | Prep: | Cook: | Ready in: 15mins

Ingredients

- 6 ribs celery (about 8 ounces), as white as possible
- 2 medium-size Red Delicious apples (12 ounces)
- 1 ½ tablespoons lemon juice
- ½ cup sour cream
- ¾ teaspoon freshly ground black pepper
- ½ teaspoon salt
- 1 teaspoon sugar
- 6 lettuce leaves, for garnish

Direction

- Trim celery ribs to remove leaves (reserving the trimmings for stock), and peel ribs with vegetable peeler if outer surface is tough or fibrous. Wash and cut the ribs into 2-inch pieces. Then press the pieces flat on the table and cut them lengthwise into thin strips. You should have about 2 1/2 cups. Place in a bowl.
- Since the apples are not peeled, wash them thoroughly in warm water, scraping lightly with a knife if necessary to remove any surface wax. Stand apples up and cut them lengthwise on all sides into slices 1/2-inch thick until you reach core. Discard it, pile apple slices together and cut into 1/2-inch strips. Add pieces to

celery along with the all ingredients except lettuce leaves and mix well.
- To serve, arrange lettuce leaves on six individual plates and spoon the salad onto the leaves.

Nutrition Information

- 77: calories;
- 234 milligrams: sodium;
- 4 grams: fat;
- 2 grams: dietary fiber;
- 1 gram: protein;
- 0 grams: polyunsaturated fat;
- 10 grams: carbohydrates;
- 7 grams: sugars;

66. Charcoal Roasted Eggplant

Serving: 8 servings | Prep: | Cook: | Ready in: 1hours30mins

Ingredients

- 1 tablespoon kosher salt, plus more to taste
- 8 large eggplants, sliced in half lengthwise
- 48 stems of lemon balm, enough to make 3 cups of julienned leaves
- ½ cup extra-virgin olive oil
- 24 anchovy fillets, finely chopped
- ½ cup capers, or more to taste
- Freshly ground pepper to taste

Direction

- Salt the open face of each eggplant half, set them on end and allow to drain at least a half-hour. Meanwhile, make a fire in a grill. Chiffonade the lemon balm leaves by stacking them, rolling them up and slicing the roll crosswise as thinly as possible. Separate.
- Rub the salt off the eggplants and cut slits lengthwise 1/2-inch apart on the opened halves. Do not cut through. Repeat crosswise to create a grid of 1/2-inch squares.
- Press about 2 tablespoons of the lemon balm into the slits of each eggplant half and drizzle 1 or 2 tablespoons of olive oil on top. Roast until the cubes are juicy and yield under light pressure, about 30 minutes.
- Meanwhile, julienne the remaining cup of lemon balm and place in a bowl big enough to contain all the eggplants. When the eggplants are done, scoop the cubed flesh from their skins. Separate the cubes, if desired. Add the anchovies, capers, salt and pepper. Toss, chill and serve.

Nutrition Information

- 332: calories;
- 24 grams: sugars;
- 11 grams: protein;
- 16 grams: fat;
- 10 grams: monounsaturated fat;
- 1331 milligrams: sodium;
- 2 grams: polyunsaturated fat;
- 44 grams: carbohydrates;
- 22 grams: dietary fiber;

67. Chard Leaves Stuffed With Rice And Herbs

Serving: 8 rolls, serving 4 as a side dish or appetizer | Prep: | Cook: | Ready in: 50mins

Ingredients

- 8 large chard leaves
- 2 tablespoons extra virgin olive oil
- 1 large onion, finely chopped
- Stems from the chard leaves
- 2 large garlic cloves, minced
- 1 cup, tightly packed, cooked medium-grain white or brown rice, such as Calrose
- ¼ cup finely chopped fresh parsley
- 2 tablespoons finely chopped fresh mint

- ½ teaspoon Aleppo pepper (more to taste)
- ¼ cup currants (optional)
- Greek yogurt seasoned with garlic, lemon and sumac for serving
- Optional: crumbled feta for the filling or for topping

Direction

- Bring a large pot of water to a boil and blanch the chard leaves and stems for 20 to 30 seconds. Transfer to a bowl of cold water, then drain and cut away the stems at the base. Next cut out the wide part of the stem remaining inside the leaf, cutting a V at the base where it connects with the leaf. Set aside the leaves and cut the stems into small dice (about 1/4 inch). Set aside 1/2 cup of the blanching water for the baking dish.
- Heat 1 tablespoon of the oil in a large, heavy skillet over medium-low heat and add the onion. Cook, stirring until very soft, about 8 minutes. Add the diced chard stems and a generous pinch of salt and continue to cook until the stems are tender, about 5 minutes. Stir in the garlic and cook, stirring, until fragrant, 30 seconds to a minute. Remove from the heat.
- Preheat the oven to 375 degrees. Oil a baking dish that can accommodate all of the chard rolls. In a large bowl mix together the rice, onion mixture, herbs, Aleppo pepper and currants if using. Taste and adjust seasoning.
- Place 2 tablespoons of the filling on each chard leaf. Tuck the sides over the filling and roll up the leaves. Place in the baking dish. Drizzle the remaining olive oil over the top and place 1/2 cup water in the baking dish. Cover with foil and bake 20 minutes, until the chard rolls are hot and the leaves tender. They should retain their bright green color.

68. Chard Quiche

Serving: 6 to 8 servings | Prep: | Cook: | Ready in: 1hours20mins

Ingredients

- Pastry for a 9-inch quiche
- 1 pound Swiss chard
- 2 tablespoons butter
- 1 large onion, sliced
- ½ cup dried currants
- Cayenne pepper or hot sauce
- Salt
- 3 eggs
- ½ cup heavy cream
- 1 ½ cups milk
- ⅓ cup freshly grated Gruyere cheese

Direction

- Preheat oven to 375 degrees. Line a nine-inch quiche pan with pastry. Refrigerate until ready to use.
- Rinse the Swiss chard and chop it fine.
- Melt the butter in a large skillet, add the onion and saute until just turning golden. Add the Swiss chard and continue to saute about 10 minutes, until the Swiss chard has wilted. Stir in the currants and season with Cayenne pepper and salt. Spread the Swiss chard mixture into the prepared quiche pan.
- Beat the eggs and mix with the cream and milk. Pour over the Swiss chard in the pan. Sprinkle with cheese.
- Bake about 40 minutes, until puffed and browned. Serve warm or cool.

69. Cherry Clafouti

Serving: Six servings | Prep: | Cook: | Ready in: 1hours

Ingredients

- 1 quart Bing or Queen Anne cherries, about 1 pound, stemmed and pitted
- ¼ pound, plus 1 tablespoon, unsalted butter
- 3 eggs
- ¾ cup sugar
- ¾ cup all-purpose flour, sifted
- ½ teaspoon vanilla extract
- ½ pint heavy cream, lightly whipped (optional)

Direction

- Preheat the oven to 350 degrees.
- Evenly coat a glass or porcelain 10-inch pie pan with one tablespoon of butter. Melt the remaining butter in a saucepan and reserve.
- In a medium-sized bowl, beat the eggs with the sugar until the mixture is thickened and a light lemon color. Add the butter, flour and vanilla and beat until thoroughly blended. Set aside for 15 minutes.
- Place the cherries over the bottom of the buttered pan. Pour the batter evenly over the cherries and bake for 40 minutes or until golden and puffy. Serve warm with the lightly whipped cream.

Nutrition Information

- 248: calories;
- 37 grams: sugars;
- 5 grams: protein;
- 0 grams: trans fat;
- 52 grams: carbohydrates;
- 31 milligrams: sodium;
- 3 grams: fat;
- 1 gram: polyunsaturated fat;
- 2 grams: dietary fiber;

70. Cherry Tomato And Goat Cheese Tart

Serving: 8 servings | Prep: | Cook: | Ready in: 1hours30mins

Ingredients

- For the olive oil crust:
- 2 cups flour
- 1 tablespoon unsalted butter
- 3 tablespoons olive oil
- 1 egg yolk
- Pinch of salt
- 3 tablespoons tepid water
- For the filling:
- 5 ½ ounces Montrachet goat cheese
- 1 cup heavy cream
- 2 egg yolks
- 1 tablespoon chopped garlic
- 1 pint yellow cherry or pear tomatoes
- 1 pint red cherry or pear tomatoes
- 2 tablespoons olive oil
- 2 tablespoons rosemary leaves, chopped
- 1 tablespoon thyme leaves
- Coarse salt and freshly ground pepper to taste

Direction

- Make the pie crust. Sift the flour into a mixing bowl and using the tips of your fingers, work in the butter and the olive oil. Add the egg yolk, salt and water and mix together until the dough forms a ball (do not overwork the dough). Refrigerate for one hour.
- Roll out the dough and fit it into a 10-inch pie shell. Preheat the oven to 350 degrees.
- Make the filling. Combine the goat cheese and heavy cream in a saucepan and melt the cheese over moderate heat. Remove from heat and allow to cool slightly. Beat in the egg yolks with the garlic.
- Prebake the crust for five minutes. Pour in the goat-cheese mixture and bake until it is set (about 10 minutes). Remove from the oven and turn the heat up to 375 degrees.
- While the tart is still warm, arrange the tomatoes, alternating the colors, onto the custard. Sprinkle them with olive oil, rosemary, thyme and coarse salt and pepper. Put the tart back in the oven until the tomatoes are wrinkled (about 10 minutes). Cool and serve at room temperature. Do not refrigerate.

Nutrition Information

- 403: calories;
- 27 grams: fat;
- 12 grams: saturated fat;
- 11 grams: monounsaturated fat;
- 32 grams: carbohydrates;
- 4 grams: sugars;
- 9 grams: protein;
- 0 grams: trans fat;
- 2 grams: polyunsaturated fat;
- 394 milligrams: sodium;

71. Cherry Tomatoes With Cream And Caviar

Serving: 36 hors d'oeuvres, 8 to 12 servings | Prep: | Cook: | Ready in: 20mins

Ingredients

- 36 firm but ripe cherry tomatoes about an inch in diameter
- ½ cup sour cream or creme fraiche
- ½ ounce sturgeon, salmon or whitefish caviar (see note)

Direction

- Remove any stems from the cherry tomatoes. Turn them stem-side down on a cutting board or other work surface. Carefully slice off the top third of each tomato, reserving these pieces for another use.
- Stir the sour cream or creme fraiche to make it smooth. Using a small spoon, dab a scant teaspoon of the cream carefully and neatly on the top of each tomato.
- Using the tip of a knife, place a tiny dab of the caviar on the cream. Arrange the tomatoes on a platter and serve, or refrigerate for up to one-half hour before serving.

Nutrition Information

- 36: calories;
- 3 grams: fat;
- 1 gram: protein;
- 0 grams: polyunsaturated fat;
- 2 grams: sugars;
- 29 milligrams: sodium;

72. Cherry Vanilla Semi Freddo

Serving: 12 servings | Prep: | Cook: | Ready in: 35mins

Ingredients

- 1 cup pitted dried cherries
- ¼ cup kirsch
- ¾ cup sugar
- ¼ cup water
- 3 egg whites, at room temperature
- 2 cups well-chilled heavy cream
- 1 ½ teaspoons vanilla extract
- 2 tablespoons cocoa

Direction

- Coarsely cut or chop the cherries. Place them in a bowl and stir in the kirsch. Refrigerate.
- Line the bottom and sides of a six-cup metal loaf pan with wax paper, allowing enough paper to extend beyond the pan so it will cover the top. Place the pan in the freezer.
- Mix the sugar and water in a saucepan, bring to a boil and cook until the mixture registers 237 to 239 degrees, the "soft-ball" stage, on a candy thermometer. While the sugar is cooking, beat the egg whites in a standing electric mixture until soft peaks form. As soon as the sugar has reached the proper temperature, drizzle it slowly into the egg whites, beating the egg whites at high speed while the sugar is being added. Continue beating the egg whites another five minutes, until they are stiff, glossy and have cooled. Refrigerate.

- Whip the cream with chilled beaters until firm but still creamy. Add the vanilla, beat a moment longer, then refrigerate.
- Fold the cherries and kirsch into the chilled egg whites, then fold in the whipped cream. Spread this mixture into the loaf pan, cover the top with the extra waxed paper and freeze at least six hours or up to several days.
- To serve, unmold the loaf onto a chilled platter and peel off the wax paper. Dust the top of the loaf with the cocoa. Serve in slices.

Nutrition Information

- 247: calories;
- 15 grams: fat;
- 4 grams: monounsaturated fat;
- 1 gram: dietary fiber;
- 23 grams: sugars;
- 28 milligrams: sodium;
- 9 grams: saturated fat;
- 25 grams: carbohydrates;
- 2 grams: protein;

73. Chicken Bouillabaisse

Serving: 8 to 10 servings | Prep: | Cook: | Ready in: 2hours

Ingredients

- 4 ¼ pounds cut up chicken (drumsticks, thighs, breasts - 16 pieces), skinned
- ½ cup Pernod or Pastis (anise flavored aperitif)
- Salt
- freshly ground pepper to taste
- 2 generous pinches saffron threads
- 2 tablespoons extra virgin olive oil
- 2 medium onions, sliced
- 2 medium carrots, peeled and diced
- 2 stalks celery, diced
- 6 large garlic cloves, minced
- 1 (14-ounce) can chopped tomatoes, with liquid
- 1 teaspoon fresh thyme leaves, or 1/2 teaspoon dried thyme
- ½ teaspoon fennel seeds, crushed in a mortar and pestle
- A bouquet garni made with a bay leaf and a couple of sprigs each thyme and rosemary
- 1 quart chicken or turkey stock
- 1 ½ pounds Yukon gold or new potatoes, scrubbed and sliced
- ½ pound green beans, trimmed and broken in half
- A handful of chopped fresh parsley

Direction

- Cut chicken breasts in half for smaller pieces. Season all of the chicken with salt and pepper, and toss in a very large bowl with one pinch of the saffron and the Pernod or Pastis. Transfer the chicken pieces to a large resealable bag, pour in the liquid from the bowl and seal the bag. Place the bag in a bowl, and refrigerate overnight. If possible, move the chicken around in the bag from time to time.
- Remove the chicken from the marinade, and pat dry with paper towels. Heat a large, heavy skillet over medium-high heat, and add 1 tablespoon of the oil. When the oil is hot, working in batches, brown the chicken on all sides, about five minutes per batch. Remove to a baking sheet or bowl.
- Heat a large, heavy casserole or Dutch oven over medium heat, and add the remaining tablespoon of olive oil. Add the onions and cook, stirring often until they soften, about five minutes. Add the carrots and celery and a generous pinch of salt, and cook, stirring, until tender and fragrant, five to eight minutes. Stir in the garlic, cook for another minute until fragrant, and then add the tomatoes, thyme and salt to taste. Cook, stirring, until the tomatoes have cooked down and smell fragrant, about 10 minutes. Add the dark meat pieces to the pot, along with any juice that has accumulated in the bowl or sheet pan. Add the crushed fennel seeds, the stock, bouquet garni and potatoes, and bring to a simmer. Season to

taste. Add the remaining pinch of saffron, cover and simmer 20 minutes. Add the breast meat pieces, and simmer another 30 minutes. Check to see that the potatoes are tender. If they are not, simmer for another 10 minutes. Taste and adjust seasonings. If serving the next day (recommended), use tongs to transfer the chicken pieces to a bowl, and cover tightly. Remove the bouquet garni and discard. Refrigerate the chicken and the broth with the vegetables overnight, and skim off the fat from the surface of the broth the next day. Return the chicken to the pot to reheat.
- While the chicken is simmering, or while reheating, blanch the beans for five minutes in a medium pot of boiling salted water. Transfer to the chicken stew. Taste and adjust seasonings. Stir in the parsley and serve in wide soup bowls.

Nutrition Information

- 600: calories;
- 36 grams: fat;
- 9 grams: saturated fat;
- 0 grams: trans fat;
- 16 grams: monounsaturated fat;
- 24 grams: carbohydrates;
- 5 grams: sugars;
- 37 grams: protein;
- 7 grams: polyunsaturated fat;
- 4 grams: dietary fiber;
- 1119 milligrams: sodium;

74. Chicken Breasts With Lemon

Serving: 4 servings | Prep: | Cook: | Ready in: 25mins

Ingredients

- ½ cup flour for dredging
- Salt and freshly ground pepper to taste
- 4 skinless boneless chicken breasts, about 6 ounces each
- 2 tablespoons olive oil
- 4 sprigs fresh thyme or 1 teaspoon dried
- 2 tablespoons finely chopped shallots
- 2 teaspoons finely chopped garlic
- 2 teaspoons grated lemon zest
- 3 tablespoons lemon juice
- ½ cup chicken broth, fresh or canned
- 2 tablespoons butter

Direction

- Season flour with salt and pepper, and dredge the chicken all over. Remove the excess flour.
- Heat the oil in a heavy skillet large enough to hold the chicken pieces in one layer. Add chicken and cook, uncovered, over medium heat for 5 minutes or until lightly browned.
- Flip the chicken and cook for 5 minutes more, or until cooked through. Carefully remove the oil from the skillet, leaving the chicken. Discard the oil.
- Add the thyme, shallots and garlic, and cook for about a minute. Do not burn the garlic. Add the lemon rind, the lemon juice and the broth.
- Scrape the skillet to dissolve the brown particles that cling to the bottom. Add the butter, and cook for 3 minutes longer. Serve immediately.

Nutrition Information

- 396: calories;
- 41 grams: protein;
- 584 milligrams: sodium;
- 6 grams: saturated fat;
- 0 grams: trans fat;
- 2 grams: polyunsaturated fat;
- 16 grams: carbohydrates;
- 1 gram: sugars;
- 18 grams: fat;
- 8 grams: monounsaturated fat;

75. Chicken Breasts With Sweet Red Peppers And Snow Peas

Serving: 4 servings | Prep: | Cook: | Ready in: 15mins

Ingredients

- 4 chicken breast halves, skinless and boneless, about 1 1/4 pounds
- 1 tablespoon cornstarch
- 2 tablespoons light soy sauce
- 2 tablespoons dry white wine or water
- 3 tablespoons olive oil
- ½ teaspoon red pepper flakes (optional)
- Salt and freshly ground pepper
- 2 large sweet red peppers, cored, seeded and cut into 1/2-inch cubes
- ¼ pound snow peas, trimmed and washed
- ½ cup sliced water chestnuts or bamboo shoots
- ¼ cup coarsely chopped red onion
- 1 tablespoon sesame seeds
- 1 tablespoon finely chopped garlic
- 1 tablespoon grated fresh ginger
- ¾ cup fresh or canned chicken broth
- 4 tablespoons coarsely chopped fresh coriander

Direction

- Using a sharp knife, cut chicken breasts in half lengthwise then crosswise into slices 1/2 inch thick.
- In a small mixing bowl, combine the cornstarch, soy sauce and white wine or water, blend well and set aside.
- In a wok or a large nonstick skillet, add oil over high heat. Add chicken, pepper flakes and salt and pepper. Cook and stir about 1 minute. Scoop out the chicken pieces, leaving the oil. Set aside.
- Add red peppers, snow peas, water chestnuts or bamboo shoots, onions and sesame seeds and cook over high heat, stirring, about 1 minute or until crisp and tender. Add garlic and ginger. Cook briefly over high heat. Add chicken and chicken broth. Cook stirring and tossing for 1 more minute.
- Add cornstarch mixture, cook and stir for 15 seconds. Sprinkle with coriander and serve immediately.

Nutrition Information

- 336: calories;
- 4 grams: dietary fiber;
- 0 grams: trans fat;
- 11 grams: monounsaturated fat;
- 17 grams: carbohydrates;
- 6 grams: sugars;
- 22 grams: protein;
- 711 milligrams: sodium;
- 20 grams: fat;
- 3 grams: polyunsaturated fat;

76. Chicken Fingers With Garlic Butter

Serving: 4 servings | Prep: | Cook: | Ready in: 15mins

Ingredients

- 4 skinless, boneless chicken breast halves
- Salt and freshly ground pepper to taste
- 1 tablespoon chopped fresh oregano or 2 teaspoons dried
- 2 tablespoons flour
- 2 tablespoons butter
- 2 tablespoons olive oil
- 4 ripe plum tomatoes, skinned, seeded and diced small
- 1 tablespoon chopped garlic
- 4 tablespoons chopped fresh coriander or basil
- 2 tablespoons fresh lime juice

Direction

- Using a sharp knife, cut the breast halves in half crosswise, then lengthwise into strips 1/2-inch wide.

- Blend salt, pepper, oregano and the flour well in a flat dish. Add the chicken pieces in one layer. Stir to season, keeping each strip separate.
- Heat the butter and oil over high heat in a skillet large enough to hold the chicken pieces in one layer. Add the chicken, cook and stir until lightly browned, about 3 minutes. Add the tomatoes and garlic and cook, stirring, for 3 minutes more. Add the coriander and lime juice and continue cooking. Blend well and serve immediately.

Nutrition Information

- 472: calories;
- 6 grams: saturated fat;
- 0 grams: trans fat;
- 8 grams: carbohydrates;
- 1 gram: sugars;
- 63 grams: protein;
- 818 milligrams: sodium;
- 20 grams: fat;
- 2 grams: dietary fiber;

77. Chicken With Olives, Prunes And Capers

Serving: Twelve to fourteen servings | Prep: | Cook: | Ready in: 1hours10mins

Ingredients

- 12 chicken breasts and thighs, trimmed of fat and skin
- 2 cups pitted prunes (or dried apricots or dried pears)
- 1 ¼ cups white wine
- ¾ cup dark brown sugar
- ¾ cup olive oil
- ¾ cup red-wine vinegar
- ¾ cup green olives, pitted
- ¾ cup capers
- 4 tablespoons oregano
- 1 teaspoon freshly ground pepper
- 1 teaspoon salt
- ½ teaspoon crushed red pepper
- 6 medium-size bay leaves
- 1 small garlic head, minced
- 3 tablespoons chopped cilantro

Direction

- In two or three baking pans, arrange the chicken pieces in one layer.
- Combine all the ingredients except the cilantro and one-half cup of the brown sugar. Pour over the chicken so that the prunes, olives and capers are evenly distributed. Cover and refrigerate overnight.
- Preheat the oven to 350 degrees.
- Sprinkle the remaining brown sugar over the chicken and bake for about one hour, basting often.
- To serve, arrange the chicken pieces with the sauce on a platter. Sprinkle with the cilantro.

Nutrition Information

- 514: calories;
- 8 grams: saturated fat;
- 18 grams: monounsaturated fat;
- 6 grams: polyunsaturated fat;
- 27 grams: carbohydrates;
- 3 grams: dietary fiber;
- 22 grams: protein;
- 34 grams: fat;
- 0 grams: trans fat;
- 17 grams: sugars;
- 519 milligrams: sodium;

78. Chicken And Chickpea Tagine

Serving: 4 servings | Prep: | Cook: | Ready in: 1hours

Ingredients

- 2 tablespoons corn or canola oil

- 2 tablespoons butter
- 1 large onion, peeled and thinly sliced
- 2 cloves garlic, minced
- Salt
- Pinch nutmeg
- ½ teaspoon ground cinnamon
- 1 teaspoon ground ginger
- 1 teaspoon ground cumin
- 1 teaspoon ground coriander
- ½ teaspoon ground black pepper
- Pinch cayenne
- 1 ½ to 2 cups chopped tomatoes (canned are fine; drain excess liquid)
- 4 cups chickpeas (canned are fine; drain and rinse first)
- ½ cup raisins or chopped pitted dates
- ½ vanilla bean
- 8 chicken thighs, or 4 leg-thigh pieces, cut in two
- Chopped cilantro or parsley leaves

Direction

- Put oil and butter in a large skillet or casserole, which can be covered later, and turn heat to medium high. When butter melts, add onion, and cook, stirring occasionally, until it softens, 5 to 10 minutes. Add garlic, a large pinch of salt and spices. Cook, stirring, for about 30 seconds. Add tomatoes, chickpeas, raisins and vanilla, and bring to a boil. (If mixture is very dry, add about 1/2 cup water.) Taste, and add salt as necessary.
- Sprinkle chicken pieces with salt, and nestle them into sauce. Cover, and 5 minutes later adjust heat so mixture simmers steadily. Cook until chicken is very tender, 45 minutes to an hour. Taste, and adjust seasoning. Then garnish, and serve with couscous.

79. Chicken And Three Peppers Sausage

Serving: about 12 links | Prep: | Cook: | Ready in: 45mins

Ingredients

- 2 cups mixture of red, yellow and green peppers, coarsely chopped
- 2 tablespoons butter
- 2 pounds white meat chicken
- 2 egg whites
- 2 cups heavy cream
- 2 tablespoons parsley
- 2 tablespoons ground cumin
- 2 teaspoons ground coriander seed
- Salt and white pepper to taste

Direction

- Saute peppers in butter until soft. Drain on paper towels.
- Chill processor bowl and metal blade in refrigerator.
- Remove all gristle, fat and cartilage from chilled chicken and cut the meat into large chunks. Place in processor bowl with parsley and chop chicken into coarse pieces. Then process until smooth. You may need to do this in several batches.
- With motor running slowly add egg whites and then cream.
- Place chicken in bowl and stir in peppers.
- Using sausage stuffer, stuff into casings, tie off at 2- to 3-inch intervals.
- Poach in salted water for 15 minutes.

Nutrition Information

- 328: calories;
- 10 grams: monounsaturated fat;
- 1 gram: dietary fiber;
- 16 grams: protein;
- 14 grams: saturated fat;
- 28 grams: fat;
- 0 grams: trans fat;
- 3 grams: carbohydrates;
- 2 grams: sugars;
- 346 milligrams: sodium;

80. Chicken, Greek Style

Serving: 2 servings | Prep: | Cook: | Ready in: 35mins

Ingredients

- 16 ounces whole onion or 14 ounces chopped ready-cut onion (about 3 1/3 cups)
- 1 tablespoon olive oil
- 2 cloves garlic
- 8 ounces skinless, boneless chicken breast
- 1 lemon to yield 1 teaspoon grated lemon rind
- ¼ cup dry vermouth
- ½ teaspoon cinnamon
- ¼ cup no-salt-added chicken broth plus 1 tablespoon
- 1 tablespoon cornstarch
- ½ cup nonfat plain yogurt
- ⅛ teaspoon salt
- Freshly ground black pepper to taste

Direction

- Chop the onion for this recipe along with the onion for the rice dish.
- Heat a nonstick skillet until it is very hot. Reduce the heat to medium high, and add oil.
- Add all the onion, and saute until the onion begins to brown.
- Mince garlic; remove 1/3 of onion from pan, and add to rice (see rice recipe). Add garlic to remaining onion, and stir.
- Wash, dry and cut chicken into bite-size chunks, and add to onion; brown chicken on both sides.
- Grate lemon rind, and add to pan with the vermouth and cinnamon and 1/4 cup chicken broth. Cover, and cook over low heat until the chicken is cooked through.
- Stir the remaining tablespoon of chicken broth into the cornstarch, and mix to a smooth paste; stir into pan. Then, add the yogurt, and stir to mix well. Season with salt and pepper.

Nutrition Information

- 443: calories;
- 3 grams: polyunsaturated fat;
- 5 grams: dietary fiber;
- 15 grams: sugars;
- 330 milligrams: sodium;
- 18 grams: fat;
- 4 grams: saturated fat;
- 0 grams: trans fat;
- 31 grams: protein;
- 10 grams: monounsaturated fat;
- 34 grams: carbohydrates;

81. Chocolate Lover's Angel Food Cake

Serving: 14 servings | Prep: | Cook: | Ready in: 1hours10mins

Ingredients

- ¼ cup plus 1 tablespoon unsweetened cocoa (Dutch-processed)
- 2 teaspoons instant coffee
- ¼ cup boiling water
- 2 teaspoons vanilla
- 1 ¾ cups sugar
- 1 cup sifted cake flour
- ¼ teaspoon salt
- Whites of 16 large eggs, 2 cups
- 2 teaspoons cream of tartar

Direction

- Preheat the oven to 350 degrees.
- In a medium bowl combine cocoa, coffee and boiling water and whisk until smooth. Whisk in vanilla.
- In another medium-size bowl combine 3/4 cup sugar, the flour and salt, and whisk to blend.
- In a large bowl beat the egg whites until frothy. Add the cream of tartar, and beat until soft peaks form when beater is raised. Gradually beat in the remaining 1 cup sugar, beating until very stiff peaks form when beater is raised slowly. Remove 1 heaping cup of egg

whites and place it on top of the cocoa mixture.

- Dust flour mixture over remaining whites, 1/4 cup at a time, and fold in quickly but gently, using a large balloon wire whisk or slotted skimmer. It is not necessary to incorporate every speck until last addition.
- Whisk together the egg white and cocoa mixture, and fold into the batter until uniform. Pour into an ungreased, 10-inch, two-piece tube pan (the batter will come to within 3/4 inch of the top), run a small metal spatula or knife through the batter to prevent air pockets, and bake for 40 minutes or until a cake tester inserted in the center comes out clean and the cake springs back when lightly pressed. (The center will rise above the pan while baking and sink slightly when done. The surface will have deep cracks like a souffle.)
- Invert the pan, placing the tube opening over the neck of a soda or wine bottle to suspend it well above the counter, and cool the cake completely in the pan, about 1 1/2 hours.
- Loosen the sides with a long metal spatula and remove the center core of the pan. Dislodge bottom and center core with a metal spatula or thin, sharp knife. (A wire cake tester works well around the core. To keep the sides attractive, press spatula against sides of the pan and avoid up-and-down motion.) Invert onto a serving plate. Wrap airtight.

Nutrition Information

- 222: calories;
- 6 grams: fat;
- 0 grams: trans fat;
- 35 grams: carbohydrates;
- 25 grams: sugars;
- 2 grams: monounsaturated fat;
- 1 gram: dietary fiber;
- 8 grams: protein;
- 124 milligrams: sodium;

82. Choux A La Creme

Serving: 6 servings | Prep: | Cook: |Ready in: 1hours40mins

Ingredients

- For the choux:
- ¾ cup water
- 1 tablespoon unsalted butter
- ⅛ teaspoons salt
- ¾ cup all-purpose flour (approximately 3 3/4 ounces)
- 3 large eggs
- 1 teaspoon confectioners' sugar to dust the tops of the choux puffs
- For the filling:
- 1 ½ cups heavy cream
- ¼ cup confectioners' sugar
- 2 teaspoons pure vanilla extract
- 4 tablespoons blackberry preserves
- For the chocolate sauce:
- 8 ounces bittersweet or semisweet chocolate
- 1 ¼ cups milk

Direction

- Preheat oven to 350 degrees. To make the choux, place the water, butter and salt in a saucepan, and bring the mixture to the boil over high heat. Immediately remove from the heat, and add the flour in one stroke. Mix in the flour with a sturdy wooden spatula, and return the pan to the stove over medium heat to high heat, stirring until the mixture comes up the sides of the pan and is almost the texture of modeling clay. Cook for about 20 to 30 seconds, still stirring, to dry the mixture further. Remove from the heat and transfer to the bowl of a food processor. Process for 4 to 5 seconds to cool the mixture slightly.
- In a bowl, beat the eggs with a fork until well mixed. Reserve 1 tablespoon of the beaten eggs to brush on the choux later, and add a third of the remaining egg mixture to the food processor bowl. Process for 5 to 6 seconds, just long enough to incorporate the eggs into the flour mixture. Repeat with the remainder of

the eggs, adding and incorporating half of them at a time. After the final addition, process the mixture for about 10 seconds, until very smooth.
- Lightly butter a cookie sheet. Spoon 6 rounds of the dough, each about the size of a golf ball (approximately 3 tablespoons), onto the sheet, spacing them evenly to allow for expansion. Brush with the reserved tablespoon of beaten egg to smooth the tops and coat the surface of the balls.
- Place the cookie sheet in the oven for about 40 minutes, until the choux are nicely developed, lightly browned, and cooked through. Set aside in a draft-free spot on top of the stove.
- To make the filling, place the cream, confectioner's sugar, and vanilla in a bowl, and whip until firm. Set aside.
- The dessert can be completed a few hours before serving. Remove and reserve the top of each choux puff, cutting around each about a quarter of the way down and lifting off the resulting "cap." Remove and discard some of the soft insides, or press this soft membrane against the walls of the choux. Spoon 2 teaspoons of the blackberry preserves into the base of each choux.
- Spoon the reserved cream mixture into a pastry bag fitted with a star tip, and pipe it into the choux. Replace the "caps," and sprinkle with the reserved teaspoon of confectioners' sugar.
- To make the chocolate sauce, heat the chocolate and milk in a saucepan over low to medium heat just until the chocolate melts. Mix well with a whisk, transfer to a bowl, and allow to cool off in the refrigerator, stirring occasionally.
- Arrange a choux on each of 6 individual dessert plates. Serve with the chocolate sauce.

Nutrition Information

- 589: calories;
- 139 milligrams: sodium;
- 0 grams: trans fat;
- 12 grams: monounsaturated fat;
- 3 grams: dietary fiber;
- 2 grams: polyunsaturated fat;
- 55 grams: carbohydrates;
- 37 grams: sugars;
- 9 grams: protein;
- 39 grams: fat;
- 23 grams: saturated fat;

83. Cinnamon Curry Rice

Serving: 6 servings | Prep: | Cook: |Ready in: 1hours30mins

Ingredients

- 4 sticks cinnamon or Chinese cinnamon bark, about 1/2 ounce
- 2 cups water
- 3 tablespoons corn or safflower oil
- 2 tablespoons curry powder
- 1 medium onion, diced, about 1 3/4 cups
- 1 ½ tablespoons flour
- 4 cups canned or homemade chicken broth
- 3 carrots, diced, about 1 1/2 cups
- 1 large apple, peeled, cored, and diced, about 1 cup
- 2 medium potatoes, diced, about 2 cups
- 1 ½ tablespoons minced garlic
- ½ pound boneless center-cut pork loin, trimmed of fat and diced
- 1 teaspoon salt
- ¼ teaspoon freshly ground black pepper
- 6 servings cooked white rice

Direction

- In a saucepan, bring the cinnamon and water to a boil. Simmer, partly covered, until the liquid is reduced to 1 cup, about 30 minutes. Strain the cinnamon, and reserve the liquid.
- In a heavy casserole or Dutch oven, heat 2 tablespoons of oil until hot, add the curry powder and the onion, and cook over medium heat for about 1 minute. Add the flour, and

cook for another minute, stirring constantly. Add the chicken broth, heat until boiling, and add the carrot, apple and potatoes. Partly cover, and simmer over low heat for 30 minutes.
- Heat a wok or a saute pan, add the remaining oil, and heat until hot. Add the garlic and pork, and cook over high heat, stirring until pork changes color. Remove garlic and pork with a slotted spoon.
- When the vegetables are tender, add the pork and cinnamon liquid. Turn up the heat, and cook for 20 minutes. Add salt and pepper, and serve over hot rice.

Nutrition Information

- 503: calories;
- 3 grams: saturated fat;
- 6 grams: dietary fiber;
- 14 grams: fat;
- 4 grams: monounsaturated fat;
- 76 grams: carbohydrates;
- 9 grams: sugars;
- 18 grams: protein;
- 667 milligrams: sodium;

84. Clam And Fregola Soup

Serving: 4 servings as a first course, 2 as a main course | Prep: | Cook: |Ready in: 45mins

Ingredients

- 3 tablespoons olive oil
- 4 cloves garlic, minced
- 1 medium onion, minced
- ½ teaspoon chili pepper
- 3 pounds steamer clams, well scrubbed
- ½ cup dry white wine
- ¾ cup fregola
- 2 cups stewed tomatoes, crushed, with their juice
- Salt and freshly ground black pepper to taste
- 2 cups bottled clam juice, if necessary
- 2 tablespoons minced flat leaf parsley

Direction

- In a large soup pot, warm the olive oil. Add the garlic, onion and chili pepper, and cook over medium heat 5 minutes. Raise heat to high, and add the steamers, 1 cup water and the wine. Cover pot, and cook 3 to 5 minutes, until clams begin to open.
- Use tongs to remove clams, leaving as much juice as possible in the pot. Add fregola and tomatoes and their juice to the pot, reduce heat to simmer, and adjust the seasoning with salt and black pepper to taste.
- Cover pot, and simmer 20 minutes, checking occasionally to be sure that not all the liquid has evaporated. If necessary to maintain soupy consistency, add water or bottled clam juice, a quarter cup at a time. After 20 minutes, remove lid and continue to simmer until fregola is tender.
- Meanwhile, pick the meat from the clams and discard the shells. When fregola is tender, stir in the clam meat as well as additional bottled clam juice, if necessary, and serve immediately, garnished with parsley.

Nutrition Information

- 598: calories;
- 14 grams: fat;
- 2 grams: polyunsaturated fat;
- 0 grams: trans fat;
- 47 grams: carbohydrates;
- 5 grams: sugars;
- 2944 milligrams: sodium;
- 8 grams: monounsaturated fat;
- 63 grams: protein;

85. Clams In Spinach And Garlic Broth

Serving: 8 servings | Prep: | Cook: | Ready in: 45mins

Ingredients

- 3 cups well-flavored chicken stock
- 3 ¼ cups packed spinach leaves (no stems)
- ½ cup dry white wine
- 4 pounds mahogany or littleneck clams, scrubbed
- 2 tablespoons flat-leaf parsley
- 2 tablespoons watercress leaves
- 2 tablespoons basil leaves
- 1 tablespoon chopped chives
- 1 large clove garlic, chopped
- 1 tablespoon chopped shallot
- 4 tablespoons softened unsalted butter
- Juice of 1/2 lemon
- 1 tablespoon Pernod or Ricard
- ⅓ cup heavy cream
- Fresh-ground black pepper to taste

Direction

- Place chicken stock in 4-quart saucepan. Add 3 cups spinach, and cook until wilted, about 2 minutes. Use slotted spoon to transfer spinach to blender, with 1/2 cup hot chicken stock. Puree.
- Place wine in 4-quart saucepan, add clams, cover and cook over medium heat until clams open, 3 to 5 minutes. Drain clams, and strain liquid into chicken stock. Set clams aside.
- Add parsley, watercress, basil, chives and remaining spinach to blender. Puree. Add garlic and shallots. Puree. Add butter. Puree, and pour mixture into chicken stock. Add lemon juice, Pernod and cream. Season to taste with pepper.
- Add clams to broth, reheat and serve.

Nutrition Information

- 337: calories;
- 1 gram: dietary fiber;
- 2 grams: sugars;
- 1508 milligrams: sodium;
- 13 grams: fat;
- 7 grams: saturated fat;
- 0 grams: trans fat;
- 3 grams: monounsaturated fat;
- 14 grams: carbohydrates;
- 36 grams: protein;

86. Cocoa Brownies

Serving: 16 squares | Prep: | Cook: | Ready in: 50mins

Ingredients

- ¾ cup cake flour
- ⅔ cup sugar
- ⅓ cup European-style cocoa powder
- ⅓ cup cornstarch
- 1 teaspoon baking powder
- ½ teaspoon baking soda
- ½ teaspoon salt
- 1 egg white
- ½ cup evaporated skim milk
- ¾ cup applesauce
- ½ cup light corn syrup
- 1 teaspoon pure vanilla extract

Direction

- Preheat oven to 350 degrees.
- Spray an 8-by-8 or 9-by-9-inch square pan with nonstick cooking spray.
- Thoroughly mix flour, sugar, cocoa, cornstarch, baking powder, baking soda and salt.
- In another bowl, whisk the egg white and milk and then stir in applesauce, corn syrup and vanilla. Stir in dry mixture until blended.
- Pour batter into prepared pan and bake 35 to 40 minutes, or until knife inserted in center comes out clean. Cool in pan and cut into squares.

Nutrition Information

- 109: calories;
- 0 grams: polyunsaturated fat;
- 27 grams: carbohydrates;
- 1 gram: protein;
- 18 grams: sugars;
- 119 milligrams: sodium;

87. Corn Chowder

Serving: 6 servings (7 cups) | Prep: | Cook: | Ready in: 32mins

Ingredients

- 1 pound baking potatoes, peeled and cut in 1/3-inch dice
- 1 medium red bell pepper, cored, de-ribbed and cut in 1/4-inch dice
- 1 medium green bell pepper, cored, de-ribbed and cut in 1/4-inch dice
- 1 small onion, chopped
- 1 cup water
- 4 ears corn, kernels removed from cob (2 cups), cooked
- 4 scallions, white and green parts, trimmed and thinly sliced
- 2 stalks celery, peeled and thinly sliced
- 1 ½ cups milk
- ½ cup heavy cream
- 1 tablespoon kosher salt
- 3 drops hot red pepper sauce
- Freshly ground pepper to taste
- 2 tablespoons unsalted butter, optional

Direction

- Place potatoes, peppers, onion and water in a 5-quart casserole dish with a tightly fitting lid. Cook, covered, at 100 percent power in a high-power oven for 12 minutes.
- Stir in corn, scallions, celery, milk and cream. Cook, covered, for 9 minutes.
- Remove from oven. Stir in salt, pepper sauce and black pepper. Cool slightly before serving. Stir in butter if desired.

Nutrition Information

- 247: calories;
- 6 grams: saturated fat;
- 0 grams: trans fat;
- 3 grams: monounsaturated fat;
- 4 grams: dietary fiber;
- 7 grams: protein;
- 790 milligrams: sodium;
- 10 grams: fat;
- 1 gram: polyunsaturated fat;
- 35 grams: carbohydrates;
- 11 grams: sugars;

88. Corn Pudding With Roasted Garlic And Sage

Serving: 6 servings, as a side dish | Prep: | Cook: | Ready in: 2hours

Ingredients

- 4 garlic cloves, unpeeled
- Kernels from 4 ears corn (about 4 cups)
- ¾ cup low-fat milk (1 percent or 2 percent)
- 3 eggs
- Salt to taste (about 1/2 teaspoon)
- Freshly ground pepper
- 1 tablespoon slivered or chopped fresh sage

Direction

- Preheat the oven to 350 degrees. Oil or butter a 2-quart soufflé dish or gratin. Set the dish in a pan and fill the pan with enough water to come partway up the sides of the dish.
- Toast the garlic: Place the unpeeled cloves in a heavy skillet over medium-high heat and toast, turning the garlic cloves often, until the skin is blackened in spots and the garlic smells

toasty, about 7 minutes. Remove from the heat. When the cloves are cool enough to handle, cut away the root end and remove the skin.
- Set aside 1 cup of the corn kernels. Place the rest, with the garlic, milk, eggs, salt and pepper in a blender and blend until smooth. Pour into a bowl and stir in the sage and the corn kernels, then transfer to the baking dish.
- Place in the oven and bake 1 hour to 1 hour 15 minutes, until the top is lightly browned and the pudding is firm. Serve hot.

89. Corn And Vegetable Gratin With Cumin

Serving: Serves six | Prep: | Cook: | Ready in: 1hours

Ingredients

- 1 tablespoon extra virgin olive oil
- 1 medium onion, finely chopped
- 1 medium red bell pepper, diced
- Salt to taste
- 1 large garlic clove, minced
- ½ pound zucchini, thinly sliced or diced
- Freshly ground pepper to taste
- Kernels from 2 ears sweet corn (about 2 cups)
- 3 large eggs
- ½ cup milk
- 1 teaspoon cumin seeds, lightly toasted and coarsely ground in a spice mill, or slightly crushed in a mortar and pestle
- 2 ounces Gruyère cheese, grated (1/2 cup, tightly packed)

Direction

- Preheat the oven to 375 degrees. Oil a 2-quart gratin or baking dish. Set aside the kernels from one of the ears of corn. Heat the olive oil in a large, nonstick skillet over medium heat and add the onion. Cook, stirring often, until it begins to soften, about three minutes, and add the red pepper and a generous pinch of salt. Cook, stirring often, until the onions and peppers are tender, about five minutes. Add the garlic and the zucchini, stir together and add another generous pinch of salt and some pepper. Cook, stirring often, until the zucchini is just beginning to look bright green and some of the slices are translucent. Stir in the kernels from one of the ears of corn. Stir together for a minute or two, and remove from the heat. Scrape into a large bowl.
- Place the remaining corn kernels in a blender jar, and add the eggs, milk and 1/2 teaspoon salt. Blend until smooth. Pour into the bowl with the vegetables. Add the cumin and the cheese, and stir everything together. Scrape into the gratin dish.
- Bake 35 to 40 minutes, until the top is browned and the gratin is firm to the touch. Serve hot or warm.

Nutrition Information

- 131: calories;
- 9 grams: fat;
- 3 grams: saturated fat;
- 0 grams: trans fat;
- 4 grams: sugars;
- 1 gram: dietary fiber;
- 6 grams: carbohydrates;
- 8 grams: protein;
- 313 milligrams: sodium;

90. Cornmeal Cranberry Drop Scones

Serving: 20 3-inch scones | Prep: | Cook: | Ready in: 50mins

Ingredients

- 130 grams (1 cup) whole-wheat pastry flour
- 130 grams (1 cup) fine stone-ground cornmeal
- 50 grams (1/4 cup) unrefined sugar
- 2 teaspoons baking powder

- ½ teaspoon baking soda
- ¼ teaspoon salt
- 2 teaspoons finely chopped lemon zest
- 3 ½ ounces (7 tablespoons) cold unsalted butter, cut into 1/2-inch pieces
- 1 egg
- ⅔ cup buttermilk
- 100 grams (3/4 cup) dried cranberries, soaked for 10 minutes in warm water and drained

Direction

- Preheat the oven to 375 degrees. Line baking sheets with parchment.
- Sift together the flour, cornmeal, sugar, baking powder, baking soda and salt. Dump any bran remaining in the strainer into the bowl. Place in the bowl of a food processor fitted with the steel blade. Add the butter and lemon zest and pulse until you have a coarse, even mixture.
- In a separate bowl, whisk together the egg and the buttermilk. Turn on the food processor and add the egg mixture to the flour mixture. As soon as the dough comes together, turn off the machine. Add the cranberries and pulse just a few times to distribute through the dough. Don't pulse too many times or the cranberries will be chopped.
- Drop the batter by heaped tablespoons onto the parchment-lined baking sheets, leaving an inch or more of space between each one. Bake one baking sheet at a time in the middle of the oven for 15 to 20 minutes, reversing the baking sheet front to back halfway through, until lightly browned.

Nutrition Information

- 112: calories;
- 3 grams: saturated fat;
- 90 milligrams: sodium;
- 6 grams: sugars;
- 5 grams: fat;
- 0 grams: polyunsaturated fat;
- 1 gram: monounsaturated fat;
- 17 grams: carbohydrates;
- 2 grams: protein;

91. Couscous Risotto

Serving: 8 cups | Prep: | Cook: | Ready in: 25mins

Ingredients

- ½ cup olive oil
- 1 medium-size onion, minced
- 10 medium-size garlic cloves, smashed, peeled and minced
- 3 tablespoons ground cumin, preferably freshly ground
- 1 tablespoon curry powder
- 2 cups couscous
- 4 cups chicken broth or vegetarian broth (see Micro-Tip)
- 1 ½ teaspoons kosher salt
- Freshly ground black pepper

Direction

- Place oil in a 14- by 9- by 2-inch oval dish. Cook, uncovered, at 100 percent in a high-power oven for 2 minutes. Stir in onion and garlic. Cook for 2 minutes. Stir in spices and cook for 3 minutes.
- Stir in couscous and pour broth over mixture. Cook for 10 minutes.
- Remove from oven. Stir in salt and pepper.

Nutrition Information

- 245: calories;
- 2 grams: saturated fat;
- 8 grams: monounsaturated fat;
- 3 grams: dietary fiber;
- 305 milligrams: sodium;
- 12 grams: fat;
- 1 gram: sugars;
- 30 grams: carbohydrates;
- 5 grams: protein;

92. Couscous With Eggplant

Serving: 4 servings | Prep: | Cook: | Ready in: 15mins

Ingredients

- 1 tablespoon olive oil
- 1 tablespoon finely chopped shallots or scallions
- 2 tablespoons finely chopped onions
- ¼ teaspoon turmeric
- ¼ teaspoon ground coriander
- 1 cup diced eggplant cut into 1/4-inch cubes
- Salt and freshly ground pepper to taste
- 1 cup water
- 1 cup precooked couscous
- 1 tablespoon butter
- 1 tablespoon fresh lemon juice

Direction

- Heat the oil in a saucepan, add the shallots, onions, turmeric, coriander, eggplant, salt and pepper. Cook over medium-high heat, stirring, until wilted, but do not brown.
- Add the water, bring to a boil, add the couscous and blend well. Cover tightly, remove from the heat and let stand 5 minutes.
- Add the butter and lemon juice, stir and blend with a fork to separate the grains. Keep warm.

Nutrition Information

- 230: calories;
- 2 grams: saturated fat;
- 3 grams: dietary fiber;
- 36 grams: carbohydrates;
- 7 grams: fat;
- 0 grams: trans fat;
- 1 gram: sugars;
- 6 grams: protein;
- 329 milligrams: sodium;

93. Couscous With Thick Tomato Vegetable Sauce

Serving: 4 servings | Prep: | Cook: | Ready in: 40mins

Ingredients

- 1 pound onions, chopped coarse
- 2 large cloves garlic, chopped fine
- 1 tablespoon olive oil
- 1 pound yellow or red and green peppers, chopped coarse
- ½ pound carrots, chopped fine
- ¾ pound mushrooms, trimmed and chopped coarse
- 1 28-ounce can no-salt-added tomato puree
- 1 teaspoon dried oregano
- 1 teaspoon dried basil
- 1 cup water
- 1 ½ cups instant couscous

Direction

- Saute onions and garlic in hot oil in a nonstick skillet until onions soften and begin to brown.
- Add peppers, carrots and mushrooms and continue cooking over medium heat for 15 minutes.
- Add tomato puree, oregano, basil and water and cook over low heat for about 15 minutes longer, until flavors are well blended.
- Meanwhile, cook couscous, following directions on package. To serve, pour the sauce over the couscous.

Nutrition Information

- 452: calories;
- 1 gram: polyunsaturated fat;
- 3 grams: monounsaturated fat;
- 14 grams: dietary fiber;
- 21 grams: sugars;
- 5 grams: fat;
- 90 grams: carbohydrates;
- 17 grams: protein;
- 430 milligrams: sodium;

94. Couscous With Tomatoes

Serving: 4 servings | Prep: | Cook: | Ready in: 15mins

Ingredients

- 3 plum tomatoes, about 1/4 pound
- 2 tablespoons butter
- ½ cup finely chopped onion
- ¼ teaspoon thread saffron
- Salt to taste if desired
- Freshly ground pepper to taste
- 1 ⅓ cups water
- 1 cup couscous
- 3 tablespoons finely chopped fresh coriander

Direction

- Cut away cores of tomatoes. Cut tomatoes into 1/4-inch cubes. There should be about 3/4 cup.
- Heat 1 tablespoon butter in a saucepan and add onion. Cook, stirring, until wilted. Add saffron and stir. Add tomatoes and cook about 2 minutes, stirring. Add salt, pepper and water and bring to boil.
- Add couscous, stir and cover closely. Remove from heat and let stand 5 minutes. Stir in coriander and remaining 1 tablespoon butter and serve.

Nutrition Information

- 228: calories;
- 0 grams: polyunsaturated fat;
- 2 grams: sugars;
- 37 grams: carbohydrates;
- 3 grams: dietary fiber;
- 420 milligrams: sodium;
- 6 grams: protein;
- 4 grams: saturated fat;

95. Couscous And Pepper Salad

Serving: 2 servings | Prep: | Cook: | Ready in: 10mins

Ingredients

- 8 ounces whole red and yellow peppers
- ½ teaspoon Dijon-style mustard
- 2 tablespoons balsamic vinegar
- 1 teaspoon sugar
- ¾ cup couscous
- 2 scallions

Direction

- Quarter peppers. Slice on thin slicing blade of food processor; if you have no processor, cut in julienne strips.
- Following package directions, bring water to boil in covered pot for couscous (each manufacturer recommends a different amount of water).
- In serving bowl, combine mustard, vinegar and sugar, mixing well to dissolve sugar.
- Add couscous to boiling water. Cover and turn off heat. Allow to sit 3 to 5 minutes, until all water has been absorbed and couscous is tender.
- Meanwhile, chop scallions.
- Stir peppers and scallions into dressing, and when couscous is ready stir into salad.

Nutrition Information

- 302: calories;
- 63 grams: carbohydrates;
- 5 grams: sugars;
- 10 grams: protein;
- 29 milligrams: sodium;
- 1 gram: fat;
- 0 grams: polyunsaturated fat;

96. Creamy Ranch Dressing

Serving: One cup | Prep: | Cook: | Ready in: 5mins

Ingredients

- ½ cup low-fat cottage cheese
- ⅓ cup low-fat buttermilk
- 1 tablespoon fresh lemon juice
- 1 tablespoon grated Parmesan cheese
- 1 shallot, peeled and coarsely chopped
- 1 garlic clove, peeled and coarsely chopped
- 2 tablespoons minced basil leaves
- ½ teaspoon minced oregano leaves
- ⅛ teaspoon freshly ground pepper

Direction

- Combine all ingredients in a blender or food processor. Puree until smooth. Store in a covered container in the refrigerator 1 day.

Nutrition Information

- 117: calories;
- 11 grams: protein;
- 7 grams: sugars;
- 353 milligrams: sodium;
- 4 grams: fat;
- 2 grams: saturated fat;
- 0 grams: polyunsaturated fat;
- 1 gram: dietary fiber;

97. Cumin Chicken With Black Bean Sauce

Serving: 2 servings | Prep: | Cook: | Ready in: 30mins

Ingredients

- 8 ounces boneless, skinless chicken breasts
- 1 teaspoon ground cumin
- ½ teaspoon ground coriander
- 1 15-ounce can no-salt-added black beans
- 1 large clove garlic
- ½ to 1 Serrano chili
- 2 tomatillos, to yield 3 tablespoons chopped
- Few sprigs cilantro, to yield 2 tablespoons chopped
- 1 small onion, to yield 1 tablespoon chopped
- 1 small green pepper, to yield 4 teaspoons chopped
- 2 teaspoons lime juice
- ⅛ teaspoon salt
- Freshly ground black pepper to taste

Direction

- Preheat broiler, if using. Wash and dry the chicken, and rub the breasts on both sides with cumin and coriander.
- Rinse and drain the beans.
- Turn on the food processor, and put garlic through feed tube. Wash, trim and seed the chili, add as much as you like to the food processor and process until finely chopped. Chop the tomatillos. Wash and chop the cilantro. Chop the onion and the green pepper.
- To the garlic and chili in the food processor add the beans, tomatillos, cilantro, onion, green pepper, lime juice, salt and pepper, and process until mixture is pureed.
- Prepare stove-top grill, if using. Broil or grill chicken, browning on both sides and cooking until chicken is no longer pink, about 10 minutes.
- Heat the bean puree in a pot slowly until warm.
- Place the bean puree in the middle of each of two dinner plates. Place the chicken on top, and top with mango salsa.

Nutrition Information

- 376: calories;
- 45 grams: carbohydrates;
- 17 grams: dietary fiber;
- 40 grams: protein;
- 496 milligrams: sodium;
- 4 grams: sugars;

- 1 gram: polyunsaturated fat;
- 0 grams: trans fat;

98. Curried Lentil And Grilled Chicken Casserole

Serving: 6 to 8 servings | Prep: | Cook: |Ready in: 55mins

Ingredients

- 2 skinless and boneless chicken breasts (about 1 1/4 pounds)
- 3 tablespoons olive oil or vegetable oil
- 1 cup finely chopped onion
- 1 medium sweet red pepper, cored, seeded and chopped
- 1 fresh hot green chili, seeded and minced
- 2 cloves garlic, minced
- 1 teaspoon minced fresh ginger
- 2 teaspoons ground cumin
- 4 cups chicken stock
- 2 cups lentils
- Salt and freshly ground black pepper
- Plain yogurt

Direction

- Preheat a grill or broiler. Brush the chicken with one tablespoon of the oil and sear the chicken, turning it once, until it is brown and just cooked through, about 10 minutes.
- Meanwhile heat the remaining oil in a large, heavy ovenproof casserole. Add the onion, sweet and hot peppers, garlic and ginger and saute until lightly browned. Stir in the cumin. Pare or cut the cooked chicken into chunks and add to the casserole.
- Preheat oven to 350 degrees.
- Stir in the broth. Pick over the lentlis and add them. Bring to a simmer, cover and bake for about 30 minutes, until the lentils are tender. Season to taste with salt and pepper. Serve with yogurt on the side.

Nutrition Information

- 375: calories;
- 2 grams: polyunsaturated fat;
- 5 grams: sugars;
- 27 grams: protein;
- 667 milligrams: sodium;
- 12 grams: fat;
- 3 grams: saturated fat;
- 0 grams: trans fat;
- 7 grams: monounsaturated fat;
- 39 grams: carbohydrates;
- 6 grams: dietary fiber;

99. Curried Rice

Serving: 4 servings | Prep: | Cook: | Ready in: 20mins

Ingredients

- 1 tablespoon butter
- ½ cup finely chopped onions
- ½ teaspoon finely chopped garlic
- 1 cup converted rice
- 2 tablespoons black or golden raisins
- 1 tablespoon curry powder
- 1 ½ cups water
- 1 bay leaf
- 2 sprigs fresh thyme or 1/2 teaspoon dried
- Salt and freshly ground pepper to taste

Direction

- Melt the butter in a saucepan. Add the onions and garlic. Cook and stir until wilted. Add the remaining ingredients and bring to a boil, stirring. Cover tightly and simmer for 17 minutes.
- Remove the bay leaf and thyme sprigs. Mix well and serve hot.

Nutrition Information

- 232: calories;

- 3 grams: fat;
- 2 grams: dietary fiber;
- 0 grams: polyunsaturated fat;
- 1 gram: monounsaturated fat;
- 46 grams: carbohydrates;
- 4 grams: protein;
- 395 milligrams: sodium;

100. Curry Laced Moules À La Marinière With Fresh Peas

Serving: 4 main-course servings | Prep: | Cook: |Ready in: 45mins

Ingredients

- 3 ½ pounds black mussels
- 1 to 1 ½ cups freshly shelled peas
- 2 tablespoons unsalted butter
- 1 small onion or 2 to 4 shallots, minced
- 1 ½ teaspoons curry powder (more to taste)
- 2 cups dry white wine
- 2 to 3 garlic cloves, peeled and crushed
- 4 sprigs fresh parsley
- 2 sprigs fresh thyme
- 1 small bay leaf
- 6 whole peppercorns
- 3 tablespoons finely chopped fresh parsley

Direction

- Clean the mussels. Inspect each one carefully and discard any that have opened (if some are partly open, tap them with your finger, and if they close back up they are O.K.) or have cracked shells. Place in a large bowl, fill the bowl with cold water and rinse several times, swishing the mussels around in the water, pouring out the water and refilling. Clean the shells, if necessary, with a brush or the end of one of the mussels, and pull out the beards – the hairy attachments emerging from the shells. Do not do this until just before cooking, or the mussels will die and spoil.
- Steam the peas or cook them in lightly salted boiling water until tender, 4 to 10 minutes, depending on the size and age of the peas. Drain and set aside.
- Heat 1 tablespoon of the butter over medium heat in a large Dutch oven or pot and add the onion or shallots. Cook, stirring occasionally, until they begin to soften, 2 to 3 minutes, and add the curry powder. Stir together for a minute, until fragrant, and add the wine, garlic, bay leaf, sprigs of parsley and thyme, and the peppercorns. Bring to a boil over high heat, reduce the heat to medium and boil for 2 minutes.
- Add the mussels and cover tightly. Cook 2 minutes, shake the pot vigorously and cook another 2 minutes. Uncover and use tongs to transfer all of the mussels that have opened to wide soup bowls. Cover the pot and cook for another minute, or until all of the mussels have opened. Transfer them to the bowls with the other mussels. Discard any mussels that have not opened. Cover the mussels to keep warm.
- Line a strainer with a few thicknesses of damp cheesecloth and place over a bowl. Strain the liquid from the pot into the bowl, return to the pot and bring to a boil. Stir in the remaining tablespoon of butter and simmer until it melts. Stir in the peas. Taste and adjust seasoning. You may want to add more pepper or curry powder. Spoon the broth and peas over the mussels, sprinkle with parsley and serve.

Nutrition Information

- 542: calories;
- 29 grams: carbohydrates;
- 15 grams: fat;
- 0 grams: trans fat;
- 4 grams: dietary fiber;
- 3 grams: polyunsaturated fat;
- 5 grams: sugars;
- 51 grams: protein;
- 1149 milligrams: sodium;

101. Dark Chocolate Cherry Ganache Bars

Serving: 18 bars | Prep: | Cook: | Ready in: 1hours

Ingredients

- 150 grams all-purpose flour (about 1 1/2 cups)
- 90 grams confectioners' sugar (about 3/4 cup)
- 26 grams unsweetened cocoa powder (about 1/4 cup)
- ½ teaspoon fine sea salt
- 12 tablespoons cold unsalted butter
- 1 teaspoon vanilla extract
- 52 grams cherry jam (about 2 tablespoons)
- 340 grams bittersweet chocolate, at least 62 percent, chopped (12 ounces)
- ⅔ cup heavy cream
- 3 tablespoons kirsch, rum, brandy or other spirit
- ½ teaspoon fleur de sel, for sprinkling

Direction

- In a food processor, pulse together the flour, sugar, cocoa powder and fine sea salt. Pulse in the butter and vanilla until the mixture just comes together into a smooth mass. Line an 8-inch square baking pan with parchment or wax paper. Press the dough into the pan. Prick all over with a fork. Chill for at least 20 minutes and up to 3 days.
- Heat the oven to 325 degrees. Bake the shortbread until firm to the touch and just beginning to pull away from the sides, 35 to 40 minutes.
- Cool in the pan for 20 minutes on a wire rack. Brush jam over shortbread's surface and let cool thoroughly.
- Place chocolate in a heatproof bowl. In a saucepan, bring the cream to a simmer. Pour over the chocolate and whisk until smooth. Whisk in the kirsch. Spread over shortbread. Sprinkle fleur de sel on. Cool to room temperature; cover and chill until firm. Slice and serve.

Nutrition Information

- 261: calories;
- 0 grams: trans fat;
- 72 milligrams: sodium;
- 17 grams: sugars;
- 10 grams: saturated fat;
- 1 gram: polyunsaturated fat;
- 28 grams: carbohydrates;
- 2 grams: protein;
- 5 grams: monounsaturated fat;

102. Dark Fruit And Creamy Cheese

Serving: 6 servings | Prep: | Cook: | Ready in: 20mins

Ingredients

- 1 cup fromage blanc (fat-free white cheese, sold in cheese shops)
- 1 cup nonfat plain yogurt
- ¼ cup honey
- 12 Italian prune plums, pitted and quartered
- 8 fresh black figs, quartered
- ½ cup blackberri

Direction

- Mix the fromage blanc and yogurt together in a bowl until very smooth. Sweeten the mixture with two tablespoons of the honey.
- Spoon the cheese and yogurt mixture into the middle of a shallow serving dish. Allow a border of about two inches all around.
- Arrange the plums, figs and berries around the cheese mixture. Drizzle with honey and serve.

103. Deconstructed Pumpkin Pie

Serving: 8 to 10 servings | Prep: | Cook: |Ready in: 2hours30mins

Ingredients

- FOR CHOCOLATE GANACHE
- 12 ounces 70 percent bittersweet chocolate, in pieces
- 1 ⅓ cups heavy cream
- ¼ cup agave syrup
- FOR PUMPKIN AND CRANBERRY CONFIT
- 2 ½ cups sugar
- ½ vanilla bean, scraped
- Zest of 1/2 orange
- Zest of 1/2 lemon
- 1 small pumpkin, about 1 1/2 pounds, or winter squash, peeled, seeded and diced
- ½ cup fresh cranberries
- FOR THE PUMPKIN MOUSSE
- 1 ⅓ cup unseasoned canned pumpkin purée
- ½ packet unflavored gelatin
- 1 cup heavy cream
- ½ vanilla bean, scraped
- ⅓ cup sugar
- ¼ teaspoon cinnamon
- ⅛ teaspoon nutmeg
- ⅛ teaspoon ground ginger
- FOR THE PUMPKIN CAKE
- Butter for pan
- 1 ½ cups flour
- ¾ teaspoon baking soda
- ½ teaspoon salt
- 1 teaspoon cinnamon
- ½ teaspoon nutmeg
- ½ teaspoon ground ginger
- 1 ½ cups sugar
- 2 large eggs, beaten
- 1 cup unseasoned pumpkin purée
- 4 ounces (1 stick) unsalted butter, melted and cooled
- FOR FINISHING
- Reserved chocolate from ganache
- 6 thin ginger or speculaas cookies

Direction

- Make the ganache: Place 10 ounces of the chocolate in a bowl. Reserve the rest for decoration.
- Bring cream and syrup to a boil. Pour over chocolate. Mix well with a whisk without incorporating any air. Place a piece of plastic wrap on the surface. Refrigerate until well chilled and fairly firm, about 4 hours.
- Make the confit: Mix sugar with 2 cups water in a 2-quart saucepan. Add vanilla bean, orange and lemon zest. Bring to a boil and when sugar has dissolved, add pumpkin. Reduce heat to very low and simmer until pumpkin is translucent, about 2 hours. Use a slotted spoon to remove pumpkin to a small container, cover with about half the sugar syrup, cover container and set aside.
- Add cranberries to remaining syrup, simmer 5 minutes, then set aside for 15 minutes. Drain cranberries into a small container, cover with some syrup, cover container and set aside.
- Make the mousse: Preheat oven to 250 degrees. Line a small baking sheet with foil, spread the 1 1/3 cup of pumpkin purée on foil and bake about 25 minutes to remove some moisture. Transfer to a bowl.
- Place gelatin in a small dish, stir in 1 1/2 tablespoons cold water and set aside. Place 1/3 cup cream, the vanilla, sugar and spices in a small saucepan and bring to a boil. Remove from heat. Stir in softened gelatin. Mix thoroughly into pumpkin purée. Cover and refrigerate until cold, about 2 hours. When cold, whip remaining cream. Fold into pumpkin purée. Refrigerate until ready to use.
- Make the cake: Butter a 9-by-13-by-2-inch baking pan. Line with parchment, allowing overhang on the long sides. Butter the paper. Preheat oven to 325 degrees.
- Place flour, baking soda, salt and spices in a sieve. Sieve into a large bowl. Stir in sugar. Mix eggs with pumpkin purée. Fold into dry ingredients. Add melted butter and mix well.
- Spread batter in pan and bake 20 minutes, until a cake tester comes out clean. Cake will

not rise to the rim of pan. Cool in pan at least 1 hour. Use parchment overhang to help remove from pan. Refrigerate until ready to assemble.
- Assemble the dessert: Place pumpkin confit in a strainer. Rinse briefly in cold water, drain and place on paper towels. Repeat with cranberry confit. Set aside.
- Place cake on a cutting board. Trim 1/2 inch from all sides. Nibble trimmings or let the army of assistants have at them. Cut cake in half lengthwise. Place half the cake on a large platter.
- Use a spatula to spread or a pastry bag to pipe ganache in a thick layer all over the top of the cake half on the platter. Place second half on top and press lightly.
- Place mousse in a pastry bag and pipe peaks or rows all over the top of the cake. Alternatively, form ovals with 2 teaspoons to cover top of cake, or simply spread the mousse on the cake and use the point of a knife to make peaks.
- Break up reserved chocolate and the ginger cookies and stick them randomly into the pumpkin mousse. Place some of the pumpkin and cranberry confit on the mousse and scatter the rest on the platter around the cake. Refrigerate until ready to serve.

104. Denesse Willey's Fresh Plum Cake

Serving: | Prep: | Cook: | Ready in: 40mins

Ingredients

- 1 cup all-purpose flour
- 1 cup whole-wheat flour
- 2 teaspoons baking powder
- ½ teaspoon table salt
- ¾ cup granulated sugar
- 12 tablespoons cold butter
- 2 eggs
- 2 teaspoons vanilla
- About 6 ounces milk
- 5 to 6 plums, sliced
- ½ cup old-fashioned oatmeal
- 1 teaspoon ground ginger
- ½ teaspoon ground cardamom

Direction

- Preheat oven to 425 degrees. Lightly grease an 9-inch-by 13-inch baking pan. In the bowl of a food processor, combine flours, baking powder, salt and 1/4 cup sugar. Add 6 tablespoons cold butter and pulse until it is the consistency of corn meal. In a measuring cup, beat together the eggs and vanilla; add enough milk to make 1 cup. With the processor running, pour in milk mixture; a soft sticky dough will form. Scrape the dough into the pan, and with a greased spatula press the dough to cover the bottom of the pan. Press in the fruit, skin side down until it uniformly covers the dough. (Distribute the dough more evenly by pushing it with the fruit sections.) Sprinkle oatmeal over all. Distribute 1/2 cup sugar over the oatmeal. Sprinkle on spices. Dot with remaining 6 tablespoons cold butter.
- Bake about 25 minutes. Serve warm (but not hot) with ice cream for dessert. Refrigerate leftovers for breakfast.

Nutrition Information

- 271: calories;
- 13 grams: fat;
- 0 grams: trans fat;
- 2 grams: dietary fiber;
- 8 grams: saturated fat;
- 4 grams: monounsaturated fat;
- 1 gram: polyunsaturated fat;
- 35 grams: carbohydrates;
- 16 grams: sugars;
- 5 grams: protein;
- 176 milligrams: sodium;

105. Deviled Crab

Serving: 14 to 16 appetizer servings; 6 main course servings | Prep: | Cook: | Ready in: 25mins

Ingredients

- 1 pound lump crab meat
- ¼ cup butter
- 2 tablespoons finely chopped onion
- 2 tablespoons finely chopped celery
- ½ cup plus 2 tablespoons mayonnaise (see note)
- ½ cup plus 1 tablespoon freshly grated Parmesan cheese
- 1 tablespoon finely chopped parsley
- 1 teaspoon fresh lemon juice
- 1 teaspoon dry sherry
- 1 teaspoon freshly ground pepper
- ¼ teaspoon Tabasco sauce

Direction

- Pick over the crab meat to remove cartilage and bone. Try not to break up the lumps. Put the crab in a mixing bowl.
- Melt the butter in a skillet and add the onion and celery. Cook until wilted. Set aside to cool.
- Preheat the broiler.
- Add the onion and celery mixture and 1/2 cup each of mayonnaise and cheese to the crab meat. Add the parsley, lemon juice, sherry, pepper and Tabasco. Blend carefully so as not to break up the lumps of crab.
- If you are to serve this as a canape, spoon the mixture into 14 to 16 small scallop dishes. If it is to be served as a main course, spoon it into six large scallop shells.
- Blend the remaining two tablespoons of mayonnaise and one tablespoon of cheese. Spoon equal portions of this mixture over the tops of the crab and smooth it over. Place under the broiler until bubbling and golden brown.

Nutrition Information

- 131: calories;
- 3 grams: monounsaturated fat;
- 7 grams: protein;
- 274 milligrams: sodium;
- 11 grams: fat;
- 4 grams: polyunsaturated fat;
- 0 grams: sugars;

106. Dressing

Serving: | Prep: | Cook: | Ready in: 5mins

Ingredients

- 1 tablespoon green peppercorns
- ½ cup olive oil
- 1 tablespoon chervil, chopped
- Juice of 2 lemons
- Salt to taste

Direction

- Press the peppercorns through a sieve and mix with the oil. Add chervil, lemon juice and season with salt.

Nutrition Information

- 248: calories;
- 20 grams: monounsaturated fat;
- 3 grams: carbohydrates;
- 1 gram: sugars;
- 0 grams: protein;
- 138 milligrams: sodium;
- 27 grams: fat;
- 4 grams: saturated fat;

107. Egg And Herb Salad

Serving: Serves four to six | Prep: | Cook: | Ready in: 30mins

Ingredients

- 8 large eggs, hard-boiled (see below) and finely chopped
- 1 cup finely chopped fresh herbs, such as parsley, dill, tarragon, chervil or chives
- 2 celery stalks, finely chopped
- 1 small red onion, finely chopped, soaked for five minutes in cold water, drained and rinsed
- Salt
- freshly ground pepper to taste
- 1 tablespoon white wine vinegar or sherry vinegar
- 2 tablespoons freshly squeezed lemon juice
- ⅓ cup plain low-fat yogurt or buttermilk
- 1 tablespoon Hellmann's or Best Foods mayonnaise
- 1 garlic clove, green shoot removed, minced
- 1 teaspoon Dijon mustard
- 2 tablespoons extra virgin olive oil
- 1 6-ounce bag baby arugula

Direction

- To hard-boil the eggs, place in a saucepan, cover with cold water and bring to a boil. Cover the pan tightly, and turn off the heat. Let sit for 12 minutes. Fill a bowl with ice water, drain the eggs and chill immediately in the ice water.
- Combine the chopped eggs, herbs, celery and red onion in a large bowl, and season to taste with salt and pepper.
- Whisk together the vinegar, lemon juice, yogurt, mayonnaise, mustard and olive oil. Season to taste with salt and pepper. Toss with the egg mixture.
- Line plates or a platter with arugula, top with the egg salad and serve.

Nutrition Information

- 182: calories;
- 13 grams: fat;
- 3 grams: sugars;
- 6 grams: monounsaturated fat;
- 5 grams: carbohydrates;
- 1 gram: dietary fiber;
- 371 milligrams: sodium;
- 0 grams: trans fat;
- 10 grams: protein;

108. Eggs Poached In Red Wine Sauce (Les Oeufs Poches Au Vin Rouge)

Serving: 4 servings | Prep: | Cook: | Ready in: 40mins

Ingredients

- 3 cups dry red wine
- ½ cup shallots, peeled and thinly sliced
- 4 large cloves garlic, peeled and crushed
- ¼ cup carrots, scraped and cut into very small cubes
- 1 bay leaf
- 2 sprigs fresh thyme
- 4 sprigs fresh parsley
- 6 peppercorns
- 1 teaspoon honey
- 8 fresh mushrooms, about 1/2 pound
- 5 tablespoons butter
- 8 eggs at room temperature
- 8 croutons (see recipe)
- 2 tablespoons flour
- 3 tablespoons finely chopped parsley

Direction

- Put the wine in a wide saucepan and add the shallots, garlic, carrots, bay leaf, thyme and parsley sprigs, peppercorns and honey. Cut off the stems of the mushrooms and add them. Set the caps aside. Bring to the simmer and cook 15 minutes. Strain the mixture and discard the solids. Return the wine liquid to the saucepan.
- Heat one tablespoon of the butter in a skillet large enough to hold the mushroom caps in one layer when they are added. Add the mushrooms cap-side down. Cook two to three minutes on one side or until golden brown.

Turn and continue cooking two to three minutes. Remove from the heat.
- Break each egg into a small bowl.
- It is best to poach only four eggs at a time. Bring the wine liquid to the simmer and carefully slide the eggs, one at a time, into the liquid. Let simmer until the whites are firm and the yolks remain runny, about two to three minutes. Carefully scoop out each egg, using a slotted spoon, and drain on absorbent paper towels. Repeat with the remaining eggs and drain.
- Arrange the croutons on a serving platter or arrange two croutons on each of four serving dishes. Top each crouton with a poached egg.
- Meanwhile, knead the remaining four tablespoons of butter with the flour.
- Skim off and discard any egg remnants floating on the surface of the wine liquid. Bring the liquid to the simmer and gradually add the butter-flour mixture. Stir until the sauce is thickened. Pour the sauce over the eggs on croutons and garnish with the mushrooms on the side. Sprinkle each egg with chopped parsley and serve.

Nutrition Information

- 464: calories;
- 23 grams: fat;
- 1 gram: trans fat;
- 7 grams: monounsaturated fat;
- 15 grams: protein;
- 12 grams: saturated fat;
- 2 grams: dietary fiber;
- 20 grams: carbohydrates;
- 6 grams: sugars;
- 159 milligrams: sodium;

109. Enfrijoladas

Serving: Serves 4 | Prep: | Cook: | Ready in: 2hours30mins

Ingredients

- ½ pound (1 1/8 cups) black beans, washed, picked over and soaked for 4 to 6 hours or overnight in 1 quart water
- 1 onion, cut in half
- 2 plump garlic cloves, minced
- 1 to 2 sprigs epazote or 2 tablespoons chopped cilantro, plus additional for garnish (optional)
- 1 to 2 teaspoons ground cumin, to taste
- ½ to 1 teaspoon ground mild chili powder (more to taste)
- Salt to taste
- 12 corn tortillas
- ¼ cup chopped walnuts (optional)

Direction

- In a large soup pot or Dutch oven combine the black beans with their soaking water (they should be submerged by at least 1 1/2 inches of water; add if necessary), one half of the onion, and half the garlic and bring to a boil. Reduce the heat, cover and simmer gently for 1 hour. Add the remaining garlic, epazote or cilantro if using, cumin, chili powder, and salt to taste and simmer for another hour, until the beans are very soft and the broth thick, soupy and aromatic. Remove from the heat. Remove and discard the onion.
- Using an immersion blender or a food processor fitted with the steel blade coarsely puree the beans. The mixture should retain some texture and the consistency should be thick and creamy. Heat through, stirring the bottom of the pot so the beans don't stick. Taste and adjust salt. Keep warm.
- Slice the remaining onion half crosswise into thin half-moons and cover with cold water while you assemble the enfrijoladas. Heat the corn tortillas: either wrap them in a damp dish towel and heat them, 4 at a time, in the microwave for about 30 seconds at 100 percent power, or wrap in a dish towel and steam for 1 minute, then let rest for 5 minutes.
- Assemble the enfrijoladas just before serving them. Spoon about 1/2 cup of the hot, thick beans over the bottom of a large lightly oiled

baking dish or serving platter. Using tongs, dip a softened tortilla into the beans and flip over to coat both sides with black beans. Remove from the beans and place on the baking dish or platter (this is messy; have the serving dish right next to the pot.) Fold into quarters. Use the tongs to do this, and if you find that the tortilla tears too much, then just coat one side with the black beans, transfer to the baking dish and spoon some of the black beans over the other side, then fold into quarters. Continue with the remaining tortillas, arranging the quartered bean-coated tortillas in overlapping rows. When all of the tortillas are in the dish, spoon the remaining black bean sauce over the top. Drain and rinse the onions, dry briefly on paper towels and sprinkle over the bean sauce. Garnish with cilantro and chopped walnuts if desired and serve at once.

Nutrition Information

- 369: calories;
- 3 grams: sugars;
- 1 gram: polyunsaturated fat;
- 72 grams: carbohydrates;
- 14 grams: dietary fiber;
- 17 grams: protein;
- 378 milligrams: sodium;

110. Fajitas (Meat Filled Tortillas With Hot Sauce)

Serving: 6 servings | Prep: | Cook: | Ready in: 40mins

Ingredients

- 3 skirt steaks, about 3 pounds
- 1 tablespoon finely minced garlic
- 1 ½ tablespoons fresh lime juice
- 1 tablepoon water
- Salt to taste
- Freshly ground pepper to taste
- 12 tortillas
- Chipotle chili sauce (see recipe)
- Red onion rings for garnish
- 3 large romaine lettuce leaves
- Guacamole
- Hot chili sauce (pico de gallo) (see recipe)
- Mexican table sauce (see recipe)
- Cowgirl beans (see recipe)

Direction

- The skirt steak should be as free of surface fat as possible. Place each steak on a flat surface, and carefully slice away most of the fat using a sharp knife. Trim well on both sides.
- Cut each steak crosswise into three or four pieces, each about five or six inches long.
- Place each piece of meat on the flat surface, and holding a sharp slicing knife parallel to the cutting surface, cut each piece of meat, sandwich-style, into two thin rectangles. Count on four or five slices per person.
- Blend the garlic, lime juice, water, salt and pepper in a small bowl. Spoon a small amount into a flat dish. Make one layer of meat slices and brush the tops with the mixture. Make another layer of meat, another brushing of sauce and so on. Continue until all the slices of meat and sauce are used.
- Cook the meat slices over a hot charcoal fire about 2 minutes on each side. Meanwhile, heat another grill or a skillet, and add the flour tortillas. Cook briefly just to heat through without browning. They must remain soft.
- To serve, arrange equal portions of the hot grilled meat on each of six preheated plates. Smear a generous quantity of the chipotle sauce over the meat. Garnish the top with three red onion rings. Cut each lettuce leaf crosswise in half and add a half to each plate. Spoon equal portions of guacamole (two avocados will produce the right quantities for these proportions) on top. Serve the hot chili sauce and the Mexican table sauce on the side. Serve the beans in individual small bowls to be eaten with a spoon. Serve the warm flour tortillas, covered, on the side.

- To eat, add one piece of sauce-covered, garnished meat in the center of a tortilla. Add hot chili sauce and Mexican table sauce to taste. Fold left and right sides of the tortilla over the center to enclose the meat. Fold up the bottom edge to prevent dripping.

111. Farfalle With Roasted Peppers

Serving: Serves 4 | Prep: | Cook: | Ready in: 30mins

Ingredients

- 1 large red pepper, roasted and peeled
- 2 ounces feta
- ¼ cup plain yogurt
- 1 to 2 garlic cloves (to taste), puréed
- 2 tablespoons extra virgin olive oil
- 2 tablespoons slivered basil leaves
- 2 teaspoons fresh marjoram or oregano leaves, chopped
- Freshly ground pepper
- Salt to taste
- ¾ pound farfalle
- 1 cup frozen peas

Direction

- Begin heating a large pot of water for the pasta. Meanwhile seed the pepper, holding it over a bowl to catch juices. Cut in small dice (about 1/4 inch) and place in a another bowl. Strain any juices into the bowl and season with salt and pepper.
- In a large bowl, mash together the feta and the yogurt and add the puréed garlic. Stir in the olive oil, pepper with its juice, basil and marjoram or oregano.
- When the water for the pasta comes to a boil, salt generously and add the farfalle. Set the timer for 5 minutes and add the peas. Boil for another 5 minutes, until the farfalle is cooked al dente. Ladle 2 to 4 tablespoons of the cooking water into the yogurt mixture. Drain the pasta and add to the bowl with the yogurt and peppers, toss together and serve. Garnish each serving with slivered basil and crumbled feta if desired.

Nutrition Information

- 465: calories;
- 7 grams: sugars;
- 463 milligrams: sodium;
- 73 grams: carbohydrates;
- 5 grams: dietary fiber;
- 16 grams: protein;
- 12 grams: fat;
- 4 grams: saturated fat;
- 6 grams: monounsaturated fat;
- 1 gram: polyunsaturated fat;

112. Fettucine With Salsa Cruda

Serving: Two to four servings | Prep: | Cook: | Ready in: 15mins

Ingredients

- 2 very ripe large tomatoes, seeded and finely chopped (see note below)
- ½ cup chopped imported green olives
- 2 tablespoons capers, chopped
- 2 teaspoons fresh lemon juice
- 2 garlic cloves, peeled and finely chopped
- ¼ cup finely chopped fresh parsley
- 1 tablespoon finely chopped fresh mint
- 4 anchovy fillets, chopped
- ½ cup extra-virgin olive oil
- Freshly ground black pepper to taste
- ¾ pound fettucine or tagliatelle

Direction

- Combine ingredients except pasta in a large bowl; set aside.

- Bring a large pot of salted water to a boil. Add the pasta and cook until al dente.
- Toss the pasta with the sauce and add additional black pepper, if desired. Serve immediately.

Nutrition Information

- 606: calories;
- 5 grams: sugars;
- 14 grams: protein;
- 494 milligrams: sodium;
- 31 grams: fat;
- 4 grams: polyunsaturated fat;
- 22 grams: monounsaturated fat;
- 69 grams: carbohydrates;

113. Fish And Vegetables

Serving: 4 servings | Prep: | Cook: | Ready in: 15mins

Ingredients

- 1 pound boneless swordfish or tuna steak, about 1/2-inch thick
- 2 teaspoons kosher salt
- 4 ounces mushrooms, wiped clean with a damp cloth and thinly sliced lengthwise (about 2 cups)
- 2 cups broccoli florets
- 4 ounces green beans, trimmed and quartered crosswise (about 1 1/3 cups)
- 4 ounces carrots, cut into 1-inch-thick matchsticks (about 1 1/3 cups)
- ¼ cup fresh lemon juice
- 2 tablespoons olive oil
- Freshly ground black pepper to taste
- 1 ½ tablespoons chopped fresh herbs, such as mint, dill or parsley

Direction

- Place fish in the center of an oval dish 14 by 9 by 2 inches. Sprinkle with salt. Top with the mushrooms and broccoli. Arrange green beans and carrots around the fish.
- Mix lemon juice, oil, pepper and herbs together in a small bowl. Pour over the fish and vegetables.
- Cover tightly with microwave plastic wrap. Cook at 100 percent power in a high-power oven for 8 minutes, or until carrots are cooked. Prick plastic to release steam.
- Remove from oven and uncover. Serve hot.

Nutrition Information

- 229: calories;
- 629 milligrams: sodium;
- 8 grams: fat;
- 1 gram: polyunsaturated fat;
- 0 grams: trans fat;
- 5 grams: monounsaturated fat;
- 2 grams: dietary fiber;
- 31 grams: protein;
- 10 grams: carbohydrates;
- 4 grams: sugars;

114. Flaky Pie Crust

Serving: Pastry for two 9-inch pies | Prep: | Cook: | Ready in: 4hours15mins

Ingredients

- 2 cups unbleached all-purpose flour
- ⅜ teaspoon salt
- ⅛ teaspoon sugar
- 5 tablespoons salted butter, cut in several pieces
- 6 ½ tablespoons unsalted butter, cut in several pieces
- 3 tablespoons solid vegetable shortening
- 3 tablespoons ice water (a bit more or less may be needed)

Direction

- Mix flour, salt and sugar.
- Using a processor, a pastry blender or your fingertips, cut the salted butter into the dry ingredients until the mixture resembles cornmeal. Add unsalted butter and shortening and cut them in until the lumps are the size of peas.
- If you have been using a processor, transfer the mixture to a large bowl. Sprinkle on the ice water a little at a time and toss with a fork until the mixture comes together in lumps and holds together when pressed. If necessary, add more ice water, sparingly. Avoid kneading the dough.
- Gather the dough into two balls, wrap each tightly in plastic wrap and chill for at least four hours.

Nutrition Information

- 1211: calories;
- 87 grams: fat;
- 8 grams: polyunsaturated fat;
- 96 grams: carbohydrates;
- 577 milligrams: sodium;
- 3 grams: dietary fiber;
- 1 gram: sugars;
- 14 grams: protein;
- 47 grams: saturated fat;
- 5 grams: trans fat;
- 25 grams: monounsaturated fat;

115. Focaccia With Tomatoes And Rosemary

Serving: 12 to 15 servings | Prep: | Cook: | Ready in: 2hours45mins

Ingredients

- 2 teaspoons (8 grams) active dry yeast
- 1 teaspoon (5 grams) sugar
- 1 ½ cups lukewarm water
- 2 tablespoons (25 grams) olive oil, plus an additional 2 tablespoons (25 grams) for drizzling
- 250 grams (approximately 2 cups) whole-wheat flour
- 200 to 220 grams (approximately 1 2/3 to 1 3/4 cups) unbleached all-purpose flour or bread flour, plus additional as needed for kneading
- 1 ¾ teaspoons (13 grams) salt
- ¾ pound Roma tomatoes
- Coarse salt and freshly ground pepper to taste
- 1 to 2 tablespoons chopped fresh rosemary (to taste)

Direction

- In the bowl of a standing mixer, or in a large bowl, dissolve the yeast and sugar in the water. Add the olive oil, whole-wheat flour, 200 grams of the all-purpose flour and salt and mix together briefly using the paddle attachment. Change to the dough hook and beat for 8 to 10 minutes at medium speed, adding flour as necessary. The dough should eventually form a ball around the dough hook and slap against the sides of the bowl as the mixer turns; it will be sticky. Remove from the bowl, flour your hands and knead for a minute on a lightly floured surface, and shape into a ball.
- If kneading the dough by hand, dissolve the yeast in the water with the sugar as directed. Stir in the olive oil, whole-wheat flour, salt and all-purpose flour by the half-cup, until the dough can be scraped out onto a floured work surface. Knead, adding flour as necessary, for 10 minutes, until the dough is elastic and smooth. Shape into a ball.
- Clean and dry your bowl and oil lightly with olive oil. Place the dough in it, rounded side down first, then rounded side up. Cover tightly with plastic and let rise in a warm spot for 1 1/2 to 2 hours, or in the refrigerator for 4 to 8 hours, until doubled.
- Punch down the dough. Cover with lightly oiled plastic and let the dough rest for 15 minutes.

- Preheat the oven to 425 degrees, preferably with a baking stone in it. Line a sheet pan with parchment and oil generously. Roll or press out the dough into a rectangle the size of the sheet pan or just slightly smaller. To do this efficiently, roll or press out the dough, stop and wait 5 minutes for the gluten to relax, then roll or press out again, and repeat until the dough reaches the right size. Cover with a damp towel and let rest for 30 minutes. Just before baking, use your fingertips to dimple the dough all over.
- Cut the tomatoes into rounds and place on top of the focaccia. Sprinkle with coarse salt and the rosemary. Drizzle a tablespoon or two of olive oil over all.
- Bake, setting the pan on top of the baking stone (if using), for 20 to 25 minutes, until the bread is deep golden brown. Let rest for at least 10 minutes before serving, or allow to cool completely.

Nutrition Information

- 124: calories;
- 0 grams: polyunsaturated fat;
- 26 grams: carbohydrates;
- 3 grams: dietary fiber;
- 4 grams: protein;
- 195 milligrams: sodium;
- 1 gram: sugars;

116. Fried Chicken Salad

Serving: 4 servings | Prep: | Cook: | Ready in: 30mins

Ingredients

- 1 3- to 4-pound chicken, cut up and skinned
- Juice 1 lemon
- 1 teaspoon Creole pepper (or substitute chili powder)
- Coarse salt to taste
- Flour for dredging
- Vegetable shortening for deep frying
- 1 cup mayonnaise (preferably homemade)
- 1 tablespoon fresh thyme (or half teaspoon dried)
- 1 tablespoon fresh tarragon (or half teaspoon dried)
- 1 jalapeno chili, minced
- 6 scallions, chopped
- Freshly ground pepper to taste
- 3 tablespoons olive oil
- 1 tablespoon tarragon vinegar
- 1 small head red-leaf lettuce (or bibb or Boston)

Direction

- Marinate the chicken in a mixture of the lemon juice and Creole pepper for a couple of hours.
- Heat the shortening until smoking. Season the chicken pieces with salt and dredge them lightly with flour. Fry until golden brown and drain on paper towels.
- Meanwhile, combine the mayonnaise with the thyme, tarragon, chili and scallions. Season to taste with salt and pepper. Mix the olive oil and vinegar in a separate bowl and season. Toss the lettuce leaves in the dressing and arrange on a platter.
- When the chicken is cool enough to handle, cut it in slices. Coat with the mayonnaise and place in the center of the lettuce leaves.

Nutrition Information

- 1120: calories;
- 20 grams: saturated fat;
- 0 grams: trans fat;
- 1 gram: sugars;
- 35 grams: monounsaturated fat;
- 37 grams: polyunsaturated fat;
- 11 grams: carbohydrates;
- 3 grams: dietary fiber;
- 53 grams: protein;
- 1341 milligrams: sodium;
- 96 grams: fat;

117. Fried Soft Shell Clams

Serving: 4 servings | Prep: | Cook: |Ready in: 30mins

Ingredients

- 4 pounds or 40 medium-size soft-shell (steamer) clams
- 1 can of evaporated milk or an equal amount of buttermilk
- 1 quart canola or corn oil
- 1 cup all-purpose flour
- 1 cup masa harina (fine ground yellow cornmeal)
- 1 teaspoon baking powder
- 1 teaspoon salt
- 1 cup tartar sauce (see recipe)

Direction

- Rinse the clams under cold water and drain. Fill a pot large enough to hold all the clams half full of water and bring to a boil. Add the clams, reduce the flame to low and let the clams sit for 3 or 4 minutes. Drain and place the clams in a bowl of cold water. When cool, open each shell and remove the clam. Use a small knife to cut out any that adhere. Discard the black mantle covering the neck. Soak the clams in a bowl with evaporated milk or buttermilk.
- In a heavy skillet or deep fryer, heat the oil to 360 degrees. Meanwhile, remove the clams from the milk and drain. Combine the flour, masa harina, baking powder and salt. When the oil is hot, toss the clams in the flour mixture to coat. Shake off any loose flour and immediately put the clams into the oil. Do not let floured clams sit or they will not be crisp when fried. In a minute or two, when the clams are a little darker than cornflakes, remove them, drain on paper towels and serve with tartar sauce.

118. Fried Winter Squash With Mint

Serving: 4 to 6 servings | Prep: | Cook: |Ready in: 15mins

Ingredients

- ¼ cup extra virgin olive oil
- 2 garlic cloves, peeled and crushed
- 1 ½ pounds peeled, seeded winter squash, like kabocha or butternut, cut in slices 1/4 inch thick by 2 or 3 inches long
- Salt
- freshly ground pepper
- 2 to 3 tablespoons chopped fresh mint, plus additional leaves for garnish
- Pomegranate seeds for garnish

Direction

- Heat the oil over medium-high heat in a large heavy skillet, preferably cast iron. Add the garlic cloves and cook, stirring, until golden brown. Remove the garlic from the oil and discard.
- Cook the squash slices in the hot oil, adding only 1 layer of slices at a time to the pan. Cook for about 3 minutes, or until squash is lightly browned on the first side, and flip over using a spatula or tongs. Cook until squash is lightly browned on the other side and tender all the way through. Season to taste with salt and pepper and transfer first to paper towels to drain, then to a platter. Repeat until all of the squash is used up. Sprinkle with chopped fresh mint, garnish with whole mint leaves and pomegranate seeds, and serve.

Nutrition Information

- 121: calories;
- 1 gram: protein;
- 7 grams: monounsaturated fat;
- 10 grams: carbohydrates;
- 2 grams: dietary fiber;
- 3 grams: sugars;

- 288 milligrams: sodium;
- 9 grams: fat;

119. Fruit Tarts

Serving: Six tarts | Prep: | Cook: | Ready in: 2hours

Ingredients

- The pastry:
- 2 cups flour, sifted
- ⅛ teaspoon salt
- ½ teaspoon sugar
- 1 ½ sticks unsalted butter, chilled and cut into bits
- 2 to 3 tablespoons ice water
- The pastry cream:
- 3 egg yolks
- ¼ cup sugar
- 1 tablespoon arrowroot
- 1 cup cold milk
- 1 tablespoon eau de vie. such as framboise, poire or kirsch
- ¼ teaspoon vanilla
- 1 sprig fresh mint
- The fruit:
- 3 cups, about 1 1/2 pints, fresh berries, such as strawberries, raspberries, blackberries or blueberries (see note)
- ⅓ cup currant jelly

Direction

- Preheat the oven to 425 degrees.
- To make the pastry, place the flour, salt, sugar and butter in the bowl of an electric mixer. Use a dough hook at low speed and mix until it is the consistency of cornmeal, about eight minutes. Add the ice water a tablespoon at a time. When the pastry becomes elastic and pulls away from the sides of the bowl, it is blended. Remove the pastry to a lightly floured surface and shape into a ball. Cover with waxed paper and refrigerate for 30 minutes.
- Roll out the pastry dough on a lightly floured surface to a thickness of a quarter inch. Set six five-inch fluted, loose-bottomed tart pans together to form a rectangle. Lift the dough and place it loosely over the tart pans. Gently press the dough into the pans and roll firmly over the pans with a rolling pin. Remove the excess dough and line the bottom and corners with the dough. Prick the dough surface with a fork. Line the pastry with foil and weigh down with aluminum baking weights or dry beans.
- Place the tart shells on a baking sheet and bake for eight to 10 minutes or until the dough begins to release from the sides of the pans. Remove the weights and foil and bake for another eight minutes or until the pastry is lightly browned. Remove and cool on a rack.
- To prepare the cream, bring the water to a simmer in the lower part of a double boiler. In the upper part of the boiler, whisk the egg yolks and sugar off the heat until the mixture becomes thick and lemon colored.
- Dissolve the arrowroot with the milk and add it to the egg mixture. Set the mixture over the bottom pan and whisk in the liqueur and vanilla. Continue whisking until the mixture becomes thick, about 10 minutes. Remove from the heat, bruise the mint and add to the cream mixture. Cool over a bowl of ice, whisking constantly. Cover and refrigerate until ready to assemble the tarts.
- When the shells have cooled, remove the tart pan collars and bottoms. Stir the pastry cream and divide among the pastry shells. Tightly fill each pastry shell with one layer of berries.
- In a small saucepan, melt the currant jelly with one tablespoon of water over medium-low heat. Brush the melted jelly over the berries. Set aside until ready to serve. Do not refrigerate.

Nutrition Information

- 386: calories;
- 17 grams: sugars;

- 20 grams: fat;
- 12 grams: saturated fat;
- 5 grams: monounsaturated fat;
- 60 milligrams: sodium;
- 1 gram: polyunsaturated fat;
- 46 grams: carbohydrates;
- 2 grams: dietary fiber;
- 6 grams: protein;

120. Ginger Butter Sauce

Serving: About one-half cup | Prep: | Cook: | Ready in: 15mins

Ingredients

- 4 tablespoons butter
- 1 tablespoon finely chopped shallots
- 2 teaspoons finely grated fresh ginger
- 2 tablespoons white-wine vinegar
- ¼ cup dry white wine
- 2 tablespoons heavy cream

Direction

- Heat one tablespoon of the butter in a saucepan and add the shallots and ginger. Cook briefly, stirring, and add the vinegar and wine. Cook until reduced to one-third cup. Add the cream, bring to the boil and add remaining butter. Put the sauce through a fine sieve, pressing to extract as much liquid as possible from the solids. Keep warm.

Nutrition Information

- 191: calories;
- 5 grams: monounsaturated fat;
- 2 grams: carbohydrates;
- 0 grams: protein;
- 8 milligrams: sodium;
- 19 grams: fat;
- 12 grams: saturated fat;
- 1 gram: sugars;

121. Ginger Pumpkin Ice Cream

Serving: About 1 quart | Prep: | Cook: | Ready in: 20mins

Ingredients

- 2 cups milk
- 1 cup heavy cream
- ⅔ cup sugar
- ¼ cup water
- 5 egg yolks
- 1 ¼ cup pumpkin puree (see instructions)
- ¼ teaspoon powdered ginger
- ⅛ teaspoon freshly grated nutmeg

Direction

- In a small pot, scald the milk; in another pot, scald the cream.
- In a saucepan, combine sugar and water and bring to a boil over medium heat, stirring at first until sugar dissolves. Let the mixture cook undisturbed until it caramelizes, 7 to 10 minutes.
- When the sugar has caramelized, remove pan from the heat and add the cream at once, stirring constantly. Return pan to medium heat and stir constantly until all sugar is dissolved. Add milk and bring just to the boiling point.
- In a mixing bowl, combine the egg yolks with the pumpkin puree and spices. Blend well with a wooden spoon.
- Add the cream mixture to the pumpkin mixture, a little at a time, stirring constantly. Take care not to let the egg curdle. When all is incorporated, place the mixture in a heavy saucepan over medium heat and cook, stirring constanlty, until it becomes thick and coats the back of a spoon, about 5 minutes.
- Remove from the heat, pour mixture into a large bowl and let cool at room temperature. Prepare ice cream in a manual or electric ice-

cream machine according to the manufacturer's instructions.

Nutrition Information

- 163: calories;
- 29 milligrams: sodium;
- 10 grams: fat;
- 6 grams: saturated fat;
- 3 grams: protein;
- 1 gram: dietary fiber;
- 16 grams: carbohydrates;
- 15 grams: sugars;

122. Gluten Free Pumpkin Muffins With Crumble Topping

Serving: 12 muffins | Prep: | Cook: | Ready in: 45mins

Ingredients

- Topping
- ¼ cup store-bought gluten-free flour blend
- ¼ cup packed light brown sugar
- ¼ cup granulated sugar
- ½ teaspoon pumpkin pie spice
- 4 tablespoons all-vegetable shortening
- Confectioners' sugar, for sprinkling
- Muffins
- 1 ¾ cups store-bought gluten-free flour blend
- 2 teaspoons baking powder
- 2 teaspoons pumpkin pie spice
- ¾ teaspoon salt
- 2 large eggs, at room temperature
- 1 cup canned pure pumpkin puree
- 1 cup granulated sugar
- ½ cup vegetable oil
- 1 tablespoon pure vanilla extract

Direction

- Preheat oven to 350 degrees Fahrenheit. Line a 12-cup muffin pan with paper liners.
- Prepare the crumble topping. Whisk together the flour, brown sugar, granulated sugar and pumpkin pie spice in a medium bowl. Add the shortening and, using your fingers or a fork, blend together until coarse crumbs form.
- To make the muffins: Whisk together the flour, baking powder, pumpkin pie spice and salt in a large bowl.
- In a medium bowl, whisk together the eggs, pumpkin puree, granulated sugar, oil and vanilla until smooth. Add to the flour mixture; stir until just combined.
- Fill each muffin cup almost full; top each with crumble topping. Bake until the muffins are springy to the touch and a toothpick inserted into the center comes out clean, 20 to 25 minutes. Let cool in the pan, set on a wire rack. Using a sieve, sprinkle with confectioners' sugar.

123. Gluten Free Whole Grain Cheese And Mustard Muffins

Serving: 12 muffins (1/3 cup capacity cups) | Prep: | Cook: | Ready in: 45mins

Ingredients

- 70 grams (approximately 1/2 cup) millet meal (you can grind the millet in a spice mill)
- 70 grams (approximately 1/2 cup) cornmeal
- 140 grams (approximately 1 cup) gluten-free whole grain mix or gluten-free all purpose mix
- 10 grams (2 teaspoons) baking powder
- 5 grams (1 teaspoon) baking soda
- 3 ½ grams (rounded 1/2 teaspoon) salt
- 2 eggs
- 40 grams (2 tablespoons) Dijon mustard
- 300 grams (1 1/4 cups) buttermilk
- 75 grams (1/3 cup) canola or grape seed oil
- 115 grams (1 cup, tightly packed) grated sharp cheddar cheese
- Optional
- 50 grams (1/2 cup) chopped walnuts

Direction

- Preheat the oven to 375 degrees with the rack adjusted to the middle. Oil or butter muffin tins. Sift together the flours, baking powder, baking soda and salt into a medium bowl. Add any grainy bits remaining in the sifter to the bowl.
- In a separate large bowl beat together the eggs, mustard, buttermilk and oil. Quickly whisk in the dry ingredients and mix until well combined. Do not beat for too long; a few lumps are fine but make sure there is no flour sitting at the bottom of the bowl. Fold in the cheese and walnuts.
- Using a spoon or ice cream scoop, fill muffin cups to the top. Place in the oven and bake 25 to 30 minutes, until lightly browned and well risen. Remove from the heat and if the muffins come out of the tins easily, remove from the tins and allow to cool on a rack. If they don't release easily, allow to cool and then remove from the tins.

Nutrition Information

- 188: calories;
- 11 grams: carbohydrates;
- 337 milligrams: sodium;
- 3 grams: monounsaturated fat;
- 0 grams: trans fat;
- 7 grams: polyunsaturated fat;
- 1 gram: sugars;
- 6 grams: protein;
- 14 grams: fat;

124. Goat Cheese Salad With Pancetta, Garlic And Figs

Serving: Four servings | Prep: | Cook: |Ready in: 15mins

Ingredients

- ½ pound pancetta, cut into small dice
- 4 tablespoons olive oil
- 4 teaspoons minced garlic
- 2 teaspoons minced fresh thyme
- ¾ cup sherry vinegar
- ½ pound goat cheese
- 8 cups mixed wild greens, washed and stemmed
- 12 fresh or dried figs, stemmed and halved
- Salt and freshly ground pepper to taste

Direction

- Place the pancetta in a large skillet over low heat and cook until it has browned and released half of its fat. Remove the pancetta from the skillet with a slotted spoon. Add the olive oil to the skillet and increase the heat to medium. When the pancetta is hot but not smoking, return it to the pan and cook for a few seconds.
- Add the garlic and cook until lightly browned. Add the thyme and cook just until it makes a popping sound. Stir in the vinegar and simmer until reduced to 1/4 cup, about 5 minutes. Crumble the goat cheese into the skillet and cook just until it begins to weep. Toss in the greens and immediately remove the pan from the heat. Toss in the figs and season with salt and pepper to taste. Place the salad in a bowl and serve warm.

125. Grapefruit Vinaigrette With Greens Or Broccoli

Serving: Serves 4 | Prep: | Cook: |Ready in: 15mins

Ingredients

- 1 pink grapefruit
- 1 teaspoon mild honey or agave syrup
- Pinch of salt
- 1 tablespoon plus 1 teaspoon sherry vinegar or cider vinegar
- 2 tablespoons grapeseed oil or sunflower oil
- 1 tablespoon extra virgin olive oil

- 1 bunch broccoli, broken into florets, stems peeled and chopped

Direction

- Squeeze 1/2 of the grapefruit. Measure out 1/3 cup of juice and place it in a small saucepan. Add the honey or agave and bring to a boil over medium-high heat. Reduce to 1/4 cup and remove from the heat. Whisk in salt, vinegar, and the oils.
- Cut away the peel and pith from the remaining grapefruit half. Cut the sections away from the membranes that divide them and chop fine. Stir into the vinaigrette.
- Steam the broccoli for 4 minutes and transfer to a platter or to plates. Spoon the vinaigrette over the florets and serve.

Nutrition Information

- 174: calories;
- 8 grams: sugars;
- 123 milligrams: sodium;
- 11 grams: fat;
- 1 gram: saturated fat;
- 4 grams: monounsaturated fat;
- 5 grams: protein;
- 18 grams: carbohydrates;

126. Grapefruit And Navel Orange Gratin

Serving: Serves 6 | Prep: | Cook: | Ready in: 45mins

Ingredients

- About 750 grams oranges (you may not need all of them)
- 2 pink grapefruit
- Cinnamon
- 1 vanilla bean
- 3 egg yolks
- 75 grams sugar (about 1/3 cup)
- 75 grams crème fraîche (about 1/3 cup)
- 1 tablespoon rum

Direction

- Set aside 200 grams oranges and 1 grapefruit. Slice the ends off the remaining oranges and grapefruit and remove the peel and white pith by slicing down the sides from top to bottom. Holding the fruit over a bowl, cut the sections from between the membranes that separate them.
- Place a strainer over a bowl and drain the fruit. Arrange the sectioned fruit in a lightly buttered baking dish or in 6 oven-proof crème brûlée dishes. Sprinkle the fruit lightly with cinnamon.
- Pour the strained juice from the fruit into a measuring cup. Squeeze the remaining grapefruit and enough of the remaining oranges to obtain 200 grams of juice (about 3/4 cup).
- Pour the juice into a medium saucepan and add half the sugar. Cut the vanilla bean in half lengthwise and using the tip of a knife, scrape the seeds into the juice. Add the vanilla bean pod to the juice. Bring to a simmer and immediately turn off the heat, cover the pan tightly with plastic wrap, and allow the vanilla bean to steep for 15 minutes. Remove the plastic wrap.
- Fill a bowl with ice and set another bowl in it. Place a strainer over the bowl. Beat the egg yolks with the remaining sugar in a small bowl and bring the juice back to a simmer. Remove from the heat and, making sure that the juice isn't boiling, whisk half of it into the egg yolks. Whisk the tempered egg yolks into the saucepan, scraping out every last bit from the bowl with a rubber spatula.
- Place the saucepan back over medium-low heat and heat, stirring constantly with a rubber spatula or a whisk. Do not allow the liquid to come to a boil. Insert a thermometer and when the mixture reaches 180 degrees Farenheit and coats the spatula like thick cream, remove from the heat and immediately

strain into the bowl set in the ice. Whisk in the crème fraiche and stir over the ice until the mixture cools. At this point, if you are not serving the gratin right away, cover and refrigerate the custard sauce.
- Preheat the broiler and place the rack about 3 inches away from the heat. Spoon the custard over the fruit. Just before serving place under the broiler and, watching closely, heat until the cream is lightly browned, 3 to 5 minutes. Remove from the heat and serve.

Nutrition Information

- 191: calories;
- 2 grams: saturated fat;
- 36 grams: carbohydrates;
- 3 grams: protein;
- 1 gram: monounsaturated fat;
- 0 grams: polyunsaturated fat;
- 29 grams: sugars;
- 9 milligrams: sodium;
- 5 grams: dietary fiber;

127. Grated Carrot Salad With Dates And Oranges

Serving: Serves 4 | Prep: | Cook: | Ready in: 10mins

Ingredients

- 1 pound carrots, grated on the medium blade of your grater
- 8 dates, pitted and quartered lengthwise
- 2 tablespoons fresh lemon juice
- ¼ cup fresh orange juice
- Salt to taste
- ¼ teaspoon ground cinnamon, plus additional for sprinkling
- 2 tablespoons olive oil
- 2 to 3 oranges (as needed)

Direction

- In a large bowl combine the carrots and dates.
- Whisk together the lemon juice, orange juice, salt, cinnamon and olive oil. Toss with the carrots.
- Remove the peel and pith from one of the oranges. Cut the sections away from between the membranes, holding the orange above the bowl to catch juice. Cut the orange sections into halves or thirds, depending on the size, and toss with the carrots. Transfer to a platter or a wide bowl.
- Slice the remaining orange or oranges into thin rounds. Cut the rounds in half, and arrange in an overlapping ring around the carrots. Sprinkle a little more cinnamon over the carrots and oranges, and serve.

Nutrition Information

- 286: calories;
- 46 grams: sugars;
- 3 grams: protein;
- 634 milligrams: sodium;
- 5 grams: monounsaturated fat;
- 59 grams: carbohydrates;
- 7 grams: fat;
- 1 gram: polyunsaturated fat;
- 8 grams: dietary fiber;

128. Gratin Of Zucchini And Yellow Squash

Serving: 4 servings | Prep: | Cook: | Ready in: 15mins

Ingredients

- 2 small zucchini, about 3/4 pound
- 2 small yellow squash, about 3/4 pound
- 2 tablespoons olive oil
- ½ cup finely chopped onion
- 2 teaspoons finely chopped garlic
- 2 sprigs fresh thyme, chopped, or 1/2 teaspoon dried
- Salt and freshly ground pepper to taste

- 3 medium-size ripe tomatoes, cored and cut into thin slices
- 2 tablespoons basil leaves cut into small strips
- 2 tablespoons freshly grated Parmesan cheese

Direction

- Preheat the broiler.
- Rinse the zucchini and squash and pat them dry. Trim off the ends but do not peel them. Slice them in thin slices crosswise.
- Heat 1 tablespoon olive oil in a nonstick skillet and when hot add the zucchini, squash, onion, garlic and thyme. Saute over high heat, shaking the pan and tossing the vegetables gently. Add salt and pepper and cook for a total of 5 minutes.
- Spoon the mixture into a casserole or baking dish. Smooth the top and arrange the sliced tomatoes in a circular pattern to cover the top. Add salt and pepper and sprinkle with the strips of basil leaves and the cheese. Drizzle the remaining oil over all.
- Place under the broiler for 3 to 4 minutes or until light brown.

Nutrition Information

- 158: calories;
- 9 grams: fat;
- 16 grams: carbohydrates;
- 4 grams: dietary fiber;
- 5 grams: protein;
- 701 milligrams: sodium;
- 2 grams: saturated fat;
- 6 grams: monounsaturated fat;
- 1 gram: polyunsaturated fat;

129. Greek Rizogalo

Serving: 4 servings | Prep: | Cook: | Ready in: 30mins

Ingredients

- 1 cup short-grain rice (sushi or Arborio)
- 4 cups whole milk
- 1 cup sugar
- 2 two-inch pieces of lemon peel
- Ground cinnamon, for sprinkling

Direction

- In a large saucepan (4 to 6 quarts), combine the rice and 4 cups water. Bring to a boil, and then lower heat and simmer 10 minutes.
- Add milk, sugar and lemon peel. Bring back to a boil, stirring frequently. Lower heat, continuing to stir, so milk simmers vigorously without bubbling over. Simmer until the liquid is reduced and thickened to a creamy consistency that will coat the back of a spoon, 10 to 15 minutes. Stir frequently to keep rice from sticking to bottom of pan.
- Discard lemon peel. Spoon equal amounts of rice into four serving bowls, and let sit for a minute. Sprinkle with cinnamon, and serve.

Nutrition Information

- 518: calories;
- 62 grams: sugars;
- 11 grams: protein;
- 106 milligrams: sodium;
- 8 grams: fat;
- 2 grams: monounsaturated fat;
- 1 gram: polyunsaturated fat;
- 0 grams: dietary fiber;
- 5 grams: saturated fat;
- 101 grams: carbohydrates;

130. Greek Zucchini And Herb Pie

Serving: One 10- inch pie, serving eight to ten | Prep: | Cook: | Ready in: 3hours

Ingredients

- 2 ¼ to 2 ½ pounds zucchini, ends trimmed
- Salt to taste
- 2 tablespoons extra virgin olive oil, plus additional for brushing the phyllo dough
- 1 large onion, finely chopped
- 2 garlic cloves, minced
- 1 cup finely chopped dill
- ½ cup chopped fresh mint, or a combination of mint and parsley
- 1 cup crumbled feta
- 3 eggs, beaten
- Freshly ground pepper
- 12 sheets phyllo dough or 1 recipe whole wheat yeasted olive oil pie pastry

Direction

- Grate the zucchini using a food processor or a hand grater. Place in a large colander, salt generously, and let drain for 1 hour, pressing down on it occasionally to squeeze out liquid. After an hour, take up handfuls and squeeze out moisture (or wrap in a kitchen towel and twist the towel to squeeze out the moisture). Place in a bowl.
- Heat 1 tablespoon of the oil over medium heat in a large, heavy nonstick skillet over medium heat, and add the onion. Cook, stirring, until tender, about five minutes, then add the garlic. Cook, stirring, until the garlic is fragrant, about one minute. Transfer to the bowl with the zucchini. Stir in the herbs, feta, eggs and pepper.
- Preheat the oven to 350 degrees. Oil a 10-inch pie or cake pan. If using phyllo, line the pie dish with seven pieces of phyllo, lightly brushing each piece with oil and turning the dish after each addition so that the edges of the phyllo drape evenly over the pan. Fill with the zucchini mixture. Fold the draped edges in over the filling, lightly brushing the folded in sheets of phyllo, then layer the remaining five pieces on top, brushing each piece with olive oil. Stuff the edges into the sides of the pan. If using the olive oil pastry, divide the dough into two equal pieces. Roll out the first ball to a circle 2 inches wider than the pan. Line the pan with the pastry, and brush with olive oil. Top with the filling. Roll out the remaining dough. Place over the filling. Press the edges of the top and bottom layers of dough together, and pinch to form an attractive lip around the edge.
- Make a few slashes in the top crust so that steam can escape as the pie bakes. Score in a few places with the tip of a knife, and brush with olive oil. Bake 50 to 60 minutes, until the pastry is golden brown. Remove from the heat, and allow to cool 15 to 30 minutes or to room temperature. Slice in wedges and serve.

Nutrition Information

- 167: calories;
- 0 grams: trans fat;
- 1 gram: polyunsaturated fat;
- 4 grams: sugars;
- 7 grams: protein;
- 432 milligrams: sodium;
- 6 grams: fat;
- 3 grams: saturated fat;
- 21 grams: carbohydrates;
- 2 grams: dietary fiber;

131. Green Beans And Tomatoes

Serving: 4 servings | Prep: | Cook: | Ready in: 20mins

Ingredients

- Salt to taste
- 1 pound green beans, trimmed and cut into 2-inch lengths
- 2 tablespoons butter
- 2 teaspoons finely minced garlic
- 3 medium-size tomatoes, peeled, cored, seeded and cut into 1/2-inch cubes (about 2 cups)
- 1 bay leaf
- Freshly ground pepper to taste

Direction

- Bring enough water to a boil to cover the beans when added. Add salt and the beans, and cook 5 to 10 minutes or until tender. Drain.
- Heat the butter in a skillet or casserole, and add the garlic. When it is wilted and starting to brown, add the tomatoes, salt and bay leaf. Cook, stirring, about 2 minutes, and add the beans and pepper. Stir to blend well. Remove the bay leaf and serve.

Nutrition Information

- 107: calories;
- 0 grams: polyunsaturated fat;
- 2 grams: monounsaturated fat;
- 12 grams: carbohydrates;
- 3 grams: protein;
- 500 milligrams: sodium;
- 6 grams: sugars;
- 4 grams: dietary fiber;

132. Green Goddess Dip

Serving: About 2 1/2 cups | Prep: | Cook: | Ready in: 1hours

Ingredients

- 1 cup 1-percent low-fat cottage cheese
- ¼ cup boiling water (see note above)
- 1 cup low-fat sour cream
- 2 tablespoons extra-virgin olive oil
- 1 tablespoon fresh lemon juice
- ¼ cup fresh parsley leaves
- 1 tablespoon fresh tarragon leaves
- 1 garlic clove, minced
- Salt
- Pepper
- ¼ cup minced fresh chives

Direction

- Process the cottage cheese and boiling water together in a food processor until smooth, about 30 seconds
- Add the sour cream, oil, lemon juice, parsley, tarragon, garlic, 1/4 teaspoon salt and 1/8 teaspoon pepper and continue to process until combined, about 30 seconds.
- Transfer to a bowl and stir in the chives. Cover and refrigerate until the flavors have blended, about 1 hour. Season with salt and pepper to taste before serving.

Nutrition Information

- 173: calories;
- 6 grams: carbohydrates;
- 1 gram: polyunsaturated fat;
- 13 grams: fat;
- 5 grams: saturated fat;
- 0 grams: dietary fiber;
- 2 grams: sugars;
- 8 grams: protein;
- 274 milligrams: sodium;

133. Green Mayonnaise

Serving: 1 to 1 1/2 cups | Prep: | Cook: | Ready in: 15mins

Ingredients

- ½ cup chopped chives
- 4 sprigs fresh tarragon
- ½ cup chopped parsley
- 2 teaspoons tarragon or white wine vinegar
- 1 large egg
- 1 clove garlic, chopped
- 1 tablespoon Dijon mustard
- ½ cup extra-virgin olive oil
- ½ cup good-quality vegetable oil
- Coarse salt and freshly ground pepper to taste

Direction

- Put the chives, tarragon, parsley, vinegar, egg and garlic into a blender or food processor. Add the mustard and one tablespoon olive oil. Process for 10 seconds, then add the oils in a thin stream very slowly while you process. Keep adding oil until the mayonnaise is thick.
- Season and refrigerate.

Nutrition Information

- 207: calories;
- 1 gram: protein;
- 84 milligrams: sodium;
- 23 grams: fat;
- 2 grams: saturated fat;
- 0 grams: sugars;
- 16 grams: monounsaturated fat;
- 3 grams: polyunsaturated fat;

134. Green Sauce

Serving: About 1 cup | Prep: | Cook: | Ready in: 20mins

Ingredients

- 1 clove garlic, peeled
- 1 cup, packed, fresh flat-leaf parsley leaves
- 6 scallions, coarsely chopped
- 8 pitted green olives
- 2 tablespoons capers, drained
- 1 anchovy
- Juice of 2 lemons
- ⅓ cup extra-virgin olive oil
- Salt and freshly ground black pepper to taste

Direction

- Turn on a food processor and drop in the garlic clove through the feed tube.
- Shut off machine and add parsley, scallions, olives, capers and anchovy. Process until finely chopped. You may have to stop the machine once or twice to scrape the sides.
- Add the lemon juice and olive oil, process until blended, then remove to a serving dish. Season to taste with salt and pepper.

Nutrition Information

- 386: calories;
- 12 grams: carbohydrates;
- 3 grams: protein;
- 470 milligrams: sodium;
- 38 grams: fat;
- 5 grams: dietary fiber;
- 28 grams: monounsaturated fat;
- 4 grams: polyunsaturated fat;

135. Grilled Fish With Tomato Cilantro Vinaigrette

Serving: 4 servings | Prep: | Cook: | Ready in: 15mins

Ingredients

- 1 ½ pounds tuna or swordfish
- 4 tablespoons extra-virgin olive oil
- 4 tablespoons rice vinegar
- ½ teaspoon dry mustard
- 4 scallions, chopped
- ½ cup chopped cilantro
- 4 medium-large ripe tomatoes, coarsely chopped
- Freshly ground black pepper to taste

Direction

- Either grill fish over medium-hot coals outdoors or broil it in the oven. Measure fish at thickest point and cook it 10 minutes to the inch.
- Whisk oil with vinegar and mustard. Stir in scallions, cilantro and tomatoes. Season with pepper.
- When fish is cooked, spoon some vinaigrette onto each of four dinner plates; arrange fish on top, and top with additional vinaigrette.

Nutrition Information

- 339: calories;
- 2 grams: dietary fiber;
- 0 grams: trans fat;
- 10 grams: monounsaturated fat;
- 87 milligrams: sodium;
- 15 grams: fat;
- 7 grams: carbohydrates;
- 4 grams: sugars;
- 43 grams: protein;

136. Grilled Lobster With Vietnamese Dipping Sauce

Serving: Four servings | Prep: | Cook: | Ready in: 25mins

Ingredients

- 4 cloves garlic, minced
- 4 small hot chilies, seeded and minced
- 3 tablespoons sugar
- 3 tablespoons Vietnamese fish sauce (nuoc mam)
- 3 tablespoons fresh lime juice
- 4 1 1/2-pound lobsters
- 1 teaspoon canola oil

Direction

- In a bowl, combine the garlic, chilies, sugar, fish sauce and lime juice. Set aside. Prepare a charcoal grill. Steam the lobsters for 5 minutes. When cool enough to handle, twist off the claws and tails. Cut the tails in half lengthwise and rub the exposed meat with the oil.
- Place the tails and claws on the grill over medium-hot coals and grill until just browned and cooked through, about 15 minutes, turning once. Serve hot with the dipping sauce.

Nutrition Information

- 594: calories;
- 0 grams: trans fat;
- 2 grams: polyunsaturated fat;
- 12 grams: sugars;
- 4581 milligrams: sodium;
- 6 grams: fat;
- 1 gram: dietary fiber;
- 15 grams: carbohydrates;
- 114 grams: protein;

137. Grilled Medallions Of Venison With Black Bean Pancakes

Serving: Six servings | Prep: | Cook: | Ready in: 25mins

Ingredients

- The venison:
- ¾ cup plain yogurt
- ¼ cup hoisin sauce
- 2 large cloves of garlic, peeled and crushed
- 1 tablespoon minced gingerroot
- Freshly ground black pepper to taste
- 1 ¾ to 2 pounds venison or lamb medallions, cut from the leg, about 1-inch thick and 3-inches in diameter
- Vegetable oil to grease the skillet
- The pancakes:
- 1 cup cooked black beans (soaked and cooked until tender, according to package directions)
- ¼ cup water
- 2 tablespoons dry Sherry
- 2 beaten eggs
- ¼ cup minced scallions, white and light green parts, reserving the tops for the garnish
- 1 medium clove garlic, peeled and crushed
- 2 tablespoons toasted sesame seeds
- 2 tablespoons sesame oil
- 2 tablespoons minced gingerroot
- 12 drops Tabasco sauce, or to taste
- ¾ teaspoon salt

- 3 tablespoons all-purpose flour
- Vegetable oil to grease the skillet

Direction

- In a nonreactive dish large enough to accommodate the meat in one layer, combine the yogurt, hoisin sauce, garlic, gingerroot and pepper, and add the medallions, turning to coat them on all sides. Cover and refrigerate for two to three days, turning twice during this time.
- For the pancakes, place half of the beans in the bowl of a food processor fitted with a steel chopping blade. Pour in the water and Sherry and process until smooth. Add the eggs, process until blended, then scrape the mixture into a bowl. Stir in the remaining beans, scallions, garlic, sesame seeds, oil, gingerroot, Tabasco sauce and salt. Sprinkle the flour onto the mixture, a tablespoon at a time, beating it with a fork until blended.
- Turn your oven to warm. Lightly grease a large, heavy skillet with oil and heat until it is hot. Pour in one tablespoon of the batter for each pancake. Cook them over medium-high heat until the edges begin to brown, about 30 to 45 seconds. Turn with a spatula and cook the second side for 30 seconds. Transfer the cooked pancakes to a warm plate, loosely cover it and place it in the oven. Continue until all the batter has been used.
- Heat a well-seasoned cast-iron or heavy skillet until it is very hot. Add enough oil to lightly film the pan. Place only as many medallions in the pan as will fit comfortably without crowding. Cook the meat over high heat for about four to four-and-a-half minutes on the first side, turn and cook three-and-a-half to four minutes on the second side for medium-rare. Transfer the meat to heated plates. Serve with three to four pancakes. Slice the reserved scallion tops and use them as garnish.

Nutrition Information

- 465: calories;
- 52 grams: protein;
- 564 milligrams: sodium;
- 19 grams: carbohydrates;
- 4 grams: dietary fiber;
- 0 grams: trans fat;
- 9 grams: monounsaturated fat;
- 5 grams: sugars;

138. Grilled Potatoes

Serving: 2 servings | Prep: | Cook: | Ready in: 20mins

Ingredients

- 1 pound new potatoes
- 2 teaspoons olive oil
- 1 teaspoon ground cumin

Direction

- Scrub potatoes; do not peel. If potatoes are large, slice 1/8-inch thick. If potatoes are very small, cut in quarters.
- Mix oil and cumin, and stir potatoes into mixture, coating well.
- Prepare stove-top grill. Arrange potatoes on grill; cook over medium heat, turning when potatoes brown on one side, and cook through.

Nutrition Information

- 218: calories;
- 5 grams: protein;
- 1 gram: polyunsaturated fat;
- 3 grams: monounsaturated fat;
- 40 grams: carbohydrates;
- 2 grams: sugars;
- 15 milligrams: sodium;

139. Grilled Trout With Cucumber Tomato Relish

Serving: 4 servings | Prep: | Cook: | Ready in: 25mins

Ingredients

- 1 large cucumber, seeded and diced
- 2 cups seeded, chopped tomatoes
- ¼ cup diced red onion
- 2 tablespoons fresh mint cut into ribbons
- ½ teaspoon red pepper flakes
- 1 tablespoon lemon juice
- Salt and freshly ground black pepper to taste
- 1 cup plain yogurt
- Grated zest of 1 lemon
- 1 teaspoon toasted cumin seeds
- 1 teaspoon toasted coriander seeds
- 4 whole brook trout, about 10 ounces each
- Olive oil for basting trout

Direction

- To make the cucumber-tomato relish, combine in a bowl the cucumber, tomatoes, onions, mint, red pepper flakes, lemon juice, salt and pepper. Keep cool until served.
- To make the yogurt sauce, combine in a bowl the yogurt, lemon juice, lemon zest, cumin seeds, coriander seeds, salt and pepper. Keep cool until served.
- Brush the trout with olive oil. Season with salt and pepper. Grill the trout over charcoal (or broil) for 4 minutes a side. Serve each trout with relish on the side and the yogurt sauce.

Nutrition Information

- 543: calories;
- 0 grams: trans fat;
- 12 grams: monounsaturated fat;
- 13 grams: carbohydrates;
- 1244 milligrams: sodium;
- 27 grams: fat;
- 6 grams: saturated fat;
- 5 grams: polyunsaturated fat;
- 3 grams: dietary fiber;
- 7 grams: sugars;
- 60 grams: protein;

140. Grilled Veal Kidneys With Sage And Pancetta

Serving: 4 servings | Prep: | Cook: | Ready in: 40mins

Ingredients

- 4 veal kidneys
- About 20 sage leaves
- ½ pound pancetta, thinly sliced
- Coarse salt and freshly ground pepper

Direction

- Soak about 10 small wooden skewers in water for 30 minutes. Preheat broiler.
- Trim the fat and filament from the kidneys and cut them in pieces about one-inch thick. Place the sage leaves on top of the kidneys, wrap in a slice of pancetta and thread on a skewer. Continue this way until you have threaded all the kidneys on skewers. There should be two small skewers a person.
- Broil the kidneys about six inches from the heat until they are cooked to desired doneness. Do not overcook or they will be tough. They are at their best when pink in the middle. Add salt and pepper to taste.

Nutrition Information

- 365: calories;
- 27 grams: fat;
- 9 grams: saturated fat;
- 5 grams: carbohydrates;
- 2 grams: dietary fiber;
- 26 grams: protein;
- 577 milligrams: sodium;
- 0 grams: trans fat;
- 11 grams: monounsaturated fat;

- 4 grams: polyunsaturated fat;
- 1 gram: sugars;

141. Grilled Vegetables

Serving: 4 servings | Prep: | Cook: |Ready in: 40mins

Ingredients

- 1 ½ pounds red and green peppers
- 2 tablespoons olive oil
- 1 pound onions
- 1 ½ pounds Japanese eggplant or other small eggplant
- 12 ounces reduced-fat turkey sausages (see note)
- 15 large fresh basil leaves
- Freshly ground black pepper to taste

Direction

- If cooking this meal on an outdoor grill, prepare fire in grill.
- Wash, trim and seed peppers; cut into 1/4-inch thick rings. Brush cut sides lightly with a little oil.
- Prepare oven-top grill if not using an outdoor grill.
- Peel and slice onions into 1/4-inch-thick rings. Arrange onions and peppers on grill and cook.
- Wash, trim and slice eggplant in half lengthwise. Brush with oil and add to grill. Turn vegetables as they begin to brown. They may be turned several times. As they soften remove from grill and place in serving bowl.
- Cut sausages into bite-size pieces and cook in skillet according to package directions; drain and add to vegetables.
- Wash, dry and coarsely cut basil leaves and add. Season with pepper and serve with a crusty, peasant bread.

Nutrition Information

- 318: calories;
- 3 grams: polyunsaturated fat;
- 7 grams: monounsaturated fat;
- 30 grams: carbohydrates;
- 14 grams: fat;
- 0 grams: trans fat;
- 10 grams: dietary fiber;
- 15 grams: sugars;
- 21 grams: protein;
- 518 milligrams: sodium;

142. Grits

Serving: | Prep: | Cook: |Ready in: 8mins

Ingredients

- 4 cups water
- 1 cup yellow stone-ground cornmeal
- Salt and pepper to taste

Direction

- Bring water and salt to boil. Slowly add cornmeal, stirring to prevent lumping. Cook over low heat until grits are cooked and mixture is thick. Season with pepper.
- Either serve grits from the pot or pour into 10-inch pie plate and chill.
- If chilled, cut into triangles and reheat in oven at 350 degrees for 10 minutes before serving.

Nutrition Information

- 112: calories;
- 1 gram: polyunsaturated fat;
- 0 grams: sugars;
- 24 grams: carbohydrates;
- 2 grams: dietary fiber;
- 3 grams: protein;
- 624 milligrams: sodium;

143. Hake In Vegetable And Lemon Broth

Serving: 6 servings | Prep: | Cook: | Ready in: 30mins

Ingredients

- 2 carrots (6 ounces)
- 1 lemon
- 12 scallions, trimmed (leaving most of the green), cleaned and minced (1 1/4 cups)
- 1 red onion (8 ounces), peeled and coarsely chopped (2 cups)
- ¾ cup dry white wine
- 2 teaspoons salt
- 1 teaspoon thyme leaves
- 1 teaspoon freshly ground black pepper
- 6 hake fillets (each about 6 ounces and 3/4 inch thick)
- ¼ cup olive oil
- 2 tablespoons unsalted butter

Direction

- Peel the carrots, and cut them into 3-inch pieces. Then, cut each piece into 1/8-inch slices. Stack the slices together, and cut them into 1/8-inch strips (julienne). You should have about 2 cups of julienned carrot.
- Peel the lemon with a vegetable peeler, removing the peel in long strips. Pile the strips together, and cut them into a fine julienne, making about 1 tablespoon. Cut the lemon in half, and press the halves to extract 2 tablespoons of juice.
- In a large saucepan (preferably stainless steel), combine the carrots, lemon peel, lemon juice, scallions, red onion, white wine, salt, thyme leaves and pepper with 3/4 cup water. Bring the mixture to a boil over high heat, cover, reduce the heat to low, and boil gently for 10 minutes.
- Fold each of the hake fillets in half and arrange them carefully on top of the vegetables in the saucepan. Cover, return the mixture to a boil, reduce the heat and boil gently for 5 minutes. The hake should be barely cooked through. Lift the fish from the saucepan and arrange it on a platter.
- Add the olive oil and butter to the vegetable mixture in the pan, and bring it to a strong boil over high heat. Continue to boil for about 20 to 30 seconds, until the mixture is emulsified. Pour over the fish, and serve immediately.

Nutrition Information

- 366: calories;
- 15 grams: fat;
- 0 grams: trans fat;
- 8 grams: monounsaturated fat;
- 2 grams: dietary fiber;
- 897 milligrams: sodium;
- 4 grams: sugars;
- 10 grams: carbohydrates;
- 42 grams: protein;

144. Hash Browns

Serving: 4 servings | Prep: | Cook: | Ready in: 25mins

Ingredients

- 1 ½ pounds russet potatoes, about 3, peeled and coarsely grated
- 1 tablespoon vegetable oil, more as needed
- Salt and pepper to taste

Direction

- Combine all ingredients in a bowl and mix thoroughly.
- Place a 10-inch nonstick skillet over medium-high heat for about 2 to 3 minutes. Spread potato mixture evenly in pan and press with spatula. Cook until bottom browns, about 10 minutes. If potatoes look too dry, add just enough oil to lightly coat. Flip with spatula and continue cooking until browned. Cut into wedges and serve warm.

Nutrition Information

- 167: calories;
- 1 gram: sugars;
- 31 grams: carbohydrates;
- 2 grams: dietary fiber;
- 405 milligrams: sodium;
- 4 grams: protein;
- 0 grams: trans fat;
- 3 grams: monounsaturated fat;

145. Herb Fritters

Serving: Serves 6 to 8 | Prep: | Cook: | Ready in: 2hours30mins

Ingredients

- ½ cup whole wheat flour
- ¼ cup unbleached all-purpose flour
- ½ teaspoon baking powder
- Rounded 1/2 teaspoon salt
- 1 egg, separated
- 1 tablespoon extra virgin olive oil
- ¾ cup sparkling water
- 1 ½ cups finely chopped fresh herbs or a mix of herbs and greens (such as spinach or chard)

Direction

- Mix together flours, baking powder and salt in a large bowl. Make a well in the center and add egg yolk and oil. Beat egg yolk and oil together, add sparkling water and mix in flour. Whisk until smooth. Cover with plastic and let sit for 2 hours.
- Beat egg white to stiff but not dry peaks and fold into batter. Fold in finely chopped herbs and greens.
- Pour oil into a wok or wide saucepan to a depth of 3 inches and heat over medium-high heat to 360 to 375 degrees. Set up a sheet pan with a rack on it next to pan. Cover rack with a few layers of paper towels. Have a spider or deep fry skimmer handy for removing fritters from oil.
- . Scoop up the batter by the tablespoon and carefully drop into the hot oil. You should be able to fry about 5 at a time. After a few seconds flip the fritters over, then fry until golden brown, about 2 minutes, flipping over again halfway through. Remove from oil with a spider or deep-fry skimmer and drain on the towel-covered rack. Allow to cool slightly, and serve.

Nutrition Information

- 64: calories;
- 1 gram: dietary fiber;
- 9 grams: carbohydrates;
- 108 milligrams: sodium;
- 2 grams: protein;
- 0 grams: sugars;

146. Homemade Twinkies

Serving: 12 homemade Twinkies. | Prep: | Cook: | Ready in: 1hours40mins

Ingredients

- FOR THE CAKES:
- Nonstick cooking spray or vegetable oil
- 60 grams (1/2 cup) cake flour
- 30 grams (1/4 cup) all-purpose flour
- 1 teaspoon baking powder
- ¼ teaspoon salt
- 2 tablespoons milk
- 4 tablespoons unsalted butter
- ½ teaspoon vanilla extract
- 5 large eggs at room temperature, separated
- 12 tablespoons sugar
- ¼ teaspoon cream of tartar
- FOR THE FILLING:
- 6 tablespoons unsalted butter, at room temperature
- 165 grams (1 1/2 cups) confectioners' sugar

- ¾ cup Marshmallow Fluff
- 2 tablespoons heavy cream

Direction

- For the cakes: Heat the oven to 350 degrees and adjust the oven rack to the lower-middle position.
- To make single-use Twinkie molds, cut 12 pieces of aluminum foil 12 inches wide by 14 inches long. Fold each piece of foil in half lengthwise, then fold it in half again to create a rectangle that's about 6 inches long and 7 inches wide. Repeat to make a dozen rectangles.
- Place one sheet of folded foil on a work surface with a standard-size spice jar on its side in the center of the foil. Bring the long sides of the foil up around the jar, folding the sides and ends as necessary to make a tight trough-shape from which the jar can be removed. Repeat to make 12 foil molds. Spray generously with nonstick spray or coat with vegetable oil. Place the molds on a baking sheet.
- In a mixing bowl, whisk together the cake flour, all-purpose flour, baking powder and salt. In a small saucepan over low heat, heat the milk and butter until the butter melts. Remove from the heat and add the vanilla. Cover to keep warm.
- Using a standing mixer, beat the egg whites on high speed until foamy. Gradually add 6 tablespoons of the sugar and the cream of tartar and continue to beat until the whites reach soft peaks.
- Transfer the beaten egg whites to a large bowl and add the egg yolks to the standing mixer bowl (there's no need to clean the bowl). Beat the egg yolks with the remaining 6 tablespoons sugar on medium-high speed until the mixture is very thick and a pale lemon color, about 5 minutes. Add the beaten egg whites to the yolks, but do not mix.
- Sprinkle the flour mixture over the egg whites and then mix everything on low speed for just 10 seconds. Remove the bowl from the mixer, make a well in one side of the batter, and pour the melted butter mixture into the bowl. Fold gently with a large rubber spatula until the batter shows no trace of flour and the whites and yolks are evenly mixed, about 8 strokes.
- Immediately scrape the batter into the prepared molds, filling each with about .75 inch of batter. Bake until the cake tops are light brown and feel firm and spring back when touched, 13 to 15 minutes. Transfer the pan containing the molds to a wire rack and allow the cakes to cool in the molds.
- For the filling: Using a mixer, beat together the butter, confectioners' sugar and Marshmallow Fluff. Add the cream and beat just until smooth.
- Just before filling the cakes, remove them from the foil. Using the end of a chopstick, poke three holes in the bottom of each cake. Wiggle the tip of the chopstick to make room for the filling. Transfer the frosting to a pastry bag fitted with a 1/4-inch round tip. Pipe frosting into the holes in each cake, taking care not to overfill, until it gently expands. Unlike real Twinkies, these won't last indefinitely. They're best served still slightly warm.

Nutrition Information

- 273: calories;
- 35 grams: carbohydrates;
- 28 grams: sugars;
- 7 grams: saturated fat;
- 0 grams: dietary fiber;
- 4 grams: protein;
- 1 gram: polyunsaturated fat;
- 13 grams: fat;
- 115 milligrams: sodium;

147. Hot Mayonnaise

Serving: 6 servings | Prep: | Cook: | Ready in: 5mins

Ingredients

- 1 ½ cups mayonnaise
- 2 tablespoons red wine vinegar
- 1 ½ teaspoons Tabasco sauce
- 1 tablespoon chopped fresh tarragon

Direction

- Mix ingredients in a bowl. Serve with crab boil.

Nutrition Information

- 402: calories;
- 11 grams: monounsaturated fat;
- 27 grams: polyunsaturated fat;
- 0 grams: protein;
- 341 milligrams: sodium;
- 44 grams: fat;
- 7 grams: saturated fat;

148. Hot Or Cold Leek Soup

Serving: 6 servings | Prep: | Cook: | Ready in: 45mins

Ingredients

- 1 large leek (about 8 ounces)
- 2 tablespoons olive oil
- 1 onion (6 ounces), peeled and sliced
- 6 cups chicken stock
- 1 ½ pounds potatoes, peeled and cut into 2-inch pieces
- Salt to taste, depending on the saltiness of the stock
- ½ teaspoon freshly ground black pepper
- Bread croutons, for garnish (optional)
- Additional for cold soup:
- 2 ½ cups cold milk
- 6 tablespoons chopped chives
- ¼ teaspoon Tabasco sauce

Direction

- Trim the leek to remove the root and any damaged outer leaves, but leave the remainder of the leaves intact. Split the leek in half lengthwise, and cut it into 1/4-inch pieces. Clean the leek by immersing the pieces in a bowl filled with cold water. Lift the pieces from the water and place them in a sieve.
- Heat the oil in a pot. When hot, add the leek and onion, and cook over medium heat for about 5 minutes, until they soften and begin to brown lightly. Add the stock, potatoes, salt and pepper, and bring to a boil. Boil for about 30 to 40 minutes, until tender.
- Strain off most of the juices and reserve them. Add the solids with a little of the juice to the bowl of a food processor and process briefly, just until pureed. (If too much juice is added to the processor bowl, the mixture will become too foamy.) Mix the puree with the reserved juices. You should have about 7 cups. The hot soup can be served immediately, with croutons if desired.
- For cold leek soup, cool the soup and stir in the milk, chives and Tabasco sauce. Serve cold.

Nutrition Information

- 297: calories;
- 12 grams: protein;
- 1230 milligrams: sodium;
- 11 grams: fat;
- 3 grams: dietary fiber;
- 6 grams: monounsaturated fat;
- 1 gram: polyunsaturated fat;
- 38 grams: carbohydrates;

149. Howard Bulka's Strawberry Icebox Cake

Serving: Eight servings | Prep: | Cook: | Ready in: 15mins

Ingredients

- The soaking syrup:
- 1 ½ pints strawberries, hulled and washed

- 1 tablespoon sugar
- 1 ounce strawberry liqueur or eau de vie
- The cream filling:
- 1 pound mascarpone
- 8 ounces sour cream
- 2 cups heavy cream, chilled, plus more for garnish, if desired
- ½ cup sugar
- 1 ½ packages Italian ladyfingers (about 11 ounces)
- Shaved white chocolate, for garnish

Direction

- The day before serving, make the soaking syrup. Puree the strawberries in a food processor. Push through a sieve to remove the seeds. Combine with the sugar and strawberry liqueur. Thin with a little water if necessary.
- Combine the mascarpone and sour cream. In another bowl, whip the heavy cream until it forms soft peaks. Slowly beat in the sugar. Fold the 2 mixtures together, until smooth and well blended.
- To assemble: Soak the ladyfingers for half a minute or so in the strawberry syrup. Layer half of the ladyfingers on the bottom of a 10-inch springform pan, then cover with half of the cream filling. Repeat with the remaining ladyfingers and cream filling. Smooth the top of the cake, cover with plastic wrap and refrigerate overnight.
- When ready to serve, unmold the cake onto a platter. Garnish with white chocolate and additional whipped cream, if desired.

Nutrition Information

- 478: calories;
- 8 grams: monounsaturated fat;
- 47 grams: carbohydrates;
- 9 grams: protein;
- 279 milligrams: sodium;
- 15 grams: saturated fat;
- 2 grams: dietary fiber;
- 21 grams: sugars;
- 29 grams: fat;

150. Iced Tea

Serving: 10 cups | Prep: | Cook: | Ready in:

Ingredients

- 1 bag chamomile tea
- 1 bag lemon-zinger tea
- 2 bags Darjeeling
- 1 bag English breakfast tea
- 2 bags black-currant tea
- 6 slices orange plus 1/2 an orange
- 6 slices lemon plus 1/2 a lemon
- 4 sprigs mint

Direction

- Bring 10 cups water to boil. Add all the tea and steep 5 minutes.
- In a container large enough to hold tea and ice, put lots of ice. Add lemon and orange slices and pour steeped tea over ice.
- Squeeze in the orange and lemon halves and add mint sprigs.
- Serve - over ice, if desired - in tall glasses decorated with lemon twists and mint.

151. Jacques Pepin's Banana Ice Cream

Serving: 6 servings | Prep: | Cook: | Ready in: 3hours15mins

Ingredients

- medium-size ripe bananas (about 2 pounds)
- ¾ cup sour cream
- ⅓ cup sugar
- 2 tablespoons dark rum, plus 2 tablespoons (optional) to sprinkle on top at serving time
- 6 sprigs mint (optional)

Direction

- Peel the bananas and cut them crosswise into 1-inch slices. Arrange the slices in a single layer on a tray and put the tray in the freezer for at least 2 hours, until bananas are frozen.
- Put half the frozen bananas in a food processor with half the sour cream, half the sugar and 1 tablespoon of the rum. Pulse the machine a few times, and then process the mixture for about 20 seconds, until smooth. Transfer to a cold bowl, and process the rest of the bananas, sour cream, sugar and a second tablespoon of rum. Return the ice cream to the freezer until serving time, at least one hour.
- To serve, scoop the ice cream into six chilled glasses. Garnish each, if desired, with 1 teaspoon of rum and a sprig of mint.

Nutrition Information

- 249: calories;
- 6 grams: fat;
- 2 grams: protein;
- 0 grams: polyunsaturated fat;
- 3 grams: saturated fat;
- 51 grams: carbohydrates;
- 4 grams: dietary fiber;
- 35 grams: sugars;
- 15 milligrams: sodium;

152. Jerry Anne Cardamom Cake

Serving: Ten servings | Prep: | Cook: | Ready in: 1hours30mins

Ingredients

- 1 ½ cups unsalted butter, plus some for greasing the pan
- 2 ¾ cups sifted cake flour, plus some for dusting the pan
- 1 pound confectioners' sugar
- 6 large eggs
- ½ teaspoon hulled cardamom seed, crushed
- ½ teaspoon grated orange zest
- ½ teaspoon lemon zest
- 1 ½ teaspoons vanilla extract

Direction

- Preheat the oven to 300 degrees. Grease and flour a 10- to 12-cup tube pan.
- Beat the butter until creamy. Add the confectioners' sugar and beat until very fluffy. Beat in the eggs one at a time.
- Stir in the flour. Mix in the cardamom, orange and lemon zests and the vanilla. Pour the batter into the pan.
- Bake for about 1 hour or until the cake springs back to the touch and starts to pull from the sides. Cool 10 minutes. Unmold onto a serving plate. Serve warm or cold, cut into thin slices.

Nutrition Information

- 602: calories;
- 8 grams: monounsaturated fat;
- 7 grams: protein;
- 48 milligrams: sodium;
- 1 gram: dietary fiber;
- 2 grams: polyunsaturated fat;
- 75 grams: carbohydrates;
- 45 grams: sugars;
- 31 grams: fat;
- 18 grams: saturated fat;

153. Julia Alvarez's Pudin De Pan (Bread Pudding)

Serving: Eight servings | Prep: | Cook: | Ready in: 1hours

Ingredients

- 1 loaf high-quality sliced bread, crusts removed and cut into 1-inch squares
- 6 cups whole milk

- 1 ¾ cups sugar
- ½ teaspoon salt
- 1 stick sweet butter, plus more for greasing the pan
- 1 teaspoon cinnamon
- 1 teaspoon vanilla
- ¼ cup dark rum
- Grated peel of 1 lemon
- 4 eggs, well beaten
- ¾ cup dried prunes, pitted
- 1 cup guava paste (available at Spanish groceries)
- ¼ cup brown sugar (unrefined, if possible)

Direction

- Preheat the oven to 375 degrees.
- In a large saucepan over medium-low heat, warm the bread, milk, sugar, salt, butter, cinnamon, vanilla, rum and lemon peel. When warm, remove from heat and stir in the beaten eggs. Add the prunes and stir well. Pour this mixture into an oiled 9-by-12-inch baking dish. Slice the guava paste into thin strips and press into the top of the mixture. Sprinkle with the brown sugar and bake for 50 to 60 minutes, until the top is golden and the pudding smells great.

Nutrition Information

- 633: calories;
- 15 grams: protein;
- 21 grams: fat;
- 12 grams: saturated fat;
- 0 grams: trans fat;
- 2 grams: polyunsaturated fat;
- 3 grams: dietary fiber;
- 6 grams: monounsaturated fat;
- 95 grams: carbohydrates;
- 62 grams: sugars;
- 503 milligrams: sodium;

154. Kale And Quinoa Salad With Plums And Herbs

Serving: Serves 4 to 6 | Prep: | Cook: | Ready in: 45mins

Ingredients

- ½ cup quinoa
- Salt to taste
- 3 cups stemmed, slivered kale
- 1 serrano or Thai chiles, minced (optional)
- 1 to 2 ripe but firm plums or pluots, cut in thin slices
- ½ cup basil leaves, chopped, torn or cut in slivers
- 2 to 4 tablespoons chopped chives
- 1 tablespoon chopped cilantro (optional)
- 2 tablespoons seasoned rice vinegar
- Grated zest of 1 lime
- 2 tablespoons fresh lime juice
- 1 garlic clove, minced or puréed
- 3 tablespoons sunflower or grapeseed oil

Direction

- Rinse the quinoa and cook in a pot of rapidly boiling, generously salted water for 15 minutes. Drain, return to pot, place a towel across the top and replace the lid. Let sit for 15 minutes. Transfer to a sheet pan lined with paper towels and allow to cool completely.
- To cut the kale, stem, wash and spin dry the leaves, then stack several at a time and cut crosswise into thin slivers. Toss in a large bowl with the quinoa, chile, herbs, and half the plums.
- Whisk together the vinegar, lime zest and juice, salt to taste, garlic and sunflower or grapeseed oil. Toss with the salad. Garnish with the remaining plums and serve.

Nutrition Information

- 131: calories;
- 14 grams: carbohydrates;
- 2 grams: sugars;
- 3 grams: protein;

- 164 milligrams: sodium;
- 8 grams: fat;
- 1 gram: monounsaturated fat;
- 5 grams: polyunsaturated fat;

155. Kohlrabi Home Fries

Serving: 4 to 6 servings | Prep: | Cook: |Ready in: 30mins

Ingredients

- 1 ½ to 2 pounds kohlrabi
- 1 tablespoon rice flour, chickpea flour or semolina (more as needed)
- Salt to taste
- 2 to 4 tablespoons canola oil or grapeseed oil, as needed
- Chili powder, ground cumin, curry powder or paprika to taste

Direction

- Peel the kohlrabi and cut into thick sticks, about 1/3 to 1/2 inch wide and about 2 inches long.
- Heat the oil over medium-high heat in a heavy skillet (cast iron is good). Meanwhile, place the flour in a large bowl, season with salt if desired and quickly toss the kohlrabi sticks in the flour so that they are lightly coated.
- When the oil is rippling, carefully add the kohlrabi to the pan in batches so that the pan isn't crowded. Cook on one side until browned, about 2 to 3 minutes. Then, using tongs, turn the pieces over to brown on the other side for another 2 to 3 minutes. The procedure should take only about 5 minutes if there is enough oil in the pan. Drain on paper towels, then sprinkle right away with the seasoning of your choice. Serve hot.

156. Kohlrabi Risotto

Serving: 4 to 6 servings. | Prep: | Cook: |Ready in: 1hours

Ingredients

- 1 pound kohlrabi, preferably with some greens attached
- 7 to 8 cups well-seasoned chicken or vegetable stock
- 1 tablespoon extra virgin olive oil
- ½ cup minced onion
- 1 ½ cups arborio rice
- 1 to 2 garlic cloves (to taste), minced
- Salt and freshly ground pepper to taste
- ½ cup dry white wine, like pinot grigio or sauvignon blanc
- ¼ to ½ cup freshly grated Parmesan cheese (1 to 2 ounces)
- 2 to 3 tablespoons chopped flat-leaf parsley

Direction

- Peel the kohlrabi, making sure to remove the fibrous layer just under the skin, and cut into .5-inch dice. If there are greens attached, wash, stem and blanch them for 1 minute in salted boiling water. Transfer to a bowl of cold water, drain, squeeze out water and chop coarsely. Set aside.
- Put your stock or broth into a saucepan and bring it to a simmer over medium heat, with a ladle nearby or in the pot. Make sure that it is well seasoned. Turn the heat down to low.
- Heat the olive oil over medium heat in a wide, heavy nonstick skillet or a wide, heavy saucepan. Add the onion and a pinch of salt, and cook gently until it is just tender, about 3 minutes. Do not brown. Add the diced kohlrabi and the garlic and cook, stirring, until the kohlrabi is crisp-tender, about 5 minutes.
- Add the rice and stir until the grains separate and begin to crackle. Add the wine and stir until it has evaporated and been absorbed by the rice. Begin adding the simmering stock, a couple of ladlefuls (about .5 cup) at a time. The stock should just cover the rice, and should be

bubbling, not too slowly but not too quickly. Cook, stirring often, until it is just about absorbed. Add another ladleful or two of the stock and continue to cook in this fashion, adding more stock and stirring when the rice is almost dry. You do not have to stir constantly, but stir often. After 15 minutes, stir in the greens from the kohlrabi. When the rice is just tender all the way through but still chewy, in 20 to 25 minutes, it is done. Taste now, add pepper and adjust salt.

- Add another ladleful of stock to the rice. Stir in the Parmesan and the parsley and remove from the heat. The mixture should be creamy (add more stock if it isn't). Serve right away in wide soup bowls or on plates, spreading the risotto in a thin layer rather than a mound.

Nutrition Information

- 381: calories;
- 4 grams: monounsaturated fat;
- 15 grams: protein;
- 1097 milligrams: sodium;
- 8 grams: fat;
- 3 grams: saturated fat;
- 1 gram: polyunsaturated fat;
- 58 grams: carbohydrates;
- 5 grams: dietary fiber;
- 7 grams: sugars;

157. Lapin A La Bourguignonne (Rabbit With Red Wine Sauce)

Serving: Four servings | Prep: | Cook: |Ready in: 1hours25mins

Ingredients

- 1 rabbit, 2 pounds, cut into 10 or 12 serving pieces
- Salt to taste, if desired
- Freshly ground pepper to taste
- ½ pound salt pork, cut into 1/2-inch cubes, about 1 cup
- 2 tablespoons butter
- 24 small, white pearl onions, about 1/2 pound, peeled and left whole
- ¾ pound fresh mushrooms, left whole
- 3 tablespoons flour
- 2 ½ cups dry red wine
- 2 whole cloves
- 10 sprigs fresh parsley
- 4 sprigs fresh thyme
- 1 bay leaf

Direction

- Sprinkle the rabbit pieces with salt and pepper.
- Put the salt-pork cubes in a saucepan and add water to cover. Bring to the boil and simmer about one minute. Drain thoroughly.
- Heat the butter in a large, heavy casserole and add the salt-pork pieces. Cook, stirring, until lightly browned, about three minutes. Add the onions and cook, stirring, about two minutes.
- Add the mushrooms, salt and pepper and cook, stirring, about two minutes. Transfer the onions, mushrooms and salt-pork pieces to a bowl and set aside.
- To the fat remaining in the casserole, add the rabbit pieces in one layer and cook, turning the pieces as necessary, until lightly browned all over, about five minutes. Scatter the mushrooms, onions and salt pork over the rabbit pieces and stir to blend.
- Cook about five minutes and sprinkle with flour, salt and pepper. Add the wine and cloves.
- Tie the parsley, thyme and bay leaf into a bundle and add it. Bring to the boil, cover closely and cook over very low heat about one hour. Remove and discard the herb bunch. Uncover and cook about three minutes to reduce the sauce.

Nutrition Information

- 973: calories;

- 5 grams: sugars;
- 1630 milligrams: sodium;
- 24 grams: saturated fat;
- 0 grams: trans fat;
- 26 grams: monounsaturated fat;
- 8 grams: polyunsaturated fat;
- 18 grams: carbohydrates;
- 3 grams: dietary fiber;
- 65 grams: fat;
- 53 grams: protein;

158. Lasagna With Spicy Roasted Cauliflower

Serving: 6 servings | Prep: | Cook: | Ready in: 1hours30mins

Ingredients

- 1 ½ pounds cauliflower (3/4 of a medium head)
- 2 tablespoons extra virgin olive oil
- Salt and freshly ground pepper
- ¼ to ½ teaspoon red pepper flakes
- 3 cups marinara sauce, preferably homemade from fresh or canned tomatoes
- 7 to 8 ounces no-boil lasagna
- 8 ounces ricotta cheese
- 2 tablespoons water, vegetable stock or chicken stock
- Pinch of cinnamon
- 4 ounces (1 cup) freshly grated Parmesan

Direction

- Preheat the oven to 450 degrees. Line a baking sheet with parchment paper. Cut away the bottom of the cauliflower stem and trim off the leaves. Cut the cauliflower into slices 1/3 inch thick, letting the florets on the edges fall off. Toss all of it, including the bits that have fallen away, with the olive oil, salt and pepper. Place on the baking sheet in an even layer. Roast for about 15 minutes, stirring and flipping over the big slices after 8 minutes, until the slices are tender when pierced with a paring knife and the small florets are nicely browned. Remove from the oven, toss with the red pepper flakes and set aside. Turn the oven down to 350 degrees.
- Blend the ricotta cheese, water or stock, cinnamon, salt and pepper. Set aside.
- Oil a rectangular baking dish and spread a spoonful of tomato sauce over the bottom. Top with a layer of lasagna noodles. Spoon a thin layer of the ricotta mixture over the noodles. Top with a layer of cauliflower, then a layer of tomato sauce and a layer of Parmesan. Repeat the layers, ending with a layer of lasagna noodles topped with tomato sauce and Parmesan.
- Cover the baking dish tightly with foil and place in the oven. Bake 40 minutes, until the noodles are tender and the mixture is bubbling. Uncover and, if you wish, bake another 10 minutes, until the top begins to brown. Remove from the heat and allow to sit for 5 minutes before serving.

Nutrition Information

- 361: calories;
- 15 grams: fat;
- 7 grams: saturated fat;
- 6 grams: sugars;
- 1 gram: polyunsaturated fat;
- 39 grams: carbohydrates;
- 19 grams: protein;
- 781 milligrams: sodium;

159. Lebanese Tabbouleh

Serving: 6 appetizer spread servings, 4 salad servings | Prep: | Cook: | Ready in: 30mins

Ingredients

- ¼ cup fine bulgur wheat
- 1 small garlic clove, minced (optional)

- Juice of 2 large lemons, to taste
- 3 cups chopped fresh flat-leaf parsley (from 3 large bunches)
- ¼ cup chopped fresh mint
- ½ pound ripe tomatoes, very finely chopped
- 1 bunch scallions, finely chopped
- Salt, preferably kosher salt, to taste
- ¼ cup extra virgin olive oil
- 1 romaine lettuce heart, leaves separated, washed and dried

Direction

- Place the bulgur in a bowl, and cover with water by 1/2 inch. Soak for 20 minutes, until slightly softened. Drain through a cheesecloth-lined strainer, and press the bulgur against the strainer to squeeze out excess water. Transfer to a large bowl, and toss with the garlic, lemon juice, parsley, mint, tomatoes, scallions and salt. Leave at room temperature or in the refrigerator for two to three hours, so that the bulgur can continue to absorb liquid and swell.
- Add the olive oil, toss together, taste and adjust seasonings. Serve with lettuce leaves.

Nutrition Information

- 139: calories;
- 398 milligrams: sodium;
- 10 grams: fat;
- 1 gram: polyunsaturated fat;
- 7 grams: monounsaturated fat;
- 13 grams: carbohydrates;
- 4 grams: dietary fiber;
- 3 grams: protein;

160. Leg Of Lamb With Julienned Vegetables

Serving: Twenty servings for cocktails | Prep: | Cook: | Ready in: 1hours10mins

Ingredients

- 2 carrots, julienned, plus 1 carrot, diced
- 2 yellow squash, julienned
- 1 zucchini, julienned
- 1 4-pound leg of lamb, butterflied
- 1 garlic head
- Salt and freshly ground pepper to taste
- 2 celery stalks, diced
- 1 medium onion, diced
- ¼ cup flour

Direction

- Preheat the oven to 350 degrees.
- Combine the julienned vegetables and place them in the center of the lamb. Roll the roast and tie it securely. Place in a roasting pan along with the garlic head. Season with salt and pepper.
- Roast for 35 minutes. Add the diced vegetables to the pan and roast another 10 minutes, or until the internal temperature of the meat reaches 125 degrees for rare, 130 degrees for medium rare. Remove the roast from the pan and keep in a warm place.
- Add the flour to the pan and cook over high heat for two minutes, stirring constantly. Add two cups of water to the pan to deglaze, scraping the bottom. Simmer for 10 minutes, stirring occasionally, and adjust the seasonings. Strain.
- Cut the roast into thin slices. When ready to serve, spoon some sauce over the meat and serve the remaining sauce on the side.

Nutrition Information

- 184: calories;
- 10 grams: fat;
- 4 grams: monounsaturated fat;
- 1 gram: sugars;
- 9 grams: carbohydrates;
- 14 grams: protein;
- 388 milligrams: sodium;

161. Lemon And Garlic Chicken With Mushrooms

Serving: Serves 4 | Prep: | Cook: | Ready in: 45mins

Ingredients

- 2 boneless skinless chicken breasts (most weigh 8 to 10 ounces)
- 2 tablespoons extra-virgin olive oil
- 3 tablespoons fresh lemon juice
- 2 garlic cloves, minced or puréed
- 1 teaspoon chopped fresh rosemary
- Salt to taste
- Freshly ground pepper
- 2 tablespoons all-purpose flour or a gluten-free flour such as rice flour or corn flour
- 2 tablespoons grapeseed, sunflower or canola oil
- 1 pound mushrooms, sliced
- 1 teaspoon fresh thyme leaves or 1 tablespoon chopped flat-leaf parsley
- ¼ cup dry white wine

Direction

- Stir together olive oil, lemon juice, garlic, rosemary, and salt and pepper in a large bowl. Cut each chicken breast into 2 equal pieces (3 if they're 12 ounces or more) and place in the bowl. Stir together and refrigerate for 15 to 30 minutes.
- Remove chicken from marinade and pat dry (discard marinade). Place two sheets of plastic wrap (1 large sheet if you have extra-wide wrap) on your work surface, overlapping slightly, to make 1 wide sheet, and brush lightly with olive oil. Place a piece of chicken in the middle of plastic sheet and brush lightly with oil. Cover the chicken with another wide layer of plastic wrap. Working from the center to the outside, pound chicken breast with the flat side of a meat tenderizer until about 1/4 inch thick. (Don't pound too hard or you'll tear the meat. If that happens it won't be the end of the world, you'll just have a few pieces to cook.) Repeat with the remaining chicken breast pieces.
- Season the pounded chicken breasts with salt and pepper on one side only. Dredge lightly in the flour (you will not use all of it) and tap the breasts to remove excess.
- Turn oven on low Heat a wide, heavy skillet over high heat and add oil. When oil is hot, place one or two pieces of chicken in the pan – however many will fit without crowding. Cook for 1 1/2 minutes, until bottom is browned in spots. Turn over and brown other side, about 1 1/2 minutes. (Do not overcook or the chicken will be dry.) Transfer to the platter or sheet pan and keep warm in the oven. If there is more than a tablespoon of fat in the pan, pour some (but not all) it off into a jar or bowl.
- Turn burner heat down to medium-high. Add mushrooms to the pan. Let them sear for about 30 seconds to a minute without moving them, then stir, scraping the bottom of the pan with a wooden spoon to deglaze. When mushrooms have softened slightly and begun to sweat, add wine, thyme or parsley, and salt and pepper to taste. Continue to stir until wine has evaporated and mushrooms are tender, 5 to 10 minutes. Spoon over the chicken, and serve.

Nutrition Information

- 346: calories;
- 3 grams: sugars;
- 35 grams: protein;
- 687 milligrams: sodium;
- 18 grams: fat;
- 2 grams: dietary fiber;
- 0 grams: trans fat;
- 10 grams: carbohydrates;

162. Lentil, Celery And Tomato Minestrone

Serving: 4 to 6 servings | Prep: | Cook: |Ready in: 1hours30mins

Ingredients

- 1 cup lentils, rinsed
- 1 onion, halved
- A bouquet garni made with 2 sprigs each thyme and parsley, a bay leaf, and a Parmesan rind
- 1 ½ quarts water
- 1 tablespoon extra virgin olive oil
- 1 medium carrot, diced
- 3 celery stalks, diced
- 2 garlic cloves, minced
- Salt, preferably kosher salt, to taste
- 1 28-ounce can chopped tomatoes, with liquid
- Pinch of sugar
- 2 tablespoons tomato paste
- ¼ cup chopped fresh parsley
- Very thinly sliced celery, from the inner heart, for garnish
- Freshly grated Parmesan cheese for serving

Direction

- Combine the lentils, 1/2 onion and the bouquet garni with 1 quart water in a saucepan and bring to a boil. Reduce the heat, add salt to taste, cover and simmer 30 minutes.
- Chop the remaining onion. Heat the olive oil in a large, heavy soup pot or Dutch oven over medium heat and add the onion, carrot, and celery. Cook, stirring often, until the onion is tender, about 5 minutes, and add the garlic and a pinch of salt. Stir together until fragrant, about 1 minute, and add the canned tomatoes with their liquid and the sugar. Bring to a simmer and cook, stirring often, for about 10 minutes, until the tomatoes have cooked down somewhat and smell fragrant.
- Add the lentils with their broth, the tomato paste, salt to taste, an additional 2 cups water, and bring to a boil. Reduce the heat, cover, and simmer 30 minutes. Taste and adjust seasonings. Season to taste with freshly ground pepper, stir in the parsley and serve, garnishing each bowl with thinly sliced celery heart if you want some crunch, and passing the Parmesan at the table.

Nutrition Information

- 176: calories;
- 1077 milligrams: sodium;
- 1 gram: polyunsaturated fat;
- 7 grams: dietary fiber;
- 6 grams: sugars;
- 10 grams: protein;
- 3 grams: fat;
- 0 grams: saturated fat;
- 2 grams: monounsaturated fat;
- 30 grams: carbohydrates;

163. Lentils With Smoked Trout Rilletes

Serving: Serves 6 | Prep: | Cook: |Ready in: 45mins

Ingredients

- For the lentils
- 2 cups / 14 ounces lentils (green, brown, or black), rinsed and picked over
- 1 ½ quarts water
- 1 onion, cut in half
- 1 bay leaf
- 2 garlic cloves, crushed
- Pinch of cayenne, or 1 dried cayenne pepper (optional)
- Salt
- Freshly ground pepper
- For the rillettes
- 7 to 8 ounces smoked trout fillets, skin and bones removed
- 2 tablespoons extra virgin olive oil
- 2 tablespoons unsalted butter, at room temperature (may substitute Greek yogurt)

- 4 to 6 tablespoons plain Greek yogurt (depending on whether or not you use butter)
- 1 to 2 tablespoons fresh lemon juice (to taste)
- 1 to 2 tablespoons minced chives (to taste)
- Freshly ground pepper

Direction

- In a medium size pot, combine lentils, water, onion, bay leaf, garlic and optional cayenne. Bring to a gentle boil over medium-high heat. Add salt, cover, reduce heat to low and simmer 30 to 40 minutes, until lentils are cooked through but still have some texture. They should not be mushy but they shouldn't be crunchy either. Taste and adjust salt. Add pepper. Using tongs, remove and discard onion and bay leaf.
- While lentils are simmering make rillettes. In a medium bowl, break up trout with your fingers or with a fork. In a small bowl, mix together olive oil and butter until well amalgamated. Mash trout with a fork, then work in olive oil and butter, and yogurt. Make sure to mash well and to distribute butter, olive oil and yogurt evenly through the mixture. Work in lemon juice and stir in minced chives and pepper. Refrigerate if not using right away. Remove from refrigerator 30 minutes before serving.
- Spoon warm lentils onto plates or wide bowls. To form quenelles, dip a soup spoon into warm water and scoop up a spoonful of trout mixture. With another soup spoon, round the top of the mound, then ease off on top of the lentils. Repeat with another spoonful and serve.

Nutrition Information

- 358: calories;
- 9 grams: fat;
- 0 grams: trans fat;
- 1 gram: polyunsaturated fat;
- 25 grams: protein;
- 912 milligrams: sodium;
- 2 grams: saturated fat;
- 4 grams: monounsaturated fat;
- 47 grams: carbohydrates;
- 8 grams: dietary fiber;
- 3 grams: sugars;

164. Light Red Sauce

Serving: 2 1/2 cups | Prep: | Cook: | Ready in: 15mins

Ingredients

- 4 pounds fresh plum tomatoes, cored and peeled, or 4 cups canned Italian tomatoes
- 1 medium-size red bell pepper, diced
- 1 medium-size onion, diced
- 2 cloves garlic, minced
- 2 cups chicken broth
- 2 teaspoons sugar
- 2 tablespoons dried basil (or 1/4 cup fresh basil leaves)
- Salt and freshly ground black pepper to taste

Direction

- In large saucepan over medium heat, combine all ingredients. Simmer for 30 minutes. Remove from heat. Using a blender or food processor, puree mixture. Return to pot, adjust salt and pepper and simmer until reduced to 2 1/2 cups, about 1 1/2 hours. This sauce freezes very well.

Nutrition Information

- 130: calories;
- 0 grams: saturated fat;
- 1 gram: polyunsaturated fat;
- 6 grams: dietary fiber;
- 7 grams: protein;
- 2 grams: fat;
- 24 grams: carbohydrates;
- 15 grams: sugars;
- 1186 milligrams: sodium;

165. Ligurian Kale Pie (Torta Di Verdura)

Serving: Serves 12 | Prep: | Cook: | Ready in: 2hours

Ingredients

- 3 bunches mixed dark greens (like kale, chard, dandelion greens, collards), washed, stalks trimmed by 2 inches
- 1 ½ cups all-purpose flour
- 1 cup whole-wheat flour
- Salt
- ¼ cup plus 5 tablespoons olive oil
- 1 bunch scallions, white and light-green parts only
- 1 cup mixed fresh herbs (like thyme, parsley, marjoram)
- Salt
- 2 eggs
- 1 cup grated hard cheese (Parmesan or Asiago)
- ½ cup fresh cheese (ricotta, farmer's cheese or queso fresco)
- ½ nutmeg, grated

Direction

- Place the greens in a large pot. Add 3 cups of water, cover and set over medium heat. Bring to a boil and cook for 12 minutes, stirring occasionally, until wilted. Transfer to a colander. Once cool, wring out the greens to remove as much water as possible.
- Using a standing mixer fitted with a dough hook, mix the flours and 2 teaspoons salt until combined. Add 1 cup cold water and 1/4 cup olive oil and mix on medium speed for 8 minutes. (You can also mix by hand: Using a wooden spoon, combine the dry ingredients in a large bowl, then stir in the wet ingredients until combined. Transfer to a floured board and knead for 10 minutes.) Divide the dough into 2 equal pieces and let rest for at least 10 minutes. (The dough can be refrigerated for up to 1 day.)
- Preheat the oven to 400 degrees. Place half of the greens in a food processor and pulse until the pieces are about the size of a grain of rice. Transfer to a large mixing bowl. Repeat with the remaining greens. Process the scallions and herbs to a rough paste and mix into the greens. Stir in the egg, cheeses, 3 tablespoons olive oil and nutmeg. Season to taste with salt.
- Line a large cookie sheet with parchment paper and set aside. Flour a flat surface and roll one of dough balls into a circle about 16 inches in diameter, 1/8- to 1/16-inch thick, and lay it on the cookie sheet. Scoop the filling onto the dough and spread it evenly to 3/4 inch from the edge. Add more flour to the surface, roll out the second ball of dough and drape it across the filling. Trim the top layer so it hangs over the filling by 1/2 inch. Pinch together the layers. (If the dough doesn't stick, moisten the edges with a little water.) Slash two vents into the top of the pie and brush with the remaining 2 tablespoons olive oil.
- Bake until the pie is slightly puffy in the center and the filling has set, 40 to 50 minutes. If the top crust browns too quickly, cover it with foil. Cool before eating. It will keep 3 to 4 days at room temperature. If refrigerated, warm the slices in a skillet before eating.

Nutrition Information

- 252: calories;
- 2 grams: dietary fiber;
- 21 grams: carbohydrates;
- 8 grams: protein;
- 16 grams: fat;
- 4 grams: saturated fat;
- 0 grams: trans fat;
- 9 grams: monounsaturated fat;
- 1 gram: sugars;
- 188 milligrams: sodium;

166. Lime Marinated Chicken Over 'Creamed' Corn

Serving: Four servings | Prep: | Cook: | Ready in: 1hours30mins

Ingredients

- 5 tablespoons fresh lime juice
- 2 boneless, skinless chicken breasts (about 8 ounces each), split
- Kernels from 6 large ears of corn
- ½ cup low-fat milk
- 1 ¼ teaspoons salt
- Freshly ground pepper to taste
- 4 teaspoons chopped fresh cilantro
- 1 teaspoon minced jalapeno pepper
- ½ teaspoon grated lime zest
- 1 teaspoon olive oil

Direction

- Place 4 tablespoons of the lime juice in a small, shallow dish. Add chicken and turn to coat on both sides. Marinate for 1 hour.
- Meanwhile, place half of the corn in a food processor and pulse just enough to chop coarsely. Scrape into a medium saucepan. Put the remaining corn in the food processor with the milk. Process until pureed. Add to the saucepan.
- Place the pan over medium heat and simmer, stirring often, until the mixture is thick, about 10 minutes. Season with 1 teaspoon of the salt and pepper to taste. Keep warm.
- Preheat a grill or broiler. Remove the chicken from the lime juice and grill or broil until just cooked through, about 4 minutes per side. While the chicken is cooking, stir together the remaining lime juice and salt, the cilantro, jalapeno, lime zest and olive oil.
- Divide the corn mixture among 4 plates, placing it in the center. Lay a piece of chicken over the corn and spoon the cilantro mixture on top. Serve immediately.

Nutrition Information

- 165: calories;
- 4 grams: carbohydrates;
- 1 gram: polyunsaturated fat;
- 0 grams: dietary fiber;
- 2 grams: sugars;
- 27 grams: protein;
- 387 milligrams: sodium;

167. Lindy Boggs's Oven Fried Chicken

Serving: 2 to 3 servings | Prep: | Cook: | Ready in: 1hours10mins

Ingredients

- ¼ cup butter
- ⅓ cup flour
- 2 eggs
- Salt to taste
- 1 tablespoon paprika
- 2 tablespoons lemon juice
- 1 cup cracker crumbs
- 2 ½ pound chicken, cut in equal size pieces

Direction

- Place butter in 13-by-9-by-2-inch baking dish and place in 350-degree oven to melt butter.
- Flour chicken pieces and set aside.
- Beat together eggs, salt, paprika and lemon juice. Dip chicken pieces, one at a time, in egg mixture, then in cracker crumbs. Arrange pieces, skin side down, in melted butter in baking dish and bake for 45 minutes at 350 degrees, turning once.

Nutrition Information

- 1137: calories;
- 28 grams: saturated fat;
- 77 grams: protein;

- 1089 milligrams: sodium;
- 80 grams: fat;
- 1 gram: trans fat;
- 30 grams: monounsaturated fat;
- 16 grams: polyunsaturated fat;
- 23 grams: carbohydrates;
- 2 grams: sugars;

168. Linguine With Mussels Provencale

Serving: 4 servings | Prep: | Cook: | Ready in: 1hours10mins

Ingredients

- 2 pounds mussels, preferably small ones
- 4 tablespoons extra-virgin olive oil
- 1 medium onion, chopped
- 2 cloves garlic, minced
- 6 ripe plum tomatoes, chopped
- ½ cup dry white wine
- ¼ cup heavy cream
- ½ sweet red pepper, seeded and chopped
- 1 teaspoon fresh thyme leaves (or 1/2 teaspoon dried)
- Salt and freshly ground black pepper
- 1 pound linguine

Direction

- Scrub and debeard the mussels.
- Heat two tablespoons of the oil in a three- to four-quart pot. Add half the onions and one clove of the garlic and saute over low heat until soft but not brown. Stir in one-third of the tomatoes, cook a few minutes so they begin to soften, then add the wine.
- Bring to boil, add the mussels, cover and steam until the mussels open, about 10 minutes.
- Transfer the mussels from the pan to a large bowl with a slotted spoon. Set them aside until cool enough to handle. Meanwhile add the cream to the cooking liquid and cook until the liquid is reduced to one cup.
- Remove the mussels from their shells, reserving eight of them in their shells for garnish.
- Bring a large pot of water to a boil for the pasta.
- Heat the remaining oil in a large skillet. Add the remaining onion, garlic and the sweet red pepper and cook until they begin to brown. Stir in the remaining tomatoes and saute about 10 minutes, until the tomatoes are tender. Stir in the cooking liquid from the mussels and cook a few minutes, until the sauce begins to thicken. Stir in the mussels and thyme. Season to taste with salt and pepper. Set aside until ready to serve.
- When the water is boiling cook the linguine for six to seven minutes, until al dente. Drain and place in a warm serving dish. Reheat the mussel sauce, toss with the linguine and divide among four plates. Garnish each plate with two of the reserved mussels in their shells.

Nutrition Information

- 848: calories;
- 103 grams: carbohydrates;
- 44 grams: protein;
- 13 grams: monounsaturated fat;
- 4 grams: polyunsaturated fat;
- 7 grams: saturated fat;
- 6 grams: dietary fiber;
- 8 grams: sugars;
- 1245 milligrams: sodium;
- 26 grams: fat;

169. Linguine With Shrimp, Tomato And Fennel

Serving: Four servings | Prep: | Cook: | Ready in: 35mins

Ingredients

- 2 medium-size fennel bulbs
- ½ pound linguine
- 2 teaspoons olive oil
- 3 large cloves garlic, peeled and minced
- 1 pound large shrimp, peeled and deveined
- 1 teaspoon salt, plus more to taste
- Freshly ground pepper to taste
- 2 large tomatoes, seeded and diced
- ½ teaspoon grated orange zest
- 2 medium-size jalapeno peppers, seeded and minced
- 2 tablespoons chopped Italian parsley

Direction

- Cut the green tops off the fennel, chop and reserve. Trim the bulbs and slice them very thin on a mandoline or with a sharp knife. Set aside. Bring a large pot of lightly salted water to a boil. Add the linguine and cook until al dente, about 10 minutes. Drain and rinse.
- Meanwhile, heat 1 teaspoon of the olive oil in a large nonstick skillet over medium heat. Add the garlic and cook, stirring constantly, for 20 seconds. Add the sliced fennel bulbs and cook until crisp-tender, about 10 minutes.
- Add the shrimp and cook until just cooked through, about 3 minutes. Season with 1 teaspoon of salt and pepper to taste. In a small bowl, stir together the tomatoes, orange zest and jalapenos. Place the linguine in a large bowl. Add the shrimp mixture, the tomato mixture and the remaining oil and toss to combine. Season with additional salt and pepper to taste. Divide pasta among 4 plates. Combine the fennel tops and parsley and sprinkle over pasta. Serve immediately.

Nutrition Information

- 372: calories;
- 1 gram: polyunsaturated fat;
- 58 grams: carbohydrates;
- 884 milligrams: sodium;
- 0 grams: trans fat;
- 2 grams: monounsaturated fat;
- 7 grams: dietary fiber;
- 8 grams: sugars;
- 25 grams: protein;
- 5 grams: fat;

170. Liz Haupert's Fried Chicken

Serving: 4 servings | Prep: | Cook: | Ready in: 45mins

Ingredients

- 3 to 3 ½ pound chicken, cut in equal-size serving pieces
- 1 to 1 ½ cups flour
- Salt and pepper
- Corn oil

Direction

- Wash chicken pieces and drain but do not dry.
- Place flour in plastic bag with salt and pepper to taste and shake to mix. Add a few chicken pieces at a time and shake to coat pieces thoroughly all over with flour. Place coated pieces on wax paper and repeat until chicken is floured. Add more flour if necessary.
- Heat enough oil in deep, heavy skillet to cover chicken pieces almost entirely, until oil begins to ripple. The skillet should be large enough to accommodate all the chicken pieces in a single layer.
- Place chicken pieces in hot oil skin side down and cook over high heat 10 minutes or until golden. Turn and cook 10 minutes more or until golden. Turn and reduce heat to medium; cover and cook for 5 minutes. Turn and cook 5 minutes more.
- Remove chicken from pan and drain on several layers of paper towel on both sides. Serve warm, not hot.

171. Lobster With Pasta And Mint

Serving: 4 servings | Prep: | Cook: | Ready in: 1hours

Ingredients

- Salt
- 1 1 1/2-pound live lobster
- 4 tablespoons olive oil
- 1 tablespoon minced garlic
- Crushed red chili flakes to taste
- 1 pound long pasta, like linguine
- ½ cup chopped mint, or to taste

Direction

- Bring a large pot of water to a boil and salt it. Put about an inch of water into another large pot, add a not-too-big pinch of salt, put in lobster and cover pot. Steam lobster until it is red, about 3 minutes; you do not have to cook it through. Remove it and keep water simmering with cover off. As soon as you can, remove lobster's tail and claws; return body to simmering liquid. Remove meat from claws and tail and return shells to pot; chop meat roughly.
- Put olive oil in a large skillet over medium heat. Add garlic and lobster meat and toss; cook until it sizzles, then add chili flakes and lower heat. Strain lobster-cooking water, discarding body and shells; you will want a couple of cups.
- Meanwhile, cook pasta until it is not even close to tender, but just bending. Drain it, reserving some cooking liquid if you have less than 2 cups of lobster liquid. Add pasta to lobster/garlic mixture, with about a cup of lobster liquid. Cook, stirring occasionally, until pasta is tender, adding more liquid as necessary. Stop cooking when pasta is tender, taking care not to add too much liquid.
- Taste and add more salt, chili flakes or olive oil if you like. Stir in the mint and serve.

172. Mackerel With Mediterranean Vegetables

Serving: 2 to 3 servings | Prep: | Cook: | Ready in: 15mins

Ingredients

- 1 pound mackerel steaks
- White wine or vermouth
- 2 tablespoons olive oil
- 1 red pepper, sliced
- 1 green pepper, sliced
- 1 medium clove garlic, minced
- 1 onion, chopped coarsely
- 2 tomatoes, cut in chunks
- 2 tablespoons capers
- 2 tablespoons red wine
- Freshly ground black pepper to taste

Direction

- Poach mackerel in white wine or vermouth, almost to cover, allowing 10 minutes per inch at its thickest part. Remove from poaching liquid and cool.
- Heat oil and saute peppers, garlic and onion until vegetables are soft. Add tomatoes, capers, red wine and pepper and simmer 5 minutes longer.
- Spoon vegetable mixture over mackerel and serve at room temperature.

Nutrition Information

- 455: calories;
- 15 grams: monounsaturated fat;
- 13 grams: carbohydrates;
- 4 grams: dietary fiber;
- 7 grams: sugars;
- 280 milligrams: sodium;
- 30 grams: protein;
- 6 grams: polyunsaturated fat;

173. Mango Buttermilk Smoothie

Serving: One 16-ounce or two 8-ounce servings | Prep: | Cook: | Ready in: 5mins

Ingredients

- 1 heaped cup fresh or frozen ripe mango
- 1 cup buttermilk
- 1 teaspoon honey
- ½ medium size ripe banana
- 4 frozen strawberries
- 2 or 3 ice cubes

Direction

- Combine all of the ingredients in a blender, and blend at high speed until smooth.

174. Mango Lassi Ice

Serving: 1 quart | Prep: | Cook: | Ready in: 30mins

Ingredients

- 2 ¼ cups/425 grams diced mango (2 large mangoes)
- 3 tablespoons plus 2 teaspoons/55 grams fresh lime juice (about 1 1/2 limes)
- 2 tablespoons/50 grams corn syrup
- 5 tablespoons/100 grams honey
- 1 ¾ cups buttermilk

Direction

- Combine all ingredients in a blender and purée until completely smooth. Transfer to a bowl or container and chill overnight in refrigerator.
- Chill a 1-quart container in the freezer while you spin the ice. Remove bowl from refrigerator and blend the mango purée again for 1 to 2 minutes in a blender or with an immersion blender. Add to ice cream maker and spin for about 25 minutes. Transfer to chilled container and freeze for 2 hours or longer to pack.
- Once frozen solid, allow to soften in refrigerator for 30 minutes before serving.

Nutrition Information

- 75: calories;
- 2 grams: protein;
- 71 milligrams: sodium;
- 0 grams: polyunsaturated fat;
- 18 grams: carbohydrates;
- 1 gram: dietary fiber;
- 17 grams: sugars;

175. Marinated Lamb Chops With Fennel And Black Olives

Serving: Four servings | Prep: | Cook: | Ready in: 1hours30mins

Ingredients

- ¼ cup olive oil
- 2 large cloves garlic, peeled and minced
- ½ teaspoon freshly ground black pepper, plus more to taste
- 8 rib lamb chops, bones scraped of fat
- 2 medium fennel bulbs, tops removed and finely chopped, bulbs very finely shaved
- 1 cup white wine
- 2 cups chicken broth, homemade or low-sodium canned
- 2 tablespoons pitted and chopped Nyons olives
- Salt and pepper to taste

Direction

- Combine the olive oil, garlic and pepper in a shallow baking dish large enough to hold the lamb chops. Place the lamb chops in the dish

and coat well with the marinade. Cover and refrigerate overnight. Let stand at room temperature for 1 hour.
- Wipe the oil off the lamb chops. Heat a large, nonstick skillet over medium-high heat, add the chops and sear until medium rare, about 30 seconds per side. Remove the chops from the skillet and wrap in foil to keep warm.
- Reduce the heat to very low. Add the shaved fennel, cover the skillet with a lid and cook until the fennel is soft, about 20 minutes. Remove the fennel from the skillet with a slotted spatula and divide among 4 warmed plates.
- Increase the heat and add the white wine and chicken broth. Cook, stirring occasionally, until reduced to 1/2 cup, about 15 minutes. Stir in the olives and season with salt and pepper to taste. Place 2 lamb chops over the fennel on each plate, spoon the sauce over the top, sprinkle with the fennel tops and serve immediately.

Nutrition Information

- 1107: calories;
- 38 grams: protein;
- 94 grams: fat;
- 7 grams: sugars;
- 43 grams: monounsaturated fat;
- 8 grams: polyunsaturated fat;
- 17 grams: carbohydrates;
- 4 grams: dietary fiber;
- 1264 milligrams: sodium;
- 37 grams: saturated fat;

176. Mashed Potato And Broccoli Raab Pancakes

Serving: Makes 2 to 2 1/2 dozen small pancakes, serving 6 | Prep: | Cook: | Ready in: 15mins

Ingredients

- 2 ½ cups mashed potatoes (about 1 pound 2 ounces potatoes, peeled, cut in chunks and steamed until tender, then mashed with a potato masher or a fork)
- 1 ½ cups finely chopped steamed or blanched broccoli raab
- ¼ cup chopped chives
- 1 teaspoon baking powder
- Salt and freshly ground pepper to taste
- ⅓ to ½ cup freshly grated Parmesan, to taste
- 3 heaped tablespoons all-purpose flour
- 2 eggs
- 3 to 4 tablespoons sunflower oil, grapeseed oil or canola oil for frying

Direction

- In a large bowl, mix together the mashed potatoes, finely chopped broccoli raab, chives, baking powder, salt, pepper, Parmesan and flour. Beat the eggs and stir in.
- Begin heating a large heavy skillet over medium heat. Heat the oven to 300 degrees. Add 2 tablespoons of the oil and when it is hot carefully scoop up heaped tablespoons of the potato mixture and use a spoon or spatula to ease them out of the spoon into the pan. Gently flatten the mounds slightly with the back of a spoon or a spatula but don't worry if this is hard to do – if they stick -- because when you flip them over you can flatten them into pancakes. Brown on the first side – about 2 or 3 minutes – and using a spatula, flip the potato and broccoli raab mounds over and gently push them down so that they will be shaped like pancakes. Brown on the other side and remove to a baking sheet. Continue with the remaining potato mixture, adding oil to the pan as necessary.

Nutrition Information

- 51: calories;
- 111 milligrams: sodium;
- 3 grams: fat;
- 1 gram: polyunsaturated fat;
- 0 grams: sugars;

- 4 grams: carbohydrates;
- 2 grams: protein;

177. Mashed Potato And Cabbage Pancakes

Serving: Makes about 2 to 2 1/2 dozen small pancakes, serving 6 | Prep: | Cook: | Ready in: 30mins

Ingredients

- 2 cups finely chopped steamed cabbage (about 1 pound cabbage)
- 2 ½ cups mashed potatoes (about 1 pound 2 ounces potatoes, peeled, cut in chunks and steamed until tender – about 20 minutes – then mashed with a potato masher or a fork)
- ½ cup chopped chives
- 1 tablespoon chopped fresh marjoram (optional)
- 1 teaspoon baking powder
- Salt and freshly ground pepper to taste
- ¼ cup all-purpose flour
- 2 eggs
- 3 to 4 tablespoons sunflower oil, grapeseed oil or canola oil for frying

Direction

- To prepare the cabbage, remove the outer leaves and quarter a small head or 1/2 of a larger head. Core and place in a steamer above 1 inch of boiling water. Steam 10 to 15 minutes, until tender when pierced with a knife or skewer. Remove from the heat and allow to cool, then squeeze out water, and chop fine. Mix with the potatoes in a large bowl. Add the chives, baking powder, marjoram if using, salt, pepper, and flour. Beat the eggs and stir in.
- Begin heating a large heavy skillet over medium heat. Heat the oven to 300 degrees. Add 2 tablespoons of the oil and when it is hot carefully scoop up heaped tablespoons of the potato mixture and use a spoon or spatula to ease them out of the spoon into the pan. Gently flatten the mounds slightly with the back of a spoon or a spatula but don't worry if this is hard to do – if they stick -- because when you flip them over you can flatten them into pancakes. Brown on the first side – about 2 or 3 minutes – and using a spatula, flip the mounds over and gently push them down so that they will be shaped like pancakes. Brown on the other side and remove to a baking sheet. Continue with the remaining potato mixture, adding oil to the pan as necessary.

Nutrition Information

- 49: calories;
- 3 grams: fat;
- 0 grams: trans fat;
- 1 gram: protein;
- 5 grams: carbohydrates;
- 108 milligrams: sodium;

178. Mashed Potatoes With Chives

Serving: 4 servings | Prep: | Cook: | Ready in: 30mins

Ingredients

- 1 ½ pounds russet potatoes
- Salt to taste
- 1 cup milk
- 4 tablespoons butter
- 4 tablespoons chopped chives

Direction

- Peel the potatoes and cut them into 2-inch cubes.
- Put the potatoes in a saucepan and cover with water. Add salt and bring to a boil. Simmer 20 minutes or until the potatoes are tender. Do not overcook them.
- Meanwhile, heat the milk until it is hot.

- Drain the potatoes and put them through a food mill or ricer or mash them well with a potato masher. Return them to the saucepan. Using a wooden spatula, add the butter and chives and blend well. Mix in the milk and keep warm until ready to serve.

Nutrition Information

- 274: calories;
- 14 grams: fat;
- 8 grams: saturated fat;
- 3 grams: monounsaturated fat;
- 2 grams: dietary fiber;
- 6 grams: protein;
- 0 grams: trans fat;
- 1 gram: polyunsaturated fat;
- 34 grams: carbohydrates;
- 4 grams: sugars;
- 577 milligrams: sodium;

179. Mashed Potatoes With Scallions

Serving: 4 servings | Prep: | Cook: | Ready in: 25mins

Ingredients

- 5 Idaho or Washington potatoes, about 1 1/2 pounds
- Salt to taste
- 2 tablespoons unsalted butter
- 1 ⅓ cups milk
- ⅓ cup finely chopped scallions
- Freshly ground white pepper to taste
- ⅛ teaspoon freshly grated nutmeg

Direction

- Peel the potatoes and cut them into 2-inch cubes. Place the cubes in a saucepan. Add water to cover and salt.
- Bring to a boil and simmer 15 minutes, or until tender. Drain and put the potatoes through a food mill or mash them well with a potato masher. Add the butter and beat to blend. Stir in the milk, scallions, salt, pepper and nutmeg. Serve piping hot.

Nutrition Information

- 311: calories;
- 8 grams: protein;
- 9 grams: fat;
- 5 grams: saturated fat;
- 2 grams: monounsaturated fat;
- 1 gram: polyunsaturated fat;
- 52 grams: carbohydrates;
- 6 grams: sugars;
- 0 grams: trans fat;
- 847 milligrams: sodium;

180. Medallion Of Pork With Sesame Seeds

Serving: 4 servings | Prep: | Cook: | Ready in: 40mins

Ingredients

- 8 slices boneless loin of pork, about 3 ounces each, trimmed of excess fat
- 2 tablespoons finely chopped shallots
- 1 tablespoon grated fresh ginger root
- 4 tablespoons dry white wine
- 2 tablespoons sherry wine
- ⅛ teaspoon red hot pepper flakes
- Freshly ground pepper to taste
- 2 tablespoons dark soy sauce
- 1 egg white
- 2 tablespoons cornstarch
- 1 ¾ cups sesame seeds
- 2 tablespoons vegetable or corn oil
- 2 tablespoons butter
- 2 tablespoons coarsely chopped fresh coriander

Direction

- Place the pork slices on a flat surface. Pound the meat lightly with a mallet or meat pounder.
- Combine the shallots, ginger, white wine, sherry, pepper flakes, ground pepper and soy sauce in a bowl and blend. Place the pork in a dish. Pour the mixture over the pork and marinate for 10 minutes.
- Combine the egg white with the cornstarch in a bowl and beat well with a wire whisk to blend.
- Drain the pork medallions, reserving the marinade. Brush the medallions with the egg white mixture.
- Pour the sesame seeds into a flat dish and dip the medallions one at a time in the seeds to coat both sides generously.
- Heat the oil in a nonstick skillet large enough to hold the slices in one layer. When the oil is hot, add the slices of meat and cook over medium heat about 5 minutes or until brown. Turn the slices over and cook about 5 minutes. Reduce the heat and continue cooking for about 2 minutes longer, turning the slices occasionally. Transfer the meat to a warm serving platter.
- In a small saucepan, add the reserved marinade and bring to a simmer. Cook about 2 minutes. Stir in the butter and blend well.
- Spoon the sauce over the pork medallions and sprinkle with coriander. Serve immediately.

Nutrition Information

- 759: calories;
- 1 gram: sugars;
- 43 grams: protein;
- 11 grams: saturated fat;
- 18 grams: monounsaturated fat;
- 8 grams: dietary fiber;
- 528 milligrams: sodium;
- 56 grams: fat;
- 0 grams: trans fat;
- 19 grams: polyunsaturated fat;
- 21 grams: carbohydrates;

181. Mint Ice Cream

Serving: Six to eight servings | Prep: | Cook: | Ready in: 20mins

Ingredients

- 3 cups milk
- ¾ cup sugar
- 1 inch vanilla bean split or 1 teaspoon vanilla extract
- 3 egg yolks
- 1 bunch fresh mint leaves (about 1 cup), washed, dried and chopped
- 1 cup heavy cream

Direction

- In a heavy saucepan, scald the milk over medium-low heat with the sugar and vanilla bean, stirring with a wooden spoon until the sugar desolves. (If using extract, do not add it at this stage; wait until after chilling the mixture.)
- In a large bowl, whisk the egg yolks until they coat the whisk.
- Slowly whisk the scalded milk mixture into the beaten yolks.
- Add the mint leaves and steep until the mixture cools.
- Remove the vanilla bean and scrape the seeds into the mixture.
- Strain the mixture through a fine sieve, pressing down on the leaves to extract all the moisture, and discard the mint.
- Add the heavy cream, cover the bowl completely and chill.
- Freeze according to the manufacturer's directions, then transfer to air-tight containers for storage.

Nutrition Information

- 254: calories;
- 25 grams: carbohydrates;

- 24 grams: sugars;
- 57 milligrams: sodium;
- 15 grams: fat;
- 9 grams: saturated fat;
- 5 grams: protein;
- 1 gram: dietary fiber;

182. Mississippi Mud Pie

Serving: 16 servings | Prep: | Cook: | Ready in: 1hours30mins

Ingredients

- For the graham cracker crust:
- About 15 whole graham crackers
- ¼ cup/50 grams granulated sugar
- ½ teaspoon kosher salt
- 8 tablespoons/114 grams (1 stick) unsalted butter, melted
- For the Brownie Cake:
- 8 tablespoons/114 grams (1 stick) unsalted butter, cut into pieces
- 6 ounces/170 grams bittersweet chocolate, chopped
- ⅓ cup/67 grams dark brown sugar
- ⅓ cup/33 grams Dutch-processed cocoa powder, plus more for dusting
- 1 teaspoon pure vanilla extract
- ¾ teaspoon kosher salt
- 3 large eggs, separated
- ½ cup/100 grams granulated sugar
- ¼ cup/32 grams all-purpose flour
- For the chocolate custard:
- 4 ounces/113 grams bittersweet chocolate, chopped
- 2 tablespoons/29 grams unsalted butter, cut into pieces
- ½ cup/100 grams granulated sugar
- ¼ teaspoon kosher salt
- ¼ cup/25 grams Dutch-processed cocoa powder
- ¼ cup/28 grams cornstarch
- 2 cups/480 milliliters whole milk
- 4 large egg yolks
- To Finish:
- 1 ½ cups/360 milliliters cold heavy cream

Direction

- Heat the oven to 325 degrees. In a food processor, grind the graham crackers to fine crumbs — you should have about 2 1/4 cups crumbs — and tip into a bowl. Add sugar, salt and butter, and toss until evenly moistened. Tip the crumb mixture into a 9-inch springform pan. Use your fingers to press the crumbs into a thin, even layer on the bottom of the pan and at least 2 1/4 inches up its sides. Bake the crust until just set, about 10 minutes. (The crust will continue to cook in the next step.) Increase heat to 350 degrees.
- Prepare the cake: In a bowl set over a pot of barely simmering water but not touching it, melt together the butter and chocolate. (Alternatively, do this in short bursts in the microwave but be careful not to scorch the chocolate.) Remove the bowl from the heat and whisk in the dark brown sugar, cocoa powder, vanilla extract and salt. Let cool slightly, then whisk in the 3 large egg yolks.
- In large bowl, beat the remaining 3 large egg whites with an electric mixer on medium until foamy, about 30 seconds. While mixing, gradually add the granulated sugar in a steady stream. Increase the mixer speed to high and continue to beat until you have stiff peaks, about 3 minutes. Using a large rubber spatula, fold the egg-white mixture evenly into the chocolate mixture. Sift the flour evenly over the chocolate mixture and fold it in. Transfer the batter to the prepared crust and smooth the top. Bake until a crust has formed over the top, the center is just set and a toothpick inserted 1 inch from the edges comes out with moist crumbs attached, 30 to 35 minutes. The center of the cake, under the crust, should still be very moist and fudgy. (Peek under the crust if necessary.) Do not overbake. The cake will sink slightly as it cools. Let the cake cool completely, at least 90 minutes.

- Prepare the custard: Set the chocolate and butter in a medium bowl. Place a fine-mesh sieve over the bowl and set it aside. In a medium saucepan, whisk together the sugar, salt, cocoa powder, and cornstarch. Add the milk, little by little, while whisking to incorporate it fully. Whisk in the egg yolks. Heat the mixture over medium heat, stirring constantly, until it has thickened and just come to a low boil. Continue to cook the custard, whisking, for another minute, then immediately pour it into the sieve, pushing it through with a small spatula. Let the custard stand for 1 minute, then whisk it together with the butter and chocolate until smooth. Pour the custard over the cooled cake. Cover the custard with plastic wrap or wax paper, making sure to press it gently into the surface of the custard. Chill until the custard has set completely, at least 4 hours and up to overnight.
- Just before serving, remove the ring from springform pan base and transfer pie to a serving plate. Whip the cream to soft peaks and spoon high dollops over the top of the pie, leaving about a 1-inch border. Dust with cocoa powder.

183. Mixed Greens Galette With Onions And Chickpeas

Serving: Serves 8 to 10 | Prep: | Cook: | Ready in: 2hours30mins

Ingredients

- 1 whole wheat Mediterranean pie crust
- 1 large onion
- 1 1-pound bag washed, stemmed greens, such as a Southern greens mix (kale, collards, turnip greens and spinach)
- Salt to taste
- 1 tablespoon extra virgin olive oil
- 2 plump garlic cloves, minced
- Freshly ground pepper
- 1 ½ teaspoons za'atar (see below)
- 1 can chickpeas, drained and rinsed
- 2 eggs
- 3 ounces feta
- 1 tablespoon egg wash (1 egg beaten with 1 teaspoon milk) for brushing the crust

Direction

- Mix together the dough for the crust and set it in a warm spot to rise. Meanwhile prepare the filling.
- Bring a large pot of water to a boil. Fill a bowl with cold water. Cut the onion into quarters, cutting from root to stem end, then cut thin slices across the grain.
- When the water in the pot reaches a boil, salt generously and add the greens. Boil for about 3 minutes, until tender. Use a skimmer to transfer the greens to the bowl of cold water, then drain. Take the greens up by the handful and squeeze out excess water. You can squeeze out the water most effectively if you take up small handfuls. Then coarsely chop (they are already chopped but the stems can be big). Set aside.
- Heat the olive oil over medium heat in a wide saucepan or a large skillet and add the onions. Cook, stirring often, until soft and golden, about 10 minutes. After the first couple of minutes of cooking add a generous pinch of salt so they don't brown too quickly or stick to the pan. When the onions are nicely colored and soft add the garlic and continue to cook for another 30 seconds to a minute, until fragrant. Stir in the greens and combine well with the onions. Add the za'atar and season to taste with salt and pepper. Stir in the chickpeas, taste and adjust seasonings, and set aside.
- Beat the eggs in a large bowl. Crumble in the feta and stir in the greens mixture. Stir well to combine.
- Dust a large work surface with flour and turn out the dough. Shape into a ball and let rest for 5 minutes. Then roll out into a thin round, 16 to 18 inches in diameter. Line a sheet pan with

parchment and place the round in the middle, with the edges overlapping the pan (this will eliminate the need to lift the galette once it is filled). Place the filling in the middle of the rolled out pastry and spread it to a circle, leaving a 3 or 4-inch margin all the way around the pastry. Fold the edges in over the filling, pleating them to cover the filling and drawing them up to the middle of the galette, so that the filling is enclosed. The finished galette should be about 10 to 11 inches in diameter. There can be a small circle of exposed filling in the middle but it shouldn't be more than an inch in diameter. Cover with plastic wrap and place in the freezer for 45 minutes to an hour.

- Meanwhile, heat the oven to 375 degrees. Remove the galette from the freezer, brush with egg wash, and place in the oven. Bake 50 minutes, or until golden brown. Remove from the oven and let sit for at least 15 minutes before serving.

Nutrition Information

- 231: calories;
- 3 grams: sugars;
- 0 grams: trans fat;
- 2 grams: polyunsaturated fat;
- 5 grams: dietary fiber;
- 27 grams: carbohydrates;
- 7 grams: protein;
- 340 milligrams: sodium;
- 11 grams: fat;
- 4 grams: monounsaturated fat;

184. Moroccan Lamb

Serving: Serves 8 | Prep: | Cook: |Ready in: 1hours30mins

Ingredients

- 4 tablespoons paprika
- 2 tablespoons ground cumin
- 2 tablespoons ground coriander
- 2 teaspoons salt
- 1 teaspoon ground black pepper
- ⅛ teaspoon ground cardamom
- 1 6- to 7-pound leg of lamb, butterflied by your butcher

Direction

- Mix together the paprika, cumin, coriander, salt, pepper and cardamom. Rub lamb all over with these spices (or 1/2 cup zaatar) and refrigerate for 1 hour.
- On a very hot grill or under the broiler, grill or broil lamb, turning once, until cooked to the desired doneness, 10 to 20 minutes for medium rare depending on thickness of the lamb. Let rest on a cutting board for 10 minutes before slicing and serving.

Nutrition Information

- 621: calories;
- 2 grams: dietary fiber;
- 17 grams: monounsaturated fat;
- 4 grams: polyunsaturated fat;
- 18 grams: saturated fat;
- 3 grams: carbohydrates;
- 0 grams: sugars;
- 54 grams: protein;
- 751 milligrams: sodium;
- 42 grams: fat;

185. Mulled Cider

Serving: 6 servings | Prep: | Cook: |Ready in: 10mins

Ingredients

- 1 ½ quarts unfiltered sweet cider
- 12 allspice berries
- 12 whole cloves
- 2 sticks cinnamon, broken into pieces

- 6 tablespoons bourbon (optional)

Direction

- Place all ingredients but the bourbon in a saucepan and heat over medium heat until the mixture is just below a boil. Cover, remove from the heat and let steep 5 minutes.
- At that point, you will notice that the allspice and cloves have floated to the top; remove and discard them. Pour a tablespoon of bourbon, if desired, into each of six mugs and pour the cider mixture over it. Spoon a few cinnamon pieces into each mug, and serve immediately.

Nutrition Information

- 127: calories;
- 14 milligrams: sodium;
- 1 gram: protein;
- 0 grams: polyunsaturated fat;
- 32 grams: carbohydrates;
- 2 grams: dietary fiber;
- 24 grams: sugars;

186. Multigrain Seed Bread

Serving: Two loaves | Prep: | Cook: | Ready in: 2hours

Ingredients

- 2 ½ cups water at room temperature
- 1 6/10-ounce cake fresh yeast or 1 tablespoon granular yeast
- ½ cup sourdough (see recipe)
- 1 tablespoon salt
- ⅓ cup mild honey
- ¼ cup sunflower seeds
- ¼ cup, plus 1 tablespoon, sesame seeds
- 3 tablespoons flax seed
- 4 ⅓ cups whole-wheat bread flour, plus flour to sprinkle surface
- Corn oil for bread pans

Direction

- Place the water in a large mixing bowl, crumble in the yeast (if using dry yeast, let dissolve), then stir in the sourdough, salt, honey, seeds and flour.
- Stir the dough until it is elastic and cohesive but still very wet and sticky, about 15 minutes by hand or 10 minutes with the paddle attachment of a heavy-duty electric mixer set at medium speed. Sprinkle the surface of the dough with flour, cover the bowl with plastic wrap and allow to rest in a warm place for one hour.
- Oil a pair of metal loaf pans, 2 1/2 by 4 by 8 inches. Stir down the dough and divide it between them, cover with plastic wrap and let rise only until one-and-a-half times the original height, about 45 minutes. The dough will not fill the pans completely.
- Heat the oven to 450 degrees and make the loaves for 20 minutes. Reduce the heat to 375 and bake 20 to 30 minutes more, or until the loaves sound hollow when tapped on the bottom. Remove the loaves from the pans and cool on their sides on wire racks.

Nutrition Information

- 310: calories;
- 3 grams: fat;
- 0 grams: trans fat;
- 1 gram: monounsaturated fat;
- 2 grams: protein;
- 71 grams: carbohydrates;
- 69 grams: sugars;
- 283 milligrams: sodium;

187. Mushroom And Grain Cheeseburgers

Serving: 4 to 6 burgers. | Prep: | Cook: | Ready in: 45mins

Ingredients

- 2 to 3 tablespoons extra virgin olive oil, as needed
- ½ cup finely chopped onion
- 1 ¼ pounds mushrooms, sliced
- Salt to taste
- 2 garlic cloves, minced
- 2 teaspoons chopped fresh sage
- Freshly ground pepper
- 1 ¼ cups cooked brown rice or barley
- ¼ cup chopped fresh parsley
- 1 egg
- ¾ cup cooked chickpeas (1/2 can)
- 2 ounces Gruyère cheese, sliced very thin with a cheese slicer

Direction

- Preheat the oven to 375 degrees. Heat 1 tablespoon of the oil over medium heat in a heavy ovenproof skillet and add the onion. Cook, stirring, until it is tender, about 3 minutes. Turn the heat up to medium-high and add the mushrooms. Cook, stirring often, until the mushrooms have begun to sweat and soften, about 3 minutes. Turn the heat back down to medium, add a generous pinch of salt, the garlic and sage, and continue to cook until the mushrooms are tender, about 3 minutes. Taste, adjust seasoning and remove from the heat.
- Place half the mushrooms in a food processor fitted with the steel blade and the other half in a large bowl, along with the rice or barley and the parsley.
- Add the chickpeas and egg to the food processor and purée with the mushrooms. Stir into the rice and mushroom mixture and mix everything together. Season to taste with salt and pepper.
- Begin heating a heavy ovenproof skillet over medium-high heat. Seasoned cast iron is good, and so is a heavy nonstick pan that can go into the oven. Moisten your hands lightly and shape 4 large or 6 smaller patties. Add the remaining tablespoon of oil to the pan and, working in batches if necessary, cook the burgers for 2 minutes on one side, until nicely browned. Carefully turn the patties over and place the pan in the oven. Bake 5 minutes. Remove the pan from the oven and lay thin slices of Gruyère on top of each burger. Return to the oven and bake for another 5 minutes, or the patties are lightly browned and the cheese has melted. Remove from the heat and serve, with or without buns, ketchup and the works.

Nutrition Information

- 252: calories;
- 4 grams: saturated fat;
- 7 grams: monounsaturated fat;
- 2 grams: polyunsaturated fat;
- 12 grams: protein;
- 13 grams: fat;
- 5 grams: dietary fiber;
- 3 grams: sugars;
- 595 milligrams: sodium;
- 0 grams: trans fat;
- 25 grams: carbohydrates;

188. Mushroom And Wild Rice Strudel

Serving: Serves 6 | Prep: | Cook: | Ready in: 2hours

Ingredients

- 3 ounces feta, crumbled (about 3/4 cup)
- 1 egg, beaten
- 2 cups mushroom ragoût
- ¼ cup chopped fresh parsley, dill, or chives, or a combination
- 1 ½ cups cooked wild rice (1/2 cup uncooked)
- 2 tablespoons butter, melted
- 3 tablespoons extra virgin olive oil
- 8 sheets phyllo dough

Direction

- Preheat the oven to 375 degrees.
- In a large bowl, beat the egg with the feta. Stir in the mushroom ragoût, chopped herbs and 1/2 cup of the cooked rice. Add a little freshly ground pepper.
- Combine the melted butter and olive oil in a pyrex measuring cup or microwave-safe bowl, heat very slightly at 50 percent power and stir together. Place 8 sheets of phyllo dough on your work surface. Cover with a dish towel and place another, damp dish towel on top of the first towel. Each time you take a piece of phyllo from the pile, replace the towels so that the phyllo doesn't dry out. Place a sheet of parchment on your work surface horizontally, with the long edge close to you. Take a sheet of phyllo from the pile and lay it on the parchment. Brush the first sheet of phyllo lightly with the butter and olive oil mixture and top with the next sheet. Continue to layer all eight sheets, brushing each one before topping with the next one.
- Brush the top sheet of phyllo dough with the butter and olive oil mixture. Spread the remaining wild rice over the surface, leaving a 3-inch margin at the bottom and a 2 1/2 inch margin at the top and on the sides. Spread the mushroom mixture over the rice. Fold the bottom edge of the phyllo up over the filling, then fold the ends over and roll up like a burrito. Using the parchment paper to help you lift the strudel, place both the parchment paper and the strudel on a baking sheet with the seam side down. Brush with butter and olive oil and make 3 or 4 slits on the diagonal along the length of the strudel.
- Place the strudel in the oven and bake 20 minutes. Remove from the oven, brush again with the butter and olive oil, rotate the pan and return to the oven. Continue to bake for another 25 to 30 minutes, until golden brown. Remove from the heat and allow to cool for at least 20 minutes and preferably for 30. Serve warm. Reheat in a medium (325 degrees) oven if the strudel loses its crispiness before you are ready to serve. It will crisp up in about 10 minutes.

Nutrition Information

- 277: calories;
- 17 grams: fat;
- 0 grams: trans fat;
- 8 grams: protein;
- 1 gram: polyunsaturated fat;
- 24 grams: carbohydrates;
- 2 grams: sugars;
- 309 milligrams: sodium;
- 7 grams: saturated fat;

189. Mussels With Linguine

Serving: 2 servings | Prep: | Cook: | Ready in: 1hours

Ingredients

- 2 pounds mussels
- 1 cup dry white wine
- 3 or 4 sprigs thyme
- 6 ounces whole onion or 5 ounces chopped ready-cut (1 1/3 cup)
- 1 teaspoon olive oil
- 1 large clove garlic
- 8 ounces fresh linguine
- ½ cup nonfat yogurt
- ¾ cup reduced-fat ricotta
- Several sprigs parsley, to yield 2 tablespoons chopped
- 1 ½ ounces Parmigiano Reggiano (1/2 cup coarsely grated)
- Freshly ground black pepper to taste

Direction

- Bring water to boil for pasta.
- Rinse mussels in cold water. Scrub and remove beards. Discard any mussels whose shells are open.
- Combine mussels with wine and thyme in pot, and cover. Steam mussels until they open, 5 to 7 minutes.

- Chop whole onion.
- Heat oil in nonstick pan until it is very hot; reduce heat to medium high; add onion, and saute until it begins to soften.
- Meanwhile, mince garlic, and add it to onion as it cooks.
- When mussels are cooked, remove from liquid and set aside. Add 1 cup of the cooking liquid to the onion, and boil to reduce to 1/4 cup.
- Shuck mussels, discarding any that are not open.
- Cook linguine according to package directions.
- Add mussels to onion mixture, and heat through.
- Whisk yogurt and ricotta to make a smooth mixture. Wash, dry and chop parsley. Grate cheese.
- Drain pasta.
- Remove mussel mixture from heat. Stir in yogurt-ricotta mixture, parsley, cheese and pepper, and mix well. Spoon over pasta, and serve.

Nutrition Information

- 1169: calories;
- 11 grams: sugars;
- 90 grams: protein;
- 1757 milligrams: sodium;
- 14 grams: saturated fat;
- 3 grams: dietary fiber;
- 9 grams: monounsaturated fat;
- 5 grams: polyunsaturated fat;
- 104 grams: carbohydrates;
- 33 grams: fat;

190. Napa Cabbage Salad

Serving: 6 servings | Prep: | Cook: | Ready in: 12mins

Ingredients

- 3 to 4 cloves garlic, peeled, crushed and chopped (2 teaspoons)
- ½ teaspoon salt
- ½ teaspoon freshly ground black pepper
- 2 teaspoons Dijon-style mustard
- 1 tablespoon red-wine vinegar
- 1 tablespoon soy sauce
- 3 tablespoons canola oil
- 1 firm head Napa cabbage (about 1 pound)

Direction

- Put the garlic in a large salad bowl and mix in all the remaining ingredients except the cabbage.
- Trim the cabbage, removing and discarding damaged or wilted leaves, and cut the head crosswise into 1-inch slices. You should have about 8 cups. Wash well and spin dry in a salad dryer (moisture would dilute the dressing). Ten or 15 minutes before serving, add the cabbage to the dressing, toss well and set aside, so the dressing can penetrate the cabbage and soften it slightly.

Nutrition Information

- 76: calories;
- 2 grams: carbohydrates;
- 214 milligrams: sodium;
- 7 grams: fat;
- 1 gram: protein;
- 0 grams: trans fat;
- 4 grams: monounsaturated fat;

191. Octopus, Galician Style

Serving: 4 to 8 servings | Prep: | Cook: | Ready in: 2hours

Ingredients

- 1 octopus, about 3 pounds
- Coarse salt
- 4 medium to large potatoes
- Smoked pimentón
- Olive oil

Direction

- Thaw octopus if necessary, either for 24 hours in refrigerator, or for a few hours in a couple of changes of cold water. With a scissors, remove skinny tips of tentacles and, cutting through webbing that connects them, separate the 8 tentacles and discard head. (Alternatively, you can cook the octopus whole and cut it up after cooking.)
- Bring a large pot of water to a boil and salt it well. Put octopus in water and, when it returns to boil, cover and adjust heat so water simmers gently. Cook an hour or so, until octopus is tender. Meanwhile peel potatoes and cut into 2-inch slices. Lower them into water and cook until tender, about a half hour. Remove if they're done before octopus, and keep warm.
- When octopus is tender, remove it and drain. Put potatoes on a platter and cut octopus into pieces (again, a scissors is easiest); top potatoes with it. Drizzle all liberally with pimentón, olive oil and coarse salt, and serve hot or warm.

192. Orange Chrysanthemum Iced Tea With Peach Ice Cubes

Serving: One quart | Prep: | Cook: | Ready in: 5mins

Ingredients

- 2 ½ cups peach nectar
- 4 cups cold, brewed chrysanthemum tea
- ½ cup cold, fresh orange juice
- Fresh mint leaves, for garnish

Direction

- Pour the peach nectar into an ice cube tray and freeze overnight. Whisk together the tea and orange juice. Place a few of the ice cubes in each glass and pour the tea over them. Let stand a few minutes until the cubes begin to melt. Stir, garnish with mint and serve.

Nutrition Information

- 25: calories;
- 0 grams: protein;
- 6 grams: sugars;
- 5 milligrams: sodium;

193. Orange Scented Lamb With Fennel And Greens

Serving: 2 servings | Prep: | Cook: | Ready in: 30mins

Ingredients

- 6 ounces boneless leg of lamb
- 1 teaspoon olive oil
- 1 ½ pounds fennel
- 3 scallions
- 2 medium garlic cloves
- 1 pound assorted bitter greens, like collard greens, beet greens, Swiss chard
- ½ cup no-salt-added beef stock or broth
- 2 tablespoons apple cider vinegar
- 1 orange, for the zest
- ⅛ teaspoon salt
- Freshly ground black pepper

Direction

- Wash and dry lamb, and cut into 1/8-inch-thick strips;
- Heat nonstick pan until it is very hot; reduce heat to medium-high. Add oil and saute lamb until it is brown on both sides. Remove lamb from pan (but reserve pan juices).
- Wash and trim fennel, and remove tough core. Slice into thin strips. Add to the pan with the lamb juices. Brown.
- Wash and trim scallions, and cut into thin rounds. Mince garlic. Add scallions and garlic to fennel, and continue cooking.

- Wash greens and remove tough stems. When fennel is lightly browned, add the greens, beef stock and vinegar. Cover, and reduce heat to simmer.
- Grate orange rind, and stir into pan along with salt and pepper and the reserved lamb. Continue cooking until fennel is tender.

Nutrition Information

- 406: calories;
- 2 grams: polyunsaturated fat;
- 46 grams: carbohydrates;
- 17 grams: dietary fiber;
- 23 grams: sugars;
- 27 grams: protein;
- 6 grams: saturated fat;
- 7 grams: monounsaturated fat;
- 16 grams: fat;
- 978 milligrams: sodium;

194. Pad Thai

Serving: 2 servings | Prep: | Cook: | Ready in: 25mins

Ingredients

- 8 ounces rice sticks
- 1 clove garlic
- 1 ½ cups water
- 1 tablespoon fish sauce
- 1 tablespoon lime juice
- 1 tablespoon tamarind paste
- 2 tablespoons sugar
- ⅛ to ¼ teaspoon red pepper flakes
- 1 scallion
- 5 sprigs cilantro, to yield 1 tablespoon chopped
- 1 cup bean sprouts
- 10 ounces cooked shrimp
- 1 whole egg and 1 egg white
- 1 teaspoon oil
- 1 lime

Direction

- Soak the rice sticks in enough cold water to cover well.
- To make sauce, mince garlic, and in large bowl mix it with the water, fish sauce, lime juice, tamarind paste, sugar and red pepper flakes.
- Wash, dry and thinly slice the scallion; wash, dry and chop the cilantro; wash the bean sprouts.
- Cut shrimp in half. (Buy the shrimp cooked and peeled to save time. Or to save money, buy the shrimp raw, and shell and cook them yourself.)
- Lightly whisk egg and egg white.
- Heat oil in nonstick skillet; stir in eggs, and cook, stirring, until firm.
- Drain the rice sticks, and stir into egg mixture with shrimp, the sauce and the bean sprouts. Cook until rice sticks are well coated and warm.
- Cut lime into quarters.
- Top rice stick mixture with scallion and cilantro and serve with lime wedges.

Nutrition Information

- 734: calories;
- 2324 milligrams: sodium;
- 0 grams: trans fat;
- 8 grams: fat;
- 2 grams: polyunsaturated fat;
- 3 grams: monounsaturated fat;
- 117 grams: carbohydrates;
- 4 grams: dietary fiber;
- 18 grams: sugars;
- 46 grams: protein;

195. Parsley Potatoes

Serving: 4 servings | Prep: | Cook: | Ready in: 15mins

Ingredients

- 8 red waxy new potatoes, about 1 pound
- Salt to taste if desired
- 1 tablespoon butter
- 1 tablespoon finely chopped parsley

Direction

- Cut the potatoes in half lengthwise. Strip away part of the peel lengthwise, leaving two red strips down the side of each potato half. As the potatoes are prepared, drop them into cold water.
- Drain the potatoes and put them in a saucepan. Add cold water to cover and salt. Bring to a boil and cook about 8 minutes or until tender. Drain.
- Add the butter to the potatoes and toss. Sprinkle with parsley and serve.

Nutrition Information

- 157: calories;
- 1 gram: sugars;
- 30 grams: carbohydrates;
- 4 grams: dietary fiber;
- 406 milligrams: sodium;
- 3 grams: protein;
- 2 grams: saturated fat;
- 0 grams: polyunsaturated fat;

---

196. Parsley And Cracked Wheat Salad

Serving: Four servings | Prep: | Cook: | Ready in: 15mins

Ingredients

- 1 cup cracked wheat
- 6 cups cold water
- ¾ cup chopped fresh parsley
- 2 tablespoons plus 2 teaspoons fresh lemon juice
- 1 teaspoon olive oil
- 1 teaspoon salt plus more to taste
- Freshly ground pepper to taste

Direction

- Combine the cracked wheat and the water in a large pot over medium heat and bring to a boil. Reduce heat and cook at a bare simmer for 10 minutes. Drain well, place in a medium bowl and let cool. Toss in remaining ingredients. Divide among 4 plates and serve.

Nutrition Information

- 158: calories;
- 603 milligrams: sodium;
- 2 grams: fat;
- 0 grams: polyunsaturated fat;
- 1 gram: sugars;
- 33 grams: carbohydrates;
- 6 grams: dietary fiber;
- 5 grams: protein;

---

197. Pasta With Cauliflower, Spicy Tomato Sauce And Capers

Serving: 4 servings | Prep: | Cook: | Ready in: 35mins

Ingredients

- 1 small cauliflower or 1/2 large cauliflower, broken into florets about 1 pound
- Salt to taste
- 2 tablespoons extra virgin olive oil
- 2 garlic cloves, minced
- ¼ teaspoon red chili flakes
- 1 14-ounce can chopped tomatoes with juice, pulsed a few times in a food processor or mini processor
- Pinch of sugar
- 2 tablespoons capers, rinsed and chopped
- ¾ pound perciatelli (bucatini)
- ¼ cup chopped fresh parsley
- 2 ounces pecorino, grated (1/2 cup), or 1 ounce each pecorino and Parmesan

Direction

- Bring a large pot of water to a boil while you core the cauliflower and break it into florets. Add a generous amount of salt to the water and blanch the cauliflower for 5 minutes, or until tender. Use a skimmer or strainer to scoop the cauliflower from the water and transfer to a bowl of cold water. Drain and chop the florets into small pieces. Keep the water at a simmer.
- Heat the oil over medium heat in a wide, heavy skillet and add the garlic and chili flakes. Cook, stirring, until the garlic is fragrant, about 30 seconds, and stir in the puréed tomatoes, a pinch of sugar, and salt to taste. Add the capers and cauliflower and simmer 10 to 15 minutes, until the tomatoes have cooked down and smell fragrant. Taste and adjust seasonings.
- Bring the water in the pot back to a boil and add the perciatelli. Cook al dente, usually about 7 or 8 minutes. Add about 1/2 cup of the pasta water to the pan with the cauliflower and stir. Drain the pasta and add to the pan, along with the parsley and the pecorino. Stir together and serve.

Nutrition Information

- 477: calories;
- 13 grams: fat;
- 4 grams: saturated fat;
- 6 grams: sugars;
- 1 gram: polyunsaturated fat;
- 72 grams: carbohydrates;
- 19 grams: protein;
- 659 milligrams: sodium;

198. Pasta With Fresh Tomato Sauce

Serving: 4 to 6 servings | Prep: | Cook: | Ready in: 20mins

Ingredients

- Salt
- 3 tablespoons butter or olive oil
- 1 ½ to 2 pounds tomatoes, cored and roughly chopped
- 1 pound linguine, spaghetti or other long pasta
- ½ cup freshly grated Parmigiano-Reggiano
- Salt and freshly ground black pepper to taste

Direction

- Bring a large pot of water to a boil, and salt it. Place the butter or oil in an 8- or 10-inch skillet, and turn heat to medium. When butter melts or oil is hot, add tomatoes and turn heat to high.
- Cook, stirring occasionally, until tomatoes begin to juice up, then turn the heat to low and keep warm, stirring occasionally, while you cook pasta.
- Cook pasta until it is tender but firm. Drain, and toss with tomatoes and cheese. Season with salt and pepper, toss again and serve immediately.

Nutrition Information

- 403: calories;
- 523 milligrams: sodium;
- 11 grams: fat;
- 3 grams: saturated fat;
- 1 gram: polyunsaturated fat;
- 4 grams: dietary fiber;
- 14 grams: protein;
- 6 grams: sugars;
- 62 grams: carbohydrates;

199. Pasta With Mushrooms, Cauliflower And Peas

Serving: 3 servings | Prep: | Cook: | Ready in: 45mins

Ingredients

- 1 pound fresh white mushrooms
- 1 teaspoon olive oil
- 8 ounces whole onion or 7 ounces chopped onion (1 2/3 cups)
- 4 ripe plum tomatoes
- 1 tablespoon parsley
- 3 cups cauliflower florettes
- ¼ teaspoon hot pepper flakes
- 8 ounces fresh pasta shells or other small pasta
- 1 cup nonfat yogurt
- 1 cup reduced fat ricotta
- 2 ounces Parmigiano Reggiano (or 4 tablespoons, grated)
- 1 cup frozen peas
- Freshly ground black pepper
- ¼ teaspoon salt, optional

Direction

- Wash and trim mushrooms and slice them in food processor.
- Heat oil in large nonstick pot or skillet; add mushrooms and cook over medium-high heat.
- Chop whole onions finely in food processor by pulsing and add to mushrooms; continue to saute until onions soften.
- Bring water for pasta to boil in covered pot.
- Wash, trim and quarter tomatoes; wash, dry and coarsely chop parsley; chop tomatoes and parsley finely in food processor by pulsing; add to onions and mushrooms; reduce heat to simmer.
- Chop cauliflower in food processor by pulsing; add to pot with hot pepper flakes; cover and continue cooking about 5 minutes, until vegetables are soft.
- Cook the pasta.
- In food processor, blend yogurt and ricotta. Coarsely grate Parmigiano and stir into yogurt mixture.
- Add the peas to the vegetables and cook 2 minutes longer.
- Remove from heat; stir in yogurt mixture; season with pepper and salt, if desired.
- Drain pasta and stir in.

Nutrition Information

- 703: calories;
- 20 grams: fat;
- 6 grams: monounsaturated fat;
- 94 grams: carbohydrates;
- 21 grams: sugars;
- 41 grams: protein;
- 11 grams: dietary fiber;
- 1 gram: polyunsaturated fat;
- 493 milligrams: sodium;

200. Pasta E Fagioli

Serving: 8 servings | Prep: | Cook: | Ready in: 1hours50mins

Ingredients

- 1 recipe Simmered Pintos using only 1/2 pound (about 1 1/8 cups) beans
- 1 tablespoon extra virgin olive oil
- 1 medium or large onion, chopped
- 1 ½ teaspoons chopped fresh rosemary
- 2 large garlic cloves, minced
- 1 28-ounce can chopped tomatoes with juice
- Pinch of sugar
- Salt and freshly ground pepper
- 1 tablespoon tomato paste
- 1 small dried red pepper, or 1/4 to 1/2 teaspoon red pepper flakes (optional)
- A bouquet garni made with a bay leaf, 1 or 2 Parmesan rinds, and a few sprigs of thyme and parsley
- 6 ounces elbow macaroni or small shells (1 cup)
- 2 to 3 tablespoons chopped fresh parsley
- 2 ounces Parmesan cheese, grated (1/2 cup), optional

Direction

- Make the simmered beans as directed, changing only the amount of beans (use 2 quarts water). Remove onion and bay leaf,

using tongs or a slotted spoon, as directed. Place a strainer over a bowl and drain beans. Measure broth and top up with enough water to make 6 cups.
- Heat oil over medium heat in a large, heavy casserole or Dutch oven and add chopped onion. Cook, stirring, until just tender, about 5 minutes. Add rosemary and garlic and stir together for another minute, until garlic is fragrant. Stir in tomatoes, add sugar, salt and pepper, and cook, stirring often, until tomatoes have cooked down and the mixture is very fragrant, 10 to 15 minutes.
- Add broth from the beans, tomato paste, hot pepper, bouquet garni, and salt to taste and bring to a boil. Reduce heat, cover and simmer 30 minutes. Stir in beans and heat through. Taste and adjust salt.
- 10 to 15 minutes before serving, stir in pasta. When it is cooked al dente, taste and adjust seasonings, stir in parsley, and serve, passing Parmesan in a bowl.

Nutrition Information

- 92: calories;
- 0 grams: polyunsaturated fat;
- 1 gram: monounsaturated fat;
- 16 grams: carbohydrates;
- 3 grams: protein;
- 4 grams: sugars;
- 322 milligrams: sodium;
- 2 grams: fat;

201. Paupiettes Of Sole With Spinach And Mushroom Stuffing

Serving: Four servings | Prep: | Cook: | Ready in: 30mins

Ingredients

- 4 skinless, boneless fillets of sole (or use any nonoily white-fleshed fish such as fluke or flounder), about 1/4 pound each
- Salt to taste, if desired
- Freshly ground pepper to taste
- ¾ pound fresh spinach
- 2 tablespoons butter
- 2 tablespoons finely chopped shallots
- ½ pound fresh mushrooms, thinly sliced, about 3 cups
- ⅛ teaspoon freshly grated nutmeg
- 1 egg yolk
- Ginger butter sauce (see recipe)

Direction

- Sprinkle the fillets with salt and pepper and set aside.
- Pick over the spinach. Remove and discard any tough stems and blemished leaves. Rinse and drain the spinach well. There should be about 8 cups loosely packed. Set aside.
- Heat the butter in a skillet and add the shallots. Cook briefly, stirring, and add the mushrooms, salt, pepper and nutmeg. Cook, stirring, until the mushrooms are wilted. Add the spinach and cook until wilted. Continue cooking until all the moisture evaporates.
- Scrape the mixture into a bowl and add the egg yolk. Let stand until cool.
- Place the fillets of fish on a flat surface, skinned side up. Spoon an equal portion of the spinach and mushroom mixture onto the center of each fillet. Roll the fillets jellyroll style to enclose the filling.
- Bring a quantity of water to the boil in the bottom of a steamer. Arrange the rolled fillets, seam side down, on a steamer rack. Set the rack over the steamer bottom. Steam five minutes. Serve hot with a ginger butter sauce (see recipe).

Nutrition Information

- 219: calories;
- 5 grams: saturated fat;
- 0 grams: trans fat;

- 1 gram: polyunsaturated fat;
- 8 grams: carbohydrates;
- 2 grams: sugars;
- 25 grams: protein;
- 762 milligrams: sodium;
- 10 grams: fat;
- 3 grams: dietary fiber;

202. Pear Smoothie With Spinach, Celery And Ginger

Serving: 1 generous serving | Prep: | Cook: | Ready in: 2mins

Ingredients

- ½ cup washed spinach leaves (baby or bunch)
- 1 ripe pear, peeled, quartered, cored and cut in chunks
- ¼ cup chopped celery
- 1 quarter-size slice fresh ginger, peeled
- A handful of baby arugula
- 1 to 2 tablespoons mint leaves (to taste)
- ½ teaspoon chia seeds
- ½ banana (50 g), frozen if possible, sliced
- 1 teaspoon fresh lemon juice
- 1 teaspoon honey or agave nectar
- 1 cup plain kefir or yogurt
- 1 or 2 ice cubes

Direction

- Place all of the ingredients in a blender and blend at high speed for 1 minute, or until smooth. Serve at once.

Nutrition Information

- 330: calories;
- 9 grams: dietary fiber;
- 2 grams: monounsaturated fat;
- 0 grams: trans fat;
- 1 gram: polyunsaturated fat;
- 56 grams: carbohydrates;

- 39 grams: sugars;
- 11 grams: protein;
- 151 milligrams: sodium;
- 5 grams: saturated fat;

203. Penne With Mushroom Ragout And Spinach

Serving: Serves 4 | Prep: | Cook: | Ready in: 1hours

Ingredients

- ½ ounce (about 1/2 cup) dried porcini mushrooms
- 2 tablespoons extra virgin olive oil
- ½ medium onion or 2 shallots, chopped
- 2 garlic cloves, minced
- 1 pound mixed regular and wild mushrooms or 1 pound regular white or cremini mushrooms, trimmed and cut in thick slices (or torn into smaller pieces, depending on the type of mushroom)
- Salt and freshly ground pepper
- ¼ cup fruity red wine, such as a Côtes du Rhone or Côtes du Luberon
- 2 teaspoons chopped fresh thyme or a combination of thyme and rosemary
- 6 ounces baby spinach or 12 ounces bunch spinach (1 bunch), stemmed and thoroughly cleaned
- ¾ pound penne
- Freshly grated Parmesan to taste

Direction

- Place the dried mushrooms in a Pyrex measuring cup and pour on 2 cups boiling water. Let soak 30 minutes, while you prepare the other ingredients. Place a strainer over a bowl, line it with cheesecloth or paper towels, and drain the mushrooms. Squeeze the mushrooms over the strainer to extract all the flavorful juices. Then rinse the mushrooms, away from the bowl with the soaking liquid, until they are free of sand. Squeeze dry and set aside. If very large, chop coarsely. Measure out 1 cup of the soaking liquid and set aside.

- Heat the olive oil in a large, heavy, nonstick skillet over medium heat and add the onion or shallots. Cook, stirring often, until tender, about 5 minutes. Turn up the heat to medium-high and add the fresh mushrooms. Cook, stirring often, until they begin to soften and sweat, about 5 minutes. Add the garlic and salt to taste, stir together for about 30 seconds, then add the reconstituted dried mushrooms and the wine and turn the heat to high. Cook, stirring, until the liquid boils down and glazes the mushrooms. Add the herbs and the mushroom soaking liquid. Bring to a simmer, add salt to taste, and cook over medium-high heat, stirring often, until the mushrooms are thoroughly tender and fragrant. Turn off the heat, stir in some freshly ground pepper, taste and adjust salt.
- Bring a large pot of water to a boil and salt generously. Fill a bowl with ice water. Add the spinach to the boiling water and blanch for 20 seconds only. Remove with a skimmer and transfer to the ice water, then drain and squeeze out water. Chop coarsely and add to the mushrooms. Reheat gently over low heat.
- Bring the water back to a boil and cook the pasta al dente following the timing suggestions on the package. If there is not much broth in the pan with the mushrooms and spinach, add a ladleful of pasta water. Drain the pasta, toss with the mushrooms and spinach, add Parmesan to taste, and serve at once.

Nutrition Information

- 442: calories;
- 641 milligrams: sodium;
- 8 grams: fat;
- 1 gram: polyunsaturated fat;
- 5 grams: sugars;
- 75 grams: carbohydrates;
- 16 grams: protein;

204. Penne With Sun Dried Tomatoes And Chicken

Serving: 4 main-dish servings | Prep: | Cook: | Ready in: 45mins

Ingredients

- ¼ cup sun-dried tomatoes, not packed in oil
- 6 ounces boneless, skinless chicken breast
- ¼ cup dry white wine
- 1 tablespoon Italian seasoning
- 3 tablespoons chopped shallot (1 large shallot)
- 1 ¼ cups chopped fresh portobello mushrooms (2 smallish mushrooms)
- ½ cup fresh peas or thawed frozen peas
- 8 ounces dried penne
- Light vegetable-oil cooking spray
- 5 garlic cloves, peeled and minced
- 1 tablespoon flour
- 12 ounces evaporated skim milk
- ⅛ teaspoon ground nutmeg
- ⅛ teaspoon crushed red pepper flakes
- ½ cup chopped fresh basil
- ¼ teaspoon salt, optional
- 5 medium black olives, thinly sliced

Direction

- Preheat the oven to 350 degrees.
- Put the sun-dried tomatoes in a bowl, add 1/2-cup boiling water and set the bowl aside for the tomatoes to reconstitute. Fill a large pot with water, and bring it to a boil.
- Combine the chicken and wine in a shallow baking dish. Sprinkle the Italian seasoning on top. Bake for 15 to 20 minutes, until the meat is no longer pink and the juices run clear. Remove and shred the chicken, reserving the cooking juices.
- Drain the sun-dried tomatoes, and slice them thin.
- Pour the reserved cooking juices from the chicken into a saute pan. Add the shallot, mushrooms, peas and tomatoes. Saute over

low heat for a few minutes, until the liquid has been absorbed and the vegetables are wilted. Remove the pan from the heat and cover it to keep the vegetables warm.
- Add the penne to the boiling water in the large pot, and cook over high heat to desired doneness, 8 to 12 minutes.
- While the pasta is cooking, make the sauce. Preheat a small heavy saucepan for about 1 minute over medium heat; then spray it twice with the vegetable oil. Toss in the garlic and flour; then, whisk in the evaporated milk. Add the nutmeg and red pepper flakes. Whisking constantly, bring the mixture to a boil, and continue cooking for about 5 minutes, until thickened. Reduce the heat to the lowest setting, and stir in basil.
- Drain the cooked pasta, and transfer to a warm serving bowl. Add the chicken, vegetables and sauce. Season with salt, if desired, and toss. Garnish with olive slices.

Nutrition Information

- 388: calories;
- 7 grams: fat;
- 0 grams: trans fat;
- 9 grams: sugars;
- 128 milligrams: sodium;
- 1 gram: polyunsaturated fat;
- 3 grams: monounsaturated fat;
- 57 grams: carbohydrates;
- 4 grams: dietary fiber;
- 23 grams: protein;

205. Peppers Stuffed With Rice, Zucchini And Herbs

Serving: Serves 6 | Prep: | Cook: | Ready in: 2hours

Ingredients

- 6 medium peppers, preferably green
- 2 medium zucchini (about 3/4 pound), shredded
- Salt to taste
- ⅓ cup extra virgin olive oil
- 2 garlic cloves, minced
- ½ cup finely chopped fresh mint
- ¼ cup chopped fresh dill or parsley
- 1 scant cup uncooked medium grain rice
- Freshly ground pepper
- 2 tablespoons tomato paste dissolved in 2/3 cup water
- 2 tablespoons freshly squeezed lemon juice

Direction

- Prepare the peppers. With a sharp paring knife, cut away the tops, then reach in and pull out the membranes and seeds.
- Toss the shredded zucchini with salt and let drain in a colander for 20 minutes. Take up handfuls of zucchini and squeeze out as much liquid as possible. Transfer to a medium bowl and add the garlic, mint, parsley or dill, and rice. Season with salt and pepper. Stir in 1/4 cup of the olive oil and let sit for 10 minutes.
- Meanwhile preheat the oven to 375 degrees. Oil a baking dish large enough to accommodate all of the peppers. Fill the peppers about 3/4 of the way full with the stuffing, and replace the caps. Place in the oiled baking dish. Mix together the tomato paste and water with the remaining olive oil and the lemon juice. Season to taste. Add to the baking dish. Cover the dish with foil. Place in the oven and bake 45 minutes to an hour, until the peppers are soft. Remove from the heat and allow to cool to room temperature, or serve hot. Remove the tops of the peppers and spoon the sauce in the baking dish over the rice before serving.

Nutrition Information

- 268: calories;
- 13 grams: fat;
- 9 grams: monounsaturated fat;
- 1 gram: polyunsaturated fat;

- 36 grams: carbohydrates;
- 4 grams: protein;
- 558 milligrams: sodium;
- 2 grams: saturated fat;
- 5 grams: sugars;

206. Perciatelli With Broccoli, Tomatoes And Anchovies

Serving: Serves 4 | Prep: | Cook: | Ready in: 1hours

Ingredients

- ¼ cup golden raisins or currants (optional)
- 1 pound baby broccoli
- Salt to taste
- 2 tablespoons extra virgin olive oil
- 2 garlic cloves, minced
- 2 anchovy fillets, rinsed and chopped
- 2 teaspoons fresh thyme leaves
- 1 pound tomatoes, grated, or 1 14-ounce can chopped tomatoes, with juice
- 8 imported black olives, pitted and chopped
- Freshly ground pepper to taste
- ¾ pound perciatelli (also sold as bucatini) or spaghetti
- 2 to 4 tablespoons grated pecorino or Parmesan cheese

Direction

- Place the raisins in a small bowl and cover with warm water. Let sit for 20 minutes while you prepare the other ingredients.
- Bring a large pot of water to a boil, salt generously and add the baby broccoli. Blanch for 4 minutes and, using a skimmer or tongs, transfer to a bowl of cold water. Drain and shake out excess water. If the stems are thick and hard, peel. Chop coarsely.
- Heat the olive oil over medium heat in a large, heavy skillet and add the garlic. Cook, stirring, until it smells fragrant, about 30 seconds to a minute, and add the anchovies, thyme and tomatoes. Turn the heat down to medium-low and cook, stirring often, until the tomatoes have cooked down and smell fragrant, about 10 minutes. Stir in the olives. Drain the raisins or currants and add, along with the broccoli and about 1/4 cup of the cooking water from the broccoli. Season to taste with salt and pepper. Cover, turn the heat to low and simmer 5 to 10 minutes, stirring occasionally, until the broccoli is very tender and the sauce is fragrant. Keep warm while you cook the pasta.
- Bring the water back to a boil and cook the pasta al dente, following the timing instructions on the package. Check the sauce and if it seems dry add another 1/4 to 1/2 cup of the pasta cooking water. Drain the pasta and transfer to the pan with the sauce. Toss together and serve, sprinkled with pecorino or Parmesan. If desired, drizzle a little olive oil over each serving.

Nutrition Information

- 490: calories;
- 7 grams: sugars;
- 2 grams: polyunsaturated fat;
- 77 grams: carbohydrates;
- 792 milligrams: sodium;
- 12 grams: fat;
- 3 grams: saturated fat;
- 20 grams: protein;
- 8 grams: dietary fiber;

207. Phillip Schulz's Brine Cure For Smoked Bluefish

Serving: About 1 1/2 quarts of brine | Prep: | Cook: | Ready in: 10mins

Ingredients

- 1 quart cool water
- ½ cup kosher salt
- ¼ cup honey

- ¼ cup golden rum
- ¼ cup lemon juice
- 10 cloves
- 10 black peppercorns
- 10 allspice berries
- 1 bay leaf

Direction

- Combine all ingredients in a ceramic, glass or stainless-steel bowl. Mr. Schulz marinates large bluefish fillets, more than 1 pound each, 2 days in this brine. Smaller fillets can be marinated 1 day or overnight.

208. Pickled Broccoli Stems

Serving: Makes about 1/2 cup | Prep: | Cook: | Ready in: 10mins

Ingredients

- 3 or 4 broccoli stems (from one bunch)
- ½ teaspoon salt, preferably kosher salt
- 1 medium size garlic clove, minced or pureed
- 1 tablespoon sherry vinegar
- 2 tablespoons extra virgin olive oil

Direction

- Peel the broccoli stems and cut, either crosswise into 1/4 inch thick medallions, or lengthwise in 1/4 inch thick slices (as pictured above) Place in a jar, add the salt, cover tightly and shake the jar to toss the stems with the salt. Refrigerate for several hours or overnight.
- Drain the water that has accumulated in the jar. Add the garlic, vinegar, and olive oil and toss together. Refrigerate for several hours or overnight. Serve with toothpicks.

Nutrition Information

- 149: calories;
- 231 milligrams: sodium;
- 14 grams: fat;
- 2 grams: protein;
- 10 grams: monounsaturated fat;
- 1 gram: sugars;
- 6 grams: carbohydrates;

209. Pierre Franey's Pasta With Clams

Serving: 4 appetizer servings | Prep: | Cook: | Ready in: 30mins

Ingredients

- 1 tablespoon olive oil
- 2 medium cloves garlic, chopped fine
- 1 teaspoon fresh thyme leaves
- 1 cup fresh clam juice
- ¼ cup dry white wine
- 1 cup (or more) heavy cream
- 1 cup loosely packed fresh basil leaves, plus more to taste
- 1 pint shucked chowder or cherrystone clams, coarsely chopped
- Salt and freshly ground pepper
- 1 pound fresh fettuccine
- ½ cup grated fresh Parmesan, or to taste

Direction

- In a 10- or 12-inch frying pan, heat the olive oil over medium heat and fry the garlic until fragrant, taking care not to burn it. Add the thyme and clam juice and reduce by half, about 4 minutes. Add the wine and reduce, about 2 minutes. Add 1 cup heavy cream and simmer till the mixture thickens slightly, about 5 minutes. Remove from heat.
- Combine 1 cup of the basil leaves and the clams and add to the sauce. Season with salt and pepper. Set aside and keep warm.
- Cook the fettuccine until al dente. Reserve 1 cup of the cooking water, then drain. Add the pasta to the sauce and stir to coat. Add Parmesan to taste. Correct the seasonings. If

the sauce is too thick, add some of the reserved pasta water or additional cream, sparingly. Simmer the pasta and stir until sauce is the desired thickness. Add more basil to taste and serve immediately.

Nutrition Information

- 748: calories;
- 33 grams: fat;
- 17 grams: saturated fat;
- 3 grams: polyunsaturated fat;
- 2 grams: sugars;
- 1307 milligrams: sodium;
- 10 grams: monounsaturated fat;
- 70 grams: carbohydrates;
- 40 grams: protein;
- 0 grams: dietary fiber;

210. Pizza Fantasy

Serving: 2 servings | Prep: | Cook: | Ready in: 45mins

Ingredients

- 1 pound new potatoes
- Nonstick pan spray
- 12 ounces whole red or yellow peppers, or 11 ounces ready-cut (about 3 cups)
- 1 tablespoon olive oil
- 8 ounces whole zucchini, or 7 ounces ready-cut (about 1 1/3 cups)
- 6 ounces whole mushrooms, or 5 ounces ready-cut (2 cups)
- 4 7-to-8-inch flour tortillas (the no-oil variety, if possible)
- 10 medium imported olives
- 6 ounces cooked peeled shrimp
- ⅛ teaspoon salt
- 1 ounce Parmigiano Reggiano (1/3 cup grated)

Direction

- Prepare stove-top grill; turn oven to 450 degrees.
- Scrub and slice potatoes thin (less than 1/4-inch). Spray on both sides with nonstick pan spray, and grill until brown on both sides.
- Wash, trim, seed and slice whole peppers.
- Heat a large nonstick pan until very hot. Reduce heat to medium-high; add oil and saute peppers until soft.
- Meanwhile wash, trim and slice whole zucchini, and add.
- Wash, trim and slice whole mushrooms, and add. Cook until vegetables have softened.
- Wrap two tortillas in aluminum foil, and heat in oven or toaster oven for 3 to 5 minutes.
- Pit olives and stir into vegetables along with the shrimp and the grilled potatoes. Add salt.
- Grate cheese.
- Arrange half of the topping on two hot tortillas. Sprinkle with half the cheese.
- Heat remaining two tortillas while eating the first two, and add the rest of the topping.

Nutrition Information

- 814: calories;
- 6 grams: polyunsaturated fat;
- 0 grams: trans fat;
- 16 grams: monounsaturated fat;
- 107 grams: carbohydrates;
- 1701 milligrams: sodium;
- 30 grams: fat;
- 11 grams: dietary fiber;
- 8 grams: sugars;
- 35 grams: protein;

211. Pizza On The Grill

Serving: 3 10-inch pizzas | Prep: | Cook: | Ready in: 3hours

Ingredients

- 8 grams (2 teaspoons) active dry or fresh yeast

- 225 grams (1 cup) warm water
- 5 grams (1 teaspoon) sugar
- 12 ½ grams (1 tablespoon) extra virgin olive oil, plus additional for brushing the pizza crusts
- 185 grams (approximately 1 1/2 cups) whole wheat flour
- 125 to 185 grams (approximately 1 to 1 1/2 cups) unbleached all-purpose flour
- 10 grams (1 1/4 teaspoons) salt
- ¾ cup marinara sauce made with fresh or canned tomatoes
- 5 to 6 ounces mozzarella, shredded if fresh, sliced if low-moisture
- Fresh basil leaves

Direction

-
-

Nutrition Information

- 615: calories;
- 18 grams: fat;
- 8 grams: saturated fat;
- 7 grams: monounsaturated fat;
- 4 grams: sugars;
- 719 milligrams: sodium;
- 2 grams: polyunsaturated fat;
- 90 grams: carbohydrates;
- 10 grams: dietary fiber;
- 27 grams: protein;

212. Platanos Maduros (Fried Yellow Plantains)

Serving: Six to eight servings | Prep: | Cook: | Ready in: 5mins

Ingredients

- 3 ripe yellow plantains
- Oil for frying

Direction

- Peel and slice the plantains in half crosswise, then again lengthwise. Cut each piece into 2 or 3 1/4-inch slices.
- Heat the oil (a depth of about 1/2 inch) in an cast-iron skillet until very hot. Add the plantain slices and fry until soft and golden brown, about 45 seconds to 1 minute.

Nutrition Information

- 171: calories;
- 1 gram: protein;
- 0 grams: trans fat;
- 6 grams: monounsaturated fat;
- 21 grams: carbohydrates;
- 2 grams: dietary fiber;
- 3 milligrams: sodium;
- 3 grams: polyunsaturated fat;
- 10 grams: sugars;

213. Poached Chicken Breasts With Tomatillos And Jalapeños

Serving: 4 servings | Prep: | Cook: | Ready in: 2hours

Ingredients

- 1 quart chicken stock, plus more as needed (or use salted water)
- 1 ¼ pounds boneless, skinless chicken breasts (3 medium breasts)
- 1 ½ pounds tomatillos, cut into 1/2-inch chunks
- 2 to 3 jalapeños, thinly sliced
- 6 tablespoons extra-virgin olive oil, plus more as needed
- ¾ teaspoon kosher salt, plus more as needed
- 1 teaspoon cumin seeds
- 4 garlic cloves, thinly sliced
- ¾ cup cilantro leaves, roughly chopped
- 3 scallions, thinly sliced
- Finely grated zest of 1/2 lime

- 1 avocado, sliced
- Fresh lime juice, to taste

Direction

- Place racks in the top and bottom third of the oven and heat to 275 degrees. In the microwave or in a small pot on the stove, heat chicken stock until it comes to a simmer.
- Place chicken in a small baking dish and cover with hot chicken stock.
- On a rimmed baking sheet, toss together tomatillos, jalapeños, 2 tablespoons oil, 3/4 teaspoon salt, and cumin seeds. Spread into a single layer on the sheet, then nudge the tomatillos aside to make room in 1 corner for a small ramekin. Fill ramekin with garlic and remaining 4 tablespoons oil or more as needed to cover the garlic.
- Place chicken on top oven rack until chicken is cooked through (a thermometer inserted in the center should read 155 degrees), 55 minutes to 1 hour and 10 minutes. At the same time, bake tomatillos on bottom rack, tossing occasionally, until they are tender, and garlic is light golden, 1 to 1 1/2 hours. If chicken is ready before the tomatillos, remove it from the oven and leave it in the pan covered in stock to keep it warm until everything is done.
- Use a slotted spoon to remove garlic from oil and coarsely chop. Remove chicken from stock (save stock for another use; it can be frozen for up to 3 months), and slice the meat.
- To assemble, toss together tomatillos, chopped garlic, cilantro, scallions, lime zest and salt to taste. Drizzle fresh lime juice and garlic oil all over the chicken and avocado if you like, and season with salt. Serve with the tomatillo salsa.

Nutrition Information

- 573: calories;
- 26 grams: carbohydrates;
- 8 grams: dietary fiber;
- 12 grams: sugars;
- 765 milligrams: sodium;
- 36 grams: fat;
- 6 grams: saturated fat;
- 22 grams: monounsaturated fat;
- 39 grams: protein;
- 0 grams: trans fat;
- 5 grams: polyunsaturated fat;

214. Pocket Sandwiches

Serving: 4 servings | Prep: | Cook: | Ready in: 20mins

Ingredients

- 1 ½ pounds ground turkey
- 1 large onion, chopped
- 1 large clove garlic, minced, or 1 teaspoon minced garlic in oil
- 2 large red or yellow peppers or one of each, chopped
- 1 tablespoon fresh oregano leaves or 1 teaspoon crushed, dried oregano
- 1 tablespoon fresh thyme leaves or 1 teaspoon crushed, dried thyme
- Freshly ground black pepper to taste
- 4 tablespoons red-wine vinegar
- 4 large whole-wheat pitas
- 2 large ripe tomatoes, sliced
- 8 scallions, sliced thin

Direction

- Heat nonstick skillet and saute turkey, breaking it up as you stir, until meat begins to brown.
- Add onion, garlic, peppers, oregano, thyme and pepper. Cook over medium heat until onion softens.
- Add vinegar and cook quickly to reduce liquid. Adjust seasonings.
- Toast the pitas and cut in half.
- Either serve the meat topped with cucumbers and yogurt salad (see recipe), with tomatoes and scallions on the side, or spoon some of the meat mixture into a pita half, add a tomato slice and scallions and serve the cucumber salad on the side.

Nutrition Information

- 495: calories;
- 0 grams: trans fat;
- 5 grams: sugars;
- 52 grams: carbohydrates;
- 42 grams: protein;
- 15 grams: fat;
- 4 grams: saturated fat;
- 395 milligrams: sodium;
- 9 grams: dietary fiber;

215. Polenta With Parmesan And Tomato Sauce

Serving: Serves four | Prep: | Cook: |Ready in: 1hours15mins

Ingredients

- 1 cup polenta
- 1 quart water
- 1 teaspoon salt
- 1 tablespoon butter
- ⅓ cup freshly grated Parmesan optional, plus additional for sprinkling
- 1 ½ cups Fresh Tomato Sauce or Simple Marinara Sauce

Direction

- Preheat the oven to 350 degrees. Combine the polenta, water and salt in a 2-quart baking dish. Stir together, and place in the oven. Bake 50 minutes. Remove from the oven, stir in the butter and return to the oven for 10 more minutes. Remove from the oven and stir again. Return to the oven for 10 minutes. Remove from the oven, and stir in the Parmesan, if using. Spoon onto plates, make a depression in the middle and spoon 1/4 heaped cup of simple tomato sauce into the depression. Sprinkle with Parmesan and serve.

Nutrition Information

- 219: calories;
- 4 grams: protein;
- 1 gram: polyunsaturated fat;
- 39 grams: carbohydrates;
- 3 grams: dietary fiber;
- 0 grams: trans fat;
- 6 grams: sugars;
- 880 milligrams: sodium;
- 5 grams: fat;
- 2 grams: saturated fat;

216. Pork Chops Baked With Apples And Onions

Serving: Four servings | Prep: | Cook: |Ready in: 30mins

Ingredients

- 1 teaspoon vegetable oil
- 4 1/2-inch-thick pork chops
- 1 medium onion, peeled and thinly sliced
- ¼ cup sherry
- ¼ cup apple cider
- 3 large Macintosh apples, peeled, cored and cut into 1/4-inch-thick slices
- ½ teaspoon salt, plus more to taste
- Freshly ground pepper to taste

Direction

- Preheat oven to 350 degrees. Heat the vegetable oil in a large, ovenproof skillet over medium-high heat. Add the pork chops and sear until golden brown, about 1 1/2 minutes per side. Place the pork chops on a plate and set aside.
- Add the onion to the skillet and cook, stirring often, for 2 minutes. Add the sherry and the cider and cook, stirring contantly, scraping up any browned bits stuck to the bottom of the pan. Add the apples, 1/2 teaspoon salt and

pepper to taste. Lower the heat and cook for 5 minutes.
- Push the pork chops down into the apple mixture and pour any juices accumulated on the plate over them. Cover with foil and bake until the pork chops are tender and cooked through, about 15 minutes. Uncover and season with additional salt and pepper to taste. Divide among 4 plates and serve.

Nutrition Information

- 467: calories;
- 6 grams: saturated fat;
- 3 grams: polyunsaturated fat;
- 42 grams: protein;
- 29 grams: carbohydrates;
- 5 grams: dietary fiber;
- 404 milligrams: sodium;
- 20 grams: sugars;
- 0 grams: trans fat;
- 8 grams: monounsaturated fat;

217. Pork Loin With Mustard Seed Crust

Serving: Six servings | Prep: | Cook: | Ready in: 2hours

Ingredients

- 8 ounces plain, nonfat yogurt
- 2 cloves garlic, peeled and minced
- 1 ½ teaspoons salt
- ½ teaspoon freshly ground pepper
- 1 3-pound boneless pork loin
- 2 tablespoons sugar
- 2 tablespoons mustard seeds

Direction

- Combine the yogurt, garlic, 1 teaspoon of the salt and pepper in a small bowl. Place the pork loin in a shallow baking dish and coat well with the yogurt mixture. Cover with plastic wrap and refrigerate for several hours or overnight. Let the pork stand at room temperature for 1 hour before roasting.
- Preheat the oven to 350 degrees. Wipe the marinade off of the pork and place in a roasting pan. Combine the sugar and mustard seeds and coat the pork with the mixture. Sprinkle with the remaining 1/2 teaspoon salt. Roast for 1 hour 20 minutes. Increase the oven temperature to 450 degrees and continue roasting until the pork reaches 145 to 150 degrees on a meat thermometer and the top is crisp, about 10 minutes longer. Let stand for 15 minutes, cut into slices and serve with the pan juices.

Nutrition Information

- 366: calories;
- 1 gram: polyunsaturated fat;
- 7 grams: sugars;
- 633 milligrams: sodium;
- 17 grams: fat;
- 3 grams: saturated fat;
- 0 grams: dietary fiber;
- 4 grams: monounsaturated fat;
- 8 grams: carbohydrates;
- 43 grams: protein;

218. Pork With Red Wine And Coriander

Serving: 4 servings | Prep: | Cook: | Ready in: 1hours

Ingredients

- 1 tablespoon extra virgin olive oil
- 2 pounds pork shoulder in 1-inch cubes
- 1 head garlic, papery coating removed, cut in half crosswise
- 2 cups red wine
- 3 tablespoons coriander seeds, cracked and wrapped in cheesecloth
- 1 tablespoon butter

- lemon juice to taste
- ½ cup chopped cilantro leaves

Direction

- Place oil in a large, deep skillet on medium-high heat. A minute later, add pork, and cook, undisturbed, until brown on one side, about 5 to 10 minutes. Turn and brown another side. Add garlic and cook, stirring occasionally, for a minute or two. Add 1 1/2 cups wine, then coriander.
- Turn heat to low, and cover. Simmer gently for 45 minutes to an hour, until pork is tender. Remove coriander. Stir in remaining wine; cook 2 or 3 minutes. Stir in butter.
- Add lemon juice to taste. Stir in half the cilantro, then serve, garnished with remaining cilantro.

219. Potato Salad With White Wine

Serving: 4 servings | Prep: | Cook: | Ready in: 30mins

Ingredients

- 1 ½ pounds small Idaho, Washington or Yellow Gold potatoes
- Salt and freshly ground pepper
- ¼ cup dry white wine
- 4 tablespoons vegetable or olive oil

Direction

- Preheat oven to 200 degrees.
- Rinse potatoes and place them in a large saucepan with cold water to cover. Bring to a boil and simmer for 20 minutes or longer, depending on the size. Do not overcook.
- Drain potatoes, and when they are cool enough to handle, peel them and cut them into 1/4-inch slices. Place them in a heat-proof mixing bowl. Sprinkle with salt and pepper, wine and oil. Toss while warm. Cover bowl with foil. Place it in oven briefly to warm through. Turn into a serving dish and serve while warm.

Nutrition Information

- 263: calories;
- 14 grams: fat;
- 2 grams: saturated fat;
- 10 grams: monounsaturated fat;
- 1 gram: sugars;
- 30 grams: carbohydrates;
- 4 grams: protein;
- 461 milligrams: sodium;

220. Potatoes And Carrots Family Style

Serving: 4 servings | Prep: | Cook: | Ready in: 35mins

Ingredients

- 5 Idaho russet potatoes, about 2 pounds
- 1 large onion, about 1/4 pound
- 2 carrots, about 1/2 pound, trimmed and scraped
- 3 large cloves garlic, peeled
- Salt to taste if desired
- 3 tablespoons butter
- ¼ cup heavy cream
- Freshly ground pepper to taste
- 2 tablespoons finely chopped fresh basil
- 2 tablespoons finely chopped fresh chervil
- 2 tablespoons finely chopped fresh parsley

Direction

- Peel the potatoes and cut them into quarters.
- Cut the onion crosswise into very thin slices. There should be about 2 cups.
- Cut the carrots crosswise into very thin slices. There should be about 1 2/3 cups.
- Combine the potatoes, onion, carrots and garlic in a large saucepan or small kettle. Add

water to cover, and salt. Bring to a boil and cook about 12 minutes or until tender. Drain saucepan and add the butter, cream, salt and pepper. Using a potato masher, mash the ingredients until they are coarse-fine. Add the basil, chervil and parsley. Blend thoroughly and serve.

Nutrition Information

- 167: calories;
- 14 grams: fat;
- 9 grams: carbohydrates;
- 0 grams: trans fat;
- 4 grams: sugars;
- 1 gram: polyunsaturated fat;
- 2 grams: protein;
- 279 milligrams: sodium;

221. Provencal Spinach Gratin

Serving: 4 servings | Prep: | Cook: | Ready in: 45mins

Ingredients

- 3 pounds bunch spinach, stemmed and washed in 2 changes of water, or 1 1/2 pounds baby spinach
- 3 tablespoons extra virgin olive oil
- 2 large garlic cloves, minced
- Salt and freshly ground pepper to taste
- 1 tablespoon all purpose flour
- ¼ cup low-fat milk
- ½ cup finely chopped parsley
- 2 tablespoons fresh or dry bread crumbs (preferably-whole wheat)

Direction

- Preheat the oven to 425 degrees. Oil a 2-quart baking dish or gratin and rub with a cut side of one of the garlic cloves before you chop the garlic.
- Steam the spinach above an inch of boiling water for 2 to 3 minutes, until it is wilted. You will probably have to do this in batches. I like to use a pasta pot with an insert for steaming spinach, as I can get a lot of it into the insert. Rinse briefly with cold water, squeeze gently (you don't have to squeeze dry) and chop.
- In a large bowl, toss together the spinach, 2 tablespoons of the olive oil, garlic, salt and pepper, flour, milk and parsley. Spoon into the gratin dish in an even layer. Sprinkle the bread crumbs over the top and drizzle on the remaining tablespoon of olive oil.
- Place in the oven and bake for 20 to 30 minutes, until the top is browned and the mixture is sizzling. Serve as a starter or a side.

Nutrition Information

- 204: calories;
- 19 grams: carbohydrates;
- 3 grams: sugars;
- 11 grams: protein;
- 888 milligrams: sodium;
- 12 grams: fat;
- 2 grams: polyunsaturated fat;
- 8 grams: dietary fiber;

222. Provençal Onion Pizza

Serving: One 12- to 14 inch pizza | Prep: | Cook: | Ready in: 1hours15mins

Ingredients

- 3 tablespoons olive oil
- 2 pounds sweet onions, finely chopped
- Salt
- freshly ground pepper
- 3 garlic cloves, minced
- ½ bay leaf
- 2 teaspoons fresh thyme leaves, or 1 teaspoon dried thyme

- 1 tablespoon capers, drained, rinsed and mashed in a mortar and pestle or finely chopped
- ½ recipe whole wheat pizza dough (see recipe)
- 12 anchovy fillets, soaked in water for five minutes, drained, rinsed and dried on paper towels
- 12 Niçoise olives

Direction

- Preheat the oven to 450 degrees, preferably with a pizza stone inside. Heat 2 tablespoons of the olive oil in a large, heavy nonstick skillet over medium-low heat. Add the onions and cook, stirring, until they begin to sizzle and soften, about three minutes. Add a generous pinch of salt and the garlic, bay leaf, thyme and pepper. Stir everything together, turn the heat to low, cover and cook slowly for 45 minutes, stirring often. The onions should melt down to a golden brown puree. If they begin to stick, add a few tablespoons of water. Stir in the capers, then taste and adjust seasonings. If there is liquid in the pan, cook over medium heat, uncovered, until it evaporates.
- Roll out the pizza dough and line a 12- to 14-inch pan. Brush the remaining tablespoon of oil over the bottom but not the rim of the crust. Spread the onions over the crust in an even layer. Cut the anchovies in half, and decorate the top of the crust with them, making twelve small X's and placing an olive in the middle of each X. Place on top of the pizza stone, and bake 15 to 20 minutes, until the edges of the crust are brown and the onions are beginning to brown. Remove from the heat. Serve hot, warm or room temperature.

Nutrition Information

- 189: calories;
- 9 grams: fat;
- 1 gram: polyunsaturated fat;
- 6 grams: monounsaturated fat;
- 23 grams: carbohydrates;
- 5 grams: protein;
- 2 grams: dietary fiber;
- 8 grams: sugars;
- 503 milligrams: sodium;

223. Purslane Salad With Cherries And Feta

Serving: 4 servings. | Prep: | Cook: | Ready in: 5mins

Ingredients

- 1 generous bunch purslane, thick stems cut away (12 ounces, about 4 cups), washed and dried, or 1 bag mâche
- 1 tablespoon chopped fresh mint
- 16 cherries, pitted and quartered
- 12 kalamata olives, pitted and coarsely chopped
- 1 tablespoon sherry vinegar
- 1 tablespoon fresh lemon juice
- 1 teaspoon balsamic vinegar
- 1 small garlic clove, puréed
- Salt
- ¼ cup extra virgin olive oil
- Freshly ground pepper
- 1 to 2 ounces feta, crumbled

Direction

- Toss together the purslane, 2 teaspoons of the mint, the cherries and the olives in a salad bowl, or in a large bowl if you prefer to serve this on a platter.
- Whisk together the vinegars, lemon juice, garlic, salt, olive oil and pepper. Toss with the salad. If desired, transfer to a platter. Sprinkle the feta and remaining mint over the top, and serve.

Nutrition Information

- 211: calories;
- 17 grams: fat;
- 4 grams: saturated fat;

- 2 grams: polyunsaturated fat;
- 12 grams: carbohydrates;
- 1 gram: dietary fiber;
- 11 grams: monounsaturated fat;
- 5 grams: protein;
- 481 milligrams: sodium;

224. Puréed Mushroom Soup

Serving: 16 shots or 6 to 8 bowls | Prep: | Cook: | Ready in: 1hours45mins

Ingredients

- ½ ounce dried porcinis
- 1 tablespoon extra virgin olive oil
- 1 medium onion, chopped
- 1 leek, white and light green part only, cut in half lengthwise, cleaned thoroughly and sliced or chopped
- Salt to taste
- 2 garlic cloves, minced (to taste, optional)
- 1 ½ pounds mushrooms (white or cremini) sliced or coarsely chopped
- ⅓ cup medium grain rice
- About 4 1/2 cups water, chicken stock or vegetable stock, or as needed
- A bouquet garni made with a bay leaf and a couple of sprigs each thyme and parsley and an optional Parmesan rind
- Freshly ground pepper to taste
- 1 tablespoon soy sauce (more to taste)
- 1 to 2 tablespoons dry sherry, to taste (optional)
- ½ cup milk or additional stock
- Garnish
- Chopped fresh parsley or torn leaves for garnish

Direction

- Place the dried porcinis in a bowl or pyrex measuring cup and cover with 2 cups boiling water. Let sit for 30 minutes. Line a strainer with cheesecloth and set over a bowl. Drain the porcinis through a cheesecloth-lined strainer. Squeeze the mushrooms over the strainer to extract as much flavorful liquid as possible. Rinse in several changes of water and set aside. Measure the mushroom soaking water and add water or stock to make 6 cups.
- Heat the olive oil over medium heat in a large, heavy soup pot or Dutch oven and add the onion and leek and a pinch of salt. Cook, stirring, until tender and, about 5 to 8 minutes. Do not brown. Add a generous pinch of salt and the garlic and cook, stirring, until the garlic smells fragrant, about 30 seconds. Add the fresh and reconstituted mushrooms and cook, stirring, until they begin to sweat and smell fragrant, 3 to 5 minutes.
- Add the rice, stock, bouquet garni, soy sauce and salt to taste, and bring to a boil. Reduce the heat, cover and simmer 45 minutes. Remove the bouquet garni and the parmesan rind if using.
- In batches, blend the soup until smooth. Fill the blender less than half way and cover the top with a towel pulled down tight, rather than airtight with the lid, because hot soup will jump and push the top off if the blender is closed airtight. Return to the pot, taste and adjust salt, and add pepper and the sherry, if using. Add the milk or another half cup of stock and heat through, stirring. If the soup still seems too thick, thin out a little more but remember to taste and adjust seasoning. Serve in espresso cups or in bowls, garnishing each serving with chopped or torn flat-leaf parsley.

Nutrition Information

- 44: calories;
- 2 grams: protein;
- 317 milligrams: sodium;
- 1 gram: sugars;
- 0 grams: polyunsaturated fat;
- 7 grams: carbohydrates;

225. Puréed White Bean Soup With Pistou

Serving: 6 servings. | Prep: | Cook: | Ready in: 2hours15mins

Ingredients

- 1 large onion, chopped
- 4 garlic cloves, minced
- 1 pound white beans, soaked for six hours (or overnight) and drained
- 1 bay leaf
- 1 sprig of fresh sage
- 2 ½ to 3 quarts water, as needed (or 2 1/2 quarts water and up to 2 cups milk as needed)
- Salt to taste
- Freshly ground pepper
- About 1/3 cup pistou
- Garlic croutons for garnish (optional)

Direction

- Combine the onion, garlic, drained beans, bay leaf, sage and 2 1/2 quarts water in a large, heavy soup pot or Dutch oven and bring to a boil. Add salt to taste, reduce the heat to low, cover and simmer 2 hours, until the beans are very tender and the broth is fragrant. Remove the bay leaf and sage sprig.
- Using an immersion blender, purée the soup (or you can use a regular blender, working in batches and placing a kitchen towel over the top to avoid splashing) until it is very smooth. Return to the pot, heat through, add freshly ground pepper and adjust salt. Thin out as desired with water or milk.
- Ladle the soup into bowls. Stir the pistou, and if it is very stiff, thin out with a little olive oil so that you can drizzle it into each bowl and it won't just fall in as a clump. Put about 2 teaspoons on each bowl, add a few garlic croutons if desired, and serve. Diners should stir the pistou into the soup for the best flavor.

226. Quesadilla With Mushroom Ragoût And Chipotles

Serving: 2 quesadillas | Prep: | Cook: | Ready in: 10mins

Ingredients

- 6 tablespoons mushroom ragoût
- 1 teaspoon chopped canned chipotle in adobo (more to taste)
- 4 corn tortillas
- 1 ½ ounces grated Monterey Jack or Gruyère (about 1/3 cup)

Direction

- Stir the chopped chipotles into the mushroom ragoût. Taste and add more if you want more spice.
- Using a microwave: Place a corn tortilla on a plate. Top with a heaped tablespoon of the grated cheese. Add half the mushrooms and spread in an even layer. Sprinkle another heaped tablespoon of the cheese over the mushrooms and top with another tortilla. Press down gently. Repeat with the remaining ingredients. Microwave for 1 to 1 1/2 minutes, until the cheese has melted. Remove from the microwave, cut into quarters, and serve.
Using a pan: Place a corn tortilla in a pan. Top with a heaped tablespoon of the cheese and half the mushrooms and spread in an even layer. Sprinkle on another heaped tablespoon the cheese. Turn the heat on medium-high and heat until the cheese begins to melt. Place the remaining tortilla on top of the cheese and press down lightly. Flip the quesadilla over in the pan and heat for about 30 seconds, or until the cheese has melted. Flip back over and remove to a plate. Cut into quarters or sixths, and serve. Repeat with the remaining ingredients.

Nutrition Information

- 190: calories;

- 22 grams: carbohydrates;
- 9 grams: protein;
- 182 milligrams: sodium;
- 8 grams: fat;
- 4 grams: saturated fat;
- 2 grams: monounsaturated fat;
- 1 gram: sugars;
- 3 grams: dietary fiber;

- 2 grams: fat;
- 1 gram: saturated fat;
- 5 grams: dietary fiber;
- 3 grams: sugars;
- 0 grams: polyunsaturated fat;
- 54 grams: carbohydrates;
- 10 grams: protein;
- 559 milligrams: sodium;

227. Quick Pumpkin Sage Pasta

Serving: 2 servings | Prep: | Cook: |Ready in: 30mins

Ingredients

- 4 ounces whole-wheat pasta
- ¾ cup vegetable broth
- ¾ cup canned pumpkin
- 1 to 2 tablespoons minced fresh sage
- ⅛ teaspoon pumpkin pie spice
- Pinch of dried oregano
- Pinch of red pepper flakes (optional)
- Salt and pepper, to taste
- Vegan Parmesan for garnish (optional)

Direction

- Cook pasta according to package instructions.
- Meanwhile, combine remaining ingredients in a small saucepan and heat over low heat until thoroughly warm, about 5 minutes.
- Taste, adding more sage if desired, plus salt and pepper to taste.
- Cover and let sauce rest for 5 to 10 minutes, allowing the flavors to merge and sauce to thicken slightly.
- Toss cooked pasta with pumpkin sauce and taste, adding more salt and pepper as needed. Garnish with vegan Parmesan if desired.

Nutrition Information

- 251: calories;

228. Quince Compote

Serving: Serves four | Prep: | Cook: |Ready in: 1hours

Ingredients

- Juice of 1/2 lemon
- 1 pound quince
- 1 pound apples
- ⅓ cup agave syrup
- ½ cup water
- ½ teaspoon ground cinnamon
- 1 vanilla bean, split and scraped

Direction

- Fill a large bowl with water, and add the juice of 1/2 lemon. Quarter the quinces and apples, and place the pieces you aren't working with in the water while you peel, core and cut each quarter crosswise into 1 inch-thick pieces.
- Combine the agave syrup and water in a large, heavy saucepan, and bring to a boil. Turn the heat down and simmer. Drain the quinces and apples, and add to the pot with the cinnamon and vanilla. Bring to a simmer, cover, reduce the heat and simmer, stirring often, for one hour. The quince will be soft and pinkish, and the apples may have broken down into apple sauce (depending on what type you use). Serve hot or cold.

Nutrition Information

- 187: calories;

- 0 grams: polyunsaturated fat;
- 48 grams: carbohydrates;
- 5 grams: dietary fiber;
- 25 grams: sugars;
- 1 gram: protein;
- 8 milligrams: sodium;

229. Quinoa, Pea And Black Bean Salad With Cumin Vinaigrette

Serving: 6 servings | Prep: | Cook: | Ready in: 35mins

Ingredients

- 1 cup quinoa
- 1 ½ cups water
- Salt to taste
- 1 15-ounce can black beans, drained and rinsed, or 1 1/2 cups cooked black beans
- ¾ cup fresh English peas (1 pound in the pod), raw or steamed 5 minutes (to taste)
- 1 red bell pepper, diced
- 1 serrano chili, seeded if desired and finely chopped (optional)
- ½ cup chopped cilantro, plus several sprigs for garnish
- 2 tablespoons fresh lime juice
- 1 tablespoon red wine vinegar or sherry vinegar
- 1 small garlic clove, puréed
- ½ teaspoon cumin seeds, lightly toasted and ground
- 3 tablespoons extra virgin olive oil, or a combination of olive oil and grapeseed oil
- ¼ cup buttermilk

Direction

- Place the quinoa in a strainer and rinse several times with cold water. Place in a medium saucepan with 1 1/2 cups water and salt to taste. Bring to a boil, cover and simmer 15 minutes, until the grains display a threadlike spiral and the water is absorbed. Remove from the heat, remove the lid and place a dish towel over the pan, then return the lid to the pan and let sit for 10 minutes or longer undisturbed. Transfer to a salad bowl and fluff with forks.
- Toss the black beans, peas, red pepper, chili pepper and cilantro with the quinoa.
- Mix together the lime juice, vinegar, salt to taste, garlic and cumin. Whisk in the olive oil and the buttermilk. Toss with the salad and serve.

Nutrition Information

- 321: calories;
- 14 grams: protein;
- 680 milligrams: sodium;
- 9 grams: fat;
- 6 grams: polyunsaturated fat;
- 47 grams: carbohydrates;
- 13 grams: dietary fiber;
- 3 grams: sugars;
- 1 gram: saturated fat;
- 2 grams: monounsaturated fat;

230. Raspberry Lime Iced Tea

Serving: About one quart | Prep: | Cook: | Ready in: 15mins

Ingredients

- 1 ½ cups frozen raspberries, defrosted slightly
- 6 tablespoons sugar, plus more to taste
- ¼ cup fresh lime juice
- 4 cups cold, brewed tea
- Thinly sliced lime, for garnish

Direction

- Place the raspberries, 6 table spoons sugar and lime juice in a food processor and process until very smooth. Strain through a fine sieve. Whisk the raspberry mixture into the tea. Place in a pitcher and refrigerate until cold. Whisk in additional sugar if desired. Serve over ice, garnished with lime slices.

Nutrition Information

- 36: calories;
- 7 grams: sugars;
- 3 milligrams: sodium;
- 0 grams: protein;
- 9 grams: carbohydrates;
- 1 gram: dietary fiber;

231. Raspberry Rose Granita

Serving: 4 servings | Prep: | Cook: |Ready in: 4hours45mins

Ingredients

- ¼ cup water
- 65 grams (about 1/4 cup plus 1 teaspoon) sugar
- 680 grams raspberries
- ½ teaspoon rose water

Direction

- Combine the water and sugar in a saucepan and bring to a boil. Reduce the heat and simmer until the sugar has dissolved. Remove from the heat and allow to cool.
- In a blender, purée the raspberries with the sugar solution and remaining ingredients until smooth. Chill in the refrigerator for 2 hours or overnight.
- Chill a 9-by-11-inch baking dish in the freezer. Blend the purée with an immersion blender for 30 seconds and scrape into the chilled baking dish and place back in the freezer. Set the timer for 30 minutes. Using a fork, scrape the ice crystals from the outside of the baking dish toward the center. Return to the freezer and set the timer for another 30 minutes. Continue to scrape the mixture with a fork every 30 minutes until you have a uniform frozen mixture. It should not be frozen solid. If you forget to scrape and the mixture does freeze like an ice cube, cut into chunks and use a food processor fitted with the steel blade to break it up. Transfer to a container and freeze. Allow to soften for 15 minutes in the refrigerator before serving.

Nutrition Information

- 151: calories;
- 1 gram: polyunsaturated fat;
- 0 grams: monounsaturated fat;
- 37 grams: carbohydrates;
- 11 grams: dietary fiber;
- 24 grams: sugars;
- 2 grams: protein;
- 2 milligrams: sodium;

232. Raspberry Rose Sorbet

Serving: 4 servings | Prep: | Cook: |Ready in: 4hours45mins

Ingredients

- ¼ cup water
- 65 grams (about 1/4 cup plus 1 teaspoon) sugar
- 33 grams (about 1 tablespoon plus 2 teaspoons) corn syrup
- 680 grams raspberries
- ½ teaspoon rose water

Direction

- Combine the water and sugar in a saucepan and bring to a boil. Reduce the heat and simmer until the sugar has dissolved. Remove from the heat and allow to cool.
- In a blender, purée the raspberries with the syrup, corn syrup and rose water. Taste and add a few more drops of rose water if desired.

Strain into a bowl and chill in the refrigerator for 2 hours or overnight.
- Chill a container in the freezer. Blend the mixture for 30 seconds with an immersion blender, then freeze in an ice cream maker following the manufacturer's instructions. Transfer to the chilled container and place in the freezer for 2 hours to pack. Allow to soften in the refrigerator for 15 to 30 minutes before serving.

Nutrition Information

- 175: calories;
- 43 grams: carbohydrates;
- 11 grams: dietary fiber;
- 30 grams: sugars;
- 2 grams: protein;
- 8 milligrams: sodium;
- 1 gram: polyunsaturated fat;
- 0 grams: monounsaturated fat;

233. Red Pepper Coulis

Serving: 6 servings | Prep: | Cook: | Ready in: 15mins

Ingredients

- ½ pound red peppers, cored, seeded and diced
- 1 medium-size tomato, seeded and diced
- ½ large onion, diced
- 1 ¾ cup tomato juice
- ¼ cup chopped basil
- ⅛ teaspoon thyme

Direction

- In a medium-size skillet, combine red pepper, tomato, onion and tomato juice and cook until tender. Stir in the basil and thyme. Puree in a blender until smooth. Return to skillet and cook over low heat until mixture is reduced to about 1 1/2 cups.

Nutrition Information

- 33: calories;
- 2 grams: dietary fiber;
- 4 grams: sugars;
- 1 gram: protein;
- 10 milligrams: sodium;
- 0 grams: polyunsaturated fat;
- 7 grams: carbohydrates;

234. Red Quinoa, Cauliflower And Fava Bean Salad

Serving: 4 to 6 servings | Prep: | Cook: | Ready in: 1hours15mins

Ingredients

- 1 cup red quinoa
- 1 ½ cups water
- Salt to taste
- 1 ½ pounds fava beans
- ½ head cauliflower, broken into small florets
- 2 tablespoons chopped chives
- For the dressing
- 1 tablespoon freshly squeezed lemon juice
- 1 tablespoon sherry vinegar
- ½ teaspoon curry powder
- 1 teaspoon Dijon mustard
- 1 small garlic clove, puréed
- Salt to taste
- 2 tablespoons grapeseed oil
- 5 tablespoons buttermilk
- Freshly ground pepper

Direction

- Rinse the quinoa in several changes of water. Heat a heavy medium-size saucepan over medium-high heat and add the quinoa. Stir until the water on the grains has evaporated and the quinoa begins to crackle and smell toasty. Add the water and salt to taste. Bring to a boil, cover and reduce the heat to low. Simmer 20 minutes, until some of the quinoa grains display a little white spiral and the water has been absorbed. Remove from the heat, place a dish towel over the top of the pot and return the lid. Let sit for 15 minutes. Fluff the quinoa with a fork.

- Meanwhile, shell and skin the fava beans. Bring a medium pot of salted water to a boil. Fill a bowl with ice water. Drop the shelled fava beans into the boiling water and boil 5 minutes. Remove from the pot with a slotted spoon and transfer immediately to the cold water. Allow the beans to cool for several minutes, then slip off their skins by pinching off the eye of the skin and squeezing gently. Hold several beans in one hand and use your other thumb and forefinger to pinch off the eyes; have a bowl for the shelled favas close at hand, and this will not take a very long time.
- Bring the water in the pot back to a boil and drop in the cauliflower. Boil 3 to 5 minutes, until just tender. Transfer to a bowl of ice water, drain and dry on paper towels. Alternatively, steam the cauliflower for 4 to 5 minutes, or see the roasting variation below.
- Whisk together the dressing ingredients. Toss the quinoa, fava beans, cauliflower and chives in a bowl. Toss with the dressing and serve.

Nutrition Information

- 265: calories;
- 630 milligrams: sodium;
- 1 gram: monounsaturated fat;
- 0 grams: trans fat;
- 12 grams: sugars;
- 42 grams: carbohydrates;
- 14 grams: protein;
- 7 grams: fat;
- 5 grams: polyunsaturated fat;

235. Rendered Chicken Fat

Serving: Y cup | Prep: | Cook: | Ready in: 25mins

Ingredients

- ½ cup raw chicken fat
- Pinch of kosher salt

Direction

- Place the chicken fat and salt in a small, heavy saucepan.
- Cook very slowly over low heat, stirring from time to time, until the fat is completely liquified and the cracklings are golden brown.
- Strain the fat into a jar or crock and refrigerate. Reserve the cracklings - crisp, fried bits that are left after fat is rendered - to use in making chopped liver or as a garnish for salads or mashed potatoes.

Nutrition Information

- 115: calories;
- 13 grams: fat;
- 4 grams: saturated fat;
- 6 grams: monounsaturated fat;
- 3 grams: polyunsaturated fat;
- 15 milligrams: sodium;

236. Rhubarb Butterscotch Sauce

Serving: 2 cups, to serve 6 to 8 | Prep: | Cook: | Ready in: 20mins

Ingredients

- 1 pound rhubarb, trimmed and sliced 1/2-inch thick (about 4 cups)
- ½ cup dark brown sugar
- 2 tablespoons unsalted butter
- Pinch kosher salt

Direction

- In a medium saucepan over low heat, combine ingredients. Cover and cook, stirring occasionally, until rhubarb breaks down, 15 to 20 minutes.

Nutrition Information

- 145: calories;
- 0 grams: polyunsaturated fat;
- 19 grams: sugars;
- 40 milligrams: sodium;
- 4 grams: saturated fat;
- 23 grams: carbohydrates;
- 1 gram: protein;
- 6 grams: fat;
- 2 grams: dietary fiber;

237. Rhubarb Soup

Serving: Twelve servings | Prep: | Cook: |Ready in: 45mins

Ingredients

- 4 cups rhubarb, washed and diced
- 5 cups water
- 1 ½ cups granulated sugar
- 3 3-inch sticks of cinnamon
- 5 to 6 slices of lemon, seeded
- 4 cups red wine
- 16 ounces creme fraiche
- One stalk rhubarb, julienned, 2 inches long

Direction

- Place the rhubarb, water and sugar in a large pot. Stir and simmer over medium heat for 20 minutes or until the rhubarb is soft.
- Add the cinnamon, lemon slices and red wine and simmer for 15 minutes.
- Remove from the heat and strain the soup through a sieve. Allow the soup to come to room temperature, cover and refrigerate.
- Serve the soup very cold in bowls with a dollop of creme fraiche and julienned rhubarb.

Nutrition Information

- 252: calories;
- 27 milligrams: sodium;
- 8 grams: fat;
- 4 grams: saturated fat;
- 2 grams: protein;
- 0 grams: polyunsaturated fat;
- 33 grams: carbohydrates;
- 28 grams: sugars;

238. Rhubarb And Berry Crumble

Serving: 4 servings | Prep: | Cook: |Ready in: 45mins

Ingredients

- 3 tablespoons unsalted butter
- 1 pound fresh rhubarb
- 1 cup fresh strawberries, hulled and halved
- 1 cup fresh raspberries
- 1 ½ teaspoons ground ginger
- 1 cup brown sugar
- 2 tablespoons flour
- ½ cup rolled oats
- ½ pint vanilla ice cream

Direction

- Preheat oven to 400 degrees. Butter a four-cup baking dish with one-half tablespoon of the butter.
- Remove any leaves from the rhubarb stalks. Dice the rhubarb. Place in a bowl and mix with the strawberries, raspberries, a teaspoon of ginger and three-fourths cup of sugar. Spread into the baking dish. Dot with one-half tablespoon of butter.
- With a fork or your fingertips mix the remaining sugar and ginger with the flour and oats. Cut the remaining butter in bits and mix them in until crumbly. Spread this mixture over the rhubarb.

- Place in the oven and bake 25 to 30 minutes, until top is browned and fruit begins to bubble. Allow to cool 20 minutes, then serve with ice cream.

Nutrition Information

- 388: calories;
- 8 grams: saturated fat;
- 0 grams: trans fat;
- 65 grams: carbohydrates;
- 6 grams: dietary fiber;
- 47 grams: sugars;
- 5 grams: protein;
- 44 milligrams: sodium;
- 14 grams: fat;
- 4 grams: monounsaturated fat;
- 1 gram: polyunsaturated fat;

239. Rice Bowl With Oven Baked Miso Tofu

Serving: 4 servings | Prep: | Cook: | Ready in: 45mins

Ingredients

- A 14-ounce block of organic extra-firm tofu, cut into 8 slices
- 3 tablespoons soy sauce
- 1 tablespoon minced ginger
- 1 garlic clove, minced
- ⅛ teaspoon of cayenne (optional)
- 1 tablespoon honey or agave nectar
- 2 teaspoons lime juice
- 2 tablespoons white or yellow miso
- 2 tablespoon mirin
- 1 tablespoon dark sesame oil
- 3 tablespoons grapeseed oil or sunflower oil
- 1 large red bell pepper, sliced
- 3 cups cooked rice (brown or white)
- 1 cup (8 ounces) kimchi

Direction

- Preheat the oven to 375 degrees. Line a sheet pan with parchment. Pat each slice of tofu dry with paper towels.
- Whisk together the soy sauce, ginger, garlic, cayenne, honey or agave nectar, lime juice, miso, mirin, and oils. Pour into a dish that can accommodate all of the tofu slices in a single layer (such as a baking dish). Place the tofu slices in the marinade and turn them over. Leave to marinate for 15 minutes, turning once or twice. Transfer to the baking sheet. Add the peppers to the dish with the marinade and toss to coat thoroughly, then place on the baking sheet in a single layer.
- Place the baking sheet in the oven and roast for 15 to 20 minutes, turning the peppers once with tongs, until the edges of the tofu are just beginning to color and the marinade sets on the surface, and the peppers are sizzling and beginning to color on the edges. Remove from the heat.
- If desired, heat the kimchi in a small pan or saucepan. Spoon rice into 4 wide bowls or onto plates. Top with kimchi, tofu, and peppers. If desired, douse the rice with some of the remaining marinade from the tofu, and serve.

Nutrition Information

- 425: calories;
- 4 grams: monounsaturated fat;
- 11 grams: polyunsaturated fat;
- 5 grams: dietary fiber;
- 19 grams: fat;
- 3 grams: saturated fat;
- 1148 milligrams: sodium;
- 49 grams: carbohydrates;
- 7 grams: sugars;
- 15 grams: protein;

240. Risotto With Broccoli

Serving: Serves 4 to 6 | Prep: | Cook: | Ready in: 45mins

Ingredients

- 2 quarts well-seasoned chicken or vegetable stock, as needed
- 2 tablespoons extra virgin olive oil
- ½ cup minced onion
- 1 ½ cups arborio or carnaroli rice
- 1 to 2 garlic cloves (to taste), green shoots removed, minced
- Freshly ground pepper to taste
- ½ cup dry white wine, such as pinot grigio or sauvignon blanc
- 1 pound broccoli (2 good-size stalks), stems peeled and cut in small dice, flowers thinly sliced
- ½ cup freshly grated Parmesan cheese
- 2 tablespoons minced flat-leaf parsley

Direction

- Put your stock or broth into a saucepan, and bring it to a simmer over low heat with a ladle nearby or in the pot. Make sure that the stock is well seasoned.
- Heat the olive oil over medium heat in a wide, heavy skillet or in a large, wide saucepan. Add the onion and a generous pinch of salt, and cook gently until it is just tender, about three minutes. Do not brown.
- Add the rice and the garlic, and stir until the grains separate and begin to crackle. Add the wine, and stir until it has been absorbed. Begin adding the simmering stock, a couple of ladlefuls (about 1/2 cup) at a time. The stock should just cover the rice and should be bubbling, not too slowly but not too quickly. Cook, stirring often, until it is just about absorbed. Add another ladleful or two of the stock, and continue to cook in this fashion, stirring in more stock when the rice is almost dry. You do not have to stir constantly, but stir often. After 10 minutes, stir in the diced broccoli stems. Continue to add broth and stir the rice for another five minutes. Stir in the thinly sliced flowers. Continue to add broth and stir the rice for another 10 minutes or so. When the rice is tender all the way through but still chewy, it is done. Taste now and adjust seasoning, adding salt and pepper to taste. Add another ladleful of stock to the rice, along with the Parmesan and the parsley, and remove from the heat. The mixture should be creamy (add more stock if it isn't). Stir for about half a minute, then serve in wide soup bowls or on plates, spreading the risotto in a thin layer rather than a mound.

Nutrition Information

- 423: calories;
- 3 grams: saturated fat;
- 7 grams: sugars;
- 17 grams: protein;
- 614 milligrams: sodium;
- 11 grams: fat;
- 6 grams: monounsaturated fat;
- 1 gram: polyunsaturated fat;
- 59 grams: carbohydrates;
- 4 grams: dietary fiber;

241. Risotto With Pumpkin

Serving: 4 servings | Prep: | Cook: | Ready in: 35mins

Ingredients

- Generous pinch of saffron
- 5 cups boiling chicken stock
- 3 tablespoons olive oil
- 2 cloves garlic, minced
- 2 cups pumpkin, in 1/2-inch dice
- 1 ½ cups arborio rice
- 1 tablespoon butter
- Salt and freshly ground black pepper
- Freshly grated Parmesan cheese

Direction

- Place the saffron in a small dish, add a little of the chicken stock and allow to steep for a few minutes.
- Heat the oil in a heavy saucepan. Add the garlic, saute briefly then stir in the pumpkin. When the pumpkin is coated with oil, stir in the rice. Add the saffron. Stir.
- Stirring constantly, begin adding the remaining stock, about one-half cup at a time, adding additional stock as each portion is absorbed by the rice.
- After about 20 minutes, when all the stock has been added, the rice should be just tender and the pumpkin should be quite soft. Don't worry if some of the pumpkin has disintegrated.
- Stir in the butter, season to taste with salt and pepper and stir in a couple of tablespoons of Parmesan cheese. Serve at once with remaining Parmesan cheese on the side.

242. Roast Breast Of Turkey

Serving: 6 to 8 servings | Prep: | Cook: | Ready in: 1hours15mins

Ingredients

- 1 4-pound fresh turkey breast (with ribs)
- 2 tablespoons peanut, corn or vegetable oil
- Salt to taste if desired
- Freshly ground pepper to taste
- ½ teaspoon dried thyme
- 1 onion, about 1/2 pound, peeled and cut in half
- 1 clove garlic, peeled
- 1 bay leave
- 1 cup fresh or canned chicken broth

Direction

- Preheat oven to 450 degrees.
- Rub turkey breast on all sides with oil. Sprinkle with salt and pepper. Rub with thyme inside and outside. Place turkey breast, skin side up, in a roasting pan and place onion, cut side down, around it. Add garlic and bay leaf inside the breast and place in the oven. Bake 30 minutes and cover with foil.
- Continue baking 15 minutes, basting. Remove turkey from roasting pan and pour off most of the fat. Return turkey breast to the pan, skin side up, and pour the broth around it. Return to the oven and continue baking 10 minutes, basting. Remove from oven and cover with foil. Let stand 10 to 15 minutes before carving. Carve and serve with pan gravy.

Nutrition Information

- 367: calories;
- 18 grams: fat;
- 4 grams: polyunsaturated fat;
- 0 grams: trans fat;
- 45 grams: protein;
- 8 grams: monounsaturated fat;
- 3 grams: carbohydrates;
- 1 gram: sugars;
- 677 milligrams: sodium;

243. Roast Leg Of Lamb With Moroccan Marinade

Serving: 4 to 6 servings | Prep: | Cook: | Ready in: 1hours30mins

Ingredients

- 1 leg of lamb, five to six pounds
- 5 cloves garlic, peeled and cut in slivers
- 2 teaspoons ground cumin
- 2 teaspoons paprika
- 2 teaspoons freshly ground black pepper
- 1 ½ teaspoons ground coriander
- ½ teaspoon cayenne pepper
- 6 tablespoons extra-virgin olive oil
- ¼ cup fresh lemon juice
- 2 tablespoons finely minced garlic
- ½ cup chopped fresh coriander
- 1 cup boiling water, optional

Direction

- Trim excess fat from leg of lamb. Make shallow incisions into the leg and insert a garlic sliver in each.
- Combine the spices with oil, lemon juice, minced garlic and fresh coriander to make a paste. Rub the paste over the lamb, place it in a roasting pan, cover and let stand 3 to 4 hours in a cool place or overnight in the refrigerator.
- Preheat oven 350 degrees. Roast leg of lamb to the desired degree of doneness, basting once or twice during roasting. After about one hour and 10 minutes, internal temperature should be 120 to 125 degrees, medium rare. Allow to rest 10 minutes before carving. Juices can be used to make a gravy if desired. To do so pour fat from roasting pan, add the boiling water and, scraping the pan, cook over medium-high heat 2 to 3 minutes. Strain into a sauceboat.

Nutrition Information

- 816: calories;
- 61 grams: protein;
- 22 grams: saturated fat;
- 4 grams: carbohydrates;
- 1 gram: dietary fiber;
- 189 milligrams: sodium;
- 29 grams: monounsaturated fat;
- 5 grams: polyunsaturated fat;
- 0 grams: sugars;

244. Roast Rabbit With Rosemary

Serving: Four servings | Prep: | Cook: | Ready in: 1hours10mins

Ingredients

- 1 young rabbit, about 2 1/2 pounds, cleaned weight, cut into serving pieces
- Salt to taste, if desired
- Freshly ground pepper to taste
- 2 tablespoons olive oil
- 2 tablespoons butter
- 1 teaspoon finely ground rosemary
- 2 tablespoons finely chopped shallots
- 1 teaspoon finely minced garlic
- ½ cup dry white wine
- ½ cup fresh or canned chicken broth
- ¼ cup finely chopped parsley

Direction

- Preheat oven to 450 degrees.
- Sprinkle the rabbit with salt and pepper.
- Heat the oil and half of the butter in a baking dish. Add the rabbit pieces in one layer. Sprinkle with rosemary.
- Place the dish in the oven and bake 30 minutes. Turn the rabbit pieces and continue baking five minutes. Sprinkle with shallots and garlic. Bake five minutes and add the wine and broth. Bake, turning the pieces occasionally, about 20 minutes. Stir in the remaining one tablespoon of butter. Sprinkle with parsley and serve.

Nutrition Information

- 684: calories;
- 1117 milligrams: sodium;
- 35 grams: fat;
- 0 grams: trans fat;
- 3 grams: carbohydrates;
- 1 gram: sugars;
- 80 grams: protein;
- 11 grams: saturated fat;
- 12 grams: monounsaturated fat;
- 5 grams: polyunsaturated fat;

245. Roasted Brussels Sprouts And Mushrooms With Gremolata And Quinoa

Serving: Serves 4 to 6 | Prep: | Cook: |Ready in: 20mins

Ingredients

- 1 pound Brussels sprouts, trimmed and cut in half if small, quartered if large
- 1 pound mushrooms or oyster mushrooms, halved if small, quartered if large
- Salt and freshly ground pepper
- 3 tablespoons extra virgin olive oil
- 1 to 2 garlic cloves, finely minced
- ¼ cup finely minced flat-leaf parsley
- 2 teaspoons finely chopped lemon zest
- 2 to 3 cups cooked quinoa (to taste)
- Crumbled feta or goat cheese for serving (optional)

Direction

- Preheat oven to 425 degrees. Line 2 baking sheets or baking dishes with parchment or foil and brush with olive oil. Place the Brussels sprouts on one and mushrooms on the other and toss each with salt and pepper to taste and 1 1/2 tablespoons olive oil. Roast together in the oven, or 1 sheet at a time, for 20 minutes, stirring halfway through. The Brussels sprouts should be browned on the edges and tender. The mushrooms should be soft and there should be juice on the baking sheet.
- Meanwhile, in a small bowl, mix together garlic, parsley and lemon zest (this is the gremolata).
- Tip mushrooms, with the juice in the baking dish, into a large bowl. Add Brussels sprouts and gremolata and toss together. Spoon quinoa onto plates or into wide bowls, top with the Brussels sprouts and mushrooms, spoon on any juice remaining in the bowl, top with crumbled feta or goat cheese if desired and serve.

Nutrition Information

- 214: calories;
- 1 gram: saturated fat;
- 557 milligrams: sodium;
- 5 grams: monounsaturated fat;
- 2 grams: polyunsaturated fat;
- 29 grams: carbohydrates;
- 7 grams: dietary fiber;
- 3 grams: sugars;
- 9 grams: protein;

246. Roasted Cauliflower Gratin With Tomatoes And Goat Cheese

Serving: Serves 4 to 6 | Prep: | Cook: |Ready in: 1hours20mins

Ingredients

- 1 medium-size head of cauliflower
- Salt and freshly ground pepper to taste
- 3 tablespoons extra virgin olive oil
- 1 small or 1/2 large red onion, cut in half or quarters (if using a whole onion) lengthwise, then sliced thin across the grain
- 2 garlic cloves, minced
- 1 teaspoon fresh thyme leaves
- 1 (14 8/10-ounce) can chopped tomatoes in juice
- ⅛ teaspoon cinnamon
- ½ teaspoon coriander seeds, lightly toasted and coarsely ground
- 2 eggs
- 2 ½ ounces soft goat cheese (about 1/2 cup plus 2 tablespoons)
- 2 to 3 teaspoon chopped chives

Direction

- Preheat oven to 450 degrees. Line a baking sheet with parchment or foil. Cut away the bottom of the cauliflower stem and trim off leaves. Cut cauliflower into 1/3 inch thick slices, letting the florets on the edges fall off. Toss all of it, including the bits that have fallen away, with 2 tablespoons of the olive oil, salt, and pepper. Place on baking sheet in an even layer.

- Roast for 15 to 20 minutes, stirring and flipping over the big slices after 8 minutes, until the slices are tender when pierced with a paring knife and the small florets are nicely browned. Remove from oven and cut large slices into smaller pieces. You should have about 2 cups. Transfer to a large bowl. Turn oven down to 375 degrees.
- Oil a 1-1/2 to 2-quart baking dish or gratin. Heat remaining oil over medium heat in a medium-size skillet or a wide saucepan and add onion. Cook, stirring, until tender, about 5 minutes. Add a generous pinch of salt and the garlic and thyme and continue to cook, stirring, until garlic is fragrant, 30 seconds to a minute. Add tomatoes, cinnamon, ground coriander seeds, and salt and pepper to taste and bring to a simmer. Cook, stirring often, over medium-low heat, for 10 to 15 minutes, until the tomatoes have cooked down and the sauce is fragrant. Taste and adjust seasoning. Add to bowl with the cauliflower and stir everything together. Scrape into prepared baking dish.
- Set aside 2 tablespoons of the goat cheese. Beat eggs, then add the remaining cheese and beat together until smooth. Pour over cauliflower mixture, making sure to scrape out every last bit with a rubber spatula. Dot top with small pieces of the remaining goat cheese and sprinkle on chives.
- Bake 30 minutes, until top is beginning to brown in spots. Remove from oven and allow to sit for 5 to 10 minutes before serving.

Nutrition Information

- 179: calories;
- 6 grams: monounsaturated fat;
- 11 grams: carbohydrates;
- 547 milligrams: sodium;
- 13 grams: fat;
- 4 grams: dietary fiber;
- 0 grams: trans fat;
- 1 gram: polyunsaturated fat;
- 5 grams: sugars;
- 8 grams: protein;

247. Roasted Corn And Tomato Salsa

Serving: Makes a little about 2 1/2 cups | Prep: | Cook: | Ready in: 45mins

Ingredients

- 1 ½ pounds ripe tomatoes, preferably plum tomatoes
- 1 or 2 jalapeños (about 1 ounce)
- 1 ear of corn, shucked
- ½ small white onion, sliced about 1/4 inch thick (about 2 ounces)
- 4 garlic cloves, peeled
- Salt to taste
- 1 ½ teaspoons cider vinegar
- ¼ cup water (optional)
- ⅓ to ½ cup chopped cilantro (to taste)

Direction

- Preheat broiler and set rack 4 inches below. If your broiler and oven are separate, also preheat the oven to 425 degrees. Line 2 baking sheets with foil.
- Place tomatoes and jalapeños on one of the baking sheets and set under broiler, about 4 inches from heat. Broil for about 6 minutes, until skins are charred and blackened in spots. Using tongs, flip over tomatoes and jalapeño and continue to broil for another 6 minutes. The tomatoes and chiles should be softened and cooked through as well as charred. Tip tomatoes and chiles, along with any juices in the pan, into a bowl and allow to cool.
- Place corn on baking sheet and set under the broiler. Broil until you hear the kernels

beginning to pop, 2 to 4 minutes. Corn should be nicely browned on one side. Flip over and broil for 2 minutes, or until you hear popping, on the other side. Remove from heat, allow to cool, then cut kernels from cob and set aside.

- If using the same oven to roast the onions, turn heat down to 425 degrees. Break up onions into rings and place on baking sheet in a single layer. Add garlic and place in oven. Roast, stirring every 5 minutes, until onions have softened and are lightly browned and charred on edges and garlic is soft and browned in spots, about 15 minutes. If some of the smaller pieces of onion begin to char more quickly than others, remove them sooner.
- Stem jalapeños and place with onions and garlic in a food processor fitted with the bowl as necessary. Transfer to a large bowl.
- When tomatoes are cool enough to handle, core and discard skins (hold over bowl to catch juices). Place in food processor with juice and pulse to a coarse purée. Add to bowl with chopped onions, garlic and jalapeño. Add the vinegar, season generously with salt (Rick Bayless recommends a generous teaspoon), and stir in the cilantro and corn. If desired, thin out with water.

Nutrition Information

- 293: calories;
- 14 grams: dietary fiber;
- 12 grams: protein;
- 2132 milligrams: sodium;
- 0 grams: saturated fat;
- 1 gram: polyunsaturated fat;
- 3 grams: fat;
- 67 grams: carbohydrates;
- 26 grams: sugars;

248. Roasted Cornish Hens With Rosemary And Garlic

Serving: 4 servings | Prep: | Cook: | Ready in: 1hours

Ingredients

- 4 Cornish hens about 1 lb. each
- Salt and freshly ground pepper to taste
- 4 sprigs fresh rosemary or 2 tablespoons dry
- 4 garlic cloves peeled
- 2 tablespoons olive oil
- 1 medium-size onion peeled and quartered
- ¼ cup dry white wine
- ¾ cup fresh or canned chicken broth

Direction

- Preheat oven to 450 degrees.
- Rub the hens inside and out with salt and pepper and remove any excess fat inside. Place one sprig of rosemary and one garlic clove in each cavity and truss the hens, if desired.
- Place the hens in a large metal roasting pan. Brush them with the oil. Arrange the birds on their sides. Scatter the necks, gizzards, hearts, livers and onion around the birds. Place the dish on top of the stove and heat until the oil is sizzling.
- Place the pan in the oven and bake for 20 minutes, basting occasionally.
- Turn the birds on the reverse side and cook for 15 more minutes, basting occasionally.
- Remove all the fat from the dish and add the wine and chicken broth.
- Reduce the heat to 425 degrees. Place the hens on their backs for a final 10 minutes of cooking. The simmering broth will deglaze the pan as the birds roast, making a gravy. Remove from the oven and pour the cavity juices, including the rosemary and garlic, into the pan. Remove the rosemary and the trussing string, and let the hens rest in a warm place for 5 minutes before carving. Serve with the giblets and onions, if desired.

Nutrition Information

- 654: calories;
- 8 grams: polyunsaturated fat;
- 1298 milligrams: sodium;
- 46 grams: fat;
- 22 grams: monounsaturated fat;
- 6 grams: carbohydrates;
- 2 grams: sugars;
- 49 grams: protein;
- 12 grams: saturated fat;

249. Roasted Eggplant And Chickpeas With Tomato Sauce

Serving: 6 servings | Prep: | Cook: | Ready in: 1hours30mins

Ingredients

- ¼ cup extra virgin olive oil
- 2 garlic cloves, minced
- 1 28-ounce can chopped tomatoes, with juice, pulsed to a coarse purée
- 1 teaspoon mild honey (more to taste)
- ¼ to ½ teaspoon cinnamon, to taste
- Salt to taste
- 1 large or 2 medium eggplants (about 1 1/4 pounds), cut into 1/3-inch-thick slices
- 3 cups cooked chickpeas (2 cans, drained and rinsed, or, 1 1/2 cups dried – about 3/4 pound
- 4 ounces feta, crumbled (3/4 cup
- 1 teaspoon dried oregano, preferably Greek or Turkish

Direction

- Make the tomato sauce. Heat 1 tablespoon of the olive oil in a heavy skillet or wide saucepan over medium heat, and add the garlic. Cook, stirring, until it smells fragrant, about 30 seconds, and add the tomatoes, honey, salt to taste and cinnamon. Cook over medium heat until the tomatoes have cooked down and the sauce is fragrant, about 20 minutes. Taste and adjust seasonings.
- Meanwhile, heat the oven to 425 degrees. Line a baking sheet with aluminum foil and brush the boil with olive oil. Place the eggplant slices on the baking sheet, salt lightly and brush with olive oil. Place in the oven and bake 20 minutes, or until eggplant is lightly browned and soft all the way through. Remove from the heat. Fold the aluminum foil over and crimp the edges together so that the eggplant steams as it cools. Do this in batches if you need more than one baking sheet. Turn the oven down to 350 degrees.
- Oil a 2-quart baking dish or gratin. Place the chickpeas in the baking dish and stir in 1 cup of the tomato sauce. Layer the eggplant over the chickpeas and top with the remaining tomato sauce. Sprinkle the feta over the top and drizzle on any remaining olive oil. Sprinkle with the oregano and cover tightly with foil. Bake 30 minutes. Uncover and bake another 10 minutes, until the dish is bubbling.

Nutrition Information

- 310: calories;
- 4 grams: saturated fat;
- 8 grams: monounsaturated fat;
- 11 grams: dietary fiber;
- 16 grams: fat;
- 2 grams: polyunsaturated fat;
- 34 grams: carbohydrates;
- 12 grams: protein;
- 789 milligrams: sodium;

250. Roasted Mushroom Base

Serving: 1 1/4 pounds or about 3 cups | Prep: | Cook: | Ready in: 45mins

Ingredients

- 2 tablespoons extra-virgin olive oil

- 2 pounds mushrooms, sliced or quartered
- Salt to taste
- Freshly ground black pepper to taste

Direction

- Preheat oven to 400 degrees. Line 2 baking sheets with parchment.
- In a large bowl, toss mushrooms with oil, salt and pepper. Spread in an even layer on baking sheets and bake in the middle and lower racks of the oven for 20 minutes, stirring every 5 minutes and switching pans top to bottom halfway through. The mushrooms should be tender and dry when done. Remove from heat and allow to cool.
- Grind in a grinder or pulse in a food processor fitted with steel blade until broken down into small pieces resembling ground meat. What works best in my food processor is to pulse about 10 times, scrape down the sides of the bowl and then pulse another five to 10 times. Taste and adjust seasoning.

Nutrition Information

- 111: calories;
- 1 gram: polyunsaturated fat;
- 5 grams: monounsaturated fat;
- 2 grams: dietary fiber;
- 4 grams: sugars;
- 7 grams: protein;
- 545 milligrams: sodium;
- 8 grams: carbohydrates;

251. Roasted Vegetable Sandwich With Parsley Arugula Salad

Serving: Four sandwiches | Prep: | Cook: | Ready in: 2hours

Ingredients

- 3 red peppers
- 2 medium eggplants, sliced crosswise into 1/2-inch-thick disks
- 2 tablespoons coarse salt
- 2 ripe tomatoes, cored, or substitute 1 cup imported canned plum tomatoes, drained of juices
- 1 large onion cut into 1/8's
- 1 sprig fresh rosemary
- ½ head of garlic, cut along the clove
- 1 cup extra-virgin olive oil
- 1 tablespoon Sherry vinegar (or substitute red-wine vinegar)
- 2 teaspoons lemon juice (optional)
- ½ cup flat-leaf parsley, washed, dried and loosely packed
- 1 ½ cups arugula, washed, dried and loosely packed
- 8 slices crusty French or Italian bread from a large round loaf
- ¼ teaspoon freshly ground black pepper

Direction

- To roast the red peppers, place either over a gas burner, under the broiler or in a very hot oven (450 to 500 degrees), turning frequently until the pepper skins blacken. Place the peppers in a paper bag or covered bowl until they cool. Gently peel away the skin, cut in half and carefully remove the seeds. Roasted peppers can be covered with olive oil and kept in a covered container in the refrigerator for up to two weeks.
- Preheat the oven to 450 degrees.
- Sprinkle the eggplant slices with about one-and-a-half tablespoons of coarse salt and let stand for 30 minutes.
- Place the tomatoes, onion wedges and rosemary sprig in a lightly oiled oven-proof skillet or pan, just large enough to contain the vegetables. Place the garlic, cut-side down, on top of one of the tomatoes. Generously brush the vegetables with olive oil and sprinkle with salt and pepper. Roast in the oven, tossing the vegetables lightly to coat them with oil and juices. Remove when the garlic and onion are

tender and golden brown, about 45 minutes. The tomato will be very soft, its skin split.
- While the vegetables are roasting, rinse the eggplant slices under cold water and dry well with paper towels. Place the slices on an oiled baking sheet and brush the tops with olive oil. Bake in a 450-degree oven, turning once, until golden brown, about 15 to 20 minutes. Set aside.
- Take the roasted garlic and squeeze the head to release the softened cloves into the bowl of a food processor. Add the onion, flesh of tomato, discarding the skins, one teaspoon of Sherry vinegar, two teaspoons of lemon juice (if desired) and two tablespoons of olive oil. Process, using short pulses, until the mixture is the consistency of a relish.
- In a mixing bowl, lightly dress the parsley and arugula with about one teaspoon of Sherry vinegar and olive oil. Sprinkle with salt and pepper to taste.
- Brush one side of each slice of bread with olive oil and lightly toast on the rack of the 450-degree oven.
- To assemble the sandwiches, place a quarter of the eggplant and roasted pepper slices on each of four slices of bread, oil-side up. Spoon on about two or three tablespoons of sauce (see note). Top with the dressed greens and cover with a second slice of bread, oil-side inward.

Nutrition Information

- 286: calories;
- 512 milligrams: sodium;
- 23 grams: fat;
- 3 grams: protein;
- 16 grams: monounsaturated fat;
- 19 grams: carbohydrates;
- 5 grams: dietary fiber;
- 7 grams: sugars;

252. Romaine Salad With Cucumber, Red Onion And Feta

Serving: serves 4 | Prep: | Cook: | Ready in: 30mins

Ingredients

- ½ small cucumber, peeled, halved and seeded
- ½ medium red onion, very thinly sliced
- ½ teaspoon coarse kosher salt
- 4 cups torn romaine lettuce
- ¼ pound feta, preferably French goat's-milk feta
- 2 tablespoons best quality olive oil
- 1 tablespoon balsamic vinegar or red-wine vinegar
- Coarsely ground black pepper

Direction

- Thinly slice the cucumber halves. You need just 1 cup. In a bowl, combine the cucumber with the onion and sprinkle with the salt. Mix, then let sit for 15 minutes.
- Meanwhile, put the romaine in a large salad bowl. Break the feta into small (1/2-inch) pieces and drop them into the bowl. Gather the cucumber and onion in your fist and squeeze out any excess moisture. Scatter them over the romaine. Sprinkle the oil and vinegar over the salad. Grind pepper over top and then mix the salad gently so that you dress it without mashing the cheese to bits.

Nutrition Information

- 156: calories;
- 3 grams: sugars;
- 285 milligrams: sodium;
- 13 grams: fat;
- 5 grams: protein;
- 6 grams: carbohydrates;
- 1 gram: dietary fiber;

253. Rosemary Bread

Serving: 2 loaves | Prep: | Cook: | Ready in: 1hours30mins

Ingredients

- 1 cake fresh compressed yeast
- 1 cup warm water
- 2 teaspoons salt
- 3 ½ to 4 cups unbleached all-purpose flour
- ¼ cup olive oil, plus oil for the pan
- 6 sprigs fresh rosemary, crushed
- 3 tablespoons golden raisins, soaked in warm water and drained

Direction

- In a large bowl, dissolve the yeast in the water. Set aside until it bubbles, then stir in the salt.
- Stir in the flour, a cup at a time, until the mixture is firm enough to handle (you will need about 3 cups). Turn the dough out on a work surface spread with 1/2 cup of the remaining flour and knead about 10 minutes, incorporating the flour on the board. Add the remaining flour while kneading. Form the dough into a ball.
- Heat the oil in a skillet and briefly sautee the rosemary. Do not let it turn brown.
- Let the rosemary and oil cool briefly. Make a hole in the center of the dough and add the rosemary, oil and raisins. Work them into the dough.
- Divide the dough into 2 equal parts. Roll each into a ball, slightly flatten the top and cut a shallow cross into the top.
- Place the loaves on a lightly oiled baking sheet. Cover with a towel and set aside to rise about 30 minutes. Preheat oven to 350 degrees.
- Bake the bread for 30 minutes, until nicely browned. Allow to cool 2 to 3 hours before serving.

Nutrition Information

- 243: calories;
- 7 grams: fat;
- 1 gram: polyunsaturated fat;
- 0 grams: trans fat;
- 5 grams: protein;
- 39 grams: carbohydrates;
- 2 grams: sugars;
- 194 milligrams: sodium;

254. Roti

Serving: Four rotis | Prep: | Cook: | Ready in: 40mins

Ingredients

- 2 cups flour
- 1 teaspoon salt
- ½ teaspoon baking powder
- ½ to ⅔ cup of water
- About 8 tablespoons vegetable oil or ghee (clarified butter) for frying
- About 4 teaspoons ghee, melted

Direction

- In a large bowl, combine the dry ingredients
- With one hand, slowly drizzle 1/2 to 2/3 cup of water into the bowl, a few tablespoons at a time. With your other hand, mix the water into the flour in a circular motion; then, begin kneading the dough as it starts to form. Stop adding water when the dough is stiff and elastic but not sticky (more flour may be added if the dough gets too wet).
- Form the dough into four balls, cover with a dish towel and let rest on a floured board for 15 to 30 minutes.
- When the fillings are ready (the recipes follow), roll out one dough ball into a 10-inch round on a well-floured surface. The rolled-out roti should have the feel of a damp washcloth. (If it doesn't, then the dough hasn't set long enough. Punch the round back into a ball and let rest for an additional 15 minutes.)
- Grease a flat iron griddle or skillet with 1 to 2 tablespoons of the oil or ghee. Place over high

heat until a drop of water sizzles when dropped in the pan. Reduce the heat to medium high and place the dough on the griddle or skillet. Moving from the edges of the roti inward, spread 1 teaspoon of the melted ghee onto the dough, rubbing the oil in with the back of a wooden spoon. The dough will begin to bubble and release steam.
- After 1 minute, turn the roti over and cook the other side for about 1 additional minute. The finished roti will be floppy, and a light golden color. Place on a warm platter and cover with a towel. Repeat with remaining three dough balls, adding additional ghee to the pan as necessary.
- To make a roti sandwich, place the bread on a plate and add a generous portion of filling (each recipe below divides equally into 4 rotis) to the middle. Fold up the top and bottom ends of the bread till they meet, then fold up the two side flaps to form a square envelope. Serve immediately.

Nutrition Information

- 351: calories;
- 15 grams: fat;
- 0 grams: sugars;
- 6 grams: protein;
- 8 grams: monounsaturated fat;
- 2 grams: dietary fiber;
- 48 grams: carbohydrates;
- 260 milligrams: sodium;
- 3 grams: saturated fat;

255. Salad Astoria

Serving: Two servings | Prep: | Cook: | Ready in: 5mins

Ingredients

- 1 head soft-leaf lettuce (like bibb or Boston)
- Minced Bermuda onion to taste
- 1 dozen pitted calamata olives, sliced
- 1 tablespoon red-wine vinegar
- 3 tablespoons extra-virgin olive oil

Direction

- Combine all ingredients in a salad bowl and toss.

256. Salmon Cakes With Dill

Serving: 2 servings | Prep: | Cook: | Ready in: 25mins

Ingredients

- 3 ounces whole red onion or 2 ounces chopped ready-cut onion (3/4 cup)
- Several sprigs of dill to yield 2 tablespoons chopped
- 1 tablespoon capers
- 1 tablespoon horseradish
- 2 egg whites
- 10 ounces salmon fillet

Direction

- Preheat broiler or prepare grill on top of stove.
- Chop whole onion; wash and chop dill, and rinse capers. Mix ingredients together with horseradish and egg whites in a bowl large enough to hold all the ingredients.
- Grill or broil salmon following the Canadian rule: measure fish at thickest point and cook 8 minutes to the inch. When salmon is cooked, flake and stir into bowl, and mix well. Shape into 4 patties.
- Grill patties on top of stove, or preheat a nonstick skillet and saute them until brown on both sides, about 4 or 5 minutes total.

Nutrition Information

- 330: calories;
- 19 grams: fat;
- 5 grams: carbohydrates;
- 6 grams: polyunsaturated fat;

- 262 milligrams: sodium;
- 4 grams: saturated fat;
- 1 gram: dietary fiber;
- 3 grams: sugars;
- 32 grams: protein;

257. Salmon Fillets Braised In Red Wine

Serving: Six servings | Prep: | Cook: | Ready in: 1hours10mins

Ingredients

- 4 tablespoons butter
- ½ cup chopped shallots
- ½ cup chopped onions
- ½ cup chopped celery
- 1 cup diced carrots
- 1 pound fish bones, and the salmon head, gills removed
- 3 ½ cups dry red wine, such as a Cotes du Rhone
- 1 cup water
- ½ bay leaf
- ¼ teaspoon dried thyme
- 4 sprigs fresh parsley
- 4 salmon fillets, boneless and skinless, each 6 to 8 ounces, at room temperature
- ½ teaspoon salt
- Freshly ground black pepper to taste

Direction

- In a saucepan, place one tablespoon of the butter, a quarter cup of the shallots, the onions, celery and carrots. Cook, stirring, for one minute over a medium-high flame. Chop the fish bones and head coarsely and add them to the pan. Cook and stir for two minutes. Pour three cups of the wine and the water into the pan, then add the bay leaf, thyme and parsley. Reduce the cooking liquid for 45 minutes over a medium-low flame, or until it reaches about one cup. Strain the broth into a pan. Discard the vegetables.
- Select a pan large enough to hold the fish in one layer. Rub the bottom of the dish with a half teaspoon of butter and sprinkle the remaining shallots over the bottom of the pan. Arrange the fish, skin side down, in the pan. Sprinkle with salt and pepper generously. Add the remaining half cup of wine and fish broth. Dot the fish with one tablespoon of the butter.
- Place the pan over a medium-high flame and cook, covered, for about 90 seconds, flip the fillets gently and cook another 90 seconds (cooking time may vary with thickness of the fish). The salmon should be just barely cooked in the center; do not overcook.
- Transfer the fish to a serving dish, cover with foil and keep it warm.
- Over a high flame, reduce the cooking liquid to about one cup. Strain it through a fine sieve and into a saucepan. Swirl in the remaining butter and, while hot, spoon the sauce over the fish. Serve immediately.

Nutrition Information

- 916: calories;
- 53 grams: fat;
- 10 grams: carbohydrates;
- 4 grams: sugars;
- 70 grams: protein;
- 15 grams: monounsaturated fat;
- 0 grams: trans fat;
- 14 grams: polyunsaturated fat;
- 2 grams: dietary fiber;
- 426 milligrams: sodium;

258. Salmon Rillettes

Serving: 1 3/4 cups, serving 8 generously | Prep: | Cook: | Ready in: 20mins

Ingredients

- 1 6-ounce salmon fillet, bones removed
- Salt and freshly ground pepper
- 5 ounces smoked salmon, cut into thin strips, then into 1/4-inch pieces
- 1 tablespoon unsalted butter, at room temperature
- 1 tablespoon extra virgin olive oil
- 4 tablespoons plain Greek yogurt
- 1 tablespoon crème fraîche (or omit and use 5 tablespoons yogurt)
- 1 1-2 to 2 tablespoons fresh lemon juice
- 2 tablespoons chopped chives

Direction

- Lightly oil a steamer basket. Season salmon with salt and pepper and place in steamer basket over 1 inch of boiling water. Cover and steam 5 to 8 minutes, depending on thickness of the salmon. It should be just cooked through and easy to flake apart, but moist. Remove from heat and allow to cool.
- Using a fork or a whisk, cream butter and olive oil together until mixture is smooth and emulsified.
- Flake salmon into a medium-size bowl and add smoked salmon. Using a fork, mash the two together until well combined and salmon has broken down like canned tuna. Add butter and olive oil, yogurt and crème fraîche and work together with a fork until well combined. Add lemon juice to taste and the chives, and mix together well. Add pepper and mix together. Chill for 1 to 2 hours. Allow to come to room temperature before serving.
- Either spoon onto endive leaves or other vegetables, or serve with toasted bread or crackers.

Nutrition Information

- 105: calories;
- 8 grams: protein;
- 2 grams: saturated fat;
- 0 grams: sugars;
- 3 grams: monounsaturated fat;
- 1 gram: carbohydrates;
- 137 milligrams: sodium;

259. Salmon And Cucumber Tartare With Wasabi Sauce

Serving: 4 to 6 appetizer servings | Prep: | Cook: | Ready in: 10mins

Ingredients

- 1 pound salmon fillet, skin and small bones removed
- 1 cup (about 5 ounces) finely diced cucumber
- 1 medium size shallot, minced
- 2 tablespoons capers, rinsed and chopped
- 1 to 2 tablespoons minced pickled ginger (available in Japanese markets), to taste, plus additional pickled ginger for garnish
- ½ teaspoon Worcestershire sauce
- Salt and freshly ground pepper to taste
- 2 tablespoons fresh lemon juice
- 2 teaspoons wasabi paste
- 1 tablespoon seasoned rice vinegar
- 1 teaspoon soy sauce
- 2 tablespoons extra virgin olive oil
- Chopped chives for garnish

Direction

- Make sure there are no small pin bones in the salmon. Remove with tweezers if there are, then mince the fish very fine. Combine with the cucumber in a medium bowl.
- Rinse the shallot with cold water and drain on a paper towel. Add to the salmon and cucumber. Add the capers, minced pickled ginger, Worcestershire sauce, salt and pepper, and lemon juice and toss together.
- In a small bowl or measuring cup, whisk together the wasabi or horseradish, vinegar, soy sauce, and olive oil. Toss with the fish and cucumber mixture. Cover and refrigerate until ready to serve.
- To serve, spoon onto cucumber rounds or pita triangles, or mold in plastic wrap-lined

ramekins and unmold onto plates as a first course. Sprinkle with chives and garnish with pickled ginger.

Nutrition Information

- 213: calories;
- 16 grams: protein;
- 294 milligrams: sodium;
- 15 grams: fat;
- 3 grams: polyunsaturated fat;
- 6 grams: monounsaturated fat;
- 4 grams: carbohydrates;
- 1 gram: sugars;

260. Salsa Intravaia (A Meat And Wild Mushroom Sauce)

Serving: sauce for 4 to 6 portions of pasta | Prep: | Cook: | Ready in: 1hours

Ingredients

- 1 ½ cups dried Italian mushrooms, preferably porcini
- 6 tablespoons butter
- 5 tablespoons olive oil
- ¼ cup finely chopped onion
- 2 teaspoons finely minced garlic
- 2 tablespoons finely chopped celery
- 2 tablespoons finely chopped carrot
- 3 tablespoons ground beef
- ¼ cup ground lean pork
- 3 tablespoons ground prosciutto
- Salt to taste if desired
- Freshly ground pepper to taste
- 1 bay leaf
- ¼ cup dry red wine
- ½ cup peeled, seeded, finely chopped ripe tomatoes
- ¼ cup dry white wine
- 1 cup heavy cream
- 2 tablespoons finely chopped parsley
- ¼ cup freshly grated Parmesan cheese

Direction

- Place the mushrooms in a mixing bowl, and add warm water to cover. Let stand 30 minutes.
- Heat half of the butter and the oil in a skillet, and add the onion, garlic, celery and carrot. Cook, stirring, about 3 minutes.
- Add the ground meats and cook, stirring and chopping with the side of a kitchen spoon to break up any lumps. Sprinkle with salt and pepper, and cook 3 minutes. Add the bay leaf and red wine. Cook over moderately high heat, stirring, for 3 minutes. Add tomatoes and cook 3 minutes more.
- Drain the mushrooms. Squeeze and chop them. There should be about 1/2 cup. Add them to the meat mixture. Stir. Add the white wine, and continue cooking 10 minutes.
- When ready to serve, heat the remaining 3 tablespoons of butter in a large, heavy skillet, and when it starts to brown, add the meat mixture. Add the cream and parsley and blend. Add the pasta, toss, and sprinkle with cheese. Serve with more cheese on the side.

Nutrition Information

- 498: calories;
- 23 grams: saturated fat;
- 3 grams: sugars;
- 5 grams: carbohydrates;
- 374 milligrams: sodium;
- 49 grams: fat;
- 1 gram: dietary fiber;
- 20 grams: monounsaturated fat;
- 8 grams: protein;

261. Salt Baked Chicken

Serving: Four servings | Prep: | Cook: | Ready in: 2hours20mins

Ingredients

- About 4 pounds kosher salt
- 1 4-pound chicken

Direction

- Preheat the oven to 350 degrees. Put the salt in a heavy pot with a lid, slightly larger than the chicken. Place the pot, uncovered, over medium heat until the salt is very hot, stirring from time to time, about 30 minutes.
- Scoop most of the salt into a large bowl, leaving a 1 1/2-to-2-inch layer of salt in the bottom of the pot. Place the chicken over the salt layer, breast side up. Spoon the remaining salt over and around the chicken, so that it is completely buried in salt.
- Cover the pot with the lid. Bake until the chicken is cooked through, about 1 1/2 hours. Scrape the salt from the chicken and remove from the pot. Wipe off as much of the salt as possible and let stand for 10 minutes. Carve the chicken and serve.

Nutrition Information

- 663: calories;
- 0 grams: trans fat;
- 19 grams: monounsaturated fat;
- 10 grams: polyunsaturated fat;
- 57 grams: protein;
- 1055 milligrams: sodium;
- 46 grams: fat;
- 13 grams: saturated fat;

262. Sauce Rémoulade

Serving: About 2 cups | Prep: | Cook: | Ready in: 10mins

Ingredients

- 2 egg yolks
- ¼ cup vegetable oil
- 3 to 4 tablespoons prepared horseradish
- 1 to 2 tablespoons Creole mustard (or any grainy French mustard)
- ½ cup finely chopped celery
- ½ cup finely chopped green onions
- ¼ cup chopped fresh parsley
- ¼ of a large lemon, seeded and cut into 3 pieces
- 2 tablespoons ketchup
- 2 tablespoons Worcestershire sauce
- 1 tablespoon white-wine vinegar
- 1 tablespoon Tabasco sauce
- 1 tablespoon minced garlic
- 2 teaspoons sweet paprika
- 1 teaspoon salt
- 1 bay leaf, crumbled

Direction

- In a blender or food processor, process the yolks for 2 minutes. With the machine running, add the oil in a thin stream and then, one at a time, blend in the remaining ingredients until well mixed and the lemon rind is finely chopped.
- To serve, toss with chilled boiled shrimp and place on a bed of shredded lettuce, garnished with tomato wedges.

Nutrition Information

- 187: calories;
- 16 grams: fat;
- 2 grams: protein;
- 11 grams: monounsaturated fat;
- 0 grams: trans fat;
- 3 grams: polyunsaturated fat;
- 9 grams: carbohydrates;
- 5 grams: sugars;
- 319 milligrams: sodium;

263. Sausage Stuffing

Serving: 6 to 8 servings | Prep: | Cook: | Ready in: 20mins

Ingredients

- ½ pound ground sausage meat
- 2 cups finely chopped onions
- 1 teaspoon finely minced garlic
- 2 apples, preferably Granny Smiths, about 1 pound
- 2 cups bread slices cut into 1/2-inch cubes, toasted
- Salt to taste if desired
- Freshly ground pepper to taste
- 2 teaspoons finely chopped leaf sage
- 1 cup fresh or canned chicken broth
- ½ cup finely chopped parsley
- 2 tablespoons butter
- 1 egg, well beaten

Direction

- Put sausage in skillet and cook, breaking up any lumps, until the meat has lost its raw look.
- Add onions and garlic and cook, stirring, until wilted.
- Meanwhile, peel apples; remove and discard stems and cores. Cut apples into quarters. Cut apple quarters crosswise into very thin slices. There should be about 3 cups.
- Add apples and stir. Add toasted bread cubes, salt and pepper. Add sage, broth and parsley. Cover and cook over low heat about 10 minutes. Add butter and egg and blend well. Remove from heat and keep warm.

Nutrition Information

- 190: calories;
- 16 grams: carbohydrates;
- 7 grams: protein;
- 389 milligrams: sodium;
- 4 grams: monounsaturated fat;
- 0 grams: trans fat;
- 11 grams: fat;
- 2 grams: polyunsaturated fat;
- 3 grams: dietary fiber;

264. Sausages With Mushrooms And Red Wine

Serving: 4 servings | Prep: | Cook: | Ready in: 1hours

Ingredients

- 1 ounce dried porcini mushrooms
- 8 pork sausages (Italian, sweet or country)
- 1 tablespoon safflower oil
- 1 large onion, chopped
- 1 clove garlic, minced
- 4 tablespoons butter
- 1 tablespoon flour
- ½ cup pureed canned tomatoes
- ½ cup dry red wine
- 1 cup chicken stock
- Coarse salt and freshly ground pepper to taste
- 1 pound mushrooms (a mixture of cultivated plus wild, such as black chanterelles and wild oak, if possible)

Direction

- Soak the porcini mushrooms in warm water to cover for at least 15 minutes. Meanwhile, prick the sausages all over with a fork and cook them in a large skillet in the oil until well-browned on all sides. Drain on paper towels when done.
- In a heavy casserole, saute the onion and the garlic in two tablespoons of butter until soft. Sprinkle on the flour and cook for a minute, stirring, without burning.
- Add the tomatoes, wine and chicken stock. Season to taste, cover and simmer for 15 minutes. Add the sausages and simmer another 15 minutes, or until you are sure they are cooked.
- Slice the mushrooms and saute them in the remaining butter in a separate skillet. Season with salt and pepper and add to the sausages. Cook, uncovered, over low heat for 10 minutes, stirring occasionally. Correct seasonings and serve.

Nutrition Information

- 398: calories;
- 1 gram: trans fat;
- 19 grams: carbohydrates;
- 3 grams: dietary fiber;
- 808 milligrams: sodium;
- 29 grams: fat;
- 12 grams: saturated fat;
- 9 grams: monounsaturated fat;
- 6 grams: sugars;
- 15 grams: protein;

265. Sautéed Apple Rings

Serving: 6 servings | Prep: | Cook: | Ready in: 30mins

Ingredients

- 4 large apples
- 1 lemon wedge
- 2 tablespoons unsalted butter
- 1 tablespoon raw brown (turbinado) sugar
- ½ teaspoon cinnamon
- 1 teaspoon vanilla extract
- 2 tablespoons calvados or brandy (optional)

Direction

- Core apples and rub inside with lemon wedge. Peel if desired (I don't). Slice about 1/4 inch thick, or a little bit thicker.
- Melt half the butter over medium-high heat in a large, heavy skillet. When it stops foaming (wait this long so that the apples sear when you add them to the pan) add half the apples, half the sugar and half the cinnamon. Cook, flipping apple rings often, until apples are caramelized, 10 to 12 minutes. Test, using the tip of a knife or the edge of a spoon, to see if the apples are soft all the way through. Remove to a bowl. Repeat with remaining apples, butter, sugar and cinnamon. When second batch is caramelized return first batch to pan. Add vanilla and brandy if using and continue to cook, flipping apples, until the liquid evaporates. Transfer to a bowl or serving dish. Serve warm.

Nutrition Information

- 122: calories;
- 2 milligrams: sodium;
- 4 grams: dietary fiber;
- 2 grams: saturated fat;
- 0 grams: protein;
- 1 gram: monounsaturated fat;
- 23 grams: carbohydrates;
- 18 grams: sugars;

266. Sautéed Red Snapper With Rhubarb Sauce

Serving: 4 servings | Prep: | Cook: | Ready in: 30mins

Ingredients

- 1 pound rhubarb, washed and trimmed
- ⅓ cup sugar
- Pinch saffron
- Salt and pepper to taste
- 2 tablespoons olive oil
- 2 tablespoons butter (or a little more oil)
- 4 6-ounce red snapper fillets
- Chopped mint or parsley for garnish (optional)

Direction

- Combine the rhubarb, sugar and saffron in a small saucepan, cover and turn the heat to low. Cook, stirring only occasionally, for about 20 minutes, or until the rhubarb becomes saucy. Add salt to taste and a little more sugar if necessary. If the mixture is very soupy, continue to cook a little longer to make it thicker.
- When you judge the rhubarb to be nearly done, put a large skillet, preferably nonstick,

over medium-high heat. A minute later, add the oil and butter. When the butter foam subsides, add the fillets, skin side down. Cook for 4 or 5 minutes, or until the fish is nearly done; turn carefully; and lightly brown the flesh side, seasoning it with salt and pepper as it cooks. Transfer the fish to a plate lined with paper towels to absorb excess oil.
- Serve the fish napped with a bit of the sauce and garnished, if you like, with the herb.

Nutrition Information

- 371: calories;
- 0 grams: trans fat;
- 7 grams: monounsaturated fat;
- 22 grams: carbohydrates;
- 36 grams: protein;
- 732 milligrams: sodium;
- 15 grams: fat;
- 5 grams: saturated fat;
- 2 grams: dietary fiber;
- 18 grams: sugars;

267. Savory Bread Pudding With Swiss Chard And Red Pepper

Serving: 6 servings | Prep: | Cook: | Ready in: 3hours

Ingredients

- 4 ounces stale baguette
- 2 garlic cloves
- 1 ¾ cups low-fat milk (1 percent or 2 percent)
- ½ to ¾ pound Swiss chard
- 1 tablespoon extra virgin olive oil
- 1 small onion, chopped
- 1 red bell pepper, diced
- ½ teaspoon chopped fresh rosemary
- 4 eggs
- 2 ounces Gruyère, grated (1/2 cup)
- 1 ounce Parmesan, grated (1/4 cup)

Direction

- Slice the bread about 3/4 inch thick. Cut 1 of the garlic cloves in half and rub each slice of bread with the cut side of the garlic. Mince all of the remaining garlic and set aside. Place the bread in a bowl and toss with 1 cup of the milk. Refrigerate for 1 hour, tossing every once in a while.
- Meanwhile, stem and wash the chard. Steam over 1 inch of boiling water until tender, about 2 minutes, or blanch in salted boiling water for 1 minute. Transfer to a bowl of cold water, drain and squeeze out excess water. Chop medium-fine.
- Preheat the oven to 350 degrees. Oil a 2-quart baking dish or a 10-inch ceramic tart pan. Heat the olive oil over medium heat in a large, heavy skillet and add the onion. Cook, stirring often, until it begins to soften, about 3 minutes, and add the red pepper. Cook, stirring often, until the vegetables are tender, about 5 minutes. Add a generous pinch of salt, the garlic, rosemary and chopped chard and stir together until the garlic is fragrant, 30 seconds to a minute. Remove from the heat.
- Remove the bowl with the soaked bread from the refrigerator. Using a wooden spoon, a whisk or an immersion blender, mash or beat the soaked bread so that the mixture turns to mush. Add the cooked vegetables to the bowl and mix together. Scrape into the oiled baking dish. Top with the grated cheese. Break the eggs into the bowl and beat with the remaining milk, salt to taste (about 1/2 teaspoon), and freshly ground pepper. Pour over the bread mixture and place in the oven.
- Bake 50 to 60 minutes, until the mixture is puffed, golden brown on the top and set. Remove from the heat and allow to cool for 10 minutes or longer before serving.

Nutrition Information

- 227: calories;
- 431 milligrams: sodium;
- 0 grams: trans fat;

- 4 grams: monounsaturated fat;
- 18 grams: carbohydrates;
- 1 gram: polyunsaturated fat;
- 2 grams: dietary fiber;
- 7 grams: sugars;
- 14 grams: protein;
- 11 grams: fat;
- 5 grams: saturated fat;

268. Savory Oatmeal Pan Bread

Serving: Serves 8 to 10 | Prep: | Cook: | Ready in: 1hours

Ingredients

- 110 grams (1 1/8 cups) rolled oats
- 70 grams (1/2 cup plus 1 tablespoon) whole wheat pastry flour
- 10 grams (2 1/4 teaspoons) baking powder
- 4 ½ grams (scant 3/4 teaspoon) salt
- 1 gram (1/4 teaspoon) freshly ground pepper
- 150 grams (1/2 cup plus 1 tablespoon) milk
- 110 grams (2 extra large) egg
- ½ cup fresh herbs, such as parsley leaves, sage, marjoram, thyme, dill, chopped (1/3 cup chopped)
- 50 grams (3 tablespoons) grated onion
- 4 tablespoons extra virgin olive oil

Direction

- Preheat the oven to 400 degrees.
- Place the oats in the bowl of a stand mixer or into the bowl of a food processor fitted with the steel blade. Sift together the flour, baking powder, salt, and ground pepper and add to the oats. Add the remaining ingredients except 2 tablespoons of the olive oil and mix at medium speed or pulse together until well blended. Scrape down the sides of the bowl and the beater and mix again for about 30 seconds.
- Add 2 tablespoons of the oil to a 9-inch cast iron skillet and place in the oven for 5 minutes.
- Remove from the oven and spread the batter in the pan.
- Place in the oven and bake 30 minutes, until the top is nicely browned and a tester comes out clean when inserted in the middle. Remove from the heat and serve hot, or allow to cool on a rack.

Nutrition Information

- 140: calories;
- 0 grams: trans fat;
- 5 grams: monounsaturated fat;
- 1 gram: sugars;
- 14 grams: carbohydrates;
- 4 grams: protein;
- 130 milligrams: sodium;
- 8 grams: fat;
- 2 grams: dietary fiber;

269. Savory Soup, Fish And Potatoes Cold Tomato Soup

Serving: About 6 servings | Prep: | Cook: | Ready in: 15mins

Ingredients

- 5 cloves garlic, peeled
- 2 ½ pounds very ripe tomatoes, cut into 1-inch pieces (6 cups)
- 1 teaspoon salt
- ½ teaspoon freshly ground black pepper
- ½ teaspoon Tabasco sauce
- ⅓ cup peanut oil
- 1 ½ tablespoons white vinegar
- 1 cup water
- ½ cup shredded basil

Direction

- Place the garlic in the bowl of a food processor, and process it for a few seconds.

- Add the tomatoes, and process the mixture for 30 to 45 seconds, until pureed.
- For a smooth soup, push the pureed tomatoes and garlic through a food mill, or press the mixture with the back of a spoon through a conventional strainer.
- Add the salt, pepper, Tabasco, oil, vinegar and water to the pureed mixture, and stir to mix well. Refrigerate until serving time.
- Spoon into bowls, and serve with basil sprinkled on top.

Nutrition Information

- 145: calories;
- 12 grams: fat;
- 2 grams: protein;
- 6 grams: monounsaturated fat;
- 4 grams: polyunsaturated fat;
- 8 grams: carbohydrates;
- 5 grams: sugars;
- 402 milligrams: sodium;

270. Savory Waffles

Serving: 4 servings | Prep: | Cook: | Ready in: 20mins

Ingredients

- 2 cups waffle and pancake mix
- 2 eggs
- 2 cups milk
- 2 tablespoons vegetable oil
- Salt and pepper
- ¾ cup grated rennet-free Parmesan cheese
- ½ cup grated rennet-free Gruyère or similar cheese

Direction

- Preheat oven to 200 degrees and place a waiting plate to warm inside. Heat a waffle maker until a flick of water beads and bounces around.
- In a bowl, add waffle mix, eggs, milk, oil, salt and pepper, and mix until just combined, adding more milk if the mix is too thick. It should be the consistency of pudding. Then fold in the cheeses.
- Lightly butter the waffle maker, and spoon judicious dollops of the mix onto the center of the hot waffle iron and spread just a bit. The mix will spread when the lid closes and expand as it cooks, so adding too much will be a bit messy as it bubbles out the sides.
- As the waffles finish, use a fork to lift them off and put them in the oven to stay warm while the rest are made. Waffles are best served warm. Freeze any leftover waffles to enjoy later.

271. Savory Whole Wheat Buttermilk Scones With Rosemary And Thyme

Serving: 12 small scones | Prep: | Cook: | Ready in: 30mins

Ingredients

- 150 grams (approximately 1 1/4 cups) whole-wheat flour
- 100 grams (approximately 3/4 cup) unbleached all-purpose flour
- 10 grams (2 teaspoons) baking powder
- 5 grams (1/2 teaspoon) baking soda
- 4 grams (approximately 1 teaspoon) brown sugar
- 5 grams (approximately 3/4 teaspoon) salt
- 70 grams (2 1/2 ounces / 5 tablespoons) unsalted butter
- 1 tablespoon finely chopped mixed fresh rosemary and thyme
- 125 grams (approximately 1/2 cup) buttermilk

Direction

- Preheat oven to 400 degrees. Line a baking sheet with parchment.

- Sift together flours, baking powder, baking soda, sugar and salt. Rub in butter, or place in a stand mixer fitted with the paddle and beat at low speed until incorporated. Add chopped rosemary and thyme and buttermilk and mix just until the dough comes together.
- Transfer to a lightly floured work surface and gently shape into a 1/2-inch thick rectangle. Either cut 2-inch circles with a biscuit cutter or cut into 6 squares, then cut each square in half on the diagonal. Transfer to baking sheet. Bake 15 minutes, until browned on the bottom. Flip over, bake 2 more minutes, and remove from the heat. Serve warm or allow to cool.

Nutrition Information

- 121: calories;
- 0 grams: polyunsaturated fat;
- 1 gram: sugars;
- 17 grams: carbohydrates;
- 2 grams: dietary fiber;
- 201 milligrams: sodium;
- 5 grams: fat;
- 3 grams: protein;

272. Scallion Risotto

Serving: 6 first-course servings | Prep: | Cook: | Ready in: 40mins

Ingredients

- 6 cups homemade chicken broth (or use 4 cups canned with 2 cups water)
- 6 tablespoons unsalted butter
- 1 ¼ cup chopped scallions (use the lower white and light green parts)
- 1 ½ cups Arborio rice
- ½ cup dry white wine
- ⅓ cup chopped scallions (use the green tops)
- ½ cup grated Parmesan or grana cheese
- White pepper to taste

Direction

- In a large saucepan, bring the broth to a boil; lower the heat and keep at a scant simmer.
- Meanwhile, in a large saute pan (see note) heat 4 tablespoons of the butter and cook the white parts of the scallions, stirring until they're soft, about 2 minutes. Add the rice, stirring with a wooden spoon, until all the grains are coated with butter. Add the wine and cook the mixture at a low simmer, stirring until all the wine is absorbed, about 3 to 4 minutes.
- Add 1/2 cup of the simmering broth and continue to simmer the mixture, stirring until the broth is absorbed. Keep adding broth by the 1/2 cup and repeating as above until the rice is creamy and al dente The rice may not absorb all the broth, so it's best to taste the mixture before adding the last 1/2 cup.
- Remove the pan from the heat and stir in the remaining 2 tablespoons butter, the green scallion tops, cheese and white pepper.

Nutrition Information

- 431: calories;
- 5 grams: sugars;
- 2 grams: dietary fiber;
- 480 milligrams: sodium;
- 17 grams: fat;
- 10 grams: saturated fat;
- 0 grams: trans fat;
- 1 gram: polyunsaturated fat;
- 51 grams: carbohydrates;
- 13 grams: protein;

273. Schav

Serving: 4 to 6 servings | Prep: | Cook: | Ready in: 45mins

Ingredients

- 1 pound fresh sorrel

- 2 medium white potatoes
- 1 leek
- 3 tablespoons butter
- 2 cups chicken stock (preferably homemade)
- Coarse salt and freshly ground pepper to taste
- 1 tablespoon sugar, plus extra if necessary
- 1 cup heavy cream
- Juice of 1 lemon, or to taste
- 1 cup sour cream for garnishing
- 6 to 8 tablespoons chopped scallions

Direction

- Stem and wash the sorrel, and cut the leaves into ribbons. Peel the potatoes and cut them into half-inch dice. Cut the leek in half, chop it and wash it thoroughly.
- Melt the butter in a large saucepan, and cook the leek for two minutes over medium heat. Add the sorrel and potatoes and cook for five minutes. Add the stock, two cups water, salt and pepper to taste, and the sugar, and simmer for 15 to 20 minutes or until the potatoes are very tender.
- Puree the soup in a blender or food processor. (A blender works better than a food processor; if you use the processor, puree the solids first and gradually add the liquids). Stir in the cream and chill the soup for at least an hour. Just before serving, add the lemon juice and additional sugar and salt, if necessary - the soup should be refreshingly tart but a little sweet. Serve schav in bowls with dollops of sour cream. Garnish each bowl with chopped scallions.

Nutrition Information

- 324: calories;
- 22 grams: fat;
- 13 grams: saturated fat;
- 6 grams: monounsaturated fat;
- 716 milligrams: sodium;
- 0 grams: trans fat;
- 1 gram: polyunsaturated fat;
- 28 grams: carbohydrates;
- 5 grams: dietary fiber;
- 7 grams: protein;

274. Sea Scallops On Asparagus

Serving: Four servings | Prep: | Cook: | Ready in: 2hours

Ingredients

- 10 ounces common mushrooms
- 1 ¼ pounds slender asparagus spears, to make 3 1/2 cups when prepared
- 2 ½ teaspoons fragrant mild honey, preferably lavender honey
- 2 teaspoons lime juice
- 2 scant teaspoons minced fresh tarragon
- 1 teaspoon minced fresh thyme
- 1 scant tablespoon dark green olive oil
- 2 tablespoons light olive oil
- 12 large sea scallops, 12 to 14 ounces, halved horizontally
- 2 tablespoons seasoned instant flour (see note)
- 2 tablespoons unsalted butter

Direction

- Coarsely chop the mushrooms and combine them in a large, non-reactive saucepan with five cups of water. Simmer gently for about one-and-a-half hours.
- Strain the liquid, pressing to get all possible juice. Discard mushrooms or reserve. Return the liquid to the pan and boil over high heat until reduced to about a half cup. Set aside.
- Break off the woody asparagus bottoms and peel the lower third. Remove the heads and halve them the long way, then slice the stems across into coins about one-eighth-inch-thick. Combine the honey, lime juice, tarragon and thyme in a small cup.
- Put the dark olive oil in a wide, nonreactive skillet over medium-high heat. When it is hot, add the asparagus pieces and stir-fry for one-and-a-half minutes, or just until they start to

change color. Stir in the honey mixture and cook one minute more, then remove the asparagus with a slotted spoon and set aside.
- Add the mushroom essence to the asparagus pan, raise the heat to high and reduce to a generous quarter cup. Set aside.
- Right before serving, put one tablespoon of the light olive oil in a wide, nonstick skillet over medium-high heat. Dust half the scallop pieces with seasoned flour (see note), place them in the pan and add one tablespoon of the butter. Cook the scallops about one-and-a-half minutes per side, basting with the fat. They should be golden, barely cooked. Set aside, uncovered, and repeat with the remaining oil, butter and scallops.
- Add the reduced mushroom essence to the scallop pan and bring to a boil, scraping. Stir in the asparagus, plus any escaped juices, and reheat.
- Make a nest of the asparagus on each plate and pour the juices over them. Arrange six scallop pieces on each nest and serve at once.

Nutrition Information

- 277: calories;
- 18 grams: carbohydrates;
- 4 grams: dietary fiber;
- 8 grams: sugars;
- 5 grams: saturated fat;
- 2 grams: polyunsaturated fat;
- 369 milligrams: sodium;
- 17 grams: protein;
- 0 grams: trans fat;
- 9 grams: monounsaturated fat;

275. Sea Scallops With Tomatoes And Shallot Butter

Serving: 4 servings | Prep: | Cook: | Ready in: 15mins

Ingredients

- 4 ripe plum tomatoes, about 1 pound
- 2 tablespoons olive oil
- 2 tablespoons butter
- 1 ½ pounds medium-size sea scallops
- Salt and freshly ground pepper to taste
- 4 tablespoons finely chopped shallots
- 2 sprigs fresh thyme or 1/2 teaspoon dried
- 1 tablespoon fresh lemon juice
- ¼ cup finely chopped parsley

Direction

- Core and peel tomatoes. Halve them crosswise. Squeeze the halves gently to extract seeds; cut halves into 1/4-inch cubes.
- In a nonstick skillet large enough to hold scallops in one layer, heat oil and butter over high heat. When hot add scallops, salt and pepper. Cook, stirring and shaking the pan and turning scallops, until lightly brown, about 2 minutes.
- Sprinkle shallots, thyme and tomatoes evenly over scallops. Cook, stirring, for 2 minutes. Add lemon juice and cook, stirring, for another minute. Sprinkle with parsley, stir well and serve immediately. Do not overcook the scallops.

Nutrition Information

- 260: calories;
- 2 grams: dietary fiber;
- 0 grams: trans fat;
- 7 grams: monounsaturated fat;
- 5 grams: saturated fat;
- 1 gram: polyunsaturated fat;
- 13 grams: carbohydrates;
- 4 grams: sugars;
- 22 grams: protein;
- 737 milligrams: sodium;
- 14 grams: fat;

276. Seared Sea Scallops With Lime Ginger Sauce And Caramelized Endive

Serving: Six first-course servings | Prep: | Cook: | Ready in: 45mins

Ingredients

- The endive:
- 2 tablespoons unsalted butter
- 3 heads Belgian endive, halved lengthwise
- ¼ teaspoon kosher salt
- Freshly ground pepper to taste
- 1 tablespoon sugar
- 1 tablespoon fresh lime juice
- The scallops:
- 1 tablespoon canola oil
- 1 pound sea scallops
- ¼ teaspoon kosher salt
- Freshly ground pepper to taste
- The sauce and garnish:
- 1 shallot, peeled and minced
- ½ clove garlic, peeled and thinly sliced
- 1 tablespoon grated fresh ginger
- 1 ½ tablespoons fresh lime juice
- 6 tablespoons imported white port or dry white wine
- ¼ cup heavy cream
- 4 tablespoons cold unsalted butter, cut into small pieces
- ½ teaspoon kosher salt
- Freshly ground pepper to taste
- Cayenne pepper to taste
- 2 scallions, trimmed and thinly sliced on the diagonal
- 1 large ripe tomato, peeled, seeded and diced small

Direction

- To make the endive, melt the butter in a large nonstick skillet over medium-low heat. Season the endive with salt and pepper and place cut side down in the skillet. Cook until lightly browned on the bottom, about 8 minutes.
- Sprinkle the sugar and lime juice over the top and cook, turning occasionally, until the endive are caramelized and tender when pierced with a knife, about 15 minutes longer. Cover and keep warm (can be prepared ahead and reheated in the oven).
- To make the scallops, heat the oil in a large skillet over medium-high heat. Season the scallops with salt and pepper, place them in the skillet and sear until lightly browned and warm in the center, about 1 minute per side.
- To make the sauce, combine the shallot, garlic, ginger, lime juice and port in a nonreactive saucepan over medium-high heat. Simmer until nearly all of the liquid has evaporated, about 3 minutes. Add the cream, bring to a boil and remove from the heat. Whisk in the butter a few pieces at a time until all is incorporated. Strain the sauce and season with salt, pepper and a touch of cayenne. Keep warm.
- To serve, place 1 endive half on each of 6 plates. Divide the scallops among the plates and spoon the sauce over and around them. Sprinkle with the scallions and tomato. Serve immediately.

Nutrition Information

- 253: calories;
- 1 gram: polyunsaturated fat;
- 11 grams: carbohydrates;
- 2 grams: dietary fiber;
- 18 grams: fat;
- 10 grams: protein;
- 0 grams: trans fat;
- 6 grams: monounsaturated fat;
- 439 milligrams: sodium;
- 4 grams: sugars;

277. Seared Wild Mushrooms

Serving: 4 servings | Prep: | Cook: | Ready in: 12mins

Ingredients

- 2 tablespoons plus 2 teaspoons extra virgin olive oil
- 1 pound wild mushrooms, torn into smaller pieces if large, cleaned if necessary
- ½ cup chopped onion or 2 shallots, minced
- 2 garlic cloves, minced, plus 1/2 garlic clove, intact
- 1 teaspoon minced fresh thyme leaves, chopped
- 1 teaspoon minced fresh rosemary or sage
- Salt and freshly ground pepper
- ¼ cup dry white wine
- For bruschetta or big bowls
- 8 thick slices country bread or 2 to 3 cups cooked quinoa
- 2 ounces Parmesan, crumbled or grated
- 2 eggs
- Chopped flat-leaf parsley for garnish

Direction

- Heat 1 tablespoon olive oil in a wide, heavy nonstick skillet or a wok over high heat. Add mushrooms. Let sear without moving for about 30 seconds, then toss and stir in the pan until they begin to sweat, 2 to 3 minutes. Turn heat to medium, add another tablespoon oil and onion or shallots and cook, stirring, until just tender, 3 to 5 minutes. Add minced garlic, thyme and rosemary or sage. Season with salt and pepper and continue to cook over medium heat until mushrooms are soft, about 5 more minutes. Add wine and cook, stirring, until it is no longer visible in the pan. Taste and adjust seasoning. Remove from heat.
- Beat 1 of the eggs in a small bowl and season with salt and pepper. Heat an 8-inch nonstick omelet pan over medium-high heat until hot. Add 1 teaspoon olive oil, swirl pan, then add egg and swirl pan to coat evenly. Shake and tilt the pan and lift the edges of the egg pancake with a rubber spatula to allow egg to run underneath itself. When just about set flip over to briefly cook any runny egg on top, then transfer to a plate. Repeat with remaining egg. Cut egg pancakes into strips.
- For bruschette, lightly toast bread and brush with olive oil. If desired, rub with a cut clove of garlic. Top with mushrooms. Sprinkle on Parmesan and egg strips, garnish with chopped parsley, and serve. For quinoa bowls, spoon quinoa into wide bowls and top with mushrooms. Sprinkle on Parmesan and egg strips. Garnish with chopped parsley, and serve.

Nutrition Information

- 395: calories;
- 17 grams: fat;
- 0 grams: trans fat;
- 9 grams: monounsaturated fat;
- 589 milligrams: sodium;
- 5 grams: saturated fat;
- 2 grams: polyunsaturated fat;
- 42 grams: carbohydrates;
- 8 grams: dietary fiber;
- 7 grams: sugars;
- 16 grams: protein;

278. Seitan Roulade With Oyster Mushroom Stuffing

Serving: 8 servings. | Prep: | Cook: | Ready in: 2hours

Ingredients

- Seitan
- 1 cup vital wheat gluten flour
- ¾ cup vegetable stock
- Roulade
- 1 pound uncooked seitan (see recipe)
- ½ cup soy sauce
- 3 tablespoons olive oil
- 1 small yellow onion, minced
- 1 cup oyster mushrooms, coarsely chopped
- 1 cup vegan sausage, cooked and crumbled
- 1 tablespoon minced fresh parsley

- 1 teaspoon minced fresh thyme
- Salt to taste
- Freshly ground black pepper to taste
- 4 cups finely diced bread

Direction

- Make the seitan. In a large bowl, combine flour and vegetable stock. Stir to make a soft dough. Knead for 3 minutes and let rest for 5 minutes.
- Place seitan in a shallow baking dish. Cover with soy sauce and marinate for 30 minutes at room temperature.
- Preheat oven to 375 degrees Fahrenheit. In a large skillet over medium heat, heat olive oil. Add onion, cover, and cook, stirring a few times until softened, about 5 minutes.
- Add mushrooms, vegan sausage, parsley, thyme, salt and pepper. Stir for 5 minutes longer, then transfer to a large bowl. Stir in the bread and mix well. Add a small amount of water if the stuffing mixture is too dry. Set aside.
- Place the uncooked seitan (reserve the marinade) between two sheets of plastic wrap and roll out with a rolling pin until it is approximately 1/4-inch thick. Using your hands, spread the stuffing over seitan to within 1/2-inch of the edges, then roll it up. In a lightly oiled shallow baking pan, place rolled seitan seam-side down. Pierce in several places with a fork.
- Pour the reserved marinade over the roast and bake uncovered for 40 to 45 minutes, basting once after 20 minutes. When the surface of the roast is firm and golden brown, remove from oven and let rest for 10 minutes.
- Using a serrated knife, cut the roast into 1/2-inch-thick slices. Arrange on serving platter and serve with remaining marinade and your favorite vegan gravy.

279. She Crab And Corn Salad

Serving: Twenty servings | Prep: | Cook: | Ready in: 20mins

Ingredients

- ¾ cup half-and-half
- 2 large cucumbers, peeled and thinly sliced
- ½ cup dry Sherry
- 20 ears of corn
- 4 tablespoons unsalted butter
- ¼ cup vegetable oil
- 2 pounds crab meat, picked over
- 1 ½ cups thinly sliced pickled sweet red peppers
- 2 to 3 teaspoons Worcestershire sauce, to taste
- ¼ teaspoon mace
- ¼ teaspoon nutmeg
- Salt and freshly ground pepper to taste
- 1 ½ pounds fresh spinach, washed and dried

Direction

- In a saucepan, bring the half-and-half to a simmer and poach the cucumbers in it for three to four minutes, until just cooked. Add the Sherry.
- Using a sharp knife, strip the kernels from the cobs. In a large pot, heat the butter and oil over medium-high heat. Saute the corn kernels for five minutes, or until heated through. Add the crab meat, red peppers and the rest of the seasonings. Saute for another two minutes, stirring constantly to blend well.
- In a large salad bowl, combine the cucumber mixture and half-and-half with the crab mixture and cool at room temperature. Place the spinach leaves on a large platter and arrange the salad over them.

Nutrition Information

- 238: calories;
- 8 grams: fat;
- 1 gram: polyunsaturated fat;
- 33 grams: carbohydrates;

- 605 milligrams: sodium;
- 3 grams: monounsaturated fat;
- 0 grams: trans fat;
- 5 grams: dietary fiber;
- 6 grams: sugars;
- 14 grams: protein;

280. Shrimp And Blue Cheese Roulade

Serving: Eight to 10 servings | Prep: | Cook: |Ready in: 20mins

Ingredients

- 1 basic sponge roll for roulades (see recipe)
- ¼ pound cooked shrimp, peeled and deveined
- 4 teaspoons cream cheese at room temperature
- 4 teaspoons blue cheese at room temperature
- 1 tablespoon finely chopped onion
- 1 tablespoon mayonnaise
- 1 tablespoon sour cream
- 2 teaspoons lemon juice
- 1 tablespoon finely chopped parsley

Direction

- Prepare the sponge roll and have it ready.
- Chop the shrimp coarse-fine and set aside. There should be about half a cup or slightly more.
- Combine the cream cheese, blue cheese, onion, mayonnaise, sour cream, lemon juice and parsley. Blend thoroughly and add the chopped shrimp.
- Spread the shrimp mixture over the sponge roll and smooth it over. Roll the cake like a jellyroll, folding the small end over and over to make a roll about 10 inches long.
- Using a knife with a serrated blade, carefully slice off the bulky ends of the roll. Cut the remaining roll into neat, one-half-inch slices. Serve lukewarm or cold.

Nutrition Information

- 57: calories;
- 1 gram: polyunsaturated fat;
- 0 grams: sugars;
- 4 grams: protein;
- 178 milligrams: sodium;
- 3 grams: fat;

281. Shrimp Broth

Serving: About four cups | Prep: | Cook: |Ready in: 30mins

Ingredients

- Shells from raw shrimp
- 5 cups water
- 6 black peppercorns
- ¼ cup coarsely chopped onions
- 2 ribs celery coarsely chopped
- 1 bay leaf

Direction

- Put all the ingredients in a saucepan and bring to a boil. Simmer for 20 minutes and strain.

282. Shrimp Risotto With Peas

Serving: Serves 4 | Prep: | Cook: |Ready in: 1hours15mins

Ingredients

- 1 pound medium shrimp, in the shell
- 1 quart chicken stock or water
- Salt to taste
- 2 tablespoons extra virgin olive oil
- ½ cup finely chopped onion
- 1 ½ cups arborio or carnaroli rice
- 2 large garlic cloves, green shoots removed, minced

- ½ cup dry white wine
- A generous pinch of saffron (optional)
- 1 cup thawed frozen peas, or fresh peas steamed for five minutes
- 2 tablespoons chopped fresh flat-leaf parsley
- Freshly ground pepper to taste

Direction

- Shell the shrimp and de-vein if necessary. Salt them lightly, and set aside in a bowl (in the refrigerator, if you won't be making and serving the risotto right away). Rinse the shells, and combine them with 5 cups of water in a medium saucepan. Bring to a boil, skim off foam, reduce the heat to low and simmer partly covered for 30 minutes. Strain and add to the chicken stock or water. Taste, add enough salt to make a well seasoned broth and bring to a simmer in a saucepan.
- Heat the oil over medium heat in a large nonstick frying pan or a large, wide saucepan. Add the onion. Cook, stirring, until the onion softens, three to five minutes, and then add the rice and the garlic. Cook, stirring, until the grains of rice are separate and beginning to crackle.
- Stir in the wine, and cook over medium heat, stirring. The wine should bubble, but not too quickly. You want some of the flavor to cook into the rice before it evaporates. When the wine has just about evaporated, stir in a ladleful or two of the simmering stock, enough to just cover the rice. The stock should bubble slowly. Cook, stirring often, until it is almost absorbed. Add another couple of ladles of the stock. Crush the saffron threads between your fingers and stir in. Continue to cook, stirring often — not too fast and not too slowly, adding more stock when the rice is almost dry — for 20 minutes.
- Taste a bit of the rice. It should taste chewy but not hard in the middle. Continue adding simmering stock and stirring until the rice reaches this al dente stage. Stir in more stock to cover, and add the peas and the shrimp. Cook, stirring, for another four to five minutes, until the shrimp are pink and cooked through but still moist and the peas are bright. Stir in the parsley and another small ladle of stock, remove from the heat, add pepper, stir for a few seconds and serve.

Nutrition Information

- 560: calories;
- 11 grams: fat;
- 78 grams: carbohydrates;
- 4 grams: dietary fiber;
- 0 grams: trans fat;
- 7 grams: sugars;
- 29 grams: protein;
- 1216 milligrams: sodium;
- 2 grams: polyunsaturated fat;

283. Shrimp A La King

Serving: 4 servings | Prep: | Cook: | Ready in: 10mins

Ingredients

- 2 tablespoons butter
- 1 ¾ pounds shrimp, shelled and deveined
- Salt and freshly ground pepper to taste
- 2 tablespoons finely chopped shallots
- 1 sweet red bell pepper, cored, seeded and cut into small strips
- ⅓ pound mushrooms, thinly sliced
- ¼ cup dry sherry
- ¾ cup heavy cream

Direction

- Heat the butter in a nonstick skillet. Add the shrimp, salt, pepper and shallots. Cook quickly, shaking and tossing the skillet, over high heat about 2 minutes.
- Using a slotted spoon, put the shrimp on a warm dish. Add the red pepper, mushrooms, salt and pepper to the skillet. Cook, stirring,

over medium-high heat until wilted, about 2 minutes.
- Add the sherry and reduce to half. Add the cream and cook over high heat about 2 minutes. Return the shrimp to the sauce and cook just to heat through. Serve with rice.

Nutrition Information

- 379: calories;
- 0 grams: trans fat;
- 2 grams: polyunsaturated fat;
- 8 grams: carbohydrates;
- 1145 milligrams: sodium;
- 25 grams: fat;
- 14 grams: saturated fat;
- 1 gram: dietary fiber;
- 4 grams: sugars;
- 30 grams: protein;
- 7 grams: monounsaturated fat;

284. Shrimp In Spicy Tomato Sauce

Serving: 4 servings | Prep: | Cook: | Ready in: 20mins

Ingredients

- 1 pound medium shrimp
- 2 teaspoons coarse salt
- 2 tablespoons olive oil
- 2 cloves garlic, minced
- 2 shallots, finely chopped
- 1 cup canned Italian plum tomatoes, drained and chopped
- ½ cup dry white wine
- ¼ teaspoon dried red pepper flakes
- Freshly ground pepper to taste

Direction

- Peel the shrimp and place in a bowl. Sprinkle with salt and cover with cold water. Set aside.

- Heat one tablespoon oil in a skillet. Add the garlic and the shallots and cook until soft. Add the tomatoes, wine and pepper and simmer gently for 10 minutes.
- Rinse and drain the shrimp. In a separate skillet, heat the remaining tablespoon oil and saute the shrimp just long enough for them to turn pink. Add them to the tomato sauce and mix well. Serve immediately.

Nutrition Information

- 195: calories;
- 1 gram: polyunsaturated fat;
- 0 grams: trans fat;
- 649 milligrams: sodium;
- 8 grams: fat;
- 2 grams: dietary fiber;
- 4 grams: sugars;
- 17 grams: protein;
- 5 grams: monounsaturated fat;
- 9 grams: carbohydrates;

285. Sirloin Steak With Crushed Peppercorns

Serving: 4 servings | Prep: | Cook: | Ready in: 15mins

Ingredients

- 4 boneless shell steaks, about 8 ounces each, with the excess fat removed
- Salt to taste
- 4 tablespoons cracked peppercorns, white or black
- 1 tablespoon vegetable oil
- 2 tablespoons finely chopped shallots
- ½ cup dry red wine
- ½ cup beef broth, fresh or canned
- 2 teaspoons tomato paste
- 2 sprigs fresh thyme or 1/2 teaspoon dried
- 2 tablespoons butter
- 2 tablespoons finely chopped parsley

Direction

- Sprinkle the steaks with salt.
- Use a mallet or meat pounder to crush the peppercorns, but not too fine. Sprinkle the peppercorns evenly over the steaks on both sides. Press down with your hands to help the peppercorns adhere to the meat.
- Heat the oil in a cast-iron skillet large enough to hold the steaks in one layer. When the skillet is hot and almost smoking, add the steaks, cook about 3 minutes until browned, then turn. Cook about 2 to 3 minutes more for medium rare. Remove to a warm platter.
- Pour the fat out of the skillet, add the shallots and cook, stirring, until they are wilted. Do not brown. Add the wine, broth, tomato paste and thyme. Reduce to half a cup. Add any liquid that may have accumulated around the steaks. Bring to a simmer. Remove from heat and swirl in the butter.
- Remove the thyme sprigs and pour the sauce over the steaks. Sprinkle with parsley.

Nutrition Information

- 619: calories;
- 0 grams: trans fat;
- 2 grams: dietary fiber;
- 1 gram: sugars;
- 41 grams: protein;
- 44 grams: fat;
- 18 grams: saturated fat;
- 19 grams: monounsaturated fat;
- 7 grams: carbohydrates;
- 729 milligrams: sodium;

286. Skillet Macaroni And Broccoli And Mushrooms And Cheese

Serving: Makes six side-dish servings. | Prep: | Cook: | Ready in: 30mins

Ingredients

- 4 ounces grated Cheddar
- 2 ounces finely grated Parmigiano-Reggiano or other hard cheese
- 1 tablespoon unsalted butter
- 1 small yellow onion, chopped
- 6 ounces cremini or white button mushrooms, sliced
- 3 tablespoons unbleached all-purpose flour
- 3 cups low-fat or fat-free milk
- 1 tablespoon Dijon mustard
- 1 tablespoon minced tarragon leaves or 2 teaspoons dried tarragon
- ½ teaspoon salt
- ½ teaspoon freshly ground black pepper
- 8 ounces dried whole-wheat pasta shells (not the large ones for stuffing), cooked and drained according to the package instructions
- 4 cups small broccoli florets, cooked in boiling water for 1 minute (broccoli can be added to the pasta during the last minute of cooking, then drained with the pasta in a colander)

Direction

- Mix the Cheddar and Parmigiano-Reggiano in a medium bowl. Set aside.
- Melt the butter in a large, high-sided, oven-safe skillet. Add the onion and cook, stirring often, until softened, about 3 minutes.
- Add the mushrooms and cook until they release their liquid and it comes to a simmer, and then reduces by about two-thirds, about 5 minutes.
- Sprinkle the flour over the vegetables in the skillet. Stir well to coat.
- Whisk in the milk in a steady, thin stream until creamy. Then whisk in the mustard, tarragon, salt and pepper. Continue whisking until the mixture starts to bubble and the liquid thickens, about 3 minutes
- Remove the skillet from the heat. Stir in three-quarters of the mixed cheeses until smooth. Then stir in the cooked pasta and broccoli.
- Preheat the broiler after setting the rack 4 to 6 inches from the heat source. Meanwhile,

sprinkle the remaining cheese over the ingredients in the skillet. Set the skillet on the rack and broil until light browned and bubbling, about 5 minutes. (If your skillet has a plastic or wooden handle, make sure it sticks outside the oven, out from under the broiler, so the handle doesn't melt.) Cool for 5 to 10 minutes before dishing up.

Nutrition Information

- 353: calories;
- 0 grams: trans fat;
- 1 gram: polyunsaturated fat;
- 42 grams: carbohydrates;
- 8 grams: sugars;
- 13 grams: fat;
- 7 grams: saturated fat;
- 3 grams: monounsaturated fat;
- 2 grams: dietary fiber;
- 19 grams: protein;
- 482 milligrams: sodium;

287. Smoked Autumn Vegetables

Serving: Four servings | Prep: | Cook: | Ready in: 1hours15mins

Ingredients

- 2 tablespoons wood chips
- ½ medium butternut squash, peeled, seeded and cut lengthwise into 1/2-inch-thick slices
- 2 medium sweet potatoes, peeled and cut into 1/2-inch-thick rounds
- Salt and freshly ground pepper to taste
- 6 shallots, peeled
- 2 portobello mushrooms, stemmed
- 4 cremini mushrooms, stemmed

Direction

- Place half of the wood chips in the bottom of a stove-top smoker and place the squash and sweet potatoes on the rack over the chips. Season lightly with salt and pepper. Place over medium heat until the wood begins to smolder. Cover and cook until tender, about 30 minutes.
- Remove the vegetables from the rack and keep warm. Add the remaining wood chips to the smoker. Place the shallots and mushrooms on the rack, season, cover and cook until tender, about 40 minutes. Thinly slice all of the vegetables and serve.

288. Smoked Salmon Roulade

Serving: Eight to 10 servings | Prep: | Cook: | Ready in: 20mins

Ingredients

- 1 basic sponge roll for roulades (see recipe)
- 3 ounces cream cheese at room temperature
- 1 cup sour cream
- ¼ pound smoked salmon
- ¼ cup finely chopped dill
- Dill sprigs for garnish

Direction

- Prepare the sponge roll and have it ready.
- Combine the cream cheese and three tablespoons of the sour cream. Blend well and spread this over the sponge roll.
- Cut the salmon lengthwise into thin, one-quarter-inch strips. Arrange the strips down the length of the sponge roll in parallel rows, leaving about an inch of space between them. Sprinkle with the chopped dill. Roll the cake like a jellyroll, folding the small end over and over to make a roll about 10 inches long.
- Using a knife with a serrated blade, carefully slice off the bulky ends of the roll. Cut the remaining roll into neat, one-half-inch slices and top each with a spoonful or so of the

remaining sour cream. Top each serving with a small sprig of dill. Serve lukewarm or cold.

Nutrition Information

- 104: calories;
- 0 grams: dietary fiber;
- 149 milligrams: sodium;
- 8 grams: fat;
- 4 grams: protein;
- 2 grams: monounsaturated fat;
- 1 gram: sugars;

289. Smoked Vegetable Salad

Serving: 2 main-course or 4 first-course servings | Prep: | Cook: | Ready in: 10mins

Ingredients

- 3 tablespoons sherry vinegar
- 2 teaspoons Dijon mustard
- 1 tablespoon olive oil
- ½ teaspoon salt
- Freshly ground pepper to taste
- ½ teaspoon chopped fresh rosemary
- 6 cups arugula, stemmed
- 1 smoked autumn vegetables (see recipe)

Direction

- Whisk the vinegar and mustard together in a small bowl. Slowly whisk in the olive oil. Add the salt, pepper and rosemary. Toss all but 1 tablespoon of the dressing with the arugula. Divide among 2 or 4 plates. Arrange the smoked vegetables over the arugula and drizzle with the remaining dressing. Serve immediately.

Nutrition Information

- 187: calories;
- 22 grams: carbohydrates;
- 7 grams: protein;
- 556 milligrams: sodium;
- 8 grams: fat;
- 1 gram: sugars;
- 0 grams: trans fat;
- 5 grams: monounsaturated fat;

290. Soft Shell Crabs With Tomato Buttermilk Sauce

Serving: 2 servings | Prep: | Cook: | Ready in: 20mins

Ingredients

- 2 medium cloves garlic
- Pan spray
- ½ teaspoon ground cumin
- ⅛ teaspoon crushed red pepper flakes
- ¼ teaspoon sugar
- ½ of a 28-ounce can of no-salt-added tomatoes
- 2 tablespoons plus 1 teaspoon flour
- ½ cup nonfat buttermilk
- 4 cleaned soft-shell crabs
- 1 teaspoon toasted sesame oil

Direction

- Mince garlic.
- Over high heat, heat nonstick saute pan large enough to hold the crabs. Spray lightly with pan spray. Stir in the garlic and cook for 30 seconds over medium heat.
- Remove from heat, and stir in cumin, red pepper and sugar. Add the tomatoes, crushing them between your fingers before adding to the pan. Simmer for a few minutes.
- Mix 1 teaspoon of flour with a little of the buttermilk to make a paste; then, add the paste to the remaining buttermilk, and stir it into the tomato mixture. Cook over low heat until mixture thickens. Remove from saute pan, and set aside.
- Wash crabs and dip into remaining flour, coating both sides.

- Return pan to medium-high heat, and add oil. When pan is hot, add the crabs, and brown on both sides, allowing 2 to 3 minutes a side, depending on the size of the crabs.
- Spoon the reserved tomato sauce over the crabs, and cook just to heat sauce through.

Nutrition Information

- 148: calories;
- 5 grams: sugars;
- 1 gram: dietary fiber;
- 2 grams: polyunsaturated fat;
- 14 grams: carbohydrates;
- 11 grams: protein;
- 297 milligrams: sodium;

291. Sole With Julienne Of Pumpkin

Serving: Serves 2 | Prep: | Cook: | Ready in: 20mins

Ingredients

- 1 pound gray sole (about 3 fillets)
- 2 teaspoons lemon juice
- ½ cup water
- ¼ cup white wine
- Salt and white pepper to taste
- 5 tablespoons sweet butter
- 1 ½ cups loosely packed julienne of pumpkin flesh (strips about 2 inches long)

Direction

- Place the sole fillets in a pan just large enough to hold them. Add the lemon juice, water, white wine, sacreamlt and pepper. Bring to a boil, reduce to simmer and cook for 4 to 5 minutes. Carefully remove sole from the pan and place on a dish in a warm oven. Reserve cooking liquid.
- Meanwhile, melt 2 tablespoons of the butter in a skillet and saute the julienne strips of pumpkin over medium heat, stirring occasionally, for 3 to 5 minutes, or until they are soft. Remove pumpkin and keep warm.
- Add any juice that has accumulated in the dish holding the sole to the cooking liquid and reduce the liquid over high heat by half. Pour the reduced liquid into an electric blender. Add about 1/2 cup of the pumpkin strips and 3 tablespoons of cold butter. Blend well.
- Put fillets on warm plates, garnish with sauce and arrange remaining pumpkin strips on top.

Nutrition Information

- 473: calories;
- 19 grams: saturated fat;
- 1 gram: trans fat;
- 7 grams: carbohydrates;
- 0 grams: dietary fiber;
- 32 grams: protein;
- 34 grams: fat;
- 9 grams: monounsaturated fat;
- 2 grams: polyunsaturated fat;
- 3 grams: sugars;
- 1069 milligrams: sodium;

292. Sonia's Phyllo And Feta Torte With Dill And Nutmeg

Serving: 10 to 12 servings | Prep: | Cook: | Ready in: 1hours30mins

Ingredients

- 1 pound Greek feta cheese, crumbled
- 3 cups cottage cheese
- 3 large eggs
- ⅓ cup chopped fresh dill
- ¼ cup grated Romano cheese
- ½ teaspoon freshly grated nutmeg
- ½ teaspoon freshly ground black pepper
- 1 1-pound box phyllo dough, thawed overnight in refrigerator if necessary
- 1 ½ cups (3 sticks) unsalted butter, melted

- Greek honey, for serving (optional)

Direction

- Heat oven to 375 degrees. In a food processor, combine feta, cottage cheese, eggs, dill, 2 tablespoons Romano, the nutmeg and pepper and pulse just to combine (you can also use a large bowl and a fork). Mixture should be well combined, but still chunky, not smooth.
- Sprinkle remaining 2 tablespoons Romano into a Bundt pan. Drape a sheet of phyllo on top of Bundt pan, poke a hole into phyllo where center tube is and push phyllo into pan to line it. Do this with another phyllo sheet, but place it perpendicular to first sheet. Continue adding phyllo sheets in this crisscross manner until all sheets are used. Edges of phyllo should hang over edges of pan.
- Scrape cheese filling into pan, and fold edges of phyllo over filling. Using a sharp knife, poke many holes (at least 20) in dough that reach all the way to bottom of pan. Slowly pour melted butter over torte; some butter will seep through holes and some will remain on top of dough.
- Place Bundt pan on a baking sheet and bake for about 1 hour 15 minutes, or until torte is puffy and golden brown. Allow torte to cool in pan for 1 to 2 hours before inverting onto a plate and slicing. Serve warm or at room temperature, with honey if desired.

Nutrition Information

- 501: calories;
- 17 grams: protein;
- 23 grams: saturated fat;
- 1 gram: dietary fiber;
- 10 grams: monounsaturated fat;
- 24 grams: carbohydrates;
- 794 milligrams: sodium;
- 38 grams: fat;
- 2 grams: polyunsaturated fat;
- 3 grams: sugars;

293. Sour Cream Cheesecake With Vanilla Bean

Serving: 12 servings | Prep: | Cook: | Ready in: 1hours10mins

Ingredients

- 18 Nabisco chocolate wafers, finely crushed
- ¼ teaspoon cinnamon
- ¼ cup butter, melted
- 1 pound cream cheese, room temperature
- 2 eggs at room temperature, lightly beaten
- ⅔ cup plus 3 tablespoons sugar
- 1 vanilla bean, split in half lengthwise and seeds scraped
- 1 ½ cups sour cream

Direction

- In a bowl stir together crushed wafers and cinnamon with a fork. Pour in butter, and stir until mixture is moist. Press mixture into a 9-inch springform pan, forming a crust just over 1 inch high around the sides. You might think you need more wafers, but you don't. Press patiently until a tight, thin layer forms. Chill until needed.
- Heat oven to 350 degrees with baking sheet on center rack. In an electric mixer, beat cream cheese until creamy and fluffy. Add eggs, 2/3 cup sugar and seeds from vanilla bean, and beat until very smooth. Scrape bowl with a spatula to break up lumps. Pour into crust, and place on baking sheet. Bake 25 minutes.
- Meanwhile, blend sour cream with 3 tablespoons sugar. After 25 minutes, remove cake from oven, and let sit 5 minutes. Increase oven heat to 450 degrees. Gently spoon sour cream mixture on top, and spread evenly. Return cake to oven, and bake 7 minutes. Cool on a wire rack.

Nutrition Information

- 324: calories;
- 24 grams: fat;
- 0 grams: dietary fiber;
- 1 gram: polyunsaturated fat;
- 23 grams: carbohydrates;
- 20 grams: sugars;
- 14 grams: saturated fat;
- 6 grams: monounsaturated fat;
- 4 grams: protein;
- 215 milligrams: sodium;

294. Southern Mesclun Salad

Serving: Four servings | Prep: | Cook: | Ready in: 5mins

Ingredients

- 8 cups mesclun (choose a variety of tender young greens, herbs and flowers like purslane, pokeweed, dandelion, watercress, mustard greens, chickweed, creeping thyme, clover flowers, chicory flowers, chervil and the tiny, inner leaves of bibb lettuce heads
- ½ cup light olive oil
- ¼ cup unseasoned Japanese rice wine vinegar (see note)
- Salt, freshly ground pepper to taste

Direction

- Remove the tough stems from greens, herbs and flowers and discard. Wash and dry carefully.
- In a serving bowl, combine oil, vinegar, salt and pepper. Add mesclun and toss to coat lightly.

Nutrition Information

- 252: calories;
- 27 grams: fat;
- 4 grams: saturated fat;
- 20 grams: monounsaturated fat;
- 3 grams: polyunsaturated fat;
- 2 grams: carbohydrates;
- 1 gram: protein;
- 265 milligrams: sodium;

295. Spaghetti With Cauliflower, Almonds, Tomatoes And Chickpeas

Serving: 4 servings | Prep: | Cook: | Ready in: 30mins

Ingredients

- 24 raw almonds (about 3 tablespoons), blanched, skinned* and chopped
- 1 small or 1/2 large head cauliflower, broken into florets
- 2 tablespoons extra virgin olive oil
- 2 garlic cloves, minced
- 1-14 1/2-ounce can chopped tomatoes in juice
- ¼ teaspoon sugar
- Pinch of cinnamon
- Salt to taste
- ½ to 1 teaspoon dried oregano (to taste)
- Freshly ground pepper to taste
- ½ cup cooked chickpeas (canned or freshly cooked)
- ¾ pound spaghetti
- Crumbled feta or freshly grated Parmesan for serving

Direction

- Fill a large pasta pot with water and bring to a boil. Add salt to taste and cauliflower. Boil 5 minutes, then using a Chinese skimmer, a strainer or a slotted spoon, transfer cauliflower to a bowl of cold water (do not drain the pot; you'll use the water for the pasta). Drain the cauliflower and chop medium-fine. Set aside.
- (You can do this step while you are waiting for the water to come to a boil for the cauliflower). Heat 1 tablespoon of the olive oil over medium heat in a large, heavy skillet or a wide saucepan and add garlic. Cook, stirring, until

fragrant, about 30 seconds, and stir in tomatoes with liquid, sugar, cinnamon, salt and oregano. Turn up heat to medium-high and stir often as tomatoes come to a brisk boil. Turn heat down to medium and cook, stirring often, until tomatoes have cooked down and taste very fragrant, about 10 minutes. Add pepper to taste.
- Add cauliflower and almonds to the tomato sauce, along with 1/4 cup cooking water from the cauliflower, and stir together. Stir in chickpeas.
- Bring water in the pot back to a boil and add spaghetti. Cook al dente, following timing instructions on the package but checking for doneness a minute before indicated time on the package. Set aside 1/2 cup of the cooking water from the pasta, in case you want to moisten the sauce more, drain pasta and toss with the tomato and cauliflower sauce and the remaining tablespoon of olive oil. Add water from pasta only if you think the mixture seems dry. Serve, passing crumbled feta or grated Parmesan at the table for sprinkling.

Nutrition Information

- 489: calories;
- 6 grams: monounsaturated fat;
- 84 grams: carbohydrates;
- 9 grams: sugars;
- 896 milligrams: sodium;
- 10 grams: dietary fiber;
- 2 grams: polyunsaturated fat;
- 0 grams: trans fat;
- 18 grams: protein;

296. Spaghetti With Turkey And Tomato Sauce

Serving: 2 servings | Prep: | Cook: | Ready in: 25mins

Ingredients

- 3 tablespoons olive oil
- ¾ cup finely chopped celery, about two ribs
- Dash of garlic powder
- 3 tablespoons tomato paste
- 1 cup water
- ½ teaspoon dried rosemary
- 2 dashes Tabasco sauce
- 2 tablespoons capers, crushed
- 2 teaspoons Dijon-style mustard
- Pepper to taste
- ⅓ pound of spaghetti
- Salt to taste
- 1 teaspoon butter
- ¼ pound cooked turkey, julienned

Direction

- Put 2 tablespoons of olive oil in a saucepan over medium heat.
- Add the celery and garlic powder and saute 1 minute over low heat. Add the tomato paste and water and blend together. Add the rosemary, Tabasco and capers and simmer 10 minutes. Add mustard and pepper to taste, and continue simmering a minute or two.
- Meanwhile, bring 2 quarts water to a boil in pot. Add the spaghetti with a dash of salt. Cook 7 or 8 minutes or until done.
- While the spaghetti cooks, melt the butter in a saucepan and cook the turkey enough to warm it.
- Drain the spaghetti and mix in the remaining olive oil. Place the spaghetti on a platter. Pour sauce around it and in a central well. Place turkey in a ring around the central well.

Nutrition Information

- 708: calories;
- 34 grams: protein;
- 35 grams: fat;
- 8 grams: saturated fat;
- 0 grams: trans fat;
- 20 grams: monounsaturated fat;
- 63 grams: carbohydrates;
- 5 grams: sugars;

- 4 grams: dietary fiber;
- 824 milligrams: sodium;

297. Spaghettini With Spicy Lentil Sauce

Serving: 6 servings | Prep: | Cook: |Ready in: 35mins

Ingredients

- 2 tablespoons olive oil
- 1 cup chopped fresh fennel
- ½ pound carrots, scraped and chopped fine
- ⅔ pound onions, chopped fine
- 2 large cloves garlic, chopped fine
- ¼ pound chunk prosciutto, diced
- ¼ to ½ teaspoon crushed red pepper flakes
- 1 teaspoon Hungarian sweet paprika
- ¼ teaspoon Hungarian hot paprika
- 1 heaping cup red lentils
- 5 cups water
- 1 teaspoon salt (optional)
- 1 pound spaghettini

Direction

- Heat oil in nonstick skillet and saute fennel, carrots, onions, garlic, prosciutto and red pepper flakes until vegetables are soft, 10 to 15 minutes.
- Add paprikas and saute for another 2 minutes to coat vegetables.
- Add lentils and 5 cups of water; bring to boil, lower heat and simmer until lentils are soft but not mushy, 10 to 12 minutes. Season with salt if desired.
- Meanwhile, bring water to boil for pasta in covered pot. Cook pasta and drain. Stir into lentil sauce and toss. Serve immediately or sauce will thicken too much.

Nutrition Information

- 514: calories;
- 4 grams: monounsaturated fat;
- 87 grams: carbohydrates;
- 7 grams: sugars;
- 24 grams: protein;
- 560 milligrams: sodium;
- 8 grams: dietary fiber;
- 1 gram: polyunsaturated fat;

298. Spartina's Roasted Cod With Nicoise Vinaigrette

Serving: 4 servings | Prep: | Cook: |Ready in: 30mins

Ingredients

- 8 marinated anchovy fillets, minced
- 1 tablespoon capers, minced
- 1 tablespoon nicoise olives, minced
- 1 tablespoon minced shallot
- 1 teaspoon finely slivered garlic
- ½ cup extra-virgin olive oil
- 3 tablespoons sherry wine vinegar
- Salt and freshly ground black pepper
- 4 cod fillets, each about 6 ounces

Direction

- Preheat oven to 500 degrees. Mix anchovies, capers, olives, shallot and garlic with 1/3 cup olive oil and the vinegar. Season with salt and pepper.
- Heat remaining oil in an oven-proof skillet. Season cod with salt and pepper, place in skillet and sear on one side until golden, about 2 minutes. Turn and place in oven until done, about 5 minutes.
- Place a cod fillet on each of 4 plates. Spoon about 2 tablespoons of anchovy sauce on top.

Nutrition Information

- 404: calories;
- 4 grams: saturated fat;
- 20 grams: monounsaturated fat;

- 3 grams: polyunsaturated fat;
- 1 gram: carbohydrates;
- 33 grams: protein;
- 29 grams: fat;
- 0 grams: sugars;
- 522 milligrams: sodium;

299. Spiced Iced Tea

Serving: About one quart | Prep: | Cook: |Ready in: 30mins

Ingredients

- 1 quart water
- 2 tablespoons sugar
- 1 cinnamon stick
- ½ teaspoon freshly grated ginger
- 1 teaspoon cloves
- 1 teaspoon hulled cardamom seeds
- ⅛ teaspoon freshly ground black pepper
- Thinly sliced orange, for garnish

Direction

- Bring the water to a boil in a saucepan. Reduce to a simmer, add the remaining ingredients and simmer slowly for 20 minutes. Line a strainer with a thin, wet cloth and strain into a pitcher. Refrigerate until cold. Serve over ice, garnished with orange slices.

Nutrition Information

- 12: calories;
- 0 grams: protein;
- 3 grams: sugars;
- 4 milligrams: sodium;

300. Spiced Lamb Sausage With Green Lentils

Serving: Six to eight servings | Prep: | Cook: |Ready in: 2hours

Ingredients

- For the sausages:
- 1 pound lean lamb (leg or shoulder), trimmed of sinew and cut into 1-inch cubes
- ¼ pound pancetta, cut into 1-inch cubes
- ¼ pound fatback, cut into 1-inch cubes
- 1 teaspoon salt
- ¼ teaspoon freshly ground black pepper
- 1 teaspoon cayenne pepper
- ½ teaspoon cinnamon powder
- 1 pinch dried oregano
- 1 pinch dried thyme
- 1 pinch ground clove
- 1 pinch ground cardamom
- 3 tablespoons fresh flat-leaf parsley, chopped
- 3 tablespoons fresh coriander, chopped
- For the lentils:
- 1 ½ cups green lentils (or substitute brown lentils)
- 2 tablespoons rendered duck fat (or substitute lard or vegetable oil)
- 6 shallots, peeled and left whole (separate cloves)
- 2 medium carrots, cut into 3/8-inch pieces (approximately 1 1/2 to 2 cups)
- 6 cups chicken stock, preferably homemade and unsalted
- 1 bouquet garni: 1 whole clove, 1 bay leaf, 2 sprigs parsley, 1 sprig thyme, all wrapped in cheesecloth
- 1 teaspoon coarse salt
- ¼ teaspoon freshly ground black pepper
- ¼ cup fresh bread crumbs

Direction

- To prepare the sausages, in a mixing bowl, combine the lamb, pancetta, fatback, salt and pepper and the dried herbs and spices, except for the parsley and coriander. Stir to blend.

- Put a third of the sausage mixture into the bowl of a food processor and process until it is very finely chopped but not pureed. Do the same with the second third of the meat mixture. Process the last third, leaving it chunkier. In a large bowl, combine by hand the three batches of meat until the larger chunks are evenly distributed. Allowing the sausage mixture to stand overnight, covered in the refrigerator, enhances the flavor, but it is not crucial.
- On the same day you are serving the dish, chop and add the parsley and coriander. Mix well and form into eight patties about two-and-a-half-inches in diameter and one-inch thick. Set aside.
- To prepare the lentils, rinse them under water and remove any stones.
- In a three-to-four-quart heavy-bottomed saucepan, melt the duck fat over a medium flame. Add the peeled shallots and saute for approximately five minutes, or until slightly golden. Add the carrot pieces and saute an additional five minutes, stirring occasionally. Add the lentils, stir to coat with fat and continue cooking for three minutes.
- Add the six cups of stock, salt, pepper and bouquet garni. Bring to a boil, then lower the flame. Simmer until the lentils are tender and most of the liquid has been reduced to a thin syrup. Discard bouquet garni. This should take about one hour. The lentils may be prepared up to this point one to two days in advance. Store, covered, in the refrigerator.
- Preheat the oven to 375 degrees.
- Pour the lentil mixture into a two-quart shallow baking dish and evenly space the eight raw sausage patties on top. Sprinkle with the bread crumbs. Bake on the middle rack of the oven until the sausages are browned and the lentils are bubbly hot, about 45 minutes.
- Serve immediately, with warm bread and roasted beets dressed with Sherry vinegar and walnut oil.

Nutrition Information

- 509: calories;
- 29 grams: fat;
- 10 grams: saturated fat;
- 34 grams: carbohydrates;
- 28 grams: protein;
- 0 grams: trans fat;
- 13 grams: monounsaturated fat;
- 5 grams: sugars;
- 758 milligrams: sodium;

301. Spiced Lobster And Carrot Risotto

Serving: 4 servings | Prep: | Cook: | Ready in: 1hours

Ingredients

- 2 1 1/2-pound lobsters
- 2 medium carrots, peeled and diced
- 2 large red or yellow bell peppers, seeded, deveined and diced
- 2 medium beets, peeled and finely diced
- 7 cups basic vegetable broth (see recipe)
- 1 teaspoon olive oil
- 1 medium onion, peeled and finely minced
- 1 ½ cups Arborio rice
- ½ teaspoon salt, plus more to taste
- 1 teaspoon freshly ground black pepper
- 2 teaspoons grated ginger
- ½ cup lime juice
- ½ cup minced parsley
- ½ cup minced mint leaves

Direction

- Steam the lobsters in a large pot for 15 minutes and set aside to cool. Remove the shell, cut each tail into 6 pieces crosswise, reserve the claw meat and discard the rest.
- Put the carrots, peppers and beets into a blender, add the broth and puree until smooth. Strain into a pot. Slowly cook over low heat until hot.

- Meanwhile, heat the olive oil in an oversize, heavy-bottomed skillet or pot, over medium heat. Add the onion and saute until soft, about 5 minutes. Add the rice and stir to combine. Ladle in 1/2 cup of broth and stir. Increase the heat to medium-high and continue adding broth, 1/2 cup at a time, for the next 25 minutes, stirring constantly. Season to taste with salt and pepper.
- After 25 minutes, add the lobster. Add the remaining broth and continue to cook the rice until it is tender and the lobster is warmed through. Remove from heat immediately. Stir in grated ginger, lime juice and minced parsley. Divide among 4 bowls and garnish with the chopped mint.

pepper to taste. Store, well covered, in the refrigerator for several days, or the freezer for up to a month. Return to room temperature before serving.

Nutrition Information

- 104: calories;
- 1 gram: fat;
- 0 grams: polyunsaturated fat;
- 25 grams: carbohydrates;
- 5 grams: dietary fiber;
- 17 grams: sugars;
- 2 grams: protein;
- 467 milligrams: sodium;

302. Spiced Pepper Purée

Serving: About 1 cup | Prep: | Cook: | Ready in: 30mins

Ingredients

- 4 large bell peppers, yellow, orange or red, about 2 pounds
- 2 teaspoons cumin seeds, or 2 teaspoons ground cumin
- 1 inchlong piece of ginger, peeled
- Salt and pepper to taste

Direction

- adjust a rack about 4 inches from the heat source. Grill or broil the peppers, turning frequently as they blacken, until they collapse, about 15 minutes. Wrap in aluminum foil and let cool.
- Toast cumin seeds in a dry skillet over medium heat, shaking pan occasionally and removing from heat when fragrant. Grind to a powder in a coffee or spice grinder.
- When peppers are cool, remove core, skin and all seeds. Place peppers in a food processor with cumin and ginger; add a large pinch of salt and purée. Stop machine, adjust salt and

303. Spicy Celery With Garlic

Serving: 6 servings | Prep: | Cook: | Ready in: 35mins

Ingredients

- 1 bunch celery (2 pounds)
- 4 cloves garlic, peeled and thinly sliced (2 tablespoons)
- ½ cup chicken stock, preferably unsalted homemade stock, or canned light chicken broth
- ¼ cup hot red salsa
- ¼ cup olive oil
- Salt to taste

Direction

- Using a vegetable peeler, remove the tough, fibrous strings from the celery ribs. Cut the celery into 2-inch pieces. You should have about 8 cups.
- Place the celery pieces in a large bowl, cover with cold water and wash them thoroughly.
- Place the celery, still wet, in a large saucepan with the remainder of the ingredients. Bring the mixture to a boil, uncovered; then, reduce the heat, cover and cook gently for about 25

minutes until most of the liquid has evaporated and the celery is tender.
- Serve immediately, or if you want to serve the dish later, cool, cover, refrigerate and reheat briefly in a microwave oven or in a saucepan on top of the stove.

Nutrition Information

- 118: calories;
- 10 grams: fat;
- 1 gram: polyunsaturated fat;
- 7 grams: carbohydrates;
- 3 grams: sugars;
- 2 grams: protein;
- 451 milligrams: sodium;

304. Spicy Pork

Serving: 2 servings | Prep: | Cook: | Ready in: 15mins

Ingredients

- 1 tablespoon coarsely grated fresh or frozen ginger
- 1 large garlic clove
- 8 ounces pork tenderloin
- 1 teaspoon olive oil
- 1 teaspoon ground cumin
- ¼ teaspoon turmeric
- ⅛ teaspoon hot pepper flakes
- ½ teaspoon ground coriander
- ½ cup no-salt-added beef stock or broth
- Freshly ground black pepper to taste
- 1 teaspoon lime juice

Direction

- Grate ginger; mince garlic.
- Trim fat from pork and cut remainder into bite-size chunks.
- Heat oil until it is very hot in nonstick pot. Saute ginger and garlic for 30 seconds. Add the pork and brown on both sides.
- Stir in cumin, turmeric, hot pepper flakes and coriander and cook about 30 seconds.
- Stir in beef stock and cook over medium-high heat until stock is reduced a little. Season with pepper and lime juice. Serve.

Nutrition Information

- 178: calories;
- 2 grams: saturated fat;
- 1 gram: dietary fiber;
- 25 grams: protein;
- 7 grams: fat;
- 0 grams: sugars;
- 3 grams: monounsaturated fat;
- 4 grams: carbohydrates;
- 181 milligrams: sodium;

305. Spinach Basil Pesto

Serving: 4 cups | Prep: | Cook: | Ready in: 30mins

Ingredients

- ¼ cup roughly chopped walnuts
- 4 cups baby spinach leaves
- 2 cups fresh basil
- 1 teaspoon salt or to taste
- ½ cup olive oil
- ¼ cup grated rennet-free Parmesan cheese

Direction

- Preheat oven to 350 degrees. Spread out the walnuts on a small rimmed baking sheet and roast in oven for about 12 minutes, giving them a shake after 6 minutes. Continue roasting until golden brown and toasted. Set aside and allow to cool thoroughly.
- Fill a large stockpot three-quarters full with water, and bring to a boil over high heat. Meanwhile, fill a large bowl half way up with ice and water and set close to the sink.

- Dump the spinach and basil into the boiling water and stir. After 1 minute, strain the greens, and plunge them into the bowl with ice water. Drain the greens again and squeeze them tightly to get as much water out as possible. Chop the greens roughly.
- Combine the greens and walnuts with the salt, olive oil and Parmesan in a food processor and process until a smooth consistency is reached. Taste and season with additional salt, if desired.

Nutrition Information

- 40: calories;
- 0 grams: sugars;
- 18 milligrams: sodium;
- 4 grams: fat;
- 1 gram: protein;
- 3 grams: monounsaturated fat;

306. Spring Lamb With Baby Greens

Serving: Six to eight servings | Prep: | Cook: | Ready in: 1hours45mins

Ingredients

- The stuffing:
- 1 ½ pounds fresh tender spinach leaves
- 2 cups fresh mint leaves, chopped
- ½ cup minced orange zest
- 2 cloves garlic, peeled and finely chopped
- 1 small red onion, peeled and finely chopped
- ¼ teaspoon ground cinnamon
- ¼ teaspoon ground ginger
- 2 tablespoons Dijon mustard
- ½ teaspoon salt
- 1 teaspoon freshly ground pepper
- The greens:
- 1 pound fresh tender dandelion leaves, trimmed and rinsed
- ½ pound fresh tender chicory, trimmed and rinsed
- The lamb:
- 1 butterflied leg of spring lamb, about 4 pounds, trimmed of all fat, at room temperature
- 2 tablespoons olive oil
- The sauce:
- ¼ cup wine vinegar
- ½ cup red wine
- 2 ½ cups chicken broth, homemade or low-sodium canned
- ½ cup apple cider
- The parsnips:
- 1 pound parsnips, peeled and cut diagonally into 1/2-inch pieces

Direction

- Preheat the oven to 375 degrees. Steam two-thirds of the spinach for a few minutes, or until it is just wilted. Rinse under cold running water. Squeeze out all of the excess water and chop coarsely. Put the chopped spinach in a large bowl, add the rest of the stuffing ingredients and mix well.
- Steam the remaining spinach leaves along with the dandelion leaves and chicory until barely wilted. Rinse under cold running water until cool. Pat dry and set aside.
- Lay the leg of lamb, fat side down, on a flat surface. Spread the stuffing over the meat. Starting with the smallest end, roll up the meat lengthwise like a jellyroll. Tie it tightly with butcher's string.
- Heat the oil in a large cast-iron skillet over medium-high heat until it is hot. Carefully put the lamb in the skillet and sear it on 4 sides, about 4 minutes per side, until golden brown all over.
- Lower the heat, take the leg out of the pan and set it aside. Gently scrape any burned pieces or fat from the bottom of the pan and discard. Add the vinegar and wine. Bring the liquid to a boil and simmer until it reduces to 1/4 cup, about 3 minutes. Add the chicken broth and apple cider. Put the lamb back into the skillet.

- Drape the greens on top of the meat, crosswise. Lay the remaining greens in the bottom of the pan. Set the pan in the oven and roast the lamb for 30 minutes, basting continually.
- Turn the lamb over, add the parsnips to the skillet and continue to roast for an additional 20 minutes. Test for doneness by inserting a meat thermometer in the large end of the leg. The thermometer should read 125 degrees for rare meat, or 130 degrees for medium rare. Let the lamb rest for at least 20 minutes before carving. Keep the greens and parsnips warm and serve alongside the sliced lamb.

Nutrition Information

- 287: calories;
- 6 grams: saturated fat;
- 0 grams: trans fat;
- 7 grams: sugars;
- 10 grams: dietary fiber;
- 15 grams: fat;
- 1 gram: polyunsaturated fat;
- 30 grams: carbohydrates;
- 9 grams: protein;
- 436 milligrams: sodium;

307. Spy Wednesday Biscuits

Serving: About 40 biscuits | Prep: | Cook: | Ready in: 3hours

Ingredients

- ½ cup currants
- 1 package active dry yeast
- 1 cup warm water
- 4 cups flour
- ½ cup sugar
- 1 teaspoon baking soda
- 4 teaspoons baking powder
- 1 teaspoon salt
- 1 cup chilled vegetable shortening, cut into bits
- 1 cup buttermilk
- ⅔ cup butter, melted and cooled

Direction

- Place the currants in a dish, cover with hot water and set aside.
- Mix the yeast with the cup of warm water in a bowl, and set aside for 5 minutes, until frothy.
- Sift the flour, sugar, baking soda, baking powder and salt together in a bowl. Cut in the shortening with a pastry blender until the mixture has the texture of coarse cornmeal. This can also be done in a food processor.
- Drain the currants, and mix them into the dough. Then, lightly stir in the yeast mixture and the buttermilk just until all the ingredients are moist. Transfer the dough to a floured surface and knead gently and briefly.
- Line two large baking sheets with parchment paper. Roll or pat the dough into a rectangle about 1/2 inch thick. Cut rounds with a 2 1/2-inch-diameter biscuit cutter. Scraps can be gently kneaded together and rolled and cut. Dip each cut biscuit into the melted butter; then, place them an inch apart on the parchment-lined baking sheets. Set aside to rise for 2 hours.
- Preheat oven to 425 degrees. Bake about 15 minutes, until golden brown. Serve warm.

Nutrition Information

- 138: calories;
- 14 grams: carbohydrates;
- 4 grams: sugars;
- 91 milligrams: sodium;
- 8 grams: fat;
- 3 grams: monounsaturated fat;
- 1 gram: dietary fiber;
- 2 grams: protein;

308. Steamed Cucumbers With Dill

Serving: 4 servings | Prep: | Cook: | Ready in: 15mins

Ingredients

- 2 large firm cucumbers
- 1 tablespoon butter
- Salt and freshly ground pepper to taste
- ¼ teaspoon ground cumin
- 3 tablespoons chopped dill

Direction

- Wash the cucumbers. Trim off the ends, and remove the skins. Cut the cucumbers into 1 1/2-inch thick rounds. Quarter each slice lengthwise, and remove the seeds.
- Place the cucumbers in the rack of a steamer over boiling water. Steam for 2 minutes. Do not overcook.
- Melt the butter in a skillet. Add the cucumbers, salt, pepper, cumin and dill. Toss well for 30 seconds. Serve immediately.

Nutrition Information

- 51: calories;
- 3 grams: sugars;
- 2 grams: saturated fat;
- 0 grams: polyunsaturated fat;
- 1 gram: protein;
- 6 grams: carbohydrates;
- 365 milligrams: sodium;

309. Stracciatella With Spinach

Serving: 4 servings | Prep: | Cook: | Ready in: 1hours

Ingredients

- 1 ½ quarts chicken or turkey stock
- Salt
- freshly ground pepper to taste
- 2 large or extra large eggs
- 1 ½ tablespoons semolina
- ⅓ cup freshly grated Parmesan (1 1/2 ounces)
- 1 6-ounce bag baby spinach, or 1 bunch spinach, stemmed, washed, dried and coarsely chopped

Direction

- Place the stock in a large saucepan or soup pot. Remove 1/3 cup and set aside. Bring the rest to a simmer. Season to taste with salt and freshly ground pepper. If there is any visible fat, skim it away.
- Beat the eggs in a bowl, and stir in the 1/3 cup of stock, the semolina and the cheese.
- Stir the spinach into the simmering stock, then drizzle in the egg mixture, scraping all of it in with a rubber spatula. Stir very slowly with the spatula, paddling it back and forth until the little "rags" form. Taste, adjust seasoning and serve at once.

Nutrition Information

- 238: calories;
- 6 grams: sugars;
- 1038 milligrams: sodium;
- 10 grams: fat;
- 4 grams: monounsaturated fat;
- 0 grams: trans fat;
- 1 gram: dietary fiber;
- 18 grams: protein;

310. Strata With Mushrooms And Chard

Serving: Serves four to six | Prep: | Cook: | Ready in: 2hours

Ingredients

- ½ pound stale bread, sliced about 3/4 to 1 inch thick

- ¾ ounce dried mushrooms
- 8 ounces Swiss chard, stemmed and cleaned
- 2 garlic cloves, 1 cut in half, green shoots removed, the other minced
- 1 ½ cups low-fat milk
- 2 ounces Gruyère cheese, grated (1/2 cup, tightly packed)
- 1 ounce Parmesan cheese, grated (1/4 cup, tightly packed)
- 2 tablespoons extra virgin olive oil
- 1 teaspoon chopped fresh rosemary
- Salt
- freshly ground pepper
- 4 large eggs
- ½ teaspoon salt

Direction

- If the bread is soft, toast it lightly and rub each slice front and back with the cut clove of garlic. Cut in 1-inch dice. If the bread is stale, just rub the slices with garlic and cut them into 1-inch dice. Place in a very large bowl, and toss with 2/3 cup of the milk. Set aside.
- Place the dried mushrooms in a bowl or a Pyrex measuring cup, and cover with 1 1/2 cups boiling water. Allow to sit for 30 minutes. Set a strainer over a bowl, line with cheesecloth, a coffee filter or paper towels, and drain the mushrooms. Squeeze the mushrooms over the strainer to extract all of the broth. Rinse, away from the strainer, in several changes of water to wash off sand. Squeeze out excess water. Chop coarsely. Measure out 1 cup of the mushroom broth, and combine with the remaining milk.
- Preheat the oven to 350 degrees. Oil or butter a 2-quart baking dish or gratin. Heat a large skillet over medium-high heat, and add the chard. Stir until the leaves begin to wilt in the liquid left on them after washing. Cover the pan, and let the chard steam until it has completely collapsed, about two minutes. Uncover and stir. When all of the chard has wilted, remove from the pan and rinse briefly with cold water. Press or squeeze out excess liquid. Chop coarsely and set aside.
- Add 1 tablespoon of the olive oil to the pan, turn the heat down to medium and add the minced garlic. Cook, stirring, until fragrant, about 30 seconds, and stir in the reconstituted mushrooms, the rosemary and the chard. Stir together for a couple of minutes, and season to taste with salt and pepper. Remove from the heat, and transfer to the bowl with the bread cubes. Add the cheeses, and toss together. Arrange in the baking dish.
- Beat together the eggs in a medium bowl. Add salt to taste (I use 1/2 to 3/4 teaspoon), the remaining milk and the mushroom broth. Add a few twists of the peppermill and pour over the bread. Press the bread down into the custard mixture. Sprinkle a little Parmesan over the top, and drizzle on the remaining olive oil. Place in the oven, and bake 40 to 50 minutes, until puffed and browned. Remove from the oven, and serve hot or warm.

Nutrition Information

- 292: calories;
- 27 grams: carbohydrates;
- 14 grams: fat;
- 5 grams: saturated fat;
- 0 grams: trans fat;
- 6 grams: sugars;
- 2 grams: dietary fiber;
- 15 grams: protein;
- 473 milligrams: sodium;

311. Strawberry Floating Islands

Serving: 8 servings | Prep: | Cook: | Ready in: 30mins

Ingredients

- 8 large egg whites, at room temperature
- Pinch of salt
- 1 ⅓ cups granulated sugar
- 3 pints ripe strawberries, hulled

- Juice of 1/2 lemon
- Pinch of cinnamon

Direction

- Beat the egg whites with the pinch of salt until softly peaked. Add four tablespoons of the sugar and beat until stiff. Gradually add all but one-third cup of the sugar, beating constantly, until the egg whites are stiff and glossy.
- Heat a large pan of water until the steam rises from the top but before it has come to a simmer. Using two large tablespoons or an ice cream scoop, form large ovals or rounds of the egg white mixture and drop them into the water. Poach for two minutes, turn once and poach them another two minutes. Remove the meringues as they are done and drain them on absorbent paper. Refrigerate for at least one hour. You may not be able to poach all the meringues at one time.
- Puree two pints of the strawberries and season the puree with the remaining sugar and the lemon juice. Add the cinnamon. Refrigerate the puree. Slice the remaining strawberries in half lengthwise and refrigerate. To serve, spoon the strawberry puree into a shallow serving bowl and float the meringues on top. Scatter the sliced strawberries around and over the meringues and serve.

Nutrition Information

- 190: calories;
- 0 grams: polyunsaturated fat;
- 44 grams: carbohydrates;
- 3 grams: dietary fiber;
- 40 grams: sugars;
- 5 grams: protein;
- 93 milligrams: sodium;

312. Strawberry Rhubarb Pie

Serving: 6 to 8 servings | Prep: | Cook: |Ready in: 1hours

Ingredients

- 9 stalks rhubarb, approximately 1 1/4 pounds
- 1 ½ cups sugar
- Pinch salt
- 1 pint strawberries
- 2 tablespoons instant tapioca
- 1 teaspoon finely grated orange rind
- 1 tablespoon bread crumbs
- 2 tablespoons sweet butter
- 3 to 4 tablespoons heavy cream
- 9-inch pie shell with strips for lattice top, chilled for 15 minutes

Direction

- Wash and drain rhubarb and strawberries and dry. Remove leaves and trim bottom of rhubarb. Slice 1/4-inch thick and place in a bowl with 1/4 cup sugar and salt.
- Hull berries and slice. Add to rhubarb. Mix with fingers. Let stand 15 minutes. Drain 15 minutes.
- Place remaining sugar, tapioca and orange rind in another bowl.
- Dust bottom of chilled pie shell with bread crumbs. Brush fluted edge with heavy cream.
- Toss strawberry-rhubarb mixture with tapioca-sugar mixture and spoon into pie shell. Dot with butter. Brush strips of pastry with cream. Arrange strips on top of filling to form lattice crust. Cover edges of pie with foil to prevent scorching.
- Bake at 400 degrees for 45 minutes. Remove foil. Bake an additional 10 to 15 minutes or until pastry is golden brown. Cool completely before cutting.

Nutrition Information

- 232: calories;
- 6 grams: fat;
- 3 grams: saturated fat;

- 0 grams: polyunsaturated fat;
- 1 gram: protein;
- 2 grams: dietary fiber;
- 49 milligrams: sodium;
- 46 grams: carbohydrates;
- 41 grams: sugars;

313. Strawberry Moscato Sorbet

Serving: about 1 quart | Prep: | Cook: | Ready in: 15mins

Ingredients

- 1 cup very ripe strawberries, quartered
- 1 cup moscato wine
- ½ cup orange juice
- 1 cup plus 2 tablespoons sugar
- 2 tablespoons light corn syrup

Direction

- In a food processor, puree strawberries. Add moscato, orange juice, sugar, corn syrup and 1 1/2 cups water. Puree. Strain through a fine sieve. Taste, adding sugar if necessary. Chill in refrigerator.
- Stir mixture, then pour into an ice cream maker and follow manufacturer's instructions.

Nutrition Information

- 162: calories;
- 35 grams: sugars;
- 6 milligrams: sodium;
- 0 grams: protein;
- 36 grams: carbohydrates;

314. Stuffed Shells Filled With Spinach And Ricotta

Serving: About 40 shells, serving 6 | Prep: | Cook: | Ready in: 1hours

Ingredients

- 1 pound baby spinach, rinsed, or 2 pounds bunch spinach, stemmed and washed thoroughly
- Salt to taste
- 12 ounces giant pasta shells
- 1 tablespoon extra virgin olive oil
- 1 to 2 garlic cloves, to taste, cut in half, green shoots removed
- 10 ounces ricotta cheese
- 1 egg, beaten
- 2 tablespoons minced chives
- 2 ounces Parmesan, grated about 1/2 cup
- Freshly ground pepper
- 2 cups marinara sauce, preferably homemade

Direction

- Bring a large pot of water to a boil and salt generously. Fill a bowl with ice water. Blanch the spinach for no more than 20 seconds, just until wilted, and transfer to the ice water, then drain. Squeeze out excess water. Bring the water in the pot back to a boil and add the pasta shells. Cook al dente, about 10 minutes, and drain and toss with the olive oil. Set aside.
- Turn on a food processor fitted with the steel blade and drop in the garlic. When the garlic is chopped and adhering to the sides of the bowl, stop the machine and scrape down the sides of the bowl. Add the spinach and pulse to chop finely. Add the ricotta and the egg and process until well blended. Add 1/3 cup of the Parmesan, the chives, and salt and pepper to taste. Pulse until well blended.
- Preheat the oven to 350 degrees. Oil a large baking dish or two 2-quart dishes. The shells should fit into the dish in one layer. Fill each shell with a scant tablespoon of the filling. Arrange in a single layer in the baking dish.

Top with the tomato sauce and cover the dish with foil.
- Bake 30 minutes in the preheated oven. Remove from the heat, sprinkle on the remaining Parmesan, and serve.

Nutrition Information

- 424: calories;
- 5 grams: dietary fiber;
- 54 grams: carbohydrates;
- 7 grams: sugars;
- 21 grams: protein;
- 672 milligrams: sodium;
- 14 grams: fat;
- 6 grams: saturated fat;
- 0 grams: trans fat;
- 2 grams: polyunsaturated fat;

315. Stuffed Strawberries

Serving: 12 strawberries | Prep: | Cook: | Ready in: 15mins

Ingredients

- 12 large ripe strawberries, rinsed and dried
- 4 ounces mascarpone cheese
- ½ teaspoon superfine sugar
- 2 drops vanilla extract
- 2 tablespoons grated dark (semisweet or bittersweet) chocolate

Direction

- With a paring knife remove hull and inner core of each berry to form a cavity. Remove meat of the berry from the hull. Save stem and hull.
- In a small bowl mix together cheese, sugar, vanilla and chocolate. Using a small spoon, stuff mixture into cavity of each berry. Top berries with hulls. Serve cold.

Nutrition Information

- 47: calories;
- 2 grams: sugars;
- 1 gram: protein;
- 0 grams: dietary fiber;
- 3 grams: carbohydrates;
- 35 milligrams: sodium;
- 4 grams: fat;

316. Succotash

Serving: Six or more servings | Prep: | Cook: | Ready in: 40mins

Ingredients

- 4 cups fresh corn (about 6 to 8 ears)
- 2 cups small, shelled fresh lima beans
- 2 cups fresh string beans, cut into 1-inch pieces
- ¼ pound unsalted butter
- ⅓ pound bacon cut into 1/2-inch pieces (optional)
- 4 scallions, trimmed
- 2 to 3 tablespoons heavy cream

Direction

- Husk the corn and remove all the silk. With a sharp knife, remove the kernels from the cob, slicing from the top of the ear downward and not too close to the cob. With a small spoon, scrape the pulp from the cobs into a mixing bowl. Add the kernels and reserve.
- In a medium-sized pot of lightly salted boiling water, blanch the lima beans until they are almost tender, then cool under cold water. Reserve and repeat the process with the string beans.
- In a large heavy saucepan, melt the butter over medium heat. Add the the butter over medium heat. Add the corn and its juices, and cook for 10 minutes, stirring often.

- Place the bacon pieces in a small skillet and render over medium heat until golden. Drain on paper towels and reserve.
- Slice the scallions into half-inch pieces, including some of the green, and set aside. Add both types of beans to the corn and cook for another 10 minutes, stirring often. After five minutes, add the scallions and fold in the cream to loosen the mixture. Fold in the bacon pieces and spoon the succotash into a warm serving bowl. Salt and pepper to taste. Serve immediately.

Nutrition Information

- 317: calories;
- 1 gram: polyunsaturated fat;
- 5 grams: dietary fiber;
- 8 grams: protein;
- 12 grams: saturated fat;
- 20 grams: fat;
- 33 grams: carbohydrates;
- 10 grams: sugars;
- 29 milligrams: sodium;

317. Summer Squash Medley

Serving: 4 servings | Prep: | Cook: | Ready in: 25mins

Ingredients

- 2 tablespoons olive oil
- 4 to 5 cloves garlic, smashed, peeled and chopped
- 1 ½ medium-size zucchini (3/4 pound), trimmed, quartered lengthwise and cut across into 1/2-inch pieces
- 1 medium-size yellow squash (6 1/2 ounces), trimmed, quartered lengthwise, seeded and cut across into 1/2-inch pieces
- 2 large tomatoes (8 ounces each), cored and cut in 1-inch chunks
- 1 tablespoon kosher salt
- 1 cup basil leaves, coarsely chopped

Direction

- Put oil in a 2 1/2-quart souffle dish with a tightly fitting lid. Cook, uncovered, at 100 percent power in a high-power oven for 1 minute. Stir in garlic. Cook, uncovered, 1 minute 30 seconds.
- Stir in squash. Cook, covered, 5 minutes.
- Uncover and stir in tomatoes and salt. Cook, uncovered, 6 minutes. Stir in basil and cook, uncovered, 1 minute.
- Remove from oven. Let stand, covered, 5 minutes.

Nutrition Information

- 112: calories;
- 5 grams: sugars;
- 11 grams: carbohydrates;
- 3 grams: protein;
- 606 milligrams: sodium;
- 7 grams: fat;
- 1 gram: polyunsaturated fat;

318. Summer Tomato Gratin

Serving: Serves four | Prep: | Cook: | Ready in: 1hours30mins

Ingredients

- 2 pounds ripe, firm tomatoes, sliced
- Salt
- freshly ground pepper to taste
- ½ teaspoon sugar
- ½ cup fresh or dry bread crumbs, preferably whole wheat
- 2 tablespoons chopped flat-leaf parsley
- 2 tablespoons extra virgin olive oil

Direction

- Preheat the oven to 400 degrees. Oil a 2-quart gratin or baking dish. Layer the tomatoes in

- the dish, seasoning each layer with salt, pepper and a small sprinkle of sugar.
- Toss together the bread crumbs, parsley and olive oil. Spread over the tomatoes in an even layer. Place in the oven, and bake for 1 to 1 1/2 hours, until the juices are thick and syrupy and the top is golden. Remove from the oven, and allow to cool for at least 15 minutes before serving.

Nutrition Information

- 175: calories;
- 599 milligrams: sodium;
- 8 grams: fat;
- 1 gram: polyunsaturated fat;
- 6 grams: dietary fiber;
- 5 grams: monounsaturated fat;
- 26 grams: carbohydrates;
- 7 grams: sugars;
- 4 grams: protein;

319. Sunday Black Bean Soup

Serving: 5 2-cup servings plus sausage | Prep: | Cook: | Ready in: 3hours15mins

Ingredients

- 1 pound dried black beans
- ½ pound bacon, preferably nitrite-free
- 3 cups chicken stock
- 1 to 2 tablespoons canola or corn oil
- 4 coarsely chopped carrots
- 3 coarsely chopped onions
- 3 coarsely chopped celery ribs
- ½ to 1 fresh jalapeno pepper or 1 3 1/2- to 4-ounce can mild jalapenos, minced
- 3 finely chopped garlic cloves
- 1 teaspoon ground cumin
- Salt to taste
- 1 pound spicy sausage (see note)
- 1 cup dry sherry
- Juice from 1/2 to 1 lime
- 5 tablespoons chopped fresh cilantro, optional

Direction

- To soak beans quickly, cover them with generous amount of water, cover pot, bring water to boil and boil 2 minutes. Remove cover and allow beans to sit in the liquid for one hour. Drain.
- Meanwhile, slice meaty part of bacon from fat. Discard fat.
- When beans are ready to cook, add meaty bacon to beans along with chicken stock and enough water to cover generously; cover and bring to a boil. Reduce heat and simmer.
- In hot oil, saute carrots, onions, celery, jalapeno, garlic and cumin until onions are golden. When vegetables are ready, add to pot of beans. If there is not enough water, add more. Cook beans 1 1/2 to 2 hours, or until tender. Season with salt, if desired.
- Just before beans are ready, cook sausage; slice into small chunks.
- Drain the bean mixture and reserve cooking liquid. Puree beans and vegetables, using some of the reserved liquid to make a thick soup. Return to cooking pot. Stir in sherry and lime juice. Add more reserved liquid, if necessary, and reheat to serve.
- Divide sausage chunks among bowls, and spoon soup into each bowl. Sprinkle with cilantro.

Nutrition Information

- 940: calories;
- 45 grams: protein;
- 1297 milligrams: sodium;
- 48 grams: fat;
- 19 grams: monounsaturated fat;
- 80 grams: carbohydrates;
- 12 grams: sugars;
- 14 grams: saturated fat;
- 0 grams: trans fat;
- 10 grams: polyunsaturated fat;
- 18 grams: dietary fiber;

320. Sweet Potato And Green Bean Salad

Serving: 6 servings | Prep: | Cook: | Ready in: 30mins

Ingredients

- 1 pound green beans, both ends removed, cut into pieces about 2-inches long
- 1 cup pineapple juice
- ½ teaspoon ground cumin
- 2 bay leaves
- ¼ cup maple syrup
- 2 tablespoons soy sauce
- 2 tablespoons olive oil
- 1 pound sweet potatoes, peeled and cut into 1-inch cubes
- Zest from 1 washed lemon, to yield about 2 teaspoons
- 3 cups baby arugula or watercress
- 1 teaspoon sesame seeds, toasted

Direction

- Place the green beans in boiling salted water and cook until al dente. Remove and place in ice-cold water so they keep their bright green color. Drain.
- Place the pineapple juice, cumin and bay leaves in a small saucepan. Simmer on low heat until reduced by half.
- Pour the pineapple juice reduction in a bowl and mix with maple syrup and soy sauce.
- Place the olive oil in a pan over high heat, add the sweet potatoes and cook until golden brown on all sides.
- Place the sweet potatoes in a bowl and add the green beans, lemon zest and the maple-pineapple dressing. Toss until mixed. Mixing the dressing with the sweet potatoes while they are still warm allows even distribution of the dressing throughout the salad. Cool to room temperature.
- Place the arugula or watercress on the bottom of a plate and place the vegetables on top. Sprinkle with the toasted sesame seeds. Serve immediately.

Nutrition Information

- 195: calories;
- 343 milligrams: sodium;
- 5 grams: dietary fiber;
- 1 gram: polyunsaturated fat;
- 3 grams: protein;
- 36 grams: carbohydrates;
- 18 grams: sugars;

321. Sweet Potato, Pumpkin And Apple Puree

Serving: Makes six to eight servings | Prep: | Cook: | Ready in: 1hours30mins

Ingredients

- 1 pound sweet potatoes, scrubbed
- 1 pound pumpkin, seeds removed
- 2 tart apples, such as Granny Smith or Braeburn
- 2 tablespoons lime juice
- 5 tablespoons plain Greek-style yogurt
- 2 tablespoons unsalted butter, melted
- 2 tablespoons maple syrup
- Pinch of salt
- Pinch of freshly grated nutmeg

Direction

- Preheat the oven to 400 degrees. Scrub sweet potatoes, and pierce in several places with a sharp knife. Pierce the apples in a few places. Line a baking sheet with foil, lightly oil the foil, and place the potatoes, pumpkin (cut side down) and apples on top. Bake the pumpkin and apples for 30 to 40 minutes, until a knife can easily be inserted right to the core of the apples (it's fine if the skin pops off the apples, or if they collapse) and the pumpkin is soft.

Remove the pumpkin and apples from the oven. Continue to bake the sweet potatoes until thoroughly soft and beginning to ooze, 15 minutes or longer, depending on the size. Remove from the heat, and allow to cool until you can handle them easily.

- Turn the oven down to 350 degrees. Remove the skins from the potatoes and pumpkin. Peel and core the apples, and scrape off any apple flesh that adheres to the skin. Chop everything coarsely, and place in a food processor fitted with the steel blade. Puree until smooth. Add the remaining ingredients, and blend well. Transfer to a lightly buttered 2-quart baking dish.
- Heat the puree in the 350-degree oven for 20 minutes, or until steaming. Serve hot.

Nutrition Information

- 138: calories;
- 4 grams: fat;
- 25 grams: carbohydrates;
- 12 grams: sugars;
- 75 milligrams: sodium;
- 2 grams: saturated fat;
- 0 grams: polyunsaturated fat;
- 1 gram: monounsaturated fat;
- 3 grams: protein;

322. Sweet And Pungent Apple And Cabbage Slaw

Serving: 6 to 8 servings. | Prep: | Cook: |Ready in: 10mins

Ingredients

- 3 tablespoons fresh lemon juice
- 2 teaspoons apple cider vinegar
- 1 tablespoon mild honey
- Salt to taste
- 2 teaspoons Dijon mustard
- 3 tablespoon grapeseed or canola oil
- ¼ cup plain low-fat yogurt
- 1 large carrot (about 4 ounces)
- 2 ribs celery
- 6 radishes
- ¼ medium red cabbage (about 1/2 pound)
- 2 apples, preferably tart ones like Granny Smith or Pink Lady, quartered and cored
- 1 to 2 ounces feta cheese, crumbled (optional)

Direction

- Whisk together the lemon juice, vinegar, salt, mustard, oil and yogurt.
- Shred the carrot, celery, radishes, cabbage and apples. I use a food processor for this, but you can also use a box grater, and for the cabbage you can use a chef's knife. Toss immediately with the dressing. Serve topped with crumbled feta if desired.

Nutrition Information

- 102: calories;
- 1 gram: protein;
- 299 milligrams: sodium;
- 0 grams: trans fat;
- 13 grams: carbohydrates;
- 3 grams: monounsaturated fat;
- 2 grams: dietary fiber;
- 9 grams: sugars;
- 6 grams: fat;

323. Tangerine Or Minneola Tart

Serving: 8 to 10 servings | Prep: | Cook: |Ready in: 1hours

Ingredients

- 8 or 9 Minneola tangelos or medium tangerines
- ½ cup plus 1 tablespoon sugar
- 2 1/2-ounce packages powdered gelatin

- 2 cups heavy cream
- 1 9-inch pate sucree tart shell, fully baked (recipe below)

Direction

- Grate the fruit peel on the second-finest blade of a box grater. Then, juice the fruit, yielding 2 1/2 cups of juice.
- Place 3/4 cup of the juice, all but 1 teaspoon of the rind, and the sugar in a small saucepan. Sprinkle the gelatin over the juice, and allow to sit for 1 to 2 minutes, or until the gelatin is no longer white. Over medium heat, bring the liquid just to a simmer. Lower heat slightly, and cook, stirring, for 5 minutes.
- Strain the juice and gelatin mixture into a medium stainless-steel bowl over a larger bowl filled with ice and water. Stir in the remaining juice; whisk to combine. Stirring from time to time with a rubber spatula, allow the gelatin to become firm, but not completely set. This process should take about 20 to 25 minutes.
- Meanwhile, whip the heavy cream to medium peaks.
- When the gelatin is firm, beat it slightly with a wire whisk to lighten. Beat in 1 1/2 cups of the whipped cream with a rubber spatula until fully combined, but not over-mixed.
- Smooth into the prepared tart shell, mounding slightly toward the center. Top with additional whipped cream, saving 1/2 cup for garnish if desired. Sprinkle the reserved teaspoon of zest over the top.
- Refrigerate for 1 to 2 hours, or until set.

Nutrition Information

- 271: calories;
- 8 grams: protein;
- 34 milligrams: sodium;
- 11 grams: saturated fat;
- 1 gram: dietary fiber;
- 23 grams: carbohydrates;
- 20 grams: sugars;
- 18 grams: fat;
- 5 grams: monounsaturated fat;

324. Teff Pancakes With Chia, Millet And Blueberries

Serving: about 15 pancakes | Prep: | Cook: | Ready in: 15mins

Ingredients

- ½ cup (75 grams) teff flour (I make the flour by grinding the grain in a spice mill)
- 1 cup (125 grams) white whole-wheat flour or regular whole-wheat flour
- 2 teaspoons (10 grams) baking powder
- 1 teaspoon (5 grams) baking soda
- Rounded 1/4 teaspoon salt
- 1 tablespoon sugar, honey or agave syrup
- 2 eggs
- 1 teaspoon (5 grams) vanilla
- 1 ½ cups buttermilk
- 3 tablespoons canola oil
- 1 cup (125 grams) cooked millet
- 3 tablespoons (35 grams) chia seeds
- 1 6-ounce box blueberries tossed with 1/2 teaspoon all-purpose flour

Direction

- Sift together the teff, flour, baking powder, baking soda, salt and sugar (if using sugar). In a medium bowl, beat together the eggs, buttermilk, oil, vanilla, and honey or agave nectar if using. Quickly whisk in the flour mixture and fold in the chia seeds and millet.
- Heat a large skillet or griddle over medium-high heat and brush with butter or oil. Drop the pancakes by the scant 1/4 cup onto the hot pan or griddle. Place 7 or 8 blueberries on each pancake, gently pushing them down into the batter. Cook until bubbles break through and turn the pancakes. Cook for about 1 minute on the other side, until lightly browned. Remove to a rack. Serve with maple syrup and butter.

Nutrition Information

- 156: calories;
- 0 grams: trans fat;
- 2 grams: sugars;
- 23 grams: carbohydrates;
- 3 grams: dietary fiber;
- 200 milligrams: sodium;
- 5 grams: protein;
- 1 gram: saturated fat;

---

325. Thanksgiving Roasted Root Veggies

Serving: | Prep: | Cook: | Ready in: 1hours15mins

Ingredients

- 1 head garlic, separated into cloves and peeled
- 1-2 pounds root vegetables, peeled and cut in 1 inch pieces (potatoes, carrots, parsnips, turnips, rutabagas, beets, sweet potatoes)
- 1 medium onion, peeled, in 1/4-inch wedges
- 2 Tbl olive oil
- 1-2 Tbl smoked Spanish paprika or mild red chile powder
- salt and pepper

Direction

- Heat oven to 400.
- Put vegetables (except garlic) in a bowl. Toss with oil and sprinkle with salt, pepper, and paprika or chile.
- Spread veggies in a roasting pan. (Do not crowd the pieces; use 2 pans if necessary.) Roast, stirring every 15 minutes until tender and evenly browned, 45-50 minutes.
- Add garlic cloves during last 20 minutes. Taste and adjust seasonings.

Nutrition Information

- 148: calories;
- 5 grams: protein;
- 1 gram: sugars;
- 3 grams: monounsaturated fat;
- 21 grams: carbohydrates;
- 6 grams: dietary fiber;
- 342 milligrams: sodium;

---

326. The Perfect Burger

Serving: 6 servings | Prep: | Cook: | Ready in: 25mins

Ingredients

- 3 pounds ground chuck, preferably chicken steak or blade steak, not more than 20 percent fat
- 6 four-inch Pepperidge Farm Farmhouse white rolls or Amy's Bread rolls
- 2 large sweet onions
- 2 ripe tomatoes
- 6 leaves of Boston or iceberg lettuce

Direction

- Heat a seasoned cast-iron grill pan over a high flame for five minutes. Meanwhile, place the meat in a bowl and knead lightly. (Disregard experts who warn that kneading will produce a dry burger. Kneading will not have this effect on chuck cooked rare or medium rare, but it will keep the meat from falling apart. Leaner cuts will be dry whether or not you knead them.) Divide the meat into six portions and shape burgers. Do not season.
- Add burgers three at a time to pan leaving space between them. After four minutes lift burgers from pan with pair of tongs and turn by 90 degrees. After two minutes turn burgers over. The grill marks will form an attractive tick-tac-toe matrix. Meanwhile, toast rolls. In about five minutes meat will be medium-medium rare. Add sweet onion, tomato and lettuce on roll's bottom half. Add burger. Top with other roll half. Serve with ketchup.

Nutrition Information

- 592: calories;
- 5 grams: polyunsaturated fat;
- 40 grams: carbohydrates;
- 4 grams: dietary fiber;
- 11 grams: sugars;
- 23 grams: fat;
- 6 grams: saturated fat;
- 0 grams: trans fat;
- 441 milligrams: sodium;
- 9 grams: monounsaturated fat;
- 55 grams: protein;

327. Three Cheese Ravioli

Serving: None | Prep: | Cook: | Ready in:

Ingredients

- 4 ounces fresh goat cheese
- 2 ounces blue cheese
- ⅓ cup grated Parmesan cheese
- Pulp of 1 small baked potato, mashed
- 3 eggs
- 3 tablespoons chopped fresh chervil
- 2 tablespoons chopped fresh chives
- Salt and freshly ground white pepper to taste
- Semolina flour
- 1 pound fresh egg pasta dough (see note)
- 1 tablespoon olive oil
- 1 cup chicken stock
- 8 tablespoons unsalted butter, at room temperature
- 1 teaspoon chopped fresh sage
- 1 teaspoon chopped fresh marjoram
- Chervil sprigs for garnish

Direction

- In a small bowl combine goat cheese, blue cheese, 1/4 cup of Parmesan cheese, the potato and two eggs. Mix well and add 2 tablespoons each of chervil and chives. Season to taste with salt and pepper and refrigerate.
- Dust a work surface with semolina flour and roll out half the pasta dough by hand or by machine, making a strip about 30 inches long and 5 inches wide. Lightly beat the remaining egg and brush the strip halfway along its length with half the beaten egg. Put heaping teaspoons of the cheese mixture on the dough that has been brushed with the egg, making 12 mounds of the mixture about 2 1/2 inches apart.
- Cover with the plain half of the dough by folding it back along its length and press the dough down around each mound. Using a cookie cutter or a knife, cut 3-inch rounds or squares and arrange the cut ravioli on a tray dusted with semolina. Repeat with the remaining dough and filling. Cover and refrigerate until ready to use. (The ravioli may be frozen.)
- Bring a large pot of water to a boil and add the olive oil.
- While water is coming to a boil, bring chicken stock to a simmer in a medium to large saucepan and season with pepper. Whisk in the butter and cook about 5 minutes, until slightly thickened. Remove from heat.
- Add a little salt to the boiling water; add the ravioli, reduce heat to medium and cook ravioli for 5 minutes. Remove ravioli with a slotted spoon and drain on clean towel.
- Reheat the sauce and stir in the sage, marjoram and remaining chervil. Stir in the remaining Parmesan cheese and season to taste with salt and pepper. Add the cooked, drained ravioli to the sauce; simmer a minute or two, and then spoon the ravioli into four warm bowls, spooning the sauce over each. Garnish with a sprig of chervil and serve at once.

Nutrition Information

- 808: calories;
- 47 grams: fat;
- 26 grams: saturated fat;
- 1 gram: trans fat;

- 14 grams: monounsaturated fat;
- 3 grams: sugars;
- 4 grams: dietary fiber;
- 68 grams: carbohydrates;
- 29 grams: protein;
- 1259 milligrams: sodium;

328. Tijoe's Fungi

Serving: Six servings | Prep: | Cook: | Ready in: 1hours40mins

Ingredients

- 3 tablespoons butter
- ½ cup minced onion
- 2 ½ cups water
- ¼ teaspoon salt
- 1 ¼ cups yellow stone ground cornmeal
- ⅓ cup diced tomato, seeded and drained
- ½ cup frozen cut okra, thawed and coarsely chopped and well drained

Direction

- Melt the butter in a small frying pan and cook the onion over medium heat for five minutes, stirring often. Remove from the heat.
- Bring the water to a boil in a three-and-a-half-quart heavy saucepan, preferably a nonstick one. Stir in the salt and slowly pour in the cornmeal, stirring constantly with a wooden spoon. Reduce the heat to low and stir constantly for 10 minutes.
- Stir in the onion and butter, tomatoes and okra. Continue stirring for five minutes until the mixture rolls off the side of the pan and no longer sticks to the bottom.
- Turn the mixture onto a baking sheet and smooth the top evenly with a spatula into a 10-inch circle, three-quarters of an inch thick. Cool for 15 minutes. Cover loosely with plastic wrap and let rest for one hour.
- Cut the fungi into about one-and-a-half-inch squares and serve at room temperature.

Nutrition Information

- 153: calories;
- 1 gram: sugars;
- 22 grams: carbohydrates;
- 7 grams: fat;
- 0 grams: trans fat;
- 2 grams: monounsaturated fat;
- 127 milligrams: sodium;
- 4 grams: saturated fat;
- 3 grams: protein;

329. Toasted Corn Salsa

Serving: Makes about 2 cups | Prep: | Cook: | Ready in: 1hours15mins

Ingredients

- 4 ½ teaspoons extra-virgin olive oil
- 2 ears corn, kernels removed
- 1 red bell pepper, stemmed, seeded, and chopped fine
- ½ jalapeño chile, stemmed, seeded, and minced (see note above)
- 1 scallion, sliced thin
- 2 garlic cloves, minced
- 2 tablespoons fresh lime juice
- 2 tablespoons minced fresh cilantro
- ½ teaspoon ground cumin
- Salt and pepper

Direction

- Heat 1 1/2 teaspoons of the oil in a 12-inch nonstick skillet over medium-high heat until shimmering. Following the photo, add the corn and cook, stirring occasionally, until golden brown, 6 to 8 minutes.
- Transfer the corn to a large bowl and stir in the remaining 1 tablespoon oil, bell pepper, jalapeño, scallion, garlic, lime juice, cilantro, cumin, 1/4 teaspoon salt, and 1/8 teaspoon

pepper. Cover and refrigerate until the flavors have blended, about 1 hour. Season with salt and pepper to taste before serving.

Nutrition Information

- 105: calories;
- 5 grams: sugars;
- 234 milligrams: sodium;
- 6 grams: fat;
- 0 grams: trans fat;
- 2 grams: protein;
- 1 gram: polyunsaturated fat;
- 4 grams: monounsaturated fat;
- 13 grams: carbohydrates;

330. Tofu Scramble

Serving: 2 servings | Prep: | Cook: | Ready in: 55mins

Ingredients

- 1 large baked potato
- 2 teaspoons margarine
- 10 ounces firm tofu, drained and crumbled
- Pinch of turmeric
- ¼ cup chopped green onion
- ¾ cup chopped red pepper
- 1 cup slice fresh mushrooms
- 3 tablespoons salsa

Direction

- Peel potato and cut into small cubes.
- Melt margarine in a nonstick skillet and add tofu. Add turmeric and cook over high heat 5 minutes. Add vegetables and cook 5 minutes, or until vegetables are tender but crisp. Stir in salsa and serve.

Nutrition Information

- 421: calories;
- 17 grams: fat;
- 1 gram: trans fat;
- 5 grams: monounsaturated fat;
- 8 grams: polyunsaturated fat;
- 45 grams: carbohydrates;
- 29 grams: protein;
- 268 milligrams: sodium;
- 3 grams: saturated fat;
- 9 grams: dietary fiber;
- 6 grams: sugars;

331. Tomato Salad With Turkish Tahini Dressing

Serving: Serves four to six (the recipe makes about 2/3 cup dressing) | Prep: | Cook: | Ready in: 10mins

Ingredients

- 1 ½ pounds tomatoes, or a mixture of red and green tomatoes, cored and sliced
- 4 tablespoons sesame tahini
- ⅓ cup water
- 2 tablespoons freshly squeezed lemon juice
- 1 to 2 garlic cloves
- Salt to taste
- ½ teaspoon cumin seeds, lightly toasted and ground
- Freshly ground pepper or Aleppo pepper to taste
- 1 to 2 tablespoons chopped flat-leaf parsley

Direction

- Arrange the sliced tomatoes on a platter.
- Mix together the tahini, water and lemon juice. Combine the garlic with 1/4 teaspoon salt in a mortar and pestle, and mash to a paste. Stir into the tahini mixture. Add the cumin, then salt and pepper (or Aleppo pepper) to taste. Thin out with water if the dressing is too thick to pour. Drizzle over the sliced tomatoes, sprinkle on the parsley and serve.

Nutrition Information

- 90: calories;
- 334 milligrams: sodium;
- 6 grams: fat;
- 1 gram: saturated fat;
- 2 grams: dietary fiber;
- 9 grams: carbohydrates;
- 5 grams: sugars;
- 3 grams: protein;

332. Tossed Green Salad

Serving: 4 servings | Prep: | Cook: |Ready in: 10mins

Ingredients

- 2 small heads Boston lettuce
- 2 tablespoons tarragon vinegar
- 1 teaspoon finely minced garlic
- 1 tablespoon Dijon-style mustard
- 6 tablespoons olive oil
- Salt to taste if desired
- Freshly ground pepper to taste
- 1 tablespoon finely chopped dill
- 1 tablespoon finely chopped parsley
- 1 tablespoon finely chopped chives (optional)

Direction

- Discard any blemished outer leaves of lettuce. Cut away core. Separate leaves, rinse and drain or spin dry. Place in a salad bowl.
- In a small bowl, combine vinegar, garlic and mustard. Using a wire whisk, beat in oil. Add salt, pepper, dill, parsley and chives. Pour dressing over salad and toss.

Nutrition Information

- 193: calories;
- 222 milligrams: sodium;
- 21 grams: fat;
- 3 grams: saturated fat;
- 0 grams: trans fat;
- 15 grams: monounsaturated fat;

- 2 grams: carbohydrates;
- 1 gram: protein;

333. Tunisian Winter Squash Salad

Serving: 4 servings | Prep: | Cook: |Ready in:

Ingredients

- 1 pound butternut or kabocha squash, peeled and cut into large chunks
- 1 teaspoon salt, plus more to taste
- 1 clove garlic, unpeeled
- 1 teaspoon harissa (a North African hot sauce available in specialty shops)
- ¼ teaspoon ground coriander
- Juice of 1/2 lemon
- 1 tablespoon olive oil

Direction

- Bring about 6 cups of water to a boil in a large pot. Then add the squash, salt and the garlic clove. Lower the heat and simmer until the squash is very tender.
- Remove the squash to a mesh strainer, and squeeze the garlic out of its skin into the strainer. Mash the two together to help get rid of excess water.
- Transfer the mixture to a large bowl and stir in the harissa, salt to taste, the coriander, lemon juice and olive oil. Taste, adjust the seasonings, then serve.

Nutrition Information

- 72: calories;
- 0 grams: polyunsaturated fat;
- 11 grams: carbohydrates;
- 3 grams: sugars;
- 293 milligrams: sodium;
- 4 grams: fat;
- 1 gram: protein;

- 2 grams: dietary fiber;

334. Turkey And Vegetable Burgers

Serving: 6 burgers | Prep: | Cook: | Ready in: 30mins

Ingredients

- 1 tablespoon extra virgin olive oil
- ½ cup finely diced onion
- ½ cup finely diced red bell pepper
- Salt to taste
- 1 large garlic clove, green shoot removed, minced
- ⅔ cup finely grated carrot (1 large carrot)
- 1 ¼ pounds lean ground turkey breast, preferably organic, from humanely raised turkeys
- 1 tablespoon prepared barbecue sauce
- 1 tablespoon ketchup
- Freshly ground pepper to taste
- Canola oil for the skillet
- Whole grain hamburger buns
- condiments of your choice

Direction

- Heat the olive oil over medium heat in a medium skillet and add the onion. Cook, stirring, until it begins to soften, about 3 minutes, and add the diced red pepper and a generous pinch of salt. Cook, stirring often, until the vegetables are tender, about 5 minutes. Stir in the garlic and the grated carrot and cook, stirring, for another minute or two, until the carrots have softened slightly and the mixture is fragrant. Remove from the heat.
- In a large bowl, mash the ground turkey with a fork. Add about ¾ teaspoon kosher salt if desired, and mix in the barbecue sauce, ketchup, and freshly ground pepper to taste. Add the sautéed vegetables and mix together well. Shape into 6 patties, about ¾-inch thick. Chill for 1 hour if possible to facilitate handling.
- Heat a nonstick griddle or a large nonstick frying pan over medium-high heat and brush with a small amount of canola oil, or prepare a medium-hot grill. When you can feel the heat when you hold your hand above it, cook the patties for 4 minutes on each side. Serve on whole grain buns, with the condiments of your choice.

335. Turkish Shepherd's Salad

Serving: 6 servings | Prep: | Cook: | Ready in: 35mins

Ingredients

- 1 pound tomatoes, diced
- ¾ pound cucumbers (1 European or 4 Persian), diced
- 1 green pepper, preferably a long green Italian frying pepper, seeded and diced
- ½ small red onion, sliced, soaked in cold water for 5 minutes, drained and rinsed
- ¼ cup (loosely packed) coarsely chopped flat-leaf parsley
- 1 tablespoon chopped dill
- 2 tablespoons chopped mint
- 1 teaspoon sumac
- ½ to 1 teaspoon Turkish or Aleppo pepper
- Salt to taste
- 3 tablespoons fresh lemon juice
- 3 tablespoons extra virgin olive oil
- 1 to 2 ounces feta, crumbled (1/4 to 1/2 cup) (optional)
- Black olives as desired (optional)
- Romaine lettuce leaves and pita bread for serving (optional)

Direction

- Combine all of the ingredients except the olives and romaine in a large bowl and refrigerate for 30 minutes. After 30 minutes toss together, taste and adjust seasonings.

Garnish with olives and serve, with pita bread and romaine lettuce if desired.

Nutrition Information

- 91: calories;
- 389 milligrams: sodium;
- 7 grams: carbohydrates;
- 1 gram: protein;
- 5 grams: monounsaturated fat;
- 2 grams: dietary fiber;
- 4 grams: sugars;

336. Veal Stew With Sauteed Artichokes

Serving: 4-6 servings | Prep: | Cook: | Ready in: 1hours45mins

Ingredients

- 4 shallots, finely chopped
- 2 tablespoons peanut or vegetable oil
- 1 tablespoon unsalted butter
- 4 pounds veal stew, in 2-inch cubes
- ¾ cup flour
- 1 cup dry white wine
- 2 teaspoons sage leaves
- Coarse salt and freshly ground pepper to taste
- For the garnish:
- 3 pounds baby artichokes
- Juice 1/2 lemon
- 2 tablespoons olive oil
- 1 tablespoon safflower oil
- 1 clove garlic, minced (green part removed)

Direction

- In a heavy casserole, soften the shallots in the oil and butter. Remove with a slotted spoon and set aside.
- Lightly dredge the veal pieces with flour. Brown a few pieces at a time in the casserole on all sides, turning with tongs. Set the browned pieces aside in a bowl.
- When the meat has browned, add the white wine and scrape up cooking juices. Return meat to the pan, along with the sage, shallots, salt and pepper. Cover and simmer gently for 1 hour, stirring occasionally and adding a little water if the meat gets dry.
- Meanwhile, trim the tops (cutting off about two-thirds of an inch) and stalks from the artichokes. Remove tough outer leaves. Slice the artichokes vertically in quarter-inch pieces. Place them in a large bowl filled with water and the lemon juice, to stop them from turning brown.
- Heat the olive and safflower oils in a large skillet. Saute the artichokes until browned and keep them warm. Add the garlic to the skillet and cook just enough to change color and sprinkle it over the top of the artichokes.
- Just before serving the stew, sprinkle the artichokes over the top.

Nutrition Information

- 786: calories;
- 35 grams: fat;
- 11 grams: saturated fat;
- 0 grams: trans fat;
- 15 grams: dietary fiber;
- 6 grams: sugars;
- 5 grams: polyunsaturated fat;
- 46 grams: carbohydrates;
- 69 grams: protein;
- 1497 milligrams: sodium;

337. Veal" With Capers

Serving: 3 servings | Prep: | Cook: | Ready in: 15mins

Ingredients

- 1 large onion, coarsely chopped
- 1 teaspoon Hungarian sweet paprika

- 2 tablespoons oil
- 1 pound boneless fresh turkey breast, cut in medium-thick slices
- 1 large fresh tomato, cubed
- 1 ½ teaspoons fresh rosemary minced or 1/2 teaspoon dried
- ¼ cup dry white wine or vermouth
- 1 tablespoon capers
- 2 tablespoons tomato paste
- Salt and freshly ground black pepper to taste
- ½ cup plain yogurt

Direction

- Saute onion and paprika in hot oil until onion is translucent.
- Add turkey slices and cook quickly until they lose their pink color.
- Add tomato, rosemary, wine and capers. Cook over high heat until liquid is reduced and barely covers bottom of pan.
- Stir in tomato paste.
- If you are going to finish cooking this dish later, it can be refrigerated or frozen at this point.
- To serve, defrost if frozen; heat slowly; stir in yogurt; season with salt and pepper and heat thoroughly but do not boil or yogurt will separate.

Nutrition Information

- 404: calories;
- 12 grams: carbohydrates;
- 3 grams: dietary fiber;
- 7 grams: sugars;
- 10 grams: monounsaturated fat;
- 36 grams: protein;
- 784 milligrams: sodium;
- 22 grams: fat;
- 5 grams: polyunsaturated fat;
- 0 grams: trans fat;

338. Vegan Chocolate Chip Banana Cake

Serving: 1 bundt or 5- by 10-inch loaf | Prep: | Cook: | Ready in: 1hours15mins

Ingredients

- 2 cups all-purpose flour (or gluten-free all-purpose flour plus 1 teaspoon xanthan gum)
- 1 cup sugar
- 1 teaspoon baking powder
- ½ teaspoon baking soda
- 1 teaspoon salt
- ½ teaspoon ground cinnamon
- ½ teaspoon ground nutmeg
- ½ teaspoon ground cloves
- ½ teaspoon ground ginger
- 1 cup mashed bananas (approximately 2 very ripe bananas, mashed on a plate using the back of a fork)
- 1 cup canned coconut milk, mixed well before measuring
- ½ cup canola oil
- 2 teaspoons white or apple cider vinegar
- 1 tablespoon pure vanilla extract
- 1 ½ cups semisweet chocolate chips (dairy free)
- Powdered sugar for garnish

Direction

- Heat oven to 350 degrees. Lightly grease a Bundt pan or a 5- by 10-inch loaf pan.
- In a large bowl, whisk together flour, sugar, baking powder, baking soda, salt, cinnamon, nutmeg, cloves and ginger. In a separate bowl, whisk together bananas, coconut milk, oil, vinegar and vanilla. Pour the wet mixture into the dry mixture and whisk until just combined. Fold in the chocolate chips; do not over-mix.
- Spread the batter evenly into the prepared pan. Bake for about 40 to 45 minutes in a Bundt pan or 50 to 60 minutes in a loaf pan until a toothpick inserted in the center of the cake comes out with a few crumbs clinging to

it. Check the cake often and if it gets too brown on top, cover with foil and continue to bake. Rotate the pan halfway through baking time. Let cool, then sift powdered sugar over top.

339. Vegetable Cakes

Serving: 6 servings | Prep: | Cook: | Ready in: 20mins

Ingredients

- 1 cup diced celery
- 1 cup diced carrots
- 1 cup diced onion
- 1 medium-size tomato, seeded and diced
- 1 cup fresh peas
- 3 tablespoons chopped fresh basil
- 1 teaspoon ground cumin
- ½ teaspoon turmeric
- ⅛ teaspoon red pepper flakes
- 1 pound baking potatoes, baked until tender and peeled
- 3 large egg whites
- 3 tablespoons nonfat milk
- 1 cup dried bread crumbs
- Spray of olive oil
- Red pepper coulis (see recipe)

Direction

- In a large nonstick skillet, slowly saute celery, carrots, onion and tomato until they are tender. Partly cover the pan and, if the tomatoes are not sufficiently juicy, add a dash of water to keep from burning. Transfer to a large mixing bowl and add the peas, basil, cumin, turmeric and red pepper flakes. Stir and set aside to cool.
- In another bowl, mash the potatoes.
- In small bowl, whisk together egg whites and milk. Stir into mashed potatoes until smooth. Add remaining vegetable mixture and combine well. Form into 12 two-ounce patties. Put bread crumbs in shallow pan and lightly coat both sides of patties.
- Spray a large skillet with olive oil spray and saute the patties over medium heat until brown, about 5 minutes each side. Serve with red pepper coulis.

Nutrition Information

- 196: calories;
- 1 gram: polyunsaturated fat;
- 37 grams: carbohydrates;
- 6 grams: sugars;
- 8 grams: protein;
- 198 milligrams: sodium;
- 2 grams: fat;
- 0 grams: trans fat;
- 5 grams: dietary fiber;

340. Vegetable And Ricotta Tortino

Serving: 8 servings | Prep: | Cook: | Ready in: 1hours45mins

Ingredients

- 2 cups shelled fresh peas
- 2 cups asparagus, halved and cut into 1-inch lengths
- 4 tablespoons extra-virgin olive oil
- 8 cups sliced spring onions, including white and green portions
- 6 celery ribs, diced
- 4 cups washed and stemmed watercress
- 14 cups stemmed, rinsed and coarsely chopped white Swiss chard
- Kosher salt and freshly ground black pepper to taste
- 4 large eggs
- 1 cup cream
- ½ cup finely grated Parmigiano-Reggiano
- ¾ cup ricotta, preferably sheep's milk ricotta
- 1 teaspoon Aleppo pepper (see note)

- ½ teaspoon kosher salt
- ⅛ teaspoon freshly ground black pepper
- ½ cup fresh mint leaves

Direction

- Bring a pot of salted water to a boil and add the peas and asparagus. Cook until the vegetables are just tender. Drain and immediately plunge the vegetables into a large bowl of cold water to stop the cooking. Drain and set aside.
- In a large kettle, heat 3 tablespoons of the olive oil over medium heat and add the onions, celery and watercress. Begin adding the Swiss chard, stirring until the leaves fit into the pot. Cook, stirring frequently, until the vegetables are very tender. Season with salt and pepper and drain if necessary. Set aside to cool.
- In a large bowl, combine the eggs, remaining tablespoon of olive oil, cream, 1/4 cup of the Parmigiano, ricotta, Aleppo pepper and 1/2 teaspoon kosher salt. Stir until smooth. Add the peas, asparagus and cooled vegetables and stir to combine.
- Preheat the oven to 350 degrees. Pour the tortino mixture into a large, lightly greased casserole dish, sprinkle with the black pepper and cover with foil. (Make sure it does not touch the vegetables.) Place the dish in a large roasting pan and pour in boiling water to rise halfway up the sides.
- Bake for 40 minutes. Remove the foil and continue to bake until the center of the tortino is set, an additional 10 to 15 minutes. Remove the casserole from the roasting pan and sprinkle the remaining Parmigiano on the top. Place the casserole under a broiler until the cheese is nicely browned, 2 to 3 minutes. Allow to cool slightly, cut into squares and garnish with mint and serve.

Nutrition Information

- 359: calories;
- 26 grams: fat;
- 12 grams: saturated fat;
- 0 grams: trans fat;
- 2 grams: polyunsaturated fat;
- 21 grams: carbohydrates;
- 7 grams: sugars;
- 10 grams: monounsaturated fat;
- 8 grams: dietary fiber;
- 16 grams: protein;
- 881 milligrams: sodium;

341. Vegetarian Apple Parsnip Soup

Serving: 6 to 8 servings | Prep: | Cook: | Ready in: 2hours

Ingredients

- Homemade Vegetarian broth
- 2 tablespoons olive oil
- 1 onion, peeled and diced
- 4 carrots, peeled and diced
- ½ celery stalk, diced
- 2 leeks, cleaned and diced
- 2 bay leaves
- 2 branches thyme
- 3 tomatoes, diced, or 6 ounces canned San Marzano plum tomatoes
- A few sprigs of parsley
- A few sprigs of chervil
- Salt to taste
- Freshly ground pepper to taste
- Soup
- 1 pound parsnips, peeled and diced
- Juice of 1 lemon
- 2 tablespoons olive oil
- 2 tablespoons butter or pareve margarine
- 6 shallots, diced
- 4 tart apples, peeled and diced
- 1 cup cider
- 8 cups vegetable broth (see above)
- Salt to taste
- White pepper to taste
- A few gratings of nutmeg
- 1 teaspoon cider vinegar (optional)

Direction

- To make the broth: heat the olive oil very slowly in a large pot. Add the onion, carrots, celery and leeks and sauté until the onions are transparent.
- Add 10 cups of water along with the bay leaves, thyme and tomatoes. Bring to a boil and simmer over low heat, half covered, for 45 minutes. During the last few minutes of cooking, add the parsley and chervil, and season with salt and freshly ground pepper to taste. Put everything through a sieve and set the broth aside.
- For the soup: put the parsnips and the lemon juice in a large bowl. Cover with water and let sit until you are ready to make the soup. Drain and dry the parsnips.
- Heat the olive oil and the butter in a heavy soup pot. Add the shallots, parsnips and apples and sauté for about 10 minutes, or until the onions are clear but not golden. Add the cider and cook uncovered for 5 minutes. Then add the broth, bring to a boil, cover, and simmer slowly for 40 minutes. Add salt, white pepper and nutmeg.
- Purée the soup in a blender or food processor, and, if you want more acidity, add the cider vinegar. Serve immediately.

342. Warm Chickpeas And Greens With Vinaigrette

Serving: Serves four | Prep: | Cook: | Ready in: 1hours30mins

Ingredients

- 1 pound spinach or Swiss chard (1 bunch), stemmed and thoroughly cleaned
- ½ pound (1 1/8 cups) chickpeas, soaked for at least six hours in 2 quarts water
- A bouquet garni made with a bay leaf, a couple of sprigs each of parsley and thyme, and a Parmesan rind
- Salt
- freshly ground pepper
- 2 tablespoons fresh lemon juice
- 1 tablespoon red wine vinegar or sherry vinegar
- 1 garlic clove, minced or pureed
- ⅓ cup extra virgin olive oil
- ¼ cup finely chopped flat-leaf parsley
- 1 small red onion, chopped, soaked in cold water for five minutes and drained (optional)

Direction

- Bring a large pot of water to a boil while you stem and wash the spinach or chard. Fill a bowl with ice water. When the water in the pot comes to a boil, add the greens. Cook spinach no longer than one minute. Cook chard one to two minutes. Remove from the pot with a skimmer, and transfer to the ice water. Do not drain the water. Cool the greens for a couple of minutes in the ice water, and then drain and squeeze out excess water. Chop coarsely and set aside. Allow the pot of water to cool for about 15 minutes.
- Drain the soaked chickpeas, and add to the pot along with the bouquet garni. Bring to a boil, reduce the heat to low, cover and simmer for one hour. Add salt to taste, and continue to simmer until the beans are tender, 30 minutes to an hour.
- Drain the chickpeas through a strainer or colander set over a bowl. Return the broth to the pot if you wish to serve it as a light soup. Whisk together the lemon juice, vinegar, minced garlic, salt and pepper to taste, and the olive oil. Combine the cooked chickpeas, greens, parsley and red onion in a bowl, and toss with the dressing. Serve warm.

Nutrition Information

- 401: calories;
- 3 grams: saturated fat;
- 14 grams: protein;
- 4 grams: polyunsaturated fat;
- 8 grams: sugars;

- 474 milligrams: sodium;
- 22 grams: fat;
- 41 grams: carbohydrates;
- 9 grams: dietary fiber;

343. Warm Millet, Carrot And Kale Salad With Curry Scented Dressing

Serving: Serves 4 to 5 | Prep: | Cook: | Ready in: 2hours

Ingredients

- 1 bunch of black kale (cavolo nero), 10 to 12 ounces, stemmed and washed thoroughly
- Salt to taste
- 2 teaspoons canola oil, rice bran oil or extra virgin olive oil
- ⅔ cup millet
- 2 cups water or blanching water from the kale
- 2 teaspoons extra virgin olive oil
- ½ pound carrots, peeled and thinly sliced on the diagonal
- ½ cup chopped cilantro
- 1 tablespoon nigella seeds
- For the Dressing
- 2 tablespoons fresh lemon juice
- 2 teaspoons seasoned rice vinegar
- 1 teaspoon sweet curry powder
- Salt and freshly ground pepper
- 4 tablespoons grape seed oil, rice bran oil, canola oil or extra virgin olive oil
- ¼ cup buttermilk

Direction

- Separate the kale into two unequal bunches, with about two thirds in one bunch. Wash and dry the smaller bunch, roll the leaves in paper towels and set aside. Blanch the rest in a pot of boiling salted water for 1 to 2 minutes. Remove from the pot with a slotted spoon or skimmer, transfer to a bowl of cold water, drain and squeeze out excess water. Cut the squeezed bunch of kale crosswise into thin slices and set aside. Measure out 2 cups of the blanching water.
- Heat 2 teaspoons of oil over medium-high heat in a heavy 2- or 3-quart saucepan. Add the millet and toast, stirring, until it begins to smell fragrant and toasty, 3 to 5 minutes. Add the 2 cups of kale water. If not using the kale water add 2 cups water and salt to taste, and bring back to a boil. Reduce the heat to low, cover and simmer 25 to 30 minutes, until the liquid in the saucepan has evaporated and the grains are fluffy. Turn off the heat, place a clean dish towel over the pot and return the lid. Let sit for 10 to 15 minutes, then transfer the cooked millet to a baking sheet or a shallow pan and spread out in an even layer to cool. This helps prevent clumping.
- Meanwhile, make crispy kale with the remaining kale. Heat the oven to 300 degrees. Line 2 baking sheets with parchment. Make sure that your kale leaves are dry. Tear them into medium-size pieces and toss with the olive oil. Gently knead the leaves between your thumbs and fingers to make sure they are coated with oil. Place in an even layer on the baking sheets. Do this in batches if necessary. Place in the oven and roast for 22 to 25 minutes, until the leaves are crisp but not browned. If some of the leaves crisp before others, remove them to a bowl or sheet pan and return the remaining kale to the oven. Watch closely as once the kale browns it will taste bitter. Once the kale is crisp, season to taste with salt. Allow to cool.
- Whisk the dressing ingredients together in a small bowl or measuring cup, then transfer to a wide skillet. Add the millet, blanched kale, carrots, and nigella seeds and heat everything together over medium heat, stirring to combine well, until sizzling. Stir in the cilantro just before serving. Serve with the crispy kale crumbled over the top.

Nutrition Information

- 287: calories;
- 29 grams: carbohydrates;
- 2 grams: saturated fat;
- 0 grams: trans fat;
- 6 grams: protein;
- 4 grams: sugars;
- 572 milligrams: sodium;
- 17 grams: fat;
- 5 grams: monounsaturated fat;
- 9 grams: polyunsaturated fat;

344. Warm Vanilla Cakes

Serving: 12 cakes | Prep: | Cook: | Ready in: 1hours

Ingredients

- 7 tablespoons butter; more for molds
- 10 ounces top-quality white chocolate
- 5 eggs at room temperature, separated
- 3 vanilla beans, split in half lengthwise and seeds scraped
- ¼ cup plus 2 tablespoons bread flour, sifted
- Pinch cream of tartar
- ¼ cup plus 2 tablespoons sugar
- Vanilla ice cream

Direction

- Melt butter and 7 ounces white chocolate in a double boiler over water that is hot but not boiling. When mixture is melted, remove from heat and stir until smooth. Whisk in egg yolks and half the vanilla-bean seeds. Sift flour over mixture. Whisk until smooth.
- In an electric mixer fitted with a whisk, combine egg whites and cream of tartar. Whisk until fluffy. Slowly add sugar a little at a time, until meringue is shiny and tight. Fold a little of the chocolate mixture into meringue; then fold meringue into remaining chocolate mixture, until mixture is smooth. Cover with plastic wrap, and refrigerate about 8 hours.
- Heat oven to 375 degrees. Line a baking sheet with parchment paper. Butter 12 metal rings 2 1/2 inches in diameter and 1 1/4 inches high. Place them on parchment paper. Using a spatula, spoon cool batter into a pastry bag with a tip opening of about 1/2 inch. Fill molds 1/3 full. Break remaining chocolate into pieces about 1 inch square and 1/8 inch thick. Drop a piece in each mold. Sprinkle a little cluster of vanilla seeds from remaining beans. Cover chocolate with more batter so molds are barely 2/3 full.
- Bake 12 to 14 minutes, until risen and still a bit jiggly in center. Remove from oven. Have 12 plates ready. Slip tip of a knife under cake, and lift it a little; then slide a spatula underneath, and transfer to a serving plate. Holding mold in place with tongs, run a sharp knife around top edge of mold; then lift mold off cake with tongs. Repeat with other cakes. Serve immediately with ice cream.

345. Watercress And Red Onion Salad

Serving: 4 servings | Prep: | Cook: | Ready in: 10mins

Ingredients

- 2 bunches watercress
- 2 tablespoons red-wine vinegar
- Salt and freshly ground pepper to taste
- 4 tablespoons olive oil
- ½ cup sliced red onion rings
- ¼ cup finely chopped parsley

Direction

- Cut off and discard the tough stems of the watercress. Rinse and spin dry.
- Place the vinegar in a salad bowl and add salt and pepper. Beat with a wire whisk while adding the oil. Add the watercress, onion rings and parsley and toss well to blend. Serve.

Nutrition Information

- 134: calories;
- 14 grams: fat;
- 2 grams: carbohydrates;
- 10 grams: monounsaturated fat;
- 1 gram: protein;
- 208 milligrams: sodium;

346. Watermelon Granite

Serving: Four to six servings | Prep: | Cook: | Ready in: 2hours

Ingredients

- 3 cups watermelon puree
- ⅓ cup superfine sugar
- ¼ cup fresh lemon juice
- 4 sprigs fresh mint

Direction

- Combine the watermelon puree, sugar and lemon juice in a large shallow pan. Put it in the freezer and stir every 20 minutes until no liquid remains, about 1 1/2 to 2 hours. Serve with sprigs of fresh mint.

Nutrition Information

- 67: calories;
- 16 grams: sugars;
- 1 gram: protein;
- 1 milligram: sodium;
- 0 grams: dietary fiber;
- 17 grams: carbohydrates;

347. Wehani Rice Pudding

Serving: Eight servings | Prep: | Cook: | Ready in: 4hours30mins

Ingredients

- 1 cup Wehani rice
- 2 cups water
- ½ cup currants
- ⅓ cup finely chopped dried apricots
- ¼ cup dark rum
- Unsalted butter to grease a 5-cup ring mold
- 1 cup milk
- 1 cup heavy cream
- ¼ cup sugar
- 3 egg yolks
- ¾ teaspoon salt
- 1 teaspoon orange extract
- ¼ teaspoon ground coriander
- Zest of 2 navel oranges, cut into thin strips, for garnish
- 2 navel oranges, peeled, thinly sliced and cut in half, for garnish

Direction

- Combine the rice and water in a small saucepan and bring to a boil. Reduce the heat, cover and simmer for 30 minutes, or until all the water has evaporated. Uncover and set aside.
- Meanwhile, combine the currants and apricots with the rum in a small bowl.
- Preheat the oven to 350 degrees. Butter a five-cup ring mold. Bring at least three cups of water to a boil.
- Scald the milk and cream in a saucepan. Combine the sugar and egg yolks in a large bowl and beat until light in color. Add the scalded milk and cream to the yolks in a slow steady stream, beating constantly with a wire whisk. Stir in the salt, orange extract and coriander. Add the rice and currant-apricot mixture.
- Ladle the mixture into the buttered mold, distributing the rice evenly. Place the filled mold in a large pan and pour enough boiling water around the mold to come halfway up its sides. Carefully transfer to the lower third of the preheated oven and bake for 60 to 70 minutes, or until a knife inserted into the center of the pudding comes out clean. The

edges will pull away slightly from the mold and the top will be browned.
- Remove from the oven and let the mold stand for about 20 minutes in the water. Run a sharp knife around the outside and inside edges, shaking to be sure the pudding is completely loosened. Wipe off any water. Place a large plate over the mold and carefully invert. Remove the mold, cover lightly with foil and refrigerate for one to two hours, or until cool but not cold.
- To serve, sprinkle the orange zest over the pudding and layer the orange slices evenly around the outside.

348. Wheat Berry And Tomato Salad

Serving: Serves six | Prep: | Cook: |Ready in: 2hours30mins

Ingredients

- 1 cup farro or wheat berries, rinsed, soaked for several hours or overnight in 1 quart water
- Salt
- freshly ground pepper
- 1 ½ to 2 cups diced tomatoes
- 1 tablespoon sherry vinegar
- 1 teaspoon balsamic vinegar
- 1 cup diced celery or cucumber, or a combination
- 3 tablespoons freshly squeezed lemon juice (more to taste)
- 3 tablespoons extra virgin olive oil
- 2 ounces feta, crumbled (about 1/2 cup)
- 1 to 2 tablespoons chopped fresh mint
- 3 tablespoons chopped fresh parsley

Direction

- Place the wheat berries and their soaking water in a large saucepan. Add salt to taste, and bring to a boil. Reduce the heat, cover and simmer one hour or until the grains are tender and beginning to splay. Turn off the heat, and allow the wheat berries to sit in the hot water for another 15 minutes. Drain.
- While the wheat berries are cooking, dice the tomatoes and place in a bowl. Sprinkle with salt, and add the sherry and balsamic vinegars. Toss together, and let sit for one hour.
- After you drain the wheat berries, toss with the tomatoes and juices. Allow to marinate together for one hour. Add the remaining ingredients, and toss together. Refrigerate until ready to serve, or serve at once.

Nutrition Information

- 204: calories;
- 3 grams: sugars;
- 6 grams: protein;
- 1 gram: polyunsaturated fat;
- 25 grams: carbohydrates;
- 5 grams: dietary fiber;
- 345 milligrams: sodium;
- 10 grams: fat;

349. White Bean Burgers

Serving: 6 patties | Prep: | Cook: |Ready in: 2hours30mins

Ingredients

- 2 cans white beans, drained and rinsed
- 2 tablespoons extra virgin olive oil
- 1 small onion, finely chopped
- Salt to taste
- 2 to 3 large garlic cloves (to taste), green shoots removed, minced
- ⅔ cup finely grated carrot
- 3 tablespoons freshly squeezed lemon juice
- ¼ cup finely chopped parsley
- 2 teaspoons minced fresh sage or thyme
- ½ cup fresh bread crumbs
- 1 egg, beaten
- Freshly ground pepper to taste

- Whole grain hamburger buns and the condiments of your choice

Direction

- Heat 1 tablespoon of the olive oil in a medium-size skillet and add the onion. Cook, stirring, until tender, about 5 minutes. Add a pinch of salt, the garlic and the grated carrot, and continue to cook for another minute or two, until fragrant and the carrot has softened slightly. Remove from the heat.
- In a food processor fitted with the steel blade, puree the beans with the lemon juice. Transfer to a bowl and stir in the onion mixture, the parsley, sage or thyme, the bread crumbs and the egg. Season to taste. Shape into patties, ½- to ¾-inch thick. Set on a parchment-covered baking sheet and cover with plastic wrap. Refrigerate for 1 to 2 hours.
- Heat the remaining oil in a large, heavy skillet or on a griddle over medium heat and brown the patties for 4 minutes on each side, being very careful when you turn them over. An offset spatula works well for this. Serve on whole grain buns, with the condiments of your choice.

Nutrition Information

- 219: calories;
- 5 grams: fat;
- 1 gram: polyunsaturated fat;
- 0 grams: trans fat;
- 3 grams: monounsaturated fat;
- 7 grams: dietary fiber;
- 2 grams: sugars;
- 386 milligrams: sodium;
- 34 grams: carbohydrates;
- 11 grams: protein;

350. White Beans With Celery

Serving: Serves four | Prep: | Cook: | Ready in: 2hours20mins

Ingredients

- 1/2 pound (about 1 1/8 cups) white beans, rinsed, picked over and soaked for six hours or overnight in 1 quart water
- Salt to taste
- ¼ cup extra virgin olive oil
- 4 to 5 cups chopped celery, including the leaves
- 4 large garlic cloves, minced
- 1 8-ounce can tomato sauce, or 2 tablespoons tomato paste diluted in 1 cup water
- ¼ to ½ cup finely chopped parsley (to taste)
- Juice of 1 to 2 lemons, to taste

Direction

- Drain the beans, and combine in a large saucepan with enough water to cover by 2 inches. Bring to a boil, reduce the heat to low, add salt to taste, cover and simmer until the beans are just tender, about 45 minutes to an hour. Do not let the beans boil hard or they'll fall apart before they're cooked through.
- Heat 2 tablespoons of the olive oil over medium heat in a large skillet, and add the celery and a generous pinch of salt. Cook, stirring often, until it just begins to soften, about three minutes, and add the garlic. Stir together for a minute, until the garlic is fragrant, and remove from the heat.
- Preheat the oven to 350 degrees. Drain the beans over a bowl. Place in a large baking dish, preferably earthenware, and toss with the celery and garlic, the remaining olive oil and the tomato sauce or diluted tomato paste. Add enough of the drained broth to cover by an inch, and stir in the remaining olive oil. Cover the dish tightly with foil, and place in the oven. Bake one hour, or until the beans are soft and creamy.
- Uncover the beans, stir, and add salt and pepper to taste. Add a tablespoon or 2 of

lemon juice, or more if desired, and adjust salt and pepper. Serve hot, warm or room temperature, with a little more olive oil drizzled over the top if desired.

Nutrition Information

- 377: calories;
- 50 grams: carbohydrates;
- 9 grams: sugars;
- 602 milligrams: sodium;
- 15 grams: fat;
- 2 grams: polyunsaturated fat;
- 13 grams: dietary fiber;
- 17 grams: protein;
- 10 grams: monounsaturated fat;

351. White Chocolate Spice Cupcakes

Serving: 1 dozen cupcakes | Prep: | Cook: | Ready in: 50mins

Ingredients

- Spice Cupcakes
- 1 ½ cups all purpose flour
- 1 teaspoon baking soda
- 1 teaspoon cinnamon
- ½ teaspoon freshly grated nutmeg
- ¼ teaspoon ground cloves
- ⅛ teaspoon ginger
- ¼ teaspoon salt
- ¼ cup unsulfured molasses
- ½ cup milk
- 1 stick of butter
- ⅓ cup granulated sugar
- 2 eggs
- White Chocolate Cream Cheese Frosting
- 4 ounces (1/2 stick) unsalted butter, still firm but not cold
- 8 ounces cold cream cheese
- ⅛ teaspoon salt
- ¾ pound (3/4 box) plus 2 teaspoons powdered sugar, sifted
- ½ teaspoon pure vanilla extract
- 2 ounces white chocolate, melted

Direction

- Preheat oven to 350 degrees Fahrenheit. Line cupcake pan with 12 cupcake liners.
- In a bowl, whisk together flour, baking soda, spices and salt. In another bowl, combine molasses and milk.
- With an electric mixer fitted with flat beater, cream the butter on medium to medium-high speed for 3 to 5 minutes. Gradually add the sugar. and beat until light and fluffy in texture. Beat in the eggs, one at a time.
- Reduce the mixer speed to low, and incorporate the flour mixture alternately with the molasses mixture, beating thoroughly after each addition and ending with dry ingredients.
- Divide batter among the cupcake liners and bake for about 20 minutes, or until top of cupcakes spring back when lightly touched. Cool thoroughly before frosting.
- Prepare the frosting. Using an electric mixer with flat beater, mix together butter, cream cheese and salt on medium speed for 3 to 5 minutes. Reduce speed to low, and gradually add powdered sugar until incorporated. Gradually add vanilla and melted white chocolate until just blended. Do not overwhip the frosting; the consistency should be creamy and dense, like ice cream.

Nutrition Information

- 454: calories;
- 4 grams: protein;
- 15 grams: saturated fat;
- 1 gram: dietary fiber;
- 6 grams: monounsaturated fat;
- 56 grams: carbohydrates;
- 43 grams: sugars;
- 271 milligrams: sodium;
- 25 grams: fat;

352. White Tepary Bean And Potato Purée

Serving: Yield: Serves 6 to 8 | Prep: | Cook: | Ready in: 2hours15mins

Ingredients

- ½ pound / 1 1/8 cups tepary beans or small white beans, soaked in 1 quart water for at least 4 hours or overnight
- 1 onion, cut in half
- 2 large garlic cloves, crushed
- 1 bay leaf
- 2 sprigs thyme
- Salt to taste
- ¾ pound Yukon gold or other fairly starchy potatoes, peeled and cut in large dice
- Optional garnish
- 2 tablespoons extra virgin olive oil
- ½ teaspoon red pepper flakes (more to taste)
- 2 garlic cloves, minced

Direction

- Drain soaked beans and place in a large saucepan or Dutch oven with 1 quart water, the onion and crushed garlic cloves. Bring to a gentle boil, add bay leaf and thyme, cover, reduce heat and simmer 30 minutes. Add salt to taste and simmer another 30 minutes. Add potato and continue to simmer another 30 minutes to an hour, until beans and potatoes are very tender. Using tongs, remove onion, bay leaf and thyme sprigs.
- Set a large strainer over a bowl and drain beans and potato. Transfer to a food processor, add 1/2 cup of bean broth, and process until smooth and creamy. Taste and adjust salt. Add pepper if desired. Transfer to a wide bowl or an oven-proof serving dish. Thin out as desired with more broth. Serve hot or warm.
- For optional garnish, heat olive oil over medium heat in a small frying pan and add garlic and red pepper flakes. When garlic begins to sizzle and smell fragrant, 30 seconds to a minute, remove from heat and drizzle over beans.

Nutrition Information

- 171: calories;
- 1 gram: polyunsaturated fat;
- 28 grams: carbohydrates;
- 2 grams: sugars;
- 216 milligrams: sodium;
- 4 grams: fat;
- 7 grams: protein;
- 3 grams: monounsaturated fat;
- 6 grams: dietary fiber;

353. Whole Rainbow Trout Baked In Foil

Serving: Serves four | Prep: | Cook: | Ready in: 15mins

Ingredients

- Extra virgin olive oil
- 4 small rainbow trout, boned
- Salt
- freshly ground pepper
- 2 lemons, one sliced, one cut in wedges
- 8 fresh tarragon or dill sprigs, or 4 rosemary sprigs
- Chopped fresh tarragon, dill or parsley for serving

Direction

- Preheat the oven to 450 degrees. Cut four sheets of heavy duty aluminum foil or eight sheets of lighter foil into squares that are three inches longer than your fish. If using lighter foil, make four double-thick squares. Oil the dull side of the foil with olive oil, and place a trout, skin side down, on each square. Season both sides with salt and pepper, and open them out flat. Place two tarragon or dill sprigs (or one rosemary sprig) and two lemon slices down the middle of each, and fold the two sides together. Drizzle 1/2 teaspoon olive oil over each fish.

- Making sure that the trout are in the middle of each square, fold up the foil loosely, grabbing at the edges and crimping together tightly to make a packet. Place on a baking sheet, and bake for 10 to 15 minutes, checking one of the packets after 10 minutes. The flesh should be opaque and pull apart easily when tested with a fork.
- Place each packet on a plate. Carefully cut across the top to open it, taking care not to let the steam from inside the packet burn you. Gently remove the fish from the packet, and pour the juices over it. Sprinkle with fresh tarragon, dill or parsley. Serve, passing the lemon wedges.

Nutrition Information

- 549: calories;
- 27 grams: fat;
- 5 grams: carbohydrates;
- 1 gram: sugars;
- 69 grams: protein;
- 895 milligrams: sodium;
- 0 grams: trans fat;
- 11 grams: monounsaturated fat;
- 3 grams: dietary fiber;
- 6 grams: polyunsaturated fat;

354. Whole Wheat Bread, Apple And Cranberry Dressing

Serving: | Prep: | Cook: | Ready in: 1hours30mins

Ingredients

- 8 to 9 ounces whole wheat bread (with crusts), cut into 3/4 to 1-inch cubes (4 to 5 cups)
- 3 tablespoons extra virgin olive oil
- 1 medium or large onion, finely chopped
- 2 stalks celery, diced
- Salt and freshly ground pepper to taste
- 1 large apple, peeled and diced
- ¼ cup chopped flat-leaf parsley
- 2 teaspoons minced fresh thyme
- 1 tablespoon minced fresh sage or 1 teaspoon rubbed dried sage
- ½ cup dried cranberries
- 1 egg
- 1 cup chicken or vegetable stock
- 1 tablespoon unsalted butter

Direction

- Preheat oven to 350 degrees. Oil or butter a 2-quart baking dish. Place cubed bread in a large bowl.
- Heat 2 tablespoons of olive oil over medium heat in a large, heavy skillet. Add onion and celery and cook, stirring, until onion is tender, 5 to 8 minutes. Season with salt and pepper and scrape into bowl with the bread. Add remaining olive oil to bowl and all of the other ingredients except egg and stock. Season generously with salt and pepper and toss well.
- Beat egg in a small bowl and whisk in 1/2 cup of stock. Scrape into bread mixture and mix together well. Turn into prepared baking dish. Douse mixture with remaining stock (hold back about 1/4 cup if you are going to reheat). Dot top with butter.
- Cover baking dish with foil and bake for 45 minutes. Uncover and bake another 15 minutes, until top is nicely browned. Serve hot.

Nutrition Information

- 207: calories;
- 28 grams: carbohydrates;
- 4 grams: dietary fiber;
- 6 grams: protein;
- 9 grams: fat;
- 2 grams: saturated fat;
- 5 grams: monounsaturated fat;

- 0 grams: trans fat;
- 1 gram: polyunsaturated fat;
- 11 grams: sugars;
- 329 milligrams: sodium;

355. Whole Wheat Focaccia With Cherry Tomatoes And Olives

Serving: 1 large focaccia, serving 12 | Prep: | Cook: | Ready in: 3hours50mins

Ingredients

- For the sponge
- 1 teaspoon / 4 grams active dry yeast
- ½ cup / 120 ml lukewarm water
- ¾ cup / 90 grams unbleached all-purpose flour
- For the dough
- 1 teaspoon / 4 grams active dry yeast
- 1 cup / 240 ml lukewarm water
- 3 tablespoons extra-virgin olive oil
- 1 ¼ cups / 155 grams unbleached all-purpose flour
- 2 cups / 250 grams whole wheat flour or durum flour
- 1 ¾ teaspoons / 12 grams fine sea salt
- For the topping
- 2 tablespoons extra-virgin olive oil
- 2 teaspoons chopped fresh thyme
- ½ pound cherry tomatoes, halved (about 1 1/2 cups)
- 16 imported black olives, halved lengthwise
- Coarse sea salt (optional)
- Several fresh basil leaves, cut in slivers or torn

Direction

- Make the sponge. Combine yeast and water in a large bowl or the bowl of a stand mixer and stir to dissolve. Whisk in flour. Cover with plastic wrap and let proof in a warm place until bubbly and doubled in volume, about 45 minutes.
- Make the dough. If using a stand mixer, whisk together yeast and water in a small bowl and let stand until creamy, a few minutes. Add to sponge in the mixer bowl, along with olive oil. Add flours and salt and mix in with the paddle attachment for 1 to 2 minutes, until ingredients are amalgamated. Change to the dough hook and knead on medium speed for 8 to 10 minutes. Dough should come together and slap against the sides of the bowl. It will be slightly tacky. To make the dough by hand, combine yeast and water as directed and whisk into sponge with the olive oil. Whisk in all-purpose flour. Add salt and remaining flour, one cup at a time, folding it in with a spatula or a wooden spoon. When you can scrape out the dough, add flour to the work surface, put the dough on top and knead for 8 to 10 minutes, until soft and velvety. Return to the bowl (coat bowl lightly with olive oil first).
- Cover bowl tightly with plastic wrap and let dough rise in a warm spot until doubled, about 1 1/2 hours.
- Shape the focaccia. Coat a 12-x 17-inch sheet pan (sides and bottom) with olive oil. Line with parchment and flip the parchment over so exposed side is oiled. Turn dough onto the baking sheet. Oil or moisten your hands, and press out dough until it just about covers the bottom of the pan. Dough may be sticky. Cover with a towel and allow it to relax for 10 minutes, then continue to press it out until it reaches the edges of the pan. Cover with a damp towel and let rise in a warm spot for 45 minutes to an hour, or until dough is full of air bubbles.
- Preheat oven to 425 degrees after 30 minutes of rising (30 minutes before you wish to bake), preferably with a baking stone in it. Place thyme and olive oil for the topping in a small saucepan or skillet and heat until thyme begins to sizzle. Count to 30 and remove from heat. Swirl the oil in the pan, then transfer to a measuring cup or ramekin and allow to cool.
- With lightly oiled fingertips or with your knuckles, dimple the dough, pressing down hard so that you leave indentations. Arrange

cherry tomato halves and olives on dough, pressing them into the dimples. Drizzle on olive oil and use your fingers to distribute any thyme that remains in the cup or ramekin over the tomatoes. Sprinkle with a little coarse sea salt if desired.
- Place pan in oven on baking stone. Spray oven 3 times with water during the first 10 minutes of baking and bake 20 to 25 minutes, until edges are crisp and top is golden. If you wish, remove focaccia from the pan and bake directly on the stone during the last 10 minutes. Remove from oven, remove from pan at once and cool on a rack. If you want a softer focaccia, cover with a towel when you remove it from the oven. Sprinkle torn or slivered basil leaves over the surface of the focaccia. Serve warm or at room temperature.

Nutrition Information

- 211: calories;
- 2 grams: dietary fiber;
- 242 milligrams: sodium;
- 7 grams: fat;
- 1 gram: sugars;
- 5 grams: protein;
- 33 grams: carbohydrates;

356. Whole Wheat Penne Or Fusilli With Tomatoes, Shell Beans And Feta

Serving: Serves 4 | Prep: | Cook: | Ready in: 2hours

Ingredients

- 1 ¼ pounds ripe tomatoes, peeled and chopped (see note)
- Freshly ground pepper to taste
- 2 to 3 tablespoons olive oil (to taste)
- 2 tablespoons slivered fresh mint or basil
- 1 pound shell beans (in the pod), like scarlet runners, borlotti, cannellini or other heirlooms available at your farmers' market (about 1 3/4 cups)
- 1 small onion, halved
- 7 cups water
- 3 large garlic cloves, 2 crushed, 1 minced
- A bouquet garni made with a few sprigs each parsley and thyme, a Parmesan rind, and a bay leaf
- Salt to taste
- 1 pound whole wheat penne, rigatoni or fusilli
- 2 ounces feta, crumbled (1/2 cup)

Direction

- In a large pasta bowl, toss together the tomatoes, minced garlic, salt, pepper, olive oil, and mint or basil. Allow to sit at room temperature for 30 minutes to an hour. Taste and adjust seasonings.
- Meanwhile shell the beans and combine with the onion, water, the crushed garlic cloves, bouquet garni and salt to taste in a heavy saucepan or soup pot. Bring to a boil, reduce the heat, cover and simmer 45 minutes, or until the beans are tender. Taste and adjust salt. Remove and discard the onion, the bouquet garni and the garlic cloves. Drain though a colander set over a bowl. Stir the beans into the tomato mixture.
- Bring a large pot of water to a boil, salt generously and add the pasta. Cook al dente, drain and toss with the tomatoes and beans. If desired add about 1/4 cup of the bean broth. Add the feta cheese, toss again and serve at once.

Nutrition Information

- 646: calories;
- 15 grams: fat;
- 7 grams: monounsaturated fat;
- 28 grams: protein;
- 1947 milligrams: sodium;
- 5 grams: sugars;
- 2 grams: polyunsaturated fat;
- 109 grams: carbohydrates;
- 8 grams: dietary fiber;

357. Whole Wheat Sesame Rings (Simit)

Serving: 8 to 10 rings | Prep: | Cook: | Ready in: 5hours

Ingredients

- 85 grams / about 1/2 cup semolina flour
- 95 grams / about 3/4 cup unbleached all purpose flour
- 330 grams / about 2 2/3 cups whole wheat flour
- 1 ¼ teaspoons salt
- 1 teaspoon ground mahlab (optional)
- ¾ teaspoon instant yeast
- 1 ½ cups / 355 ml lukewarm water
- 1 tablespoon agave syrup, malt syrup, or honey
- 1 egg, beaten or 2 tablespoons grape or pomegranate molasses dissolved in 1/4 cup water
- 1 cup / 100 grams toasted sesame seeds
- Optional: 1 egg white, beaten

Direction

- Combine flours, salt and optional mahlab in a large bowl or the bowl of a stand mixer fitted with the paddle and stir together or mix at low speed until combined. Dissolve yeast in water. Add agave syrup or honey and stir together.
- At low speed, add water and yeast mixture to flour and mix for 1 minute. Remove paddle and let sit for 5 minutes. Change to dough hook and mix dough (or knead by hand) for about 5 minutes. Dough will be stiff and slightly sticky. Let sit for 5 minutes.
- Lightly oil work surface and shape dough into a ball. Clean, dry and lightly oil mixing bowl and place dough in it, rounded side down first, then rounded side up. Cover bowl with plastic (plastic should not be touching dough) and let rise at room temperature for about 3 hours, until doubled.
- Line 2 baking sheets with parchment and lightly oil parchment. In a wide bowl, combine pomegranate or grape molasses and 1/4 cup water and stir together, or beat egg with 2 tablespoons water.
- Turn dough onto a lightly oiled work surface and shape into a ball. Divide into 8 to 10 equal pieces and shape each piece into a ball. Cover loosely with plastic and let sit for 20 minutes. Roll out each piece into a rope, approximately 12 to 14 inches long. Holding one end of the rope, twist it a few times, then join ends together, overlapping by about an inch and pinching together so they stay connected. The hole should be about 2 to 2 1/2 inches. Dip into molasses solution or egg, coating both sides well, then dip into sesame seeds, flip over and coat other side. Place on baking sheets, allowing at least 1 inch of space between rings. Cover loosely with plastic and let rest for 20 to 30 minutes. Meanwhile heat oven to 400 degrees with the rack arranged in the middle. Place a pan on the bottom of the oven.
- Carefully pour 1 cup of water into the tin on the floor of the oven. Bake each sheet on the middle rack of the oven for 30 to 35 minutes (you can refrigerate the second baking sheet while the first one is baking to prevent the rings from rising too much), flipping the rings over so they don't brown too much on one side after 15 to 20 minutes, and if desired, brushing with egg white halfway through. Another way to prevent too much browning on the bottom is to slide another baking sheet under baking sheet (if you have enough of them to spare). Remove pan of water after 10 minutes. Rings should be dark brown and respond to tapping on the bottom with a hollow sound. Remove from heat and cool before eating.

Nutrition Information

- 246: calories;
- 5 grams: dietary fiber;

- 8 grams: protein;
- 3 grams: sugars;
- 42 grams: carbohydrates;
- 233 milligrams: sodium;
- 6 grams: fat;
- 1 gram: saturated fat;
- 2 grams: monounsaturated fat;

358. Whole Wheat Buttermilk Scones With Raisins And Oatmeal

Serving: 12 small scones | Prep: | Cook: | Ready in: 30mins

Ingredients

- 150 grams (approximately 1 1/4 cups) whole-wheat flour
- 62 grams (approximately 1/2 scant cup) unbleached all-purpose flour
- 40 grams (approximately 1/3 cup) oatmeal
- 10 grams (2 teaspoons) baking powder
- 5 grams (1/2 teaspoon) baking soda
- 25 grams (approximately 2 tablespoons) raw brown sugar (turbinado)
- 3 grams (approximately scant 1/2 teaspoon) salt
- 70 grams (2 1/2 ounces / 5 tablespoons) unsalted butter
- 125 grams (approximately 1/2 cup) buttermilk
- 75 grams (approximately 1/2 cup) raisins

Direction

- Preheat oven to 400 degrees. Line a baking sheet with parchment.
- Sift together flours, baking powder, baking soda, sugar and salt. Stir in oatmeal. Rub in butter, or place in a stand mixer fitted with the paddle and beat at low speed, or pulse in a food processor, until incorporated. Add buttermilk and raisins and mix just until dough comes together.
- Transfer to a lightly floured work surface and gently shape into a 1/2-inch thick rectangle. Cut either into 2-inch circles with a biscuit cutter or into 6 squares, then cut each square in half on the diagonal. Transfer to baking sheet. Bake 15 minutes, until browned on the bottom. Flip over, bake 2 more minutes, and remove from the heat. Serve warm or allow to cool.

Nutrition Information

- 147: calories;
- 23 grams: carbohydrates;
- 7 grams: sugars;
- 216 milligrams: sodium;
- 5 grams: fat;
- 3 grams: protein;
- 1 gram: monounsaturated fat;
- 0 grams: polyunsaturated fat;
- 2 grams: dietary fiber;

359. Wilted Salad Soup

Serving: Two servings | Prep: | Cook: | Ready in: 25mins

Ingredients

- 1 baking potato, about 9 ounces
- 2 tablespoons cornstarch
- 1 ½ cups skim milk
- 1 ⅔ cups wilted salad greens (about 4 cups romaine lettuce leaves and 1/3 cup vinaigrette)
- 1 ½ cups chicken broth
- 1 ½ cups heavy cream
- Coarse salt to taste
- Freshly ground pepper to taste

Direction

- Prick the potato twice with a fork and place in the center of the carousel of a 650- to 700-watt oven. (If your oven does not have a carousel,

give the potato a quarter-turn every two minutes.) Cook at 100 percent power for eight minutes. Remove from the oven and cool. Cut the potato in half lengthwise, scoop out the flesh and set aside. Discard the potato skins.
- Combine the cornstarch and milk in a two-and-one-half-quart souffle dish or casserole. Set aside.
- Place the wilted salad in a blender and puree until smooth. Add the reserved potato and the chicken broth and process to combine. Add to the milk mixture. Cover tightly with microwave-safe plastic wrap. Cook at 100 percent power for eight minutes. Prick the plastic to release the steam.
- Remove from the oven and uncover. Stir in the cream, salt and pepper and serve.

Nutrition Information

- 861: calories;
- 20 grams: monounsaturated fat;
- 3 grams: polyunsaturated fat;
- 2 grams: dietary fiber;
- 18 grams: sugars;
- 42 grams: saturated fat;
- 69 grams: fat;
- 47 grams: carbohydrates;
- 17 grams: protein;
- 1654 milligrams: sodium;

360. Winter Squash, Leek And Farro Gratin With Feta And Mint

Serving: Serves 6 | Prep: | Cook: | Ready in: 1hours20mins

Ingredients

- 2 pounds winter squash, peeled and cut in small dice (about 1/2 inch)
- Salt and freshly ground pepper
- 4 tablespoons extra virgin olive oil
- 1 pound leeks (2 large), white and light green parts only, cleaned and chopped
- 2 garlic cloves, minced
- 3 to 4 tablespoons chopped fresh mint, or 1 to 2 tablespoons dried mint (to taste)
- 3 eggs
- 3 ounces feta, crumbled
- ¾ cup cooked faro

Direction

- Heat oven to 425 degrees. Oil a 2-quart baking dish or gratin. Line a sheet pan with parchment. Place squash on baking sheet, season with salt and pepper, and add 2 tablespoons olive oil. Toss squash until evenly coated with oil. Place in oven and roast until tender and lightly colored, about 25 to 30 minutes, stirring every 10 minutes. Remove from oven and set aside. Turn heat down to 375 degrees.
- Heat another tablespoon of olive oil over medium heat in a large, heavy skillet and add leeks. Cook, stirring, until they begin to soften, about 2 minutes. Add a generous pinch of salt and continue to cook, stirring often, until tender, another 3 to 4 minutes. Stir in garlic and cook, stirring, until fragrant, 30 seconds to a minute. Add squash and mint to pan and toss together. Remove from heat.
- In a large bowl beat eggs. Add salt to taste (remembering that feta is very salty) and feta, and beat together until feta has broken up into eggs. Stir in squash and leek mixture and farro. Scrape into oiled baking dish. Drizzle remaining oil over top.
- Bake 35 minutes, or until lightly browned. Remove from heat. Serve hot, warm or room temperature.

Nutrition Information

- 325: calories;
- 2 grams: polyunsaturated fat;
- 41 grams: carbohydrates;
- 6 grams: dietary fiber;
- 15 grams: fat;

- 4 grams: saturated fat;
- 0 grams: trans fat;
- 8 grams: sugars;
- 11 grams: protein;
- 688 milligrams: sodium;

361. Winter Tomato Quiche

Serving: Serves 6 to 8 | Prep: | Cook: | Ready in: 1hours40mins

Ingredients

- 1 9- or 10-inch whole wheat Mediterranean pie crust, (or gluten-free version)
- 1 tablespoon extra virgin olive oil
- ½ medium onion, finely chopped
- 2 to 3 garlic cloves (to taste), minced
- 1-14 1/2-ounce can chopped tomatoes in juice (no salt added), with juice
- 1 tablespoon tomato paste
- Pinch of sugar
- Salt to taste
- 1 sprig fresh basil or rosemary
- 1 teaspoon fresh thyme leaves or 1/2 teaspoon dried thyme
- Freshly ground pepper
- 2 eggs
- 2 egg yolks
- ¾ cup low-fat (2 percent) milk
- 2 ounces Gruyère cheese, grated (1/2 cup, tightly packed)
- 1 ounce Parmesan cheese, grated (1/4 cup, tightly packed)

Direction

- Roll out the crust and line a 9- or 10-inch tart pan. Refrigerate uncovered (place in freezer if using the yeasted crust) while you make the filling.
- Heat the olive oil over medium heat in a wide, heavy saucepan and add the onion. Cook, stirring, until it begins to soften, 2 to 3 minutes. Add a pinch of salt and continue to cook, stirring often, until tender, about 5 minutes. Meanwhile pulse the tomatoes in a food processor fitted with the steel blade or in a mini-processor.
- Add the garlic to the onions and cook, stirring, until fragrant, about 30 seconds. Add to the canned tomatoes and turn up the heat slightly. Add the tomato paste, sugar, salt, basil or rosemary spring and thyme and simmer briskly, stirring often, until the tomatoes have cooked down and smell fragrant, about 15 minutes. Taste and adjust salt, and add pepper. Remove from the heat. Remove the basil or rosemary sprig and, if you used rosemary, remove any rosemary needles that may have detached from the sprig. Allow to cool slightly. You should have about 1 cup of the sauce.
- Preheat the oven to 350 degrees. Beat the eggs and egg yolks in a large bowl. Brush the bottom of the crust with a small amount of the beaten egg and pre-bake for 10 minutes. Remove from the oven and allow to cool for 5 minutes.
- Beat the milk into the eggs. Add 1/2 teaspoon salt, freshly ground pepper to taste and beat together. Stir in the cheeses and the tomato sauce and combine well. Scrape into the crust, using a rubber spatula to scrape out every last bit from the bowl. Place the tart on a sheet pan for easier handling and place in the oven. Bake for 30 to 35 minutes, until set. Remove from the heat and allow to sit for at least 15 minutes before cutting.

Nutrition Information

- 235: calories;
- 2 grams: polyunsaturated fat;
- 19 grams: carbohydrates;
- 3 grams: sugars;
- 7 grams: protein;
- 292 milligrams: sodium;
- 15 grams: fat;
- 6 grams: monounsaturated fat;
- 0 grams: trans fat;

- 1 gram: dietary fiber;

362. Zucchini And Cheddar Cheese Soup

Serving: Six servings | Prep: | Cook: | Ready in: 40mins

Ingredients

- 2 ½ cups chicken broth
- ¼ cup chopped onion
- ⅓ cup chopped celery
- 5 cups unpeeled, sliced zucchini (about 1 1/2 pounds)
- ½ teaspoon salt
- ⅛ teaspoon pepper
- 2 tablespoons butter or margarine
- 2 tablespoons flour
- ½ cup light cream or milk
- 1 cup lightly packed, grated, medium-sharp cheddar cheese

Direction

- Place 2 cups of the broth, the onion, celery, zucchini, salt and pepper in a 3- or 4-quart saucepan. Cover and bring to a boil. Lower heat and simmer, covered, for 25 minutes.
- Puree in small batches in a blender or food processor and set aside in the saucepan.
- In a 2-quart saucepan, melt the butter. Add the flour. Cook, stirring, for 1 minute over medium heat. Remove from heat. Add the cream and the remaining 1/2 cup of broth. Return to heat and cook, stirring, until the mixture thickens and comes to a boil, about 4 to 5 minutes. Remove from heat. Add the cheese and stir to melt. Add to the pureed vegetables. Correct seasonings. Heat gently before serving.

Nutrition Information

- 237: calories;
- 10 grams: saturated fat;
- 11 grams: carbohydrates;
- 0 grams: trans fat;
- 5 grams: sugars;
- 1 gram: dietary fiber;
- 9 grams: protein;
- 479 milligrams: sodium;
- 18 grams: fat;

363. Zucchini Cake

Serving: 20 servings | Prep: | Cook: | Ready in: 1hours10mins

Ingredients

- 3 cups cake flour
- 2 teaspoons baking powder
- 1 teaspoon baking soda
- 2 teaspoons ground cinnamon
- 1 teaspoon ground nutmeg
- ½ teaspoon ground cloves
- ½ teaspoon salt
- 1 cup applesauce
- 1 cup dark brown sugar
- 1 cup granulated sugar
- 3 egg whites
- Grated rind of one orange
- 2 cups shredded zucchini
- ½ cup cut-up dates

Direction

- Preheat oven to 350 degrees.
- Spray a bundt-style pan or 10-inch spring-form pan with center hole with nonstick cooking spray.
- Combine flour, baking powder, baking soda, cinnamon, nutmeg, cloves and salt.
- Beat together applesauce, sugars, egg whites and orange rind.
- Blend in flour mixture with mixer at medium speed, beating only until smooth; do not overbeat.
- Stir in zucchini and dates.

- Pour batter into prepared pan and bake 45 to 50 minutes or until knife inserted near center comes out clean. Remove cake from pan, or if using spring-form, remove sides of pan and put cake on wire rack to cool completely.

Nutrition Information

- 167: calories;
- 22 grams: sugars;
- 2 grams: protein;
- 168 milligrams: sodium;
- 0 grams: polyunsaturated fat;
- 40 grams: carbohydrates;
- 1 gram: dietary fiber;

364. Zucchini Salad

Serving: 6 servings | Prep: | Cook: | Ready in: 12mins

Ingredients

- 2 medium zucchini (about 1 1/2 pounds total)
- ½ teaspoon salt
- ½ teaspoon ground black pepper
- 2 tablespoons white wine vinegar
- 4 tablespoons corn or safflower oil

Direction

- Preheat oven to 400 degrees.
- Wash the zucchini, trim and discard the ends, and cut crosswise into 1/4-inch thick rounds. Arrange the rounds in one layer on a large cookie sheet and sprinkle them with the salt. Place in oven for 5 to 7 minutes, until they soften slightly.
- Transfer the rounds to a bowl and toss them lightly with the pepper, vinegar and oil. Serve immediately.

Nutrition Information

- 93: calories;
- 9 grams: fat;
- 1 gram: protein;
- 7 grams: polyunsaturated fat;
- 2 grams: sugars;
- 185 milligrams: sodium;

365. Zucchini And Apricot Muffins

Serving: 14 muffins | Prep: | Cook: | Ready in: 1hours

Ingredients

- 250 grams (about 2 cups) whole-wheat pastry flour
- 2 teaspoons baking powder
- 1 teaspoon baking soda
- 2 teaspoons ground cinnamon
- 1 teaspoon freshly grated nutmeg
- ¼ teaspoon salt
- 75 grams (1/3 cup) canola or sunflower oil
- 180 grams (3 extra-large) eggs
- 75 grams (1/3 cup) raw brown sugar or muscovado sugar
- 50 grams (1/4 cup) milk
- 2 teaspoons vanilla
- 250 grams (1/2 pound) zucchini, grated (about 2 cups)
- 100 grams dried apricots, cut in 1/4-inch dice (about 1/2 cup)

Direction

- Preheat the oven to 375 degrees. Oil muffin tins. The recipe makes about 14 1/2-cup muffins.
- Sift together the flour, baking powder, baking soda, cinnamon, nutmeg and salt.
- In a medium or large bowl, whisk together the oil, eggs, sugar, milk and vanilla. Quickly whisk in the sifted dry ingredients. Fold in the grated zucchini and the dried apricots. Fill muffin tins about 3/4 full.
- Bake 20 to 25 minutes, until the muffins are brown on the edges and a tester comes out

clean. Remove from the heat and allow to cool for 10 minutes in the tin, then remove from the tins and allow to cool on a rack.

Nutrition Information

- 172: calories;
- 25 grams: carbohydrates;
- 4 grams: protein;
- 7 grams: fat;
- 0 grams: trans fat;
- 3 grams: dietary fiber;
- 2 grams: polyunsaturated fat;
- 10 grams: sugars;
- 167 milligrams: sodium;
- 1 gram: saturated fat;

Index

A

Ale 3,9,51,213,215,218,219

Almond 7,191

Anchovies 5,138

Apple 3,6,7,9,16,34,40,41,49,143,173,207,208,219,228

Apricot 3,8,9,236

Arborio rice 177,195

Artichoke 3,7,11,30,34,216

Asparagus 3,6,12,13,23,178

Avocado 3,15,48

B

Banana 3,5,7,19,20,102,217

Barley 3,21,22,23

Basil 3,7,24,25,197

Beans 3,4,7,13,17,49,91,225,230

Beef 3,26

Berry 6,7,155,224

Biscuits 7,199

Black pepper 29

Blueberry 3,20

Bread 3,5,6,7,19,35,39,101,103,125,166,174,175,210,228

Brioche 3,35

Broccoli 3,4,5,6,7,36,37,87,118,138,139,157,186

Broth 3,4,5,6,24,39,63,98,183

Brussels sprouts 160

Buckwheat 3,40,41

Burger 7,210,215,224

Butter 3,4,5,6,7,24,35,43,56,73,85,117,154,155,176,179,188,222,2
23,232

C

Cabbage 3,5,7,34,37,44,45,119,128,208

Cake 3,4,5,6,7,8,9,11,59,73,74,101,103,122,167,217,218,222,235

Capers 4,5,7,57,131,216

Caramel 3,6,40,47,180

Cardamom 5,103

Carrot 3,4,6,7,40,43,48,89,145,195,221

Cauliflower 3,5,6,7,13,21,49,107,131,132,153,160,191

Caviar 4,53

Cayenne pepper 51,180

Celery 3,5,7,30,49,110,135,196,225

Chard 3,4,6,7,50,51,174,200

Cheddar 8,186,235

Cheese 3,4,5,6,7,8,22,27,52,72,86,87,125,160,183,186,190,211,226,235

Cherry 4,7,51,52,53,72,229

Chervil 211

Chestnut 3,35

Chicken 4,5,6,54,55,56,57,58,59,69,70,82,109,113,115,136,141,154,170

Chickpea 4,5,6,7,57,123,163,191,220

Chipotle 3,6,17,78,149

Chives 5,119

Chocolate 3,4,7,43,59,72,217,226

Cider 5,124

Cinnamon 4,61,88

Clams 3,4,5,17,63,83,139

Cod 7,193

Cola 3,12

Coleslaw 3,37

Coriander 3,6,12,144

Corn oil 115,125

Coulis 6,153

Couscous 4,66,67,68

Crab 4,6,7,75,182,188

Cranberry 4,7,65,228

Cream 3,4,5,7,47,53,69,72,85,102,113,121,190,226

Crumble 4,6,22,27,86,87,123,155,160,191

Cucumber 4,6,7,96,165,169,200

Cumin 4,6,48,65,69,151

Curry 3,4,7,43,61,71,221

D

Date 4,89

Dijon mustard 26,37,42,49,76,86,92,153,186,188,198,208

Dill 3,6,7,42,167,187,189,200

E

Egg 3,4,6,50,67,75,76,163

F

Farfalle 4,79

Fat 6,154

Fennel 3,5,30,114,117,129

Feta 6,7,8,147,165,189,230,233

Fig 3,4,35,87

Fish 3,4,6,9,23,37,80,93,175

Fleur de sel 27

Flour 82,112,113

Focaccia 3,4,7,25,81,229

Fruit 4,72,84

Fusilli 7,230

G

Garlic 3,4,5,6,7,36,56,63,64,87,109,149,162,196

Gin 4,5,6,85,134,135,180

Grain 4,5,86,125

Grapefruit 4,87,88

Gratin 4,6,7,65,88,89,146,160,205,233

Guacamole 78

H

Hake 5,98

Halibut 3,18

Ham 3,19

Herbs 3,5,50,104,137

Honey 3,20

J

Jelly 3,47

Jus 31,82,89,100,123,178,206,216

K

Kale 3,5,7,15,29,41,104,112,221

Kidney 4,96

Kohlrabi 3,5,37,105

L

Lamb 5,6,7,108,117,124,129,158,194,198

Leek 3,5,7,40,101,233

Lemon 3,4,5,18,23,49,55,98,109

Lentils 5,7,110,194

Lime 5,6,113,151,180

Ling 5,114,127

Lobster 4,5,7,94,116,195

M

Macaroni 7,186

Mackerel 5,116

Mango 3,5,43,117

Marmalade 3,44

Marshmallow 100

Mayonnaise 4,5,92,100

Meat 4,6,78,170

Mesclun 7,191

Millet 3,7,45,209,221

Mince 31,34,59,129,167,174,188

Mint 4,5,8,83,116,121,233

Miso 6,156

Muffins 4,8,86,236

Mushroom 3,5,6,7,12,109,125,126,132,134,135,148,149,160,163,170,172,180,181,186,200

Mussels 5,114,127

Mustard 3,4,6,42,49,86,144

N

Nut 1,7,9,10,11,12,13,14,15,16,17,18,19,20,21,22,23,24,25,26,28,29,30,31,32,33,34,35,36,37,38,39,40,41,42,43,44,45,46,47,48,50,52,53,54,55,56,57,58,59,60,61,62,63,64,65,66,67,68,69,70,71,72,74,75,76,77,78,79,80,81,82,83,84,85,86,87,88,89,90,91,92,93,94,95,96,97,98,99,100,101,102,103,104,106,107,108,109,110,111,112,113,114,115,116,117,118,119,120,121,124,125,126,127,128,129,130,131,132,133,134,135,136,137,138,139,140,141,142,143,144,145,146,147,148,149,150,151,152,153,154,155,156,157,158,159,160,161,162,163,164,165,166,167,168,169,170,171,172,173,174,175,176,177,178,179,180,181,182,183,184,185,186,187,188,189,190,191,192,193,194,195,196,197,198,199,200,201,202,203,204,205,206,207,208,209,210,211,212,213,214,216,217,218,219,220,221,222,223,224,225,226,227,228,230,231,232,233,234,235,236,237

O

Oatmeal 6,7,175,232

Octopus 5,128

Oil 11,16,18,39,45,51,64,65,87,91,107,125,137,141,146,161,163,174,201,203,205,227,228,229,233,236

Olive 3,4,5,7,29,57,96,117,128,229

Onion 3,5,6,7,44,45,123,143,146,165,222

Orange 3,4,5,21,47,88,89,129

Oyster 6,181

P

Pancakes 3,4,5,7,28,94,118,119,209

Pancetta 4,87,96

Parmesan 3,6,15,16,21,22,25,26,29,30,32,33,46,69,75,90,105,106,107,110,112,118,131,133,134,135,136,138,139,143,148,150,157,158,170,174,176,177,181,191,192,197,198,200,201,203,204,211,220,230,234

Parsley 5,6,130,131,164

Parsnip 7,219

Pasta 5,6,116,131,132,133,139,150

Pastry 51,80

Peach 5,129

Pear 5,135

Peas 4,5,6,56,71,132,183

Peel 22,44,97,98,103,105,119,120,139,141,145,173,178,185,208,213

Penne 5,7,135,136,230

Pepper 4,5,6,7,41,56,58,68,79,92,137,153,174,185,192,196,210

Pesto 7,197

Pickle 3,5,13,35,139

Pie 4,5,7,73,80,90,112,122,139,182,202,207

Pizza 5,6,140,146

Plantain 5,141

Plum 4,5,74,104

Polenta 6,143

Pomegranate 83

Pork 5,6,7,120,143,144,197

Potato 3,4,5,6,7,13,17,95,118,119,120,130,145,175,207,227

Prosciutto 3,42

Prune 4,57

Pulse 72,103,203

Pumpkin 4,6,7,73,85,86,150,157,189,207

Q

Quince 6,150

Quinoa 3,5,6,30,37,104,151,153,160

R

Rabbit 5,6,106,159

Raisins 3,7,36,232

Raspberry 6,151,152

Red onion 78

Rhubarb 6,7,154,155,173,202

Rice 3,4,5,6,7,15,30,31,32,40,50,61,70,126,137,156,223

Ricotta 7,203,218

Risotto 3,4,5,6,7,15,21,30,32,66,105,157,177,183,195

Rosemary 4,6,81,159,162,166,176

S

Sage 4,6,64,96,150

Salad 3,4,5,6,7,8,15,23,27,29,30,33,42,45,48,49,68,75,82,87,89,104,128,131,145,147,151,153,164,165,167,182,188,191,207,213,214,215,221,222,224,232,236

Salmon 6,7,167,168,169,187

Salsa 4,6,7,79,161,170,212

Salt 6,13,14,15,17,18,21,22,23,25,27,28,29,30,31,32,33,34,37,38,40,41,43,44,45,49,50,51,54,55,56,58,62,64,65,67,68,70,75,76,77,78,79,83,87,89,91,92,93,96,97,98,101,104,105,106,107,108,109,110,111,112,113,114,115,116,117,118,119,120,123,126,131,132,133,134,135,137,138,139,145,146,147,148,149,150,151,153,157,158,159,160,161,162,163,164,169,170,172,173,176,179,181,182,183,184,185,187,189,191,192,193,196,200,201,203,205,206,208,211,212,213,214,215,217,219,220,221,222,224,225,227,228,230,233,234

Sausage 4,6,7,58,171,172,194

Savory 6,174,175,176

Scallop 6,178,179,180

Seasoning 47

Seeds 3,5,20,48,120

Semolina 211

Shallot 6,179

Sherry 94,95,164,165,182,195

Sirloin 6,185

Snapper 6,173

Sole 5,7,134,189

Sorbet 6,7,152,203

Soup 4,5,6,7,8,62,101,148,149,155,175,206,219,232,235

Spaghetti 7,191,192,193

Spinach 4,5,6,7,63,134,135,146,197,200,203

Squash 3,4,7,15,83,89,205,214,233

Steak 3,6,38,185

Stew 7,216

Strawberry 5,7,101,201,202,203

Stuffing 3,5,6,35,134,171,181

Swiss chard 51,129,174,201,218,220

T

Tabasco 14,20,46,75,94,95,101,171,175,176,192

Tahini 7,213

Tangerine 7,208

Tea 3,5,6,7,21,102,129,151,194,221

Thyme 6,176

Tofu 6,7,156,213

Tomatillo 5,141

Tomato 3,4,5,6,7,8,10,18,25,38,52,53,67,68,81,91,93,96,110,114,131,132,136,138,143,160,161,163,175,179,185,188,191,192,205,213,224,229,230,234

Trout 4,5,7,96,110,227

Turkey 6,7,158,192,215

V

Veal 4,7,96,216

Vegan 7,150,217

Vegetable oil 19,94,95

Vegetable shortening 82

Vegetables 4,5,7,80,97,108,116,187

Vegetarian 7,219

Venison 4,94

W

Waffles 6,176

Wasabi 6,169

Watercress 7,222

Watermelon 7,223

White pepper 177,219

White wine 116

Wine 3,4,5,6,21,76,106,144,145,168,172

Worcestershire sauce 20,26,46,169,171,182

Z

Zest 73,207,223

L

lasagna 107